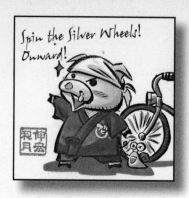

Spin the Silver Wheels!
Onward!

Bicycle

I treated myself to a new bicycle. Most of my hobbies—reading, watching movies, collecting toys—are done indoors. My only outdoor activity is riding my bike. I usually just ride it around town for a change of scenery, but something about moving at a speed faster than I can walk yet slower than a car really appeals to me. I want to use my new bike to help me lose weight.

—Nobuhiro Watsuki

Nobuhiro Watsuki earned international accolades for his first major manga series, **Rurouni Kenshin**, about a wandering swordsman in Meiji Era Japan. Serialized in Japan's *Weekly Shonen Jump* from 1994 to 1999, **Rurouni Kenshin**, available in North America from VIZ Media, quickly became a worldwide sensation, inspiring a spin-off short story ("Yahiko no Sakabatô"), an animated TV show and a series of novels. Watsuki's latest hit, **Buso Renkin**, began publication in *Weekly Shonen Jump* in 2003 and was adapted into an animated TV series in 2006.

BUSO RENKIN
VOL. 8
The SHONEN JUMP ADVANCED
Manga Edition

STORY AND ART BY
NOBUHIRO WATSUKI

English Adaptation/Lance Caselman
Translation/Toshifumi Yoshida
Touch-up Art & Lettering/James Gaubatz
Design/Yukiko Whitley
Editor/Amy Yu

Editor in Chief, Books/Alvin Lu
Editor in Chief, Magazines/Marc Weidenbaum
VP of Publishing Licensing/Rika Inouye
VP of Sales/Gonzalo Ferreyra
Sr. VP of Marketing/Liza Coppola
Publisher/Hyoe Narita

Printed in the U.S.A.

Published by VIZ Media, LLC
P.O. Box 77010
San Francisco, CA 94107

SHONEN JUMP ADVANCED Manga Edition
10 9 8 7 6 5 4 3 2
First printing, October 2007
Second printing, November 2007

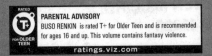

THE WORLD'S MOST
CUTTING-EDGE MANGA

SHONEN
JUMP
ADVANCED
www.shonenjump.com

SHONEN JUMP ADVANCED MANGA EDITION

STORY & ART BY
NOBUHIRO WATSUKI

Vol. 8

The Determination to Protect What's Important to the End

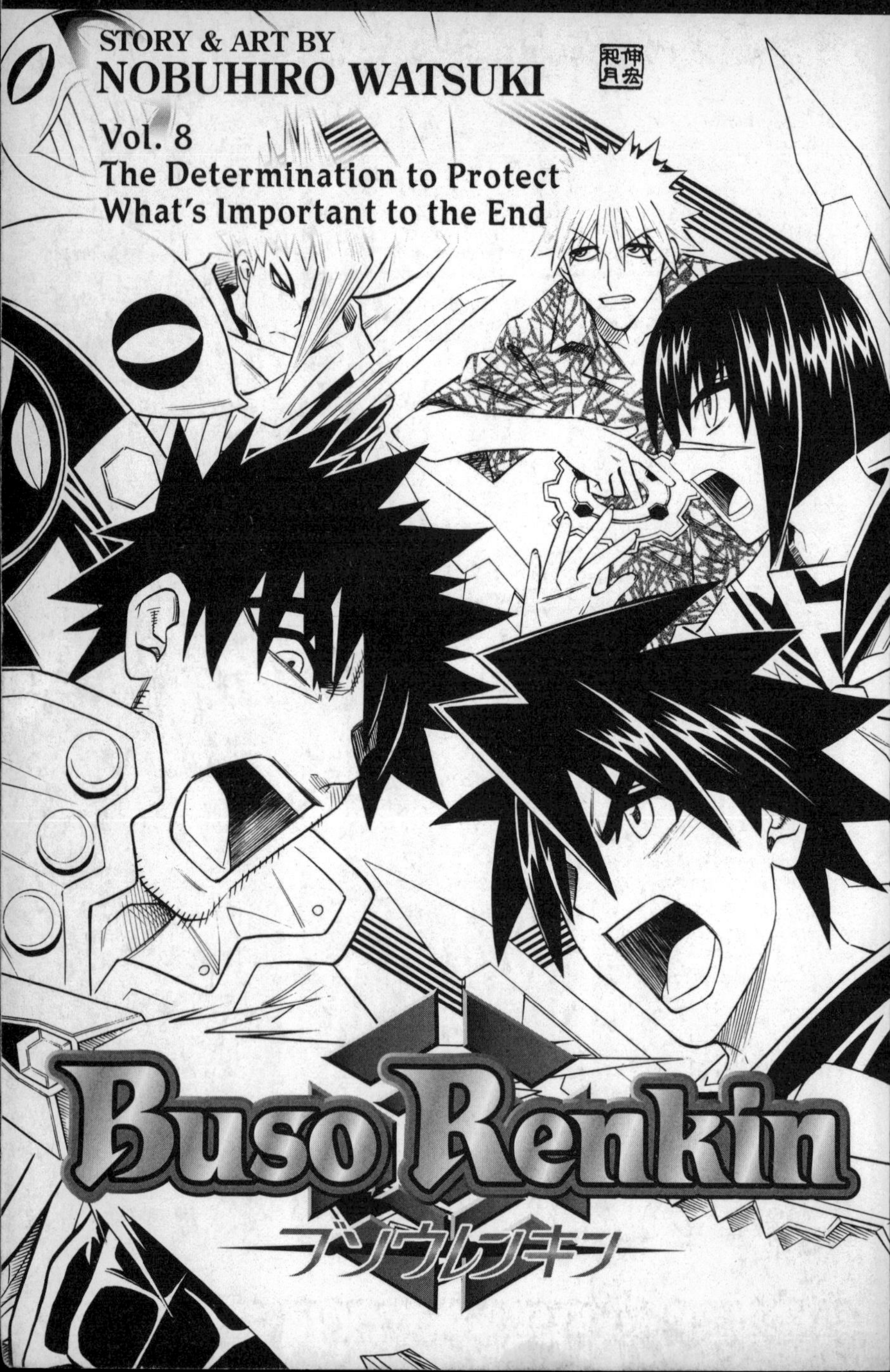
和月伸宏
Buso Renkin
ブソウレンキン

Alchemy

An early scientific practice that combines elements of various disciplines that came to Europe over the millennia. Its goals were the transmutation of base metals into gold and the creation of an Elixir of Immortality, neither of which succeeded. But unknown to the world at large, alchemy achieved two earthshaking supernatural successes–the homunculi and the kakugane.

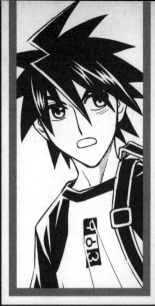

Kazuki Muto

Sixteen-year-old Kazuki was killed by a homunculus but was restored to life by Tokiko, who replaced his heart with a magical talisman called a kakugane. His Buso Renkin is a lance called "Sunlight Heart Plus."

CHARACTERS

Homunculus

An artificial being created by alchemy. The form and powers of the homunculus differ depending on the organism it was based on. Homunculi feed on human flesh and can only be destroyed by the power of alchemy.

Kakugane

The kakugane are forged from a magical alchemic alloy. They are activated by the deepest parts of the human psyche, the basic instincts. Each kakugane can materialize a unique weapon called a Buso Renkin.

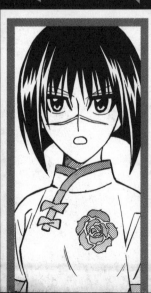

Tokiko Tsumura

A girl chosen to be an Alchemist Warrior, an expert of Buso Renkin. Her Buso Renkin is a Death Scythe called the "Valkyrie Skirt."

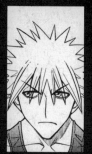

Gouta Nakamura

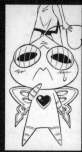

Angel Gozen

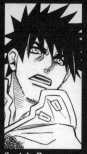

**Captain Bravo
(Mamoru Sakimori)**

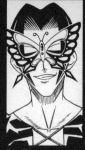

**Papillon
(Koushaku Chouno)**

S T O R Y

Following the destruction of Dr. Butterfly and the L.X.E., Kazuki battles former Alchemist Warrior Victor. Victor has become a being that draws energy directly from living creatures nearby—in this case, the students of Ginsei Academy. In the course of the battle, Kazuki's Sunlight Heart is broken, and he is only able to survive by temporarily transforming into a creature like Victor. It is discovered that the source of the transformation is the black kakugane that functions as Kazuki's heart.

Confronted with the fact that Kazuki will become a superhuman life-sucking "Victor" in a few weeks time, the Alchemist Army orders Kazuki's "re-extermination." Kazuki is defeated by Captain Bravo and hurled into the ocean, where he is rescued by Tokiko. Hoping to find answers, Kazuki, Tokiko, and Warrior Gouta Nakamura make their way through the hinterland toward the place where Tokiko originally found Kazuki's black kakugane. Unfortunately, the Re-Extermination Squad ambushes them, and Tokiko is shrunk by Maruyama's floating mines.

Now doll-size and separated from her comrades, Tokiko is found by Papillon, who offers her his protection. But as they near their destination, a new threat appears in the form of the brutal Warrior Ikusabe. A battle ensues in an abandoned industrial area, and Ikusabe's formidable power is revealed: he can quickly regenerate even after being blown to smithereens!

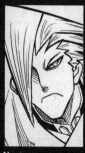

Negoro

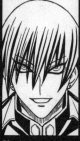

Maruyama

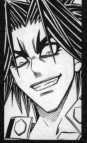

Hiwatari

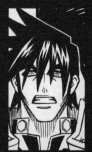

Ikusabe

BUSO RENKIN
Volume 8: The Determination to Protect What's Important to the End

CONTENTS

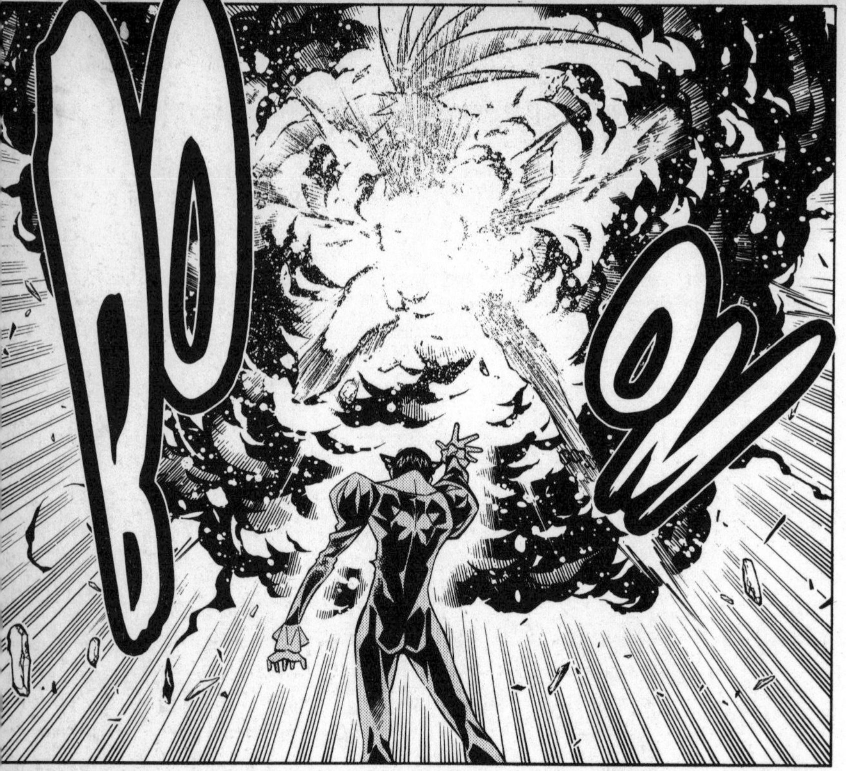
BOOM

CHAPTER 64: EATER

和月伸宏

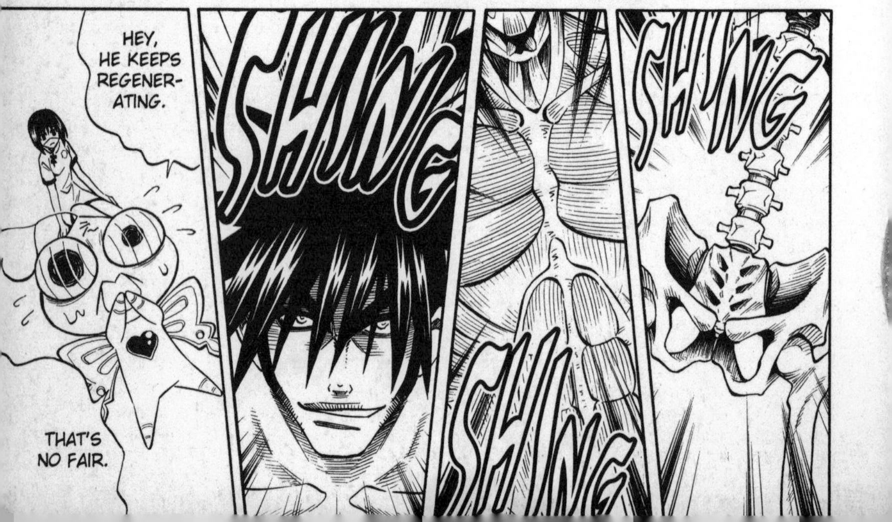
SHING
SHING
SHING
HEY, HE KEEPS REGENER-ATING.
THAT'S NO FAIR.

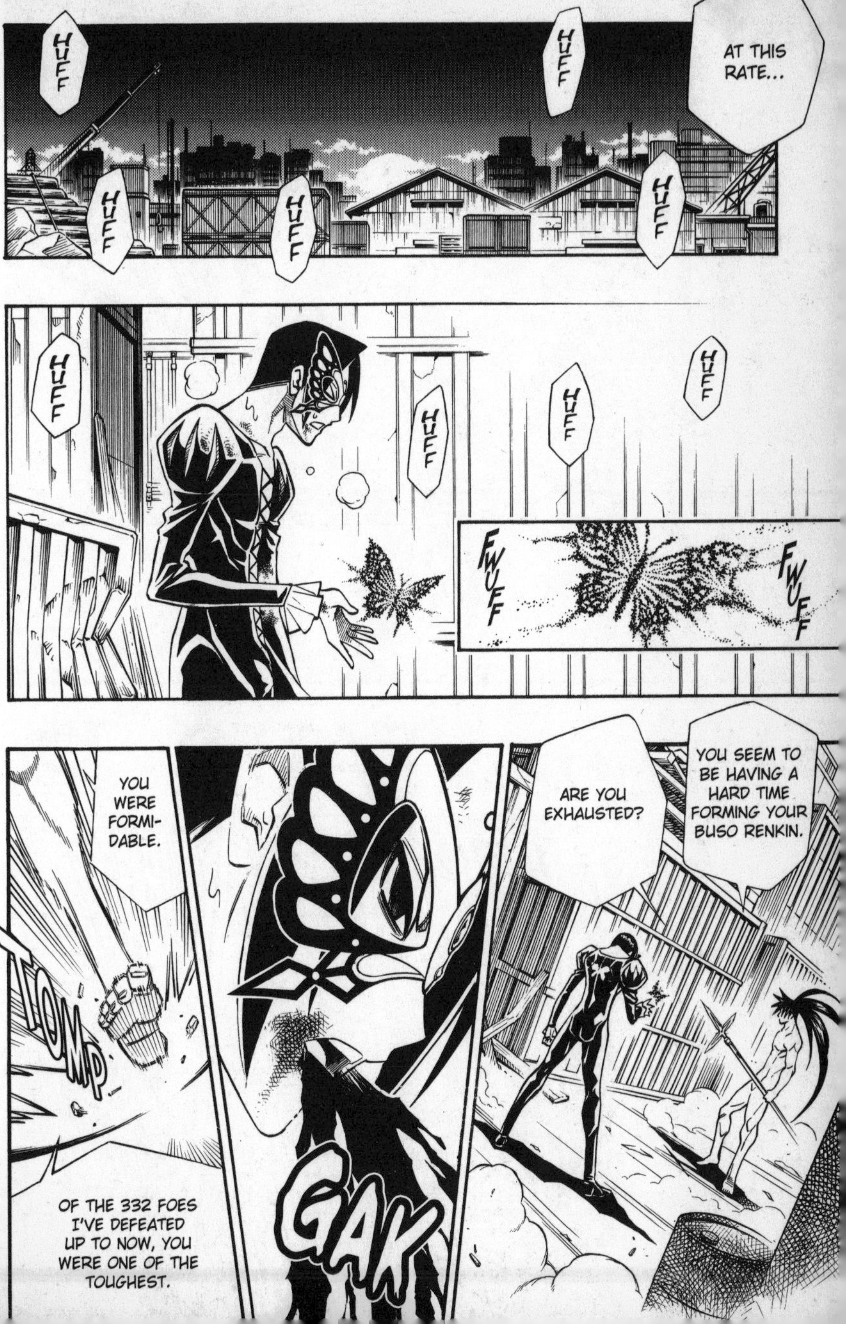
AT THIS RATE...
HUFF
HUFF
HUFF
HUFF
HUFF
HUFF
HUFF
HUFF
HUFF
FWUFF
FWUFF
YOU SEEM TO BE HAVING A HARD TIME FORMING YOUR BUSO RENKIN.
ARE YOU EXHAUSTED?
GAK
YOU WERE FORMIDABLE.
TOMP
OF THE 332 FOES I'VE DEFEATED UP TO NOW, YOU WERE ONE OF THE TOUGHEST.

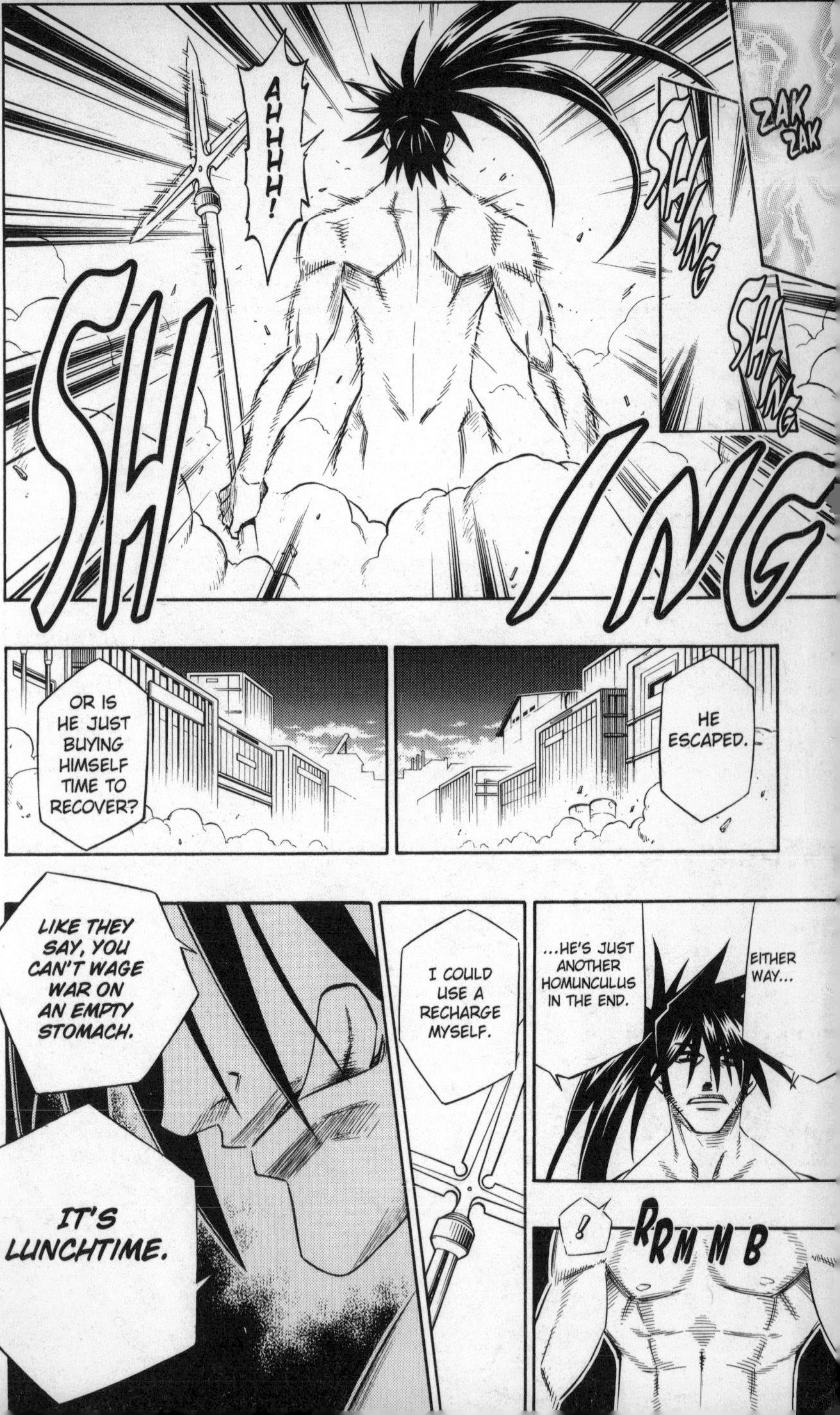
ZAK ZAK
SHING
SHING
AHHHH!
SHING
HE ESCAPED.
OR IS HE JUST BUYING HIMSELF TIME TO RECOVER?
EITHER WAY...
...HE'S JUST ANOTHER HOMUNCULUS IN THE END.
!
RRMMB
I COULD USE A RECHARGE MYSELF.
LIKE THEY SAY, YOU CAN'T WAGE WAR ON AN EMPTY STOMACH.
IT'S LUNCHTIME.

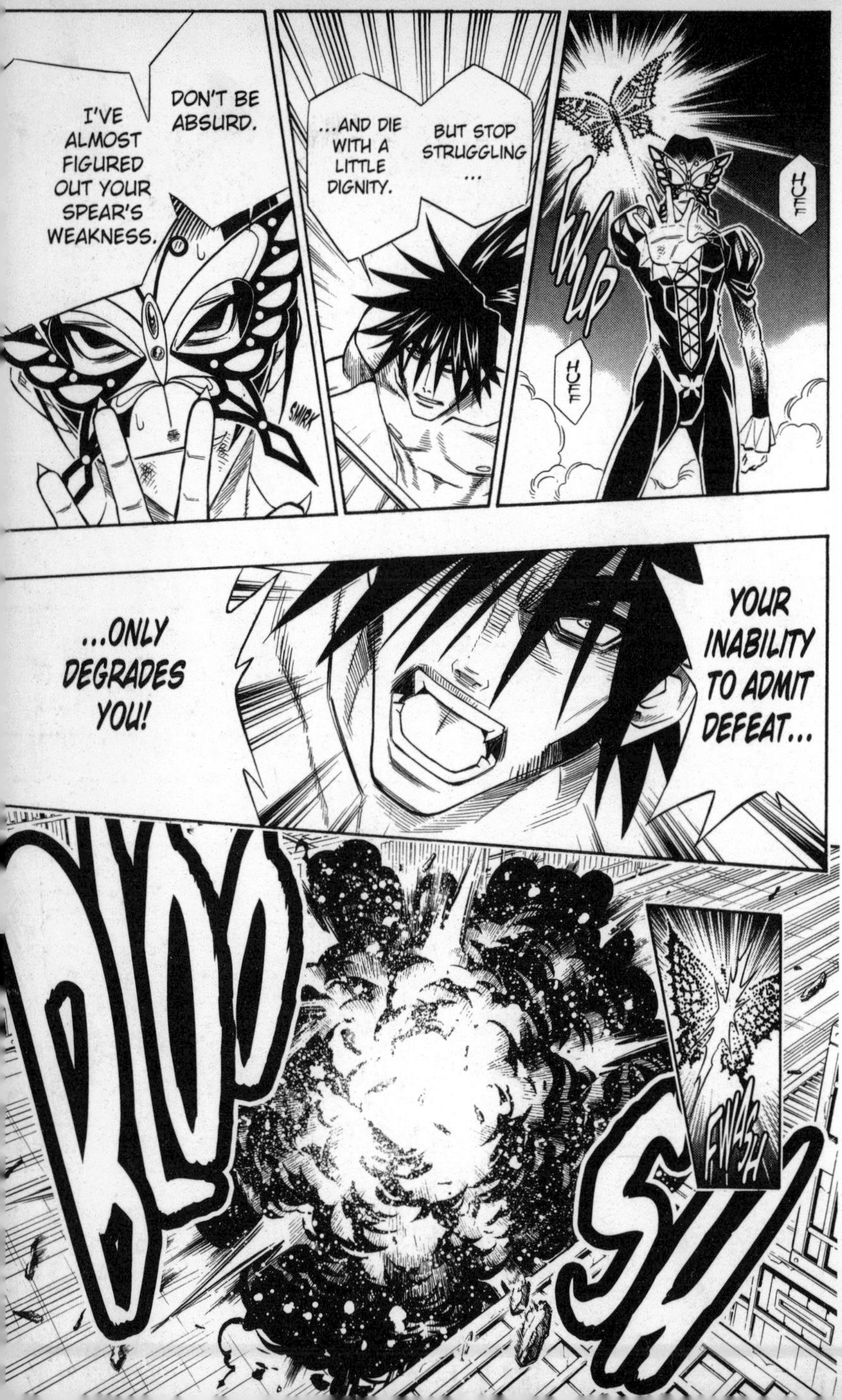
HUFF
HUFF
BUT STOP STRUGGLING...
...AND DIE WITH A LITTLE DIGNITY.
SMIRK
DON'T BE ABSURD.
I'VE ALMOST FIGURED OUT YOUR SPEAR'S WEAKNESS.
YOUR INABILITY TO ADMIT DEFEAT...
...ONLY DEGRADES YOU!

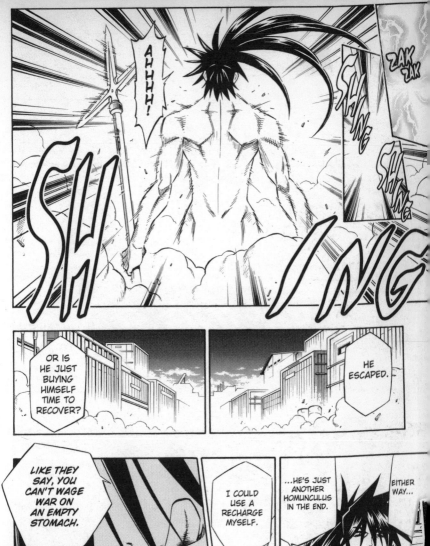

AHHHH!

ZAK ZAK

SHING

SHING

SH ING

OR IS HE JUST BUYING HIMSELF TIME TO RECOVER?

HE ESCAPED.

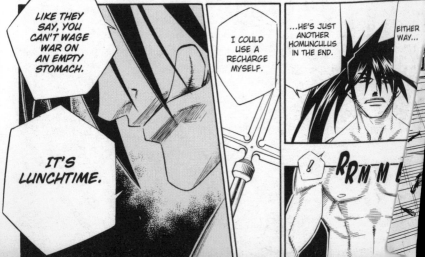

LIKE THEY SAY, YOU CAN'T WAGE WAR ON AN EMPTY STOMACH.

IT'S LUNCHTIME.

I COULD USE A RECHARGE MYSELF.

...HE'S JUST ANOTHER HOMUNCULUS IN THE END.

EITHER WAY...

RRMM

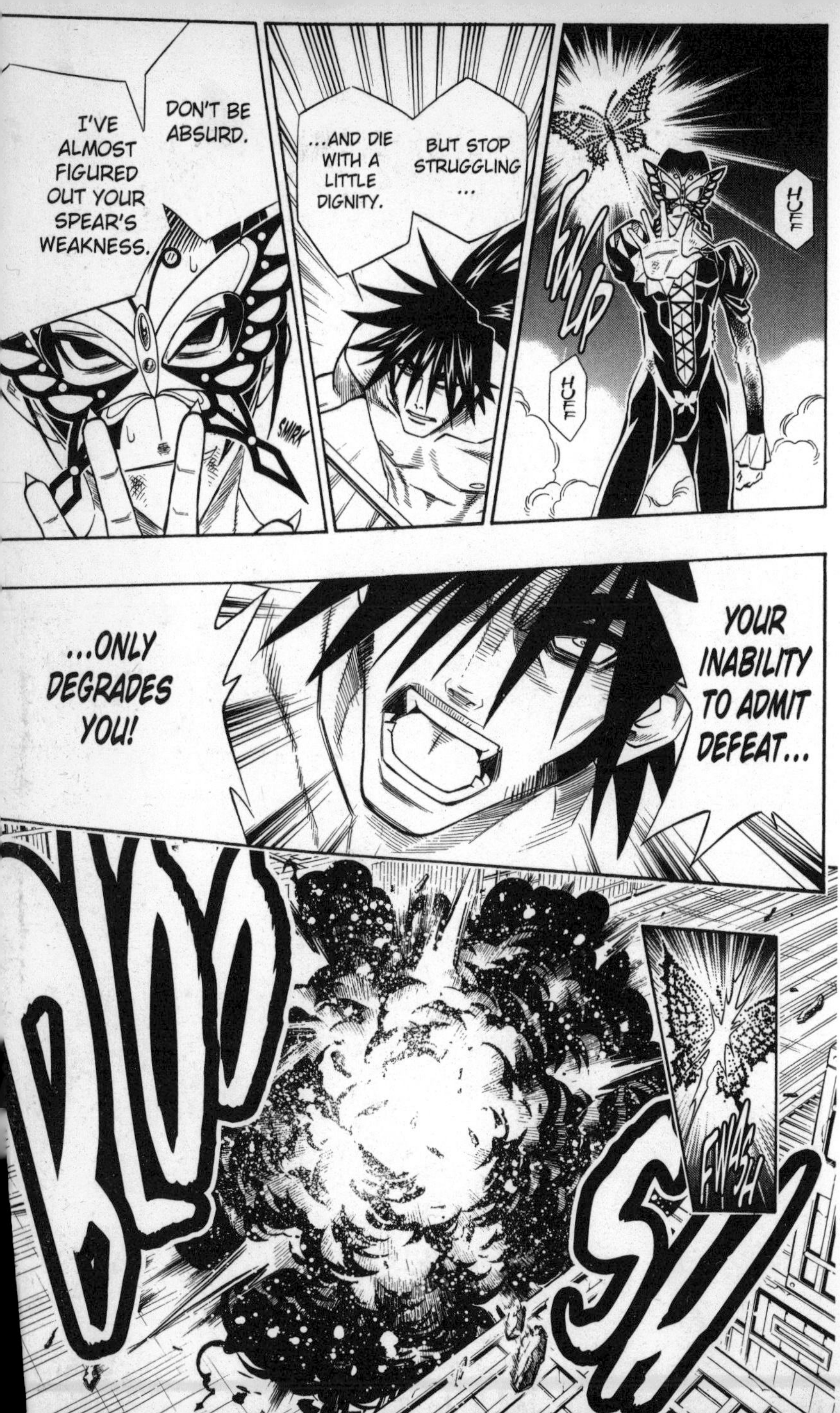
HUFF
FWUP
HUFF
BUT STOP STRUGGLING ...
...AND DIE WITH A LITTLE DIGNITY.
DON'T BE ABSURD.
I'VE ALMOST FIGURED OUT YOUR SPEAR'S WEAKNESS.
SMIRK
YOUR INABILITY TO ADMIT DEFEAT...
...ONLY DEGRADES YOU!
FWASH

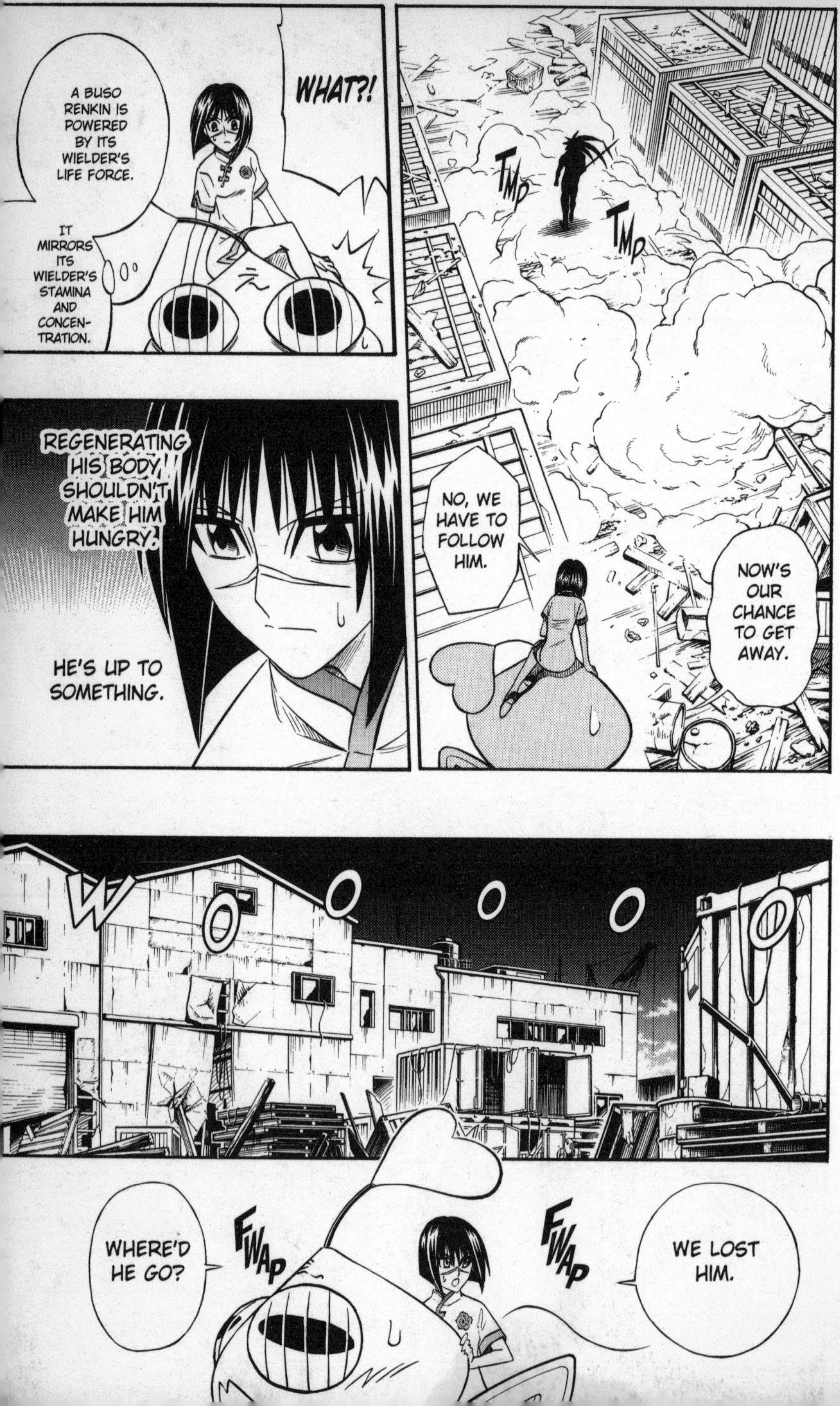
TMP
TMP
NOW'S OUR CHANCE TO GET AWAY.
NO, WE HAVE TO FOLLOW HIM.
WHAT?!
A BUSO RENKIN IS POWERED BY ITS WIELDER'S LIFE FORCE.
IT MIRRORS ITS WIELDER'S STAMINA AND CONCEN-TRATION.
REGENERATING HIS BODY SHOULDN'T MAKE HIM HUNGRY.
HE'S UP TO SOMETHING.
WOOOO
WE LOST HIM.
FWAP
FWAP
WHERE'D HE GO?

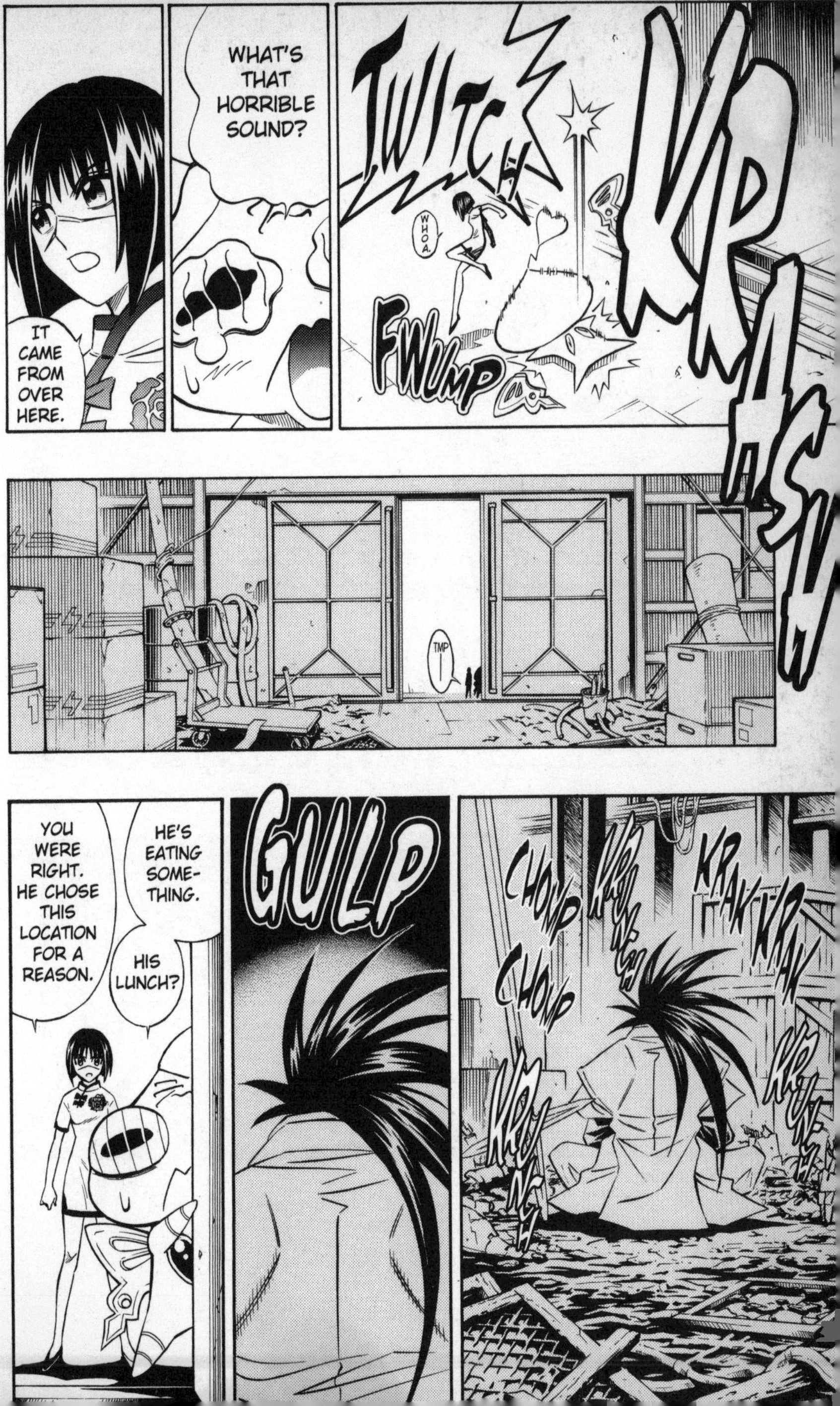
TWITCH
WHOA.
FWUMP
KRASH
WHAT'S THAT HORRIBLE SOUND?
IT CAME FROM OVER HERE.
TMP
CHOMP CHOMP
KRAK KRAK
GULP
HE'S EATING SOME-THING.
HIS LUNCH?
YOU WERE RIGHT. HE CHOSE THIS LOCATION FOR A REASON.

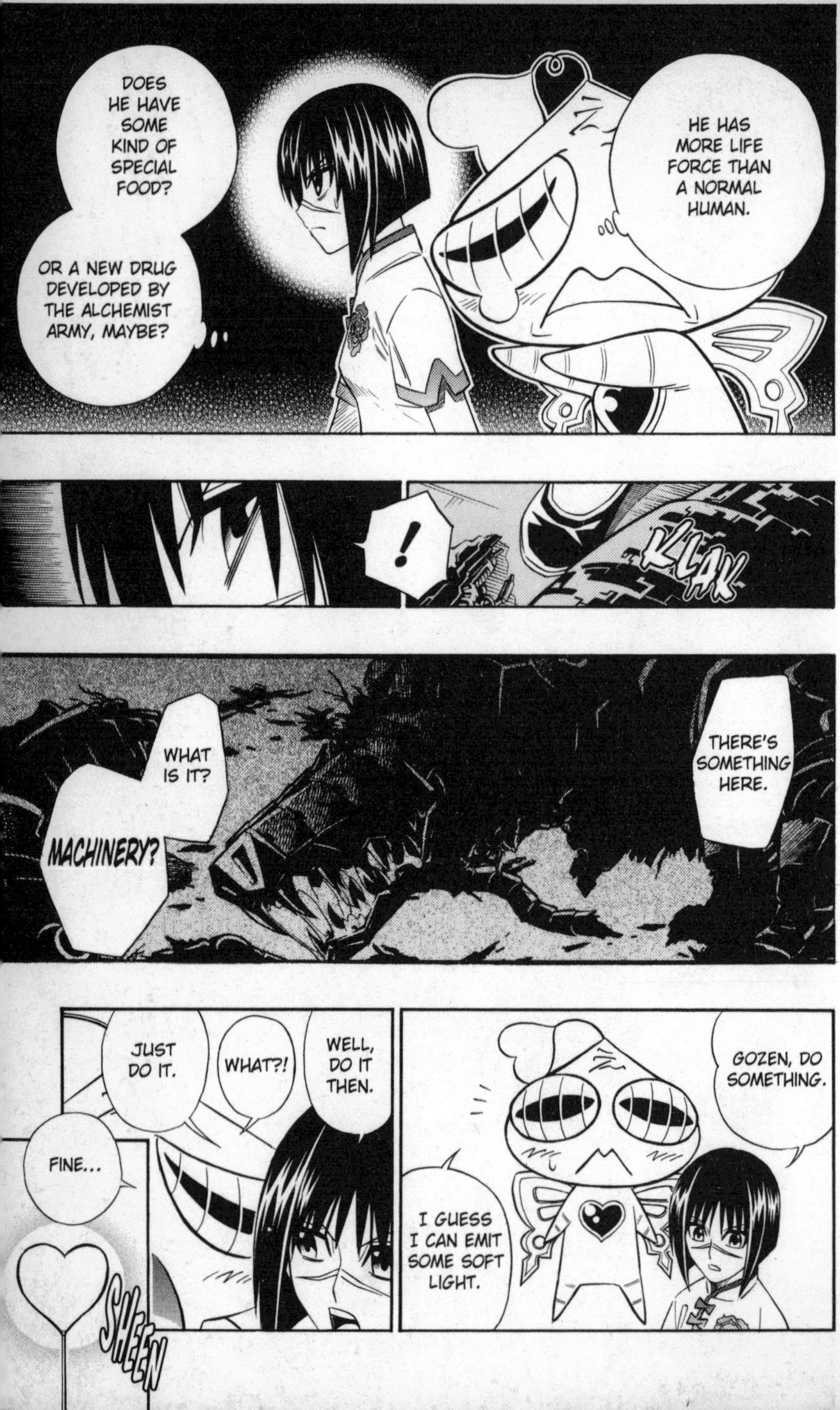
HE HAS MORE LIFE FORCE THAN A NORMAL HUMAN.
DOES HE HAVE SOME KIND OF SPECIAL FOOD?
OR A NEW DRUG DEVELOPED BY THE ALCHEMIST ARMY, MAYBE?...
KLAK
!
THERE'S SOMETHING HERE.
WHAT IS IT?
MACHINERY?
GOZEN, DO SOMETHING.
I GUESS I CAN EMIT SOME SOFT LIGHT.
WELL, DO IT THEN.
WHAT?!
JUST DO IT.
FINE...
SHEEN

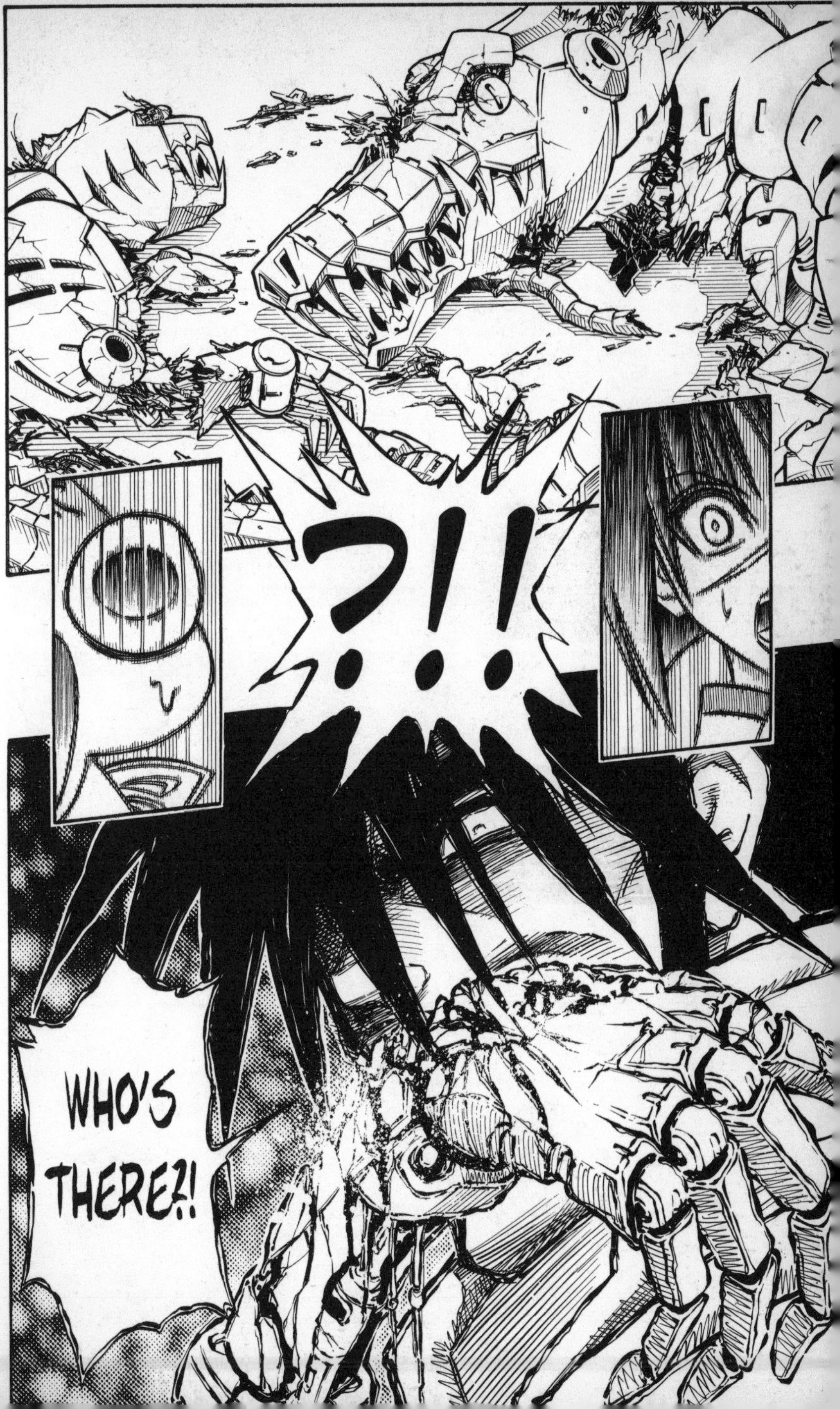
?!!
WHO'S THERE?!

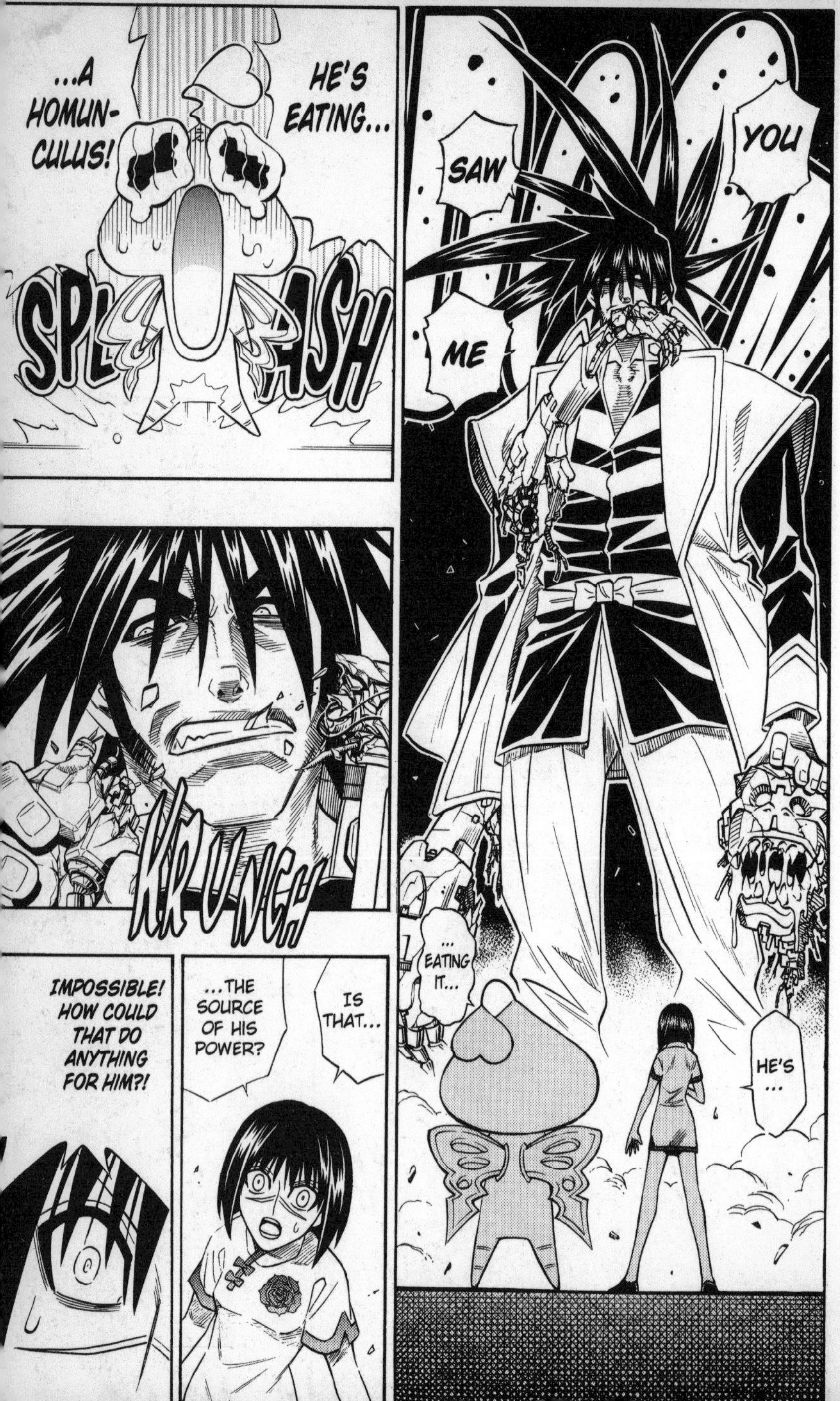
YOU
SAW
ME
HE'S...
...EATING IT...
HE'S EATING...
...A HOMUN-CULUS!
SPLASH
KRUNCH
IS THAT...
...THE SOURCE OF HIS POWER?
IMPOSSIBLE! HOW COULD THAT DO ANYTHING FOR HIM?!

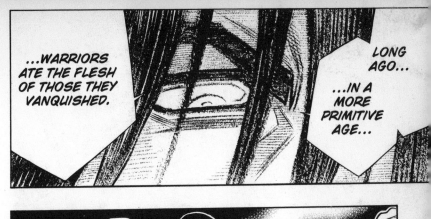

...WARRIORS ATE THE FLESH OF THOSE THEY VANQUISHED.

LONG AGO...

...IN A MORE PRIMITIVE AGE...

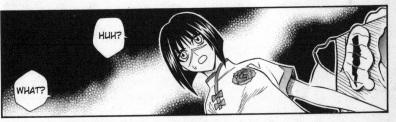

HUH?

WHAT?

AND BY DEVOURING THE FLESH, THEY ACQUIRED THE POWERS OF THE SLAIN.

BY KILLING AN ENEMY WARRIOR OR A FIERCE BEAST, THEY PROVED THEIR STRENGTH.

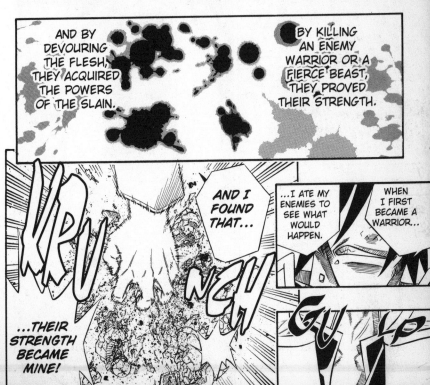

AND I FOUND THAT...

...I ATE MY ENEMIES TO SEE WHAT WOULD HAPPEN.

WHEN I FIRST BECAME A WARRIOR...

...THEIR STRENGTH BECAME MINE!

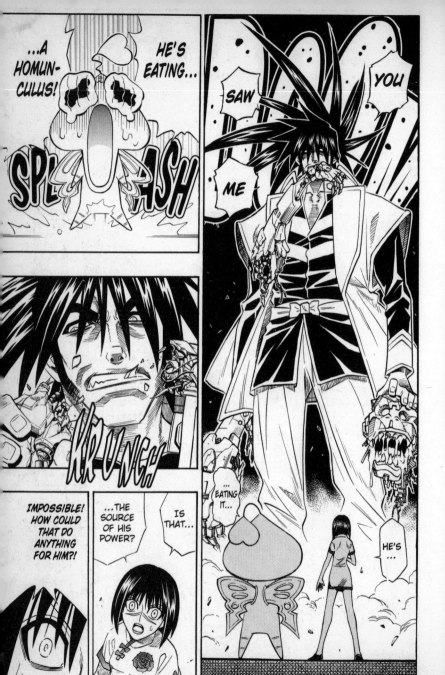

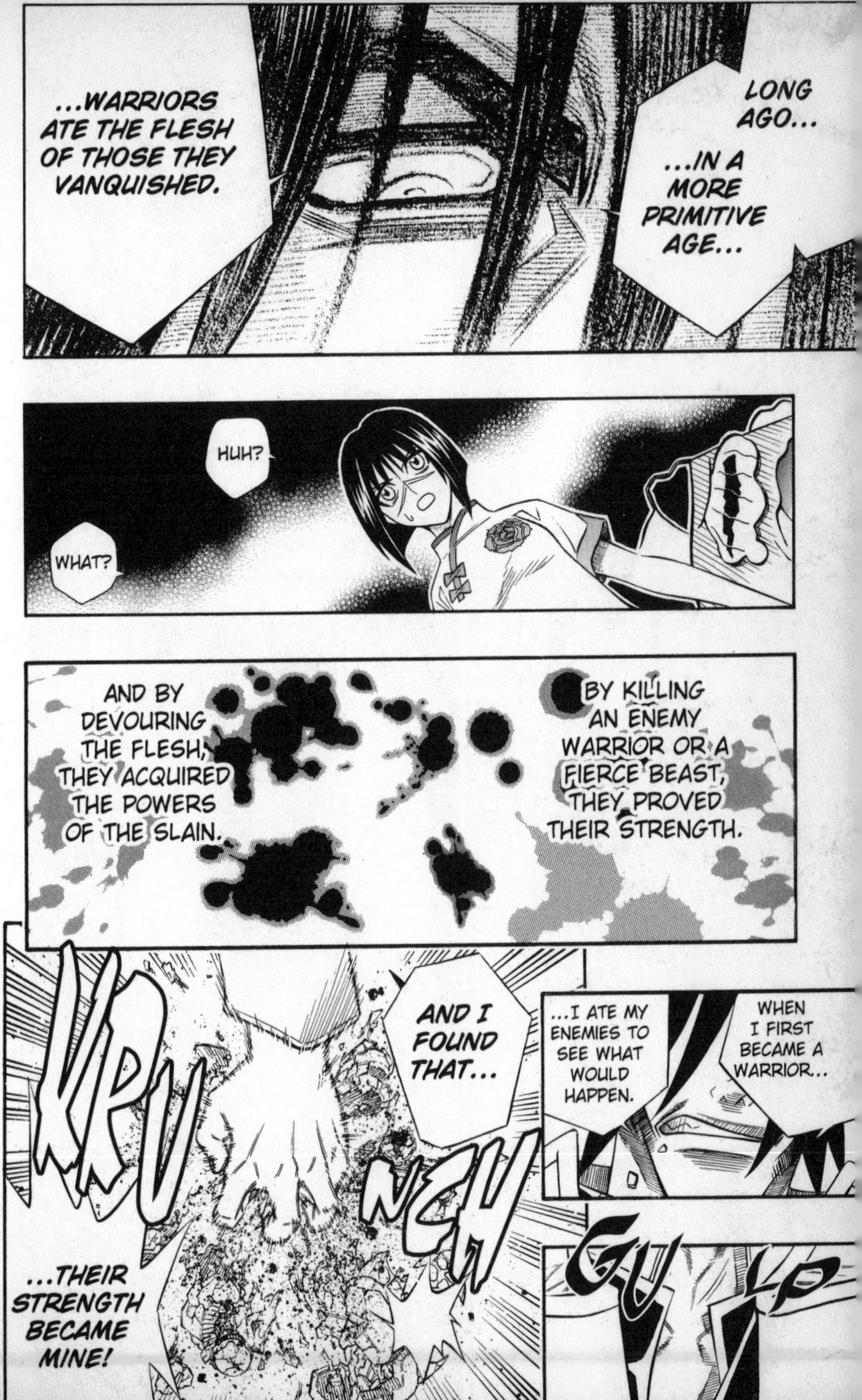
LONG AGO...
...IN A MORE PRIMITIVE AGE...
...WARRIORS ATE THE FLESH OF THOSE THEY VANQUISHED.
HUH?
WHAT?
BY KILLING AN ENEMY WARRIOR OR A FIERCE BEAST, THEY PROVED THEIR STRENGTH.
AND BY DEVOURING THE FLESH, THEY ACQUIRED THE POWERS OF THE SLAIN.
WHEN I FIRST BECAME A WARRIOR...
...I ATE MY ENEMIES TO SEE WHAT WOULD HAPPEN.
GULP
AND I FOUND THAT...
KRUNCH
...THEIR STRENGTH BECAME MINE!

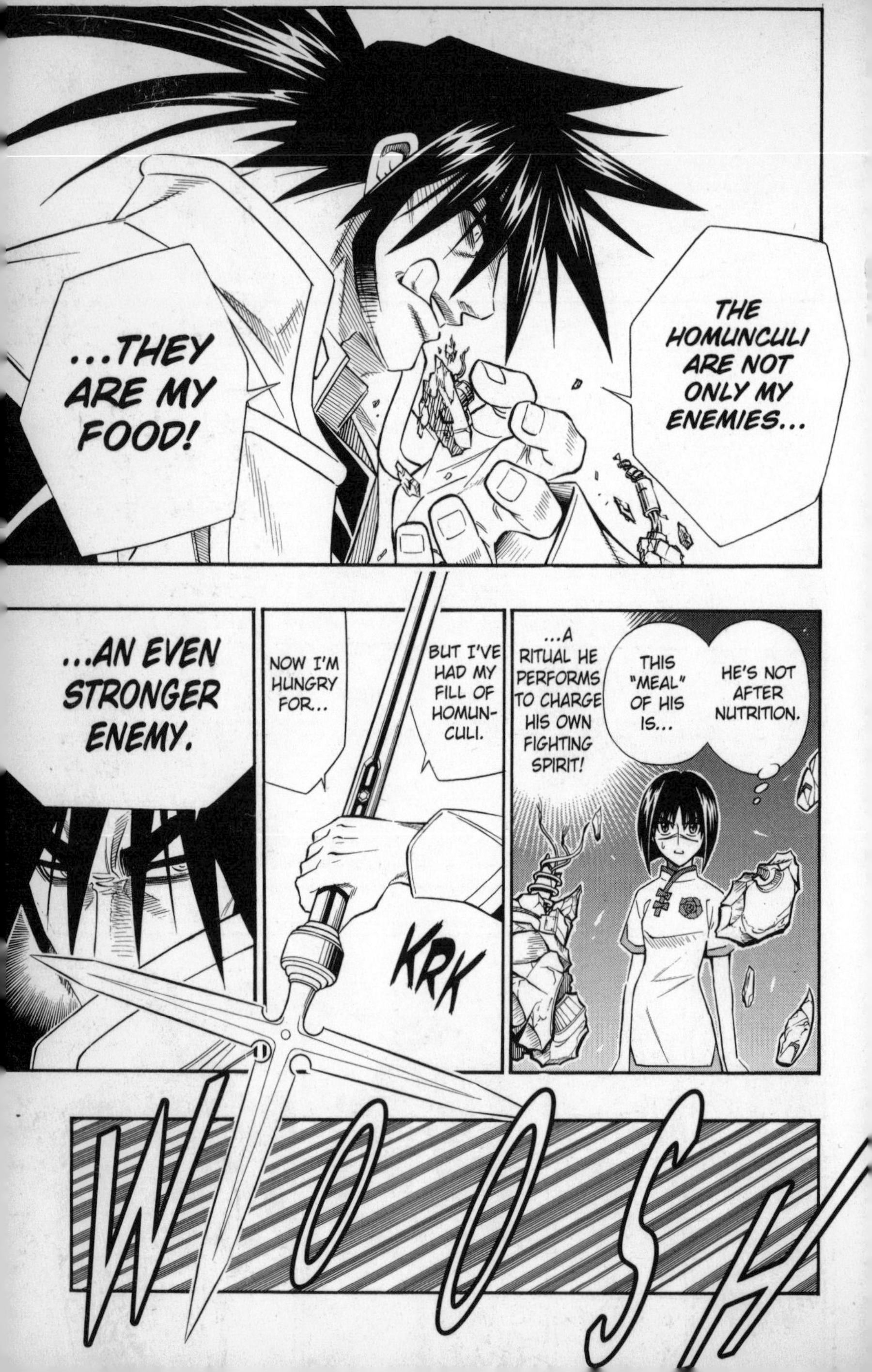
THE HOMUNCULI ARE NOT ONLY MY ENEMIES...
...THEY ARE MY FOOD!
HE'S NOT AFTER NUTRITION.
THIS "MEAL" OF HIS IS...
...A RITUAL HE PERFORMS TO CHARGE HIS OWN FIGHTING SPIRIT!
BUT I'VE HAD MY FILL OF HOMUN-CULI.
NOW I'M HUNGRY FOR...
KRK
...AN EVEN STRONGER ENEMY.
WHOOSH

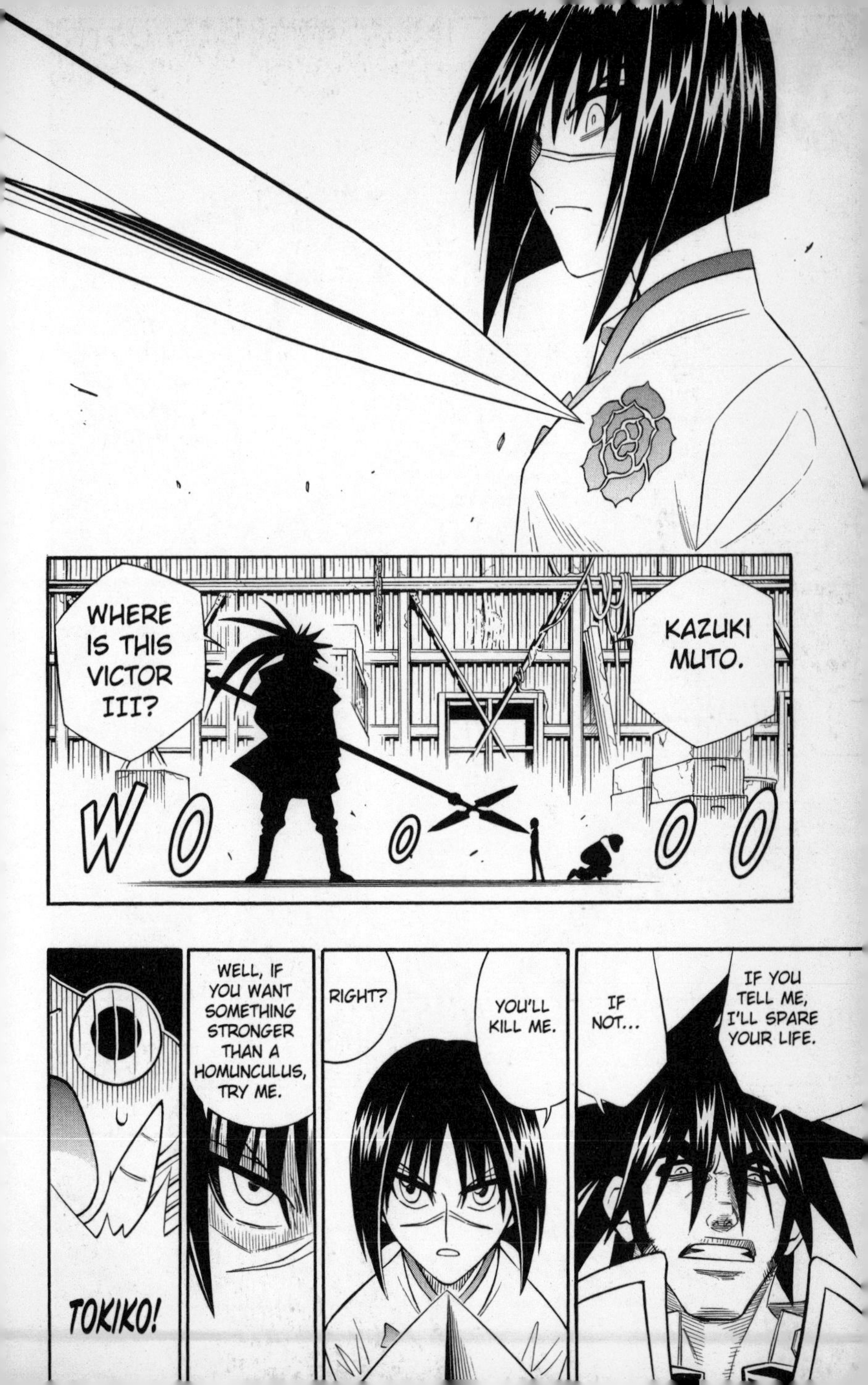
KAZUKI MUTO.
WHERE IS THIS VICTOR III?
WOOOO
IF YOU TELL ME, I'LL SPARE YOUR LIFE.
IF NOT...
YOU'LL KILL ME.
RIGHT?
WELL, IF YOU WANT SOMETHING STRONGER THAN A HOMUNCULUS, TRY ME.
TOKIKO!

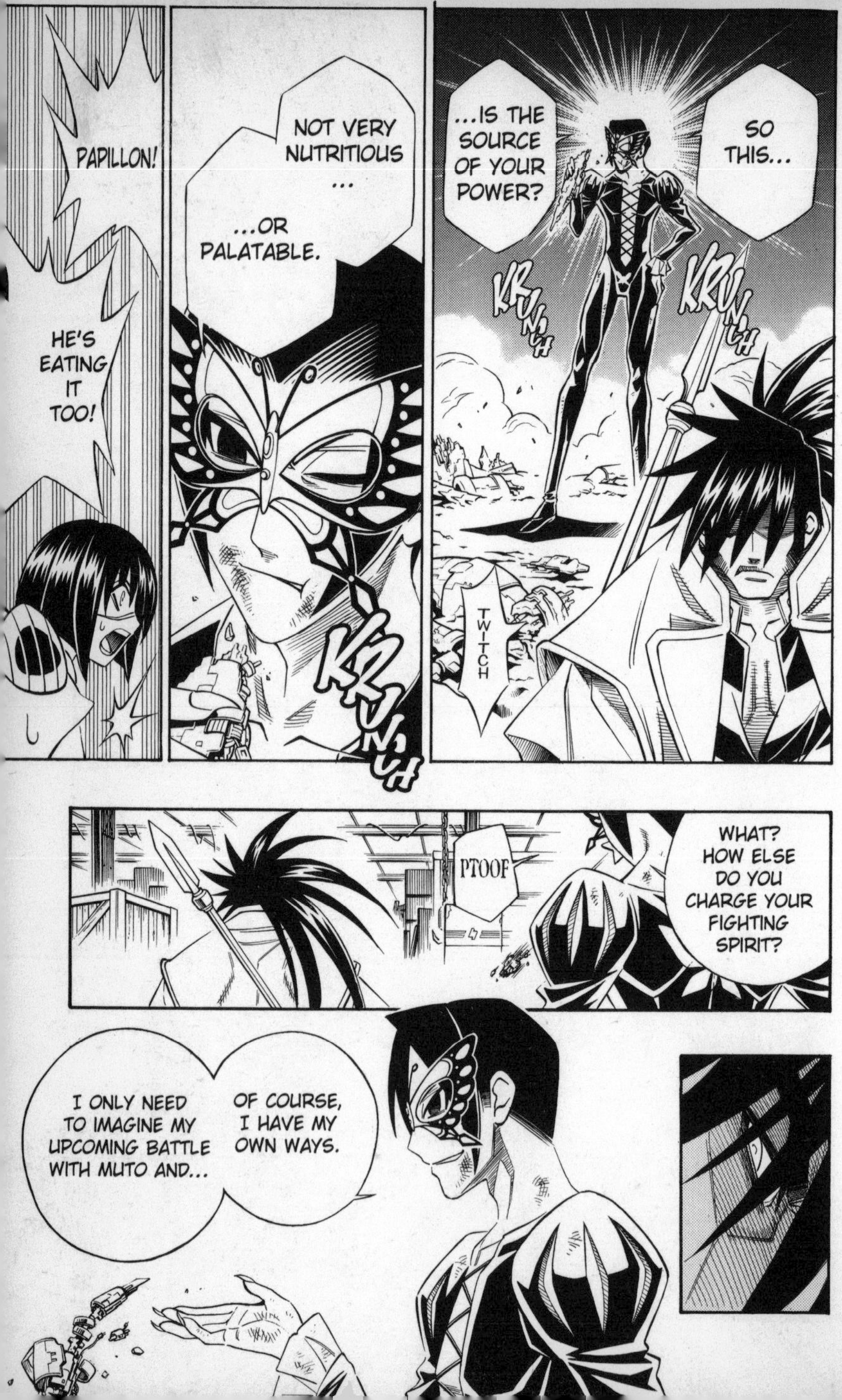
SO THIS...
...IS THE SOURCE OF YOUR POWER?
KRUNCH
KRUNCH
TWITCH
NOT VERY NUTRITIOUS ...
...OR PALATABLE.
KRUNCH
PAPILLON!
HE'S EATING IT TOO!
WHAT? HOW ELSE DO YOU CHARGE YOUR FIGHTING SPIRIT?
PTOOF
OF COURSE, I HAVE MY OWN WAYS.
I ONLY NEED TO IMAGINE MY UPCOMING BATTLE WITH MUTO AND...

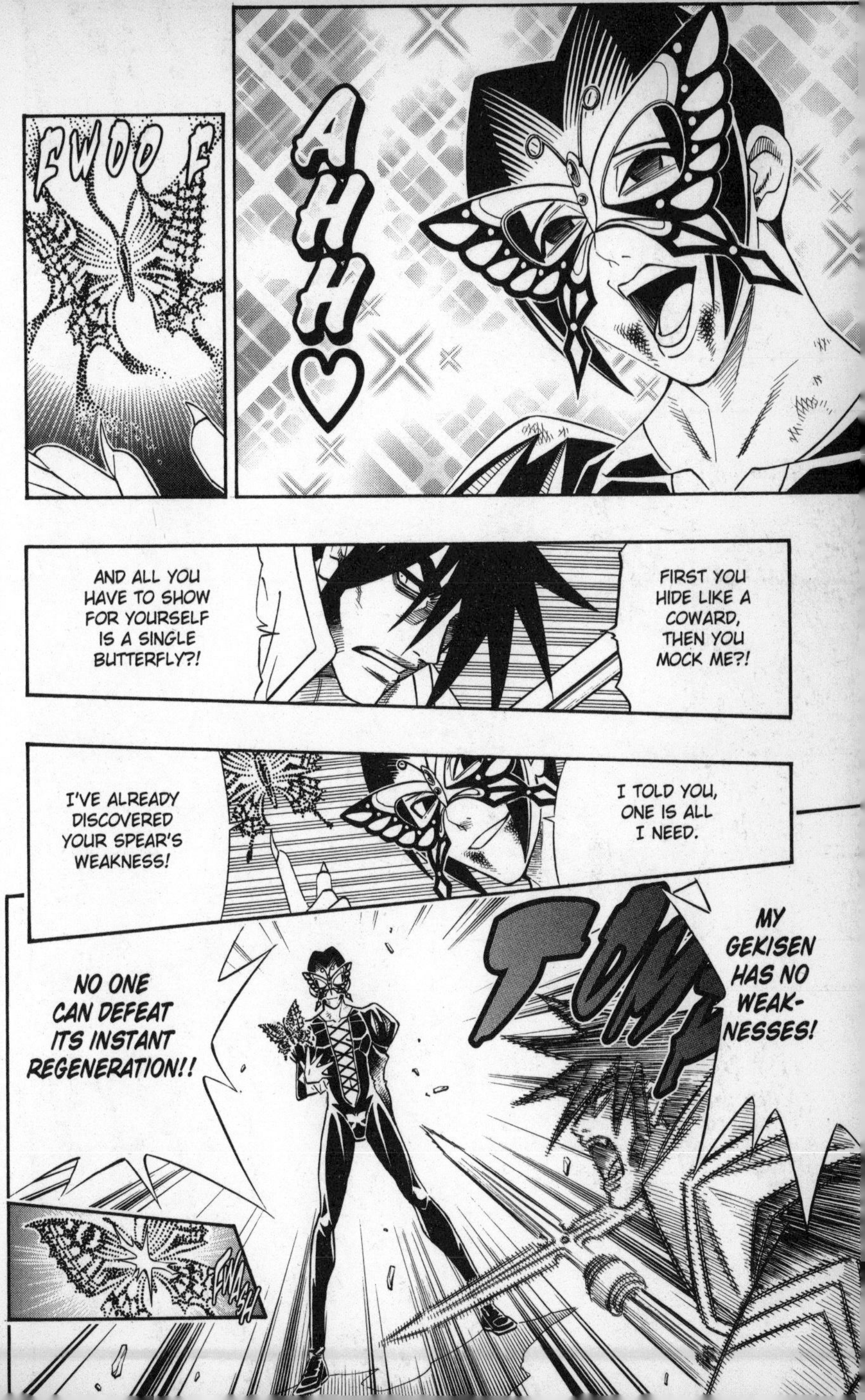
AHH♡
FWOO F
FIRST YOU HIDE LIKE A COWARD, THEN YOU MOCK ME?!
AND ALL YOU HAVE TO SHOW FOR YOURSELF IS A SINGLE BUTTERFLY?!
I TOLD YOU, ONE IS ALL I NEED.
I'VE ALREADY DISCOVERED YOUR SPEAR'S WEAKNESS!
MY GEKISEN HAS NO WEAK-NESSES!
TOMP
NO ONE CAN DEFEAT ITS INSTANT REGENERATION!!
FLASH

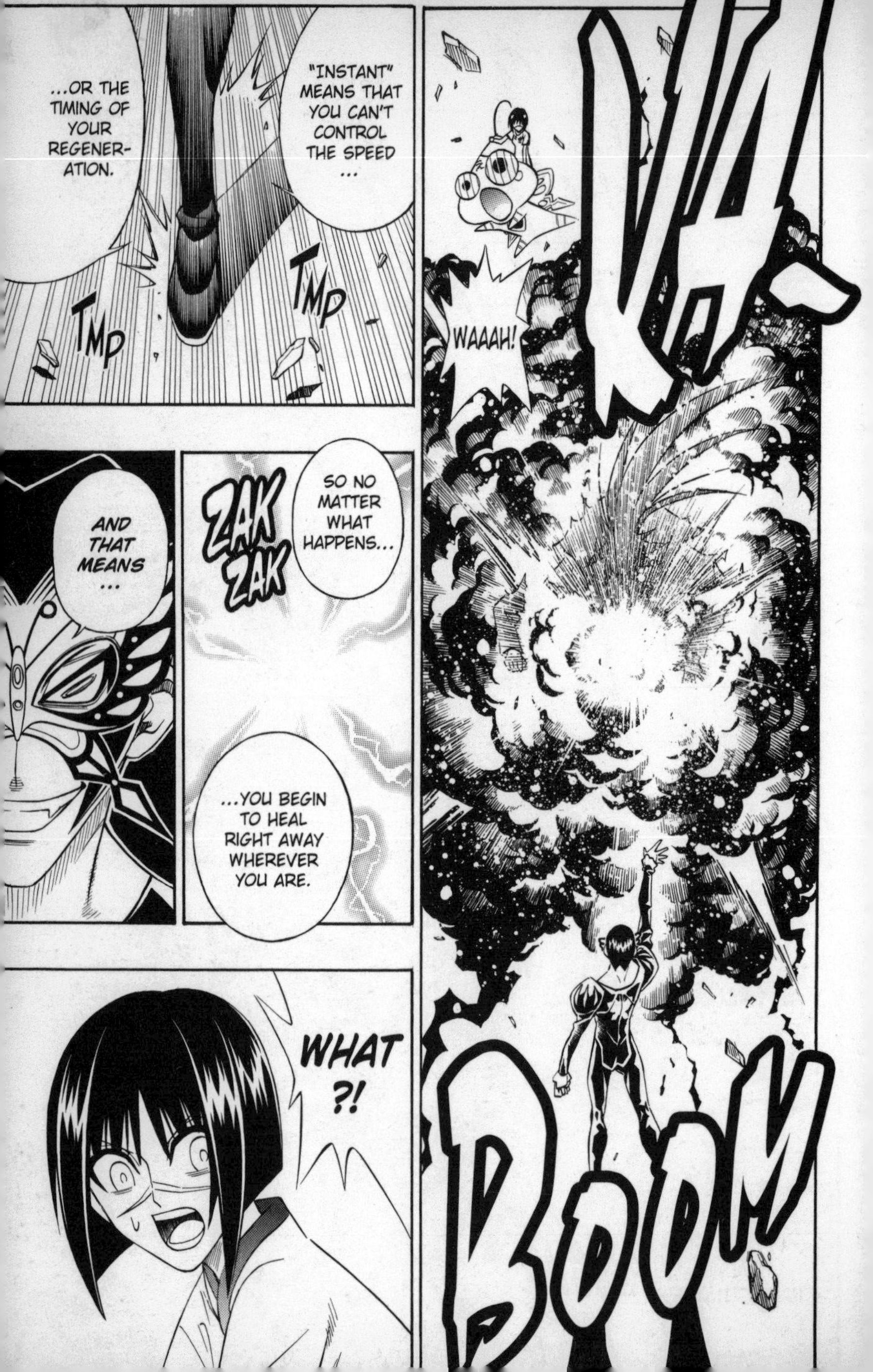
WAAAH!
BOOM
"INSTANT" MEANS THAT YOU CAN'T CONTROL THE SPEED ...
...OR THE TIMING OF YOUR REGENER-ATION.
TMP
TMP
ZAK ZAK
SO NO MATTER WHAT HAPPENS...
...YOU BEGIN TO HEAL RIGHT AWAY WHEREVER YOU ARE.
AND THAT MEANS ...
WHAT ?!

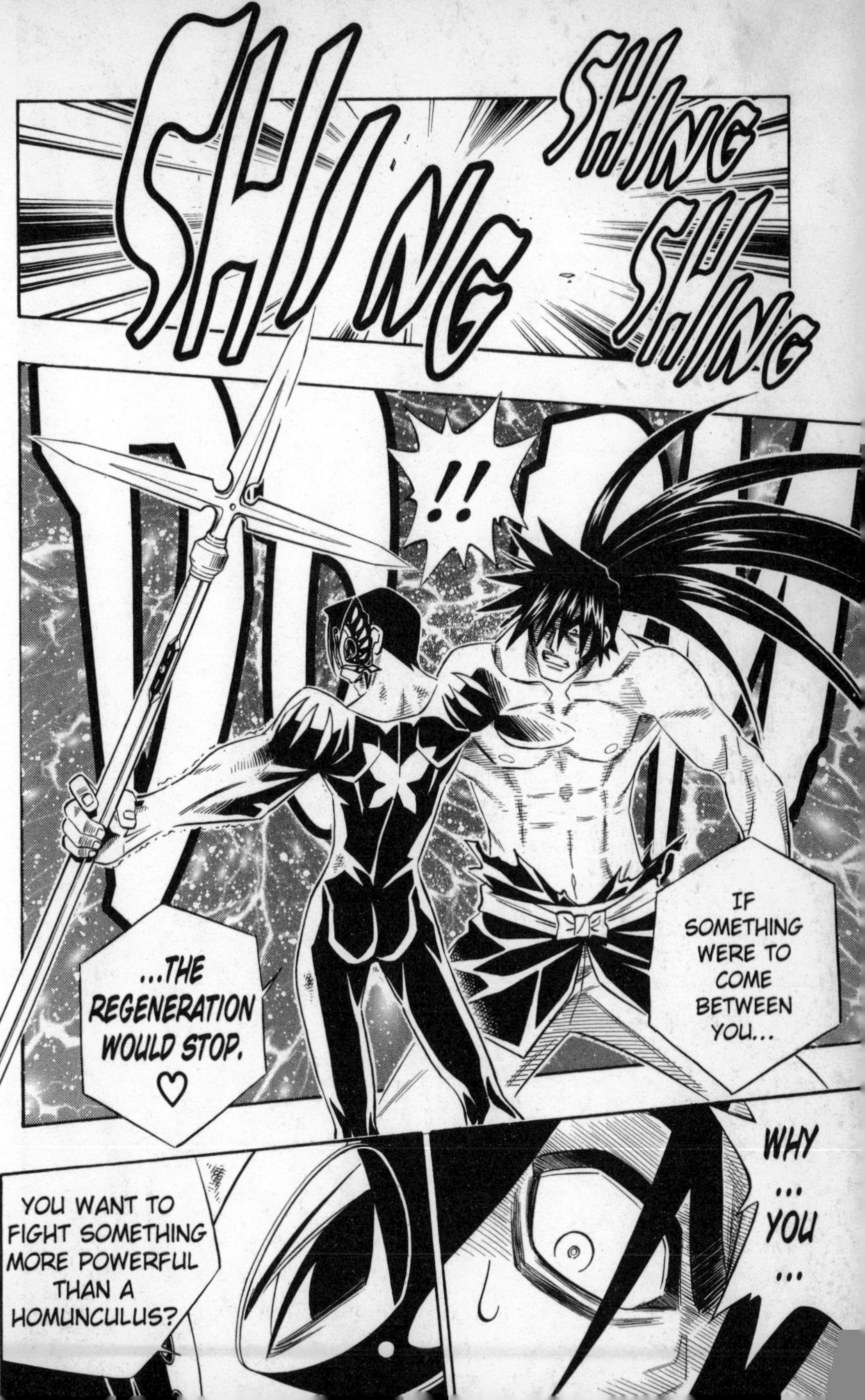
SHING
SHING
SHING SHING
!!
IF SOMETHING WERE TO COME BETWEEN YOU...
...THE REGENERATION WOULD STOP. ♡
WHY ... YOU ...
YOU WANT TO FIGHT SOMETHING MORE POWERFUL THAN A HOMUNCULUS?

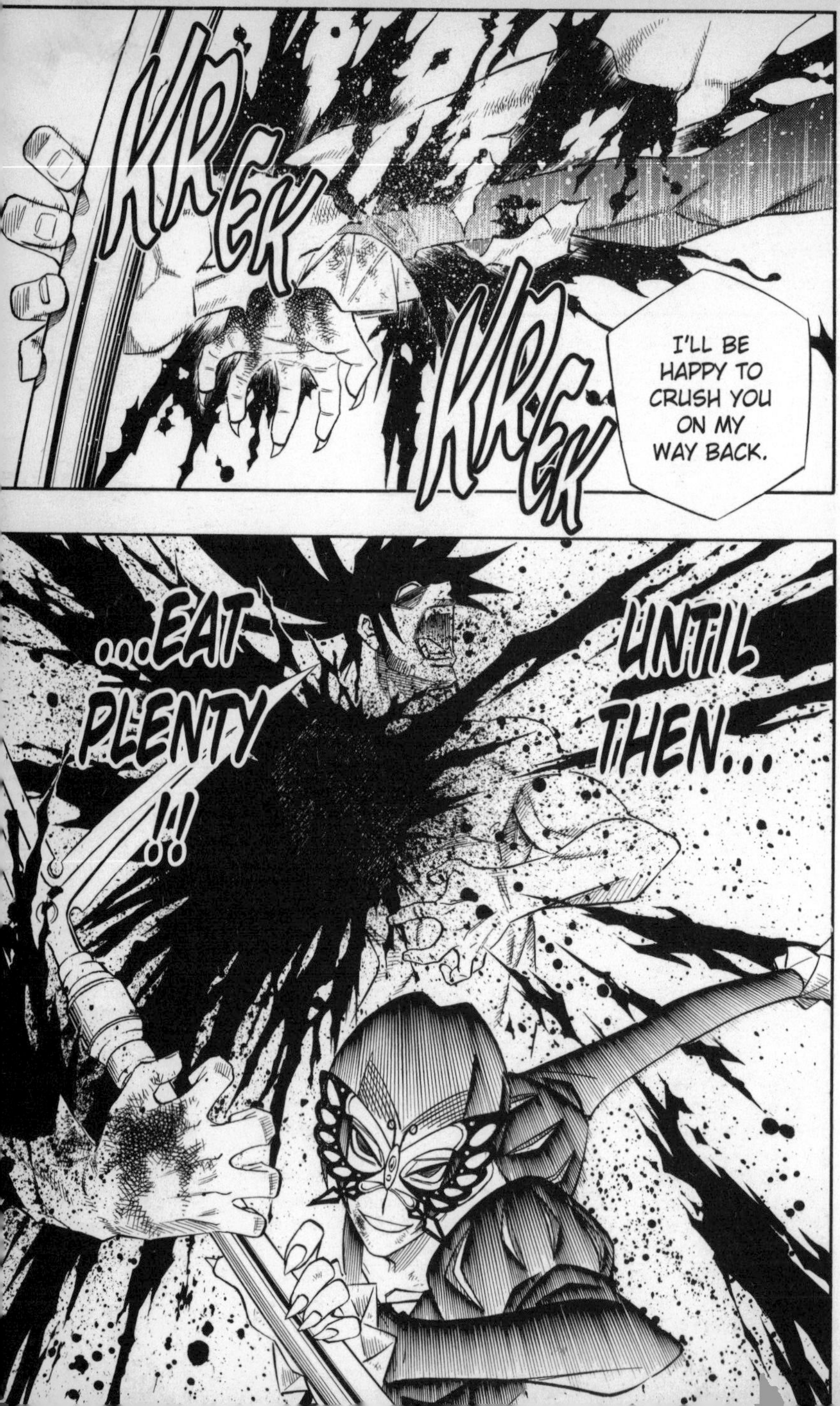
I'LL BE HAPPY TO CRUSH YOU ON MY WAY BACK.
KREEK
KREEK
UNTIL THEN...
...EAT PLENTY!!

"I have only one desire—endless battle!"

Buso Renkin File No. 14

激戦

GEKISEN

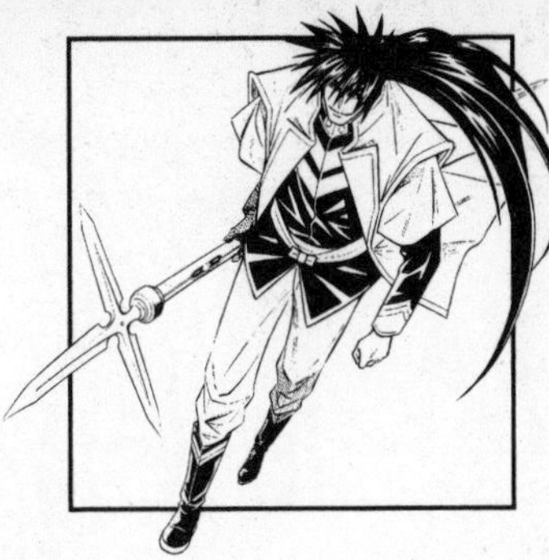

- Kakugane Serial Number: XII (12)
- Creator: Genji Ikusabe
- Form: Cross Spear
- Main Color: Lacquered Vermillion
- Special Abilities: · Instant Regeneration
- Special Traits:
  - The spear and its wielder are repaired or regenerated instantly when damaged.
  - The number of times the regeneration can be performed is dependent on the wielder's energy level. (Ikusabe is able to replenish his by ritualistically devouring homunculi.)
  - If Gekisen leaves its master's hand during regeneration, the process ceases.

- Author's Notes:
  - What abilities would suit a battle maniac who would keep fighting even after he lost a limb or two? The answer came to me in the form of Gekisen.
  - Having created it, I found myself with a new problem—how to defeat it. I could only think of one way, so I used it. I wasn't completely happy with it, but it worked. I still wonder sometimes if I could've come up with something better.
  - The design is based on a real weapon and I added some detail to the shaft. The spear head is what makes the cross spear distinctive so I didn't want to mess with that. It's cool just the way it is!

GEKISEN

CHAPTER 65: DAWN AT THE GRAVEYARD

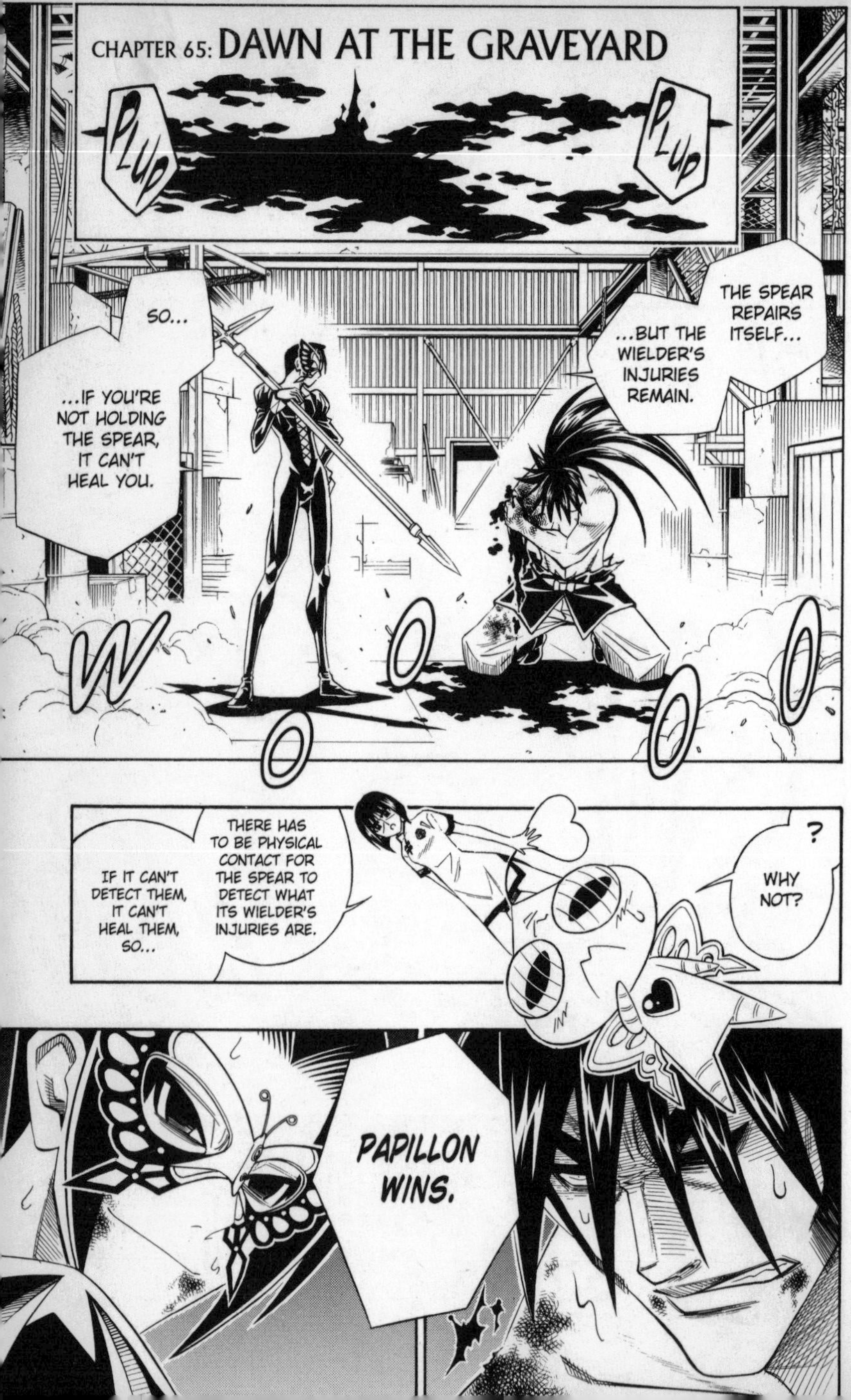

PLUP
PLUP
THE SPEAR REPAIRS ITSELF...
...BUT THE WIELDER'S INJURIES REMAIN.
SO...
...IF YOU'RE NOT HOLDING THE SPEAR, IT CAN'T HEAL YOU.
WOOOO
?
WHY NOT?
THERE HAS TO BE PHYSICAL CONTACT FOR THE SPEAR TO DETECT WHAT ITS WIELDER'S INJURIES ARE.
IF IT CAN'T DETECT THEM, IT CAN'T HEAL THEM, SO...
PAPILLON WINS.

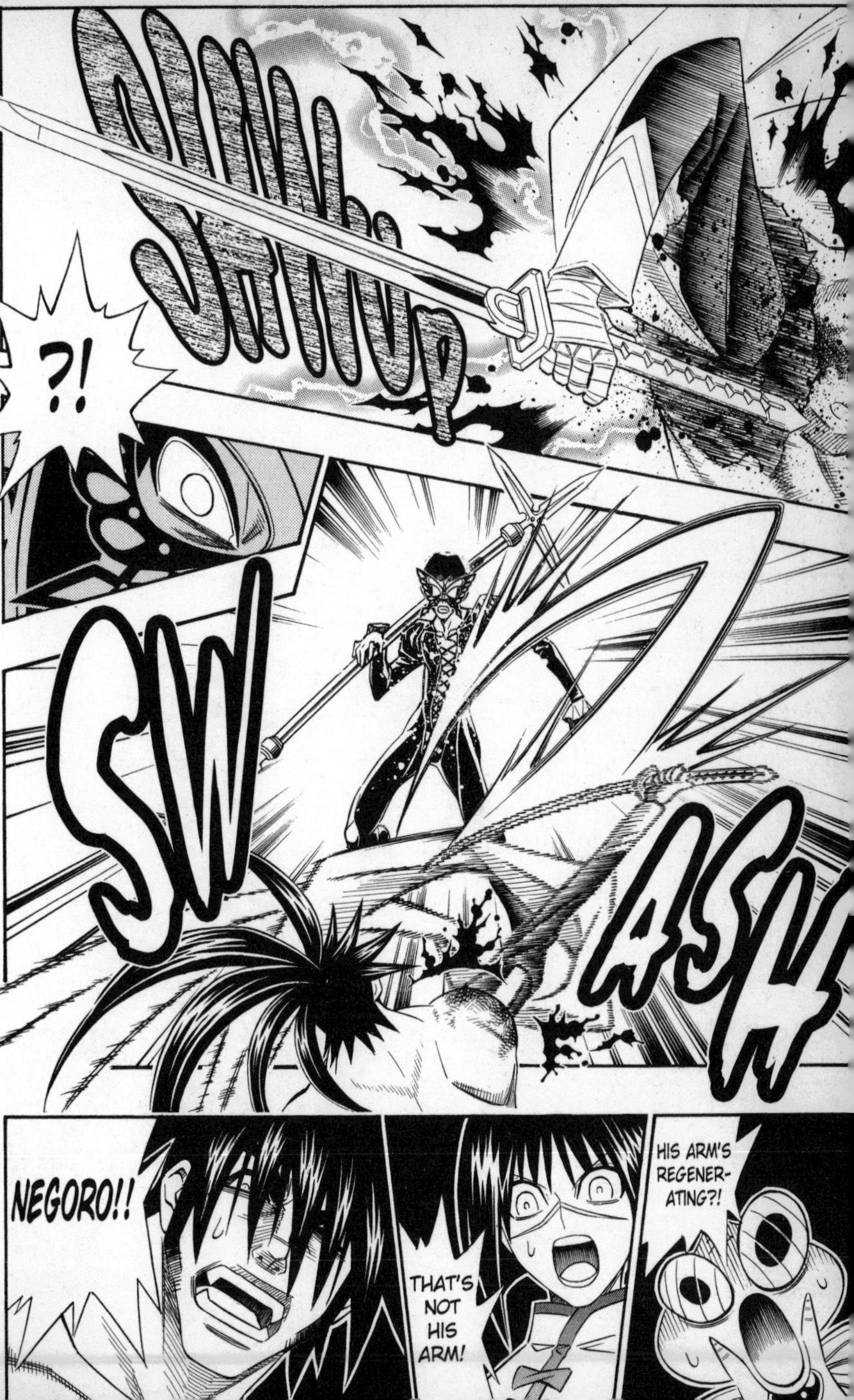
?!
SWASH
HIS ARM'S REGENER-ATING?!
THAT'S NOT HIS ARM!
NEGORO!!

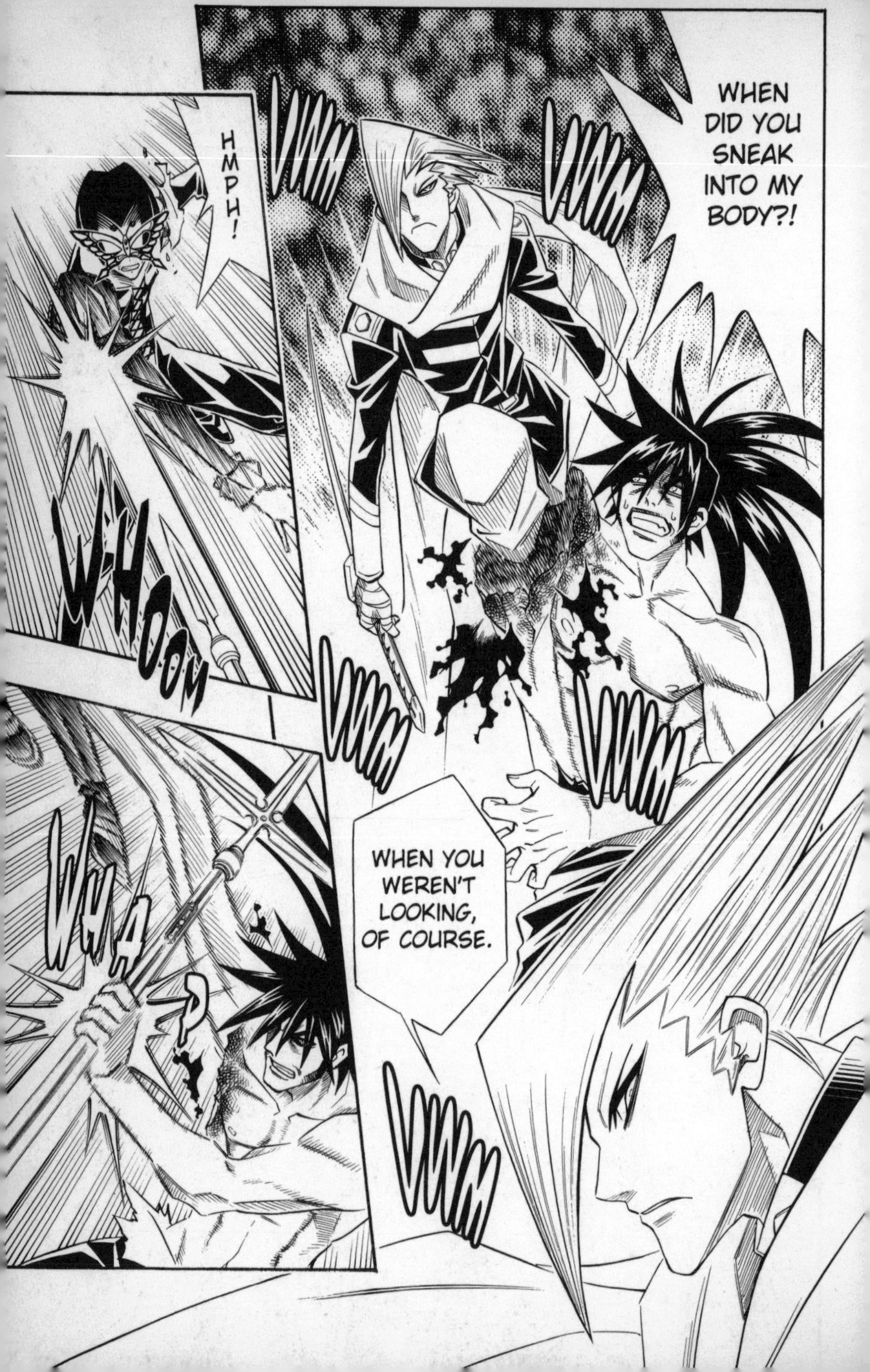
WHEN DID YOU SNEAK INTO MY BODY?!
VWWM
VWWM
HMPH!
WHOOM
VWWM
VWWM
WHEN YOU WEREN'T LOOKING, OF COURSE.
VWWM
WHA?

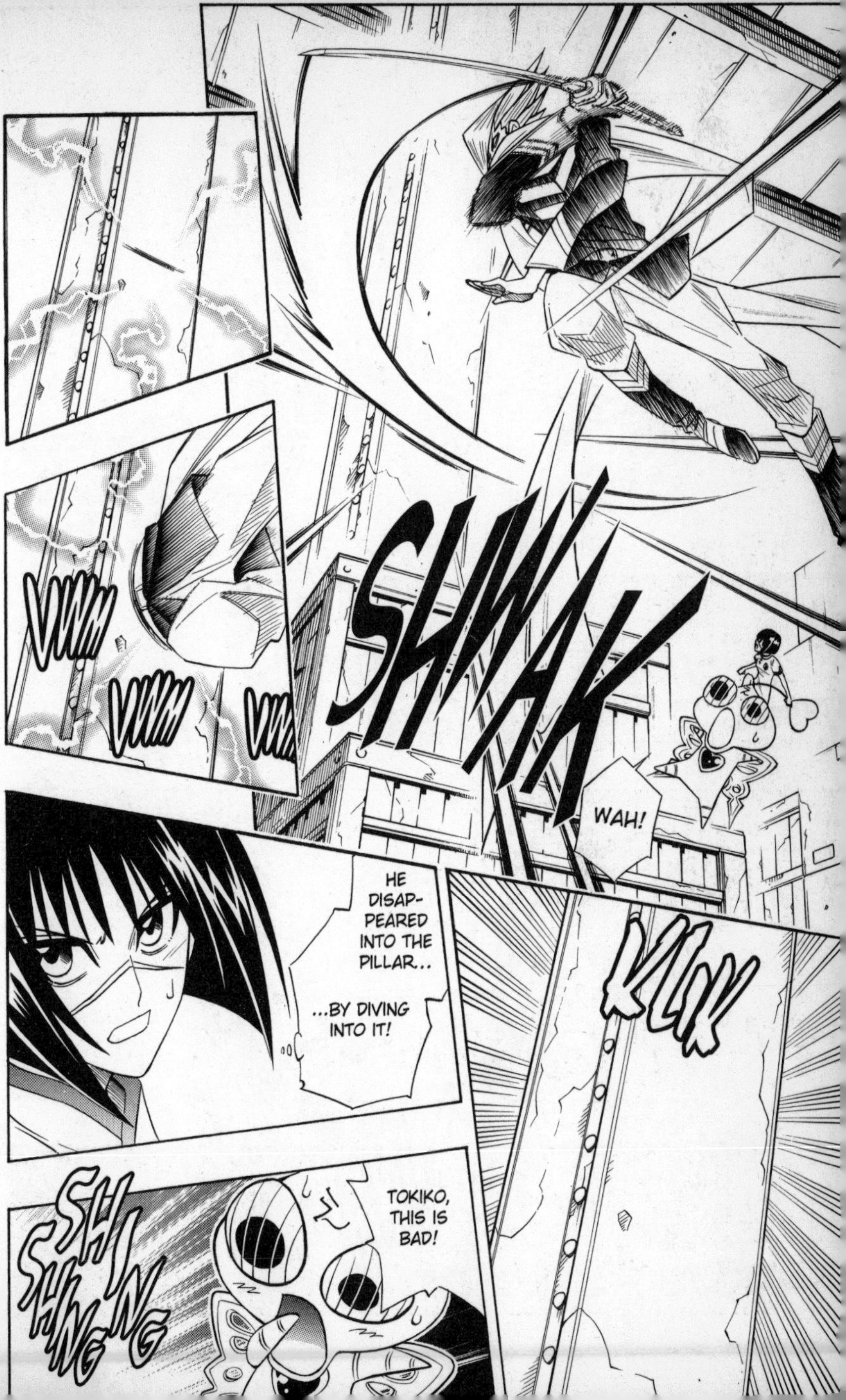
SHWAK
WAH!
VWM
VWM
VW
KLIK
HE DISAPPEARED INTO THE PILLAR...
...BY DIVING INTO IT!
TOKIKO, THIS IS BAD!
SHING SHING

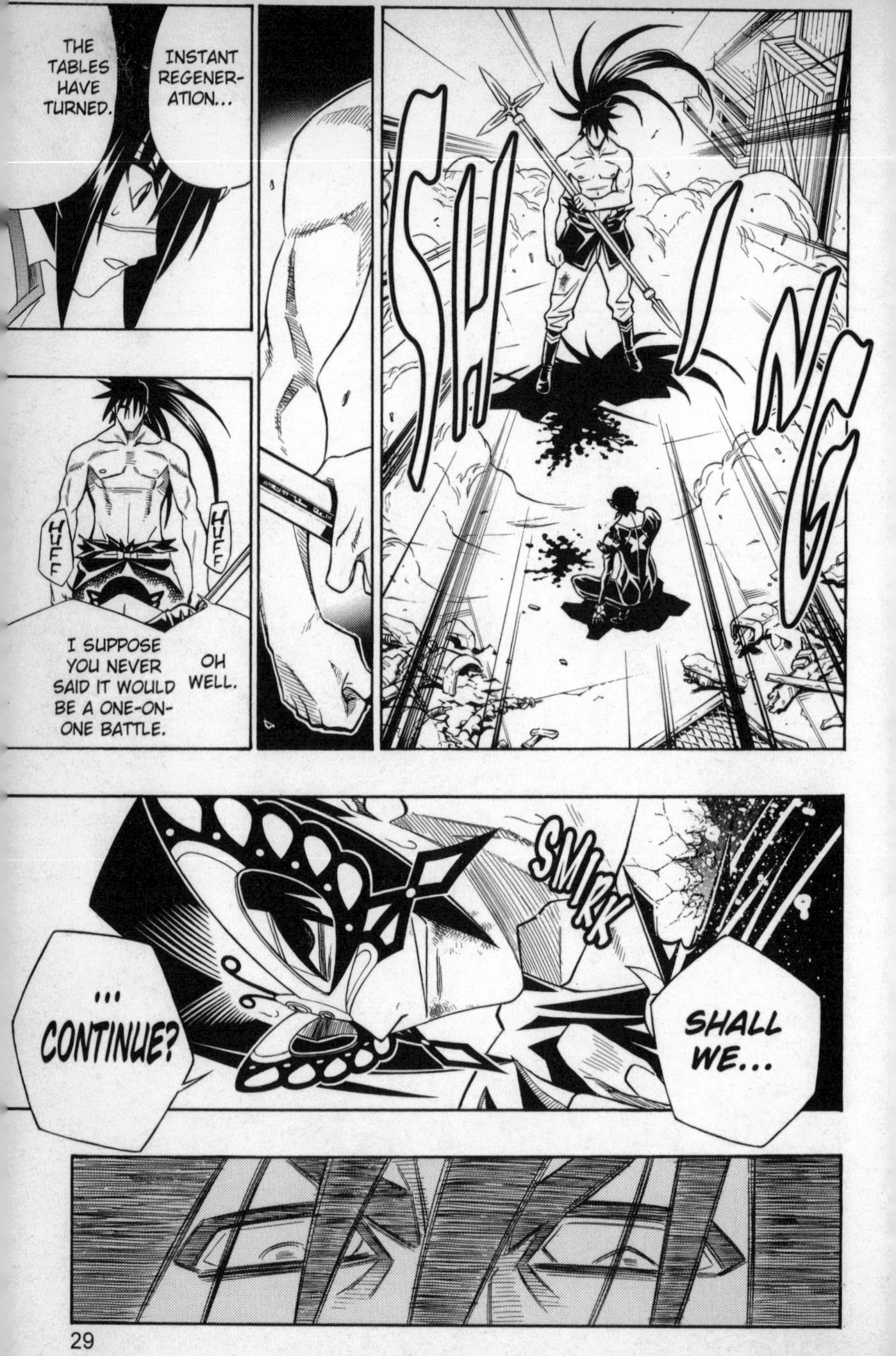
SHING
INSTANT REGENER-ATION...
THE TABLES HAVE TURNED.
HUFF
HUFF
OH WELL.
I SUPPOSE YOU NEVER SAID IT WOULD BE A ONE-ON-ONE BATTLE.
SMIRK
SHALL WE...
... CONTINUE?

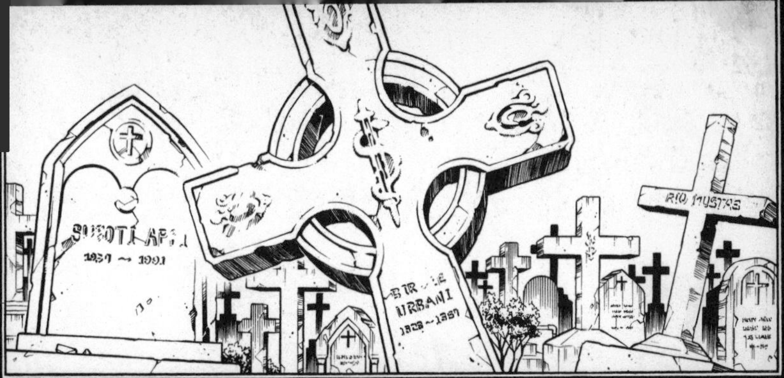

CHAPTER 65:

DAWN AT THE GRAVEYARD

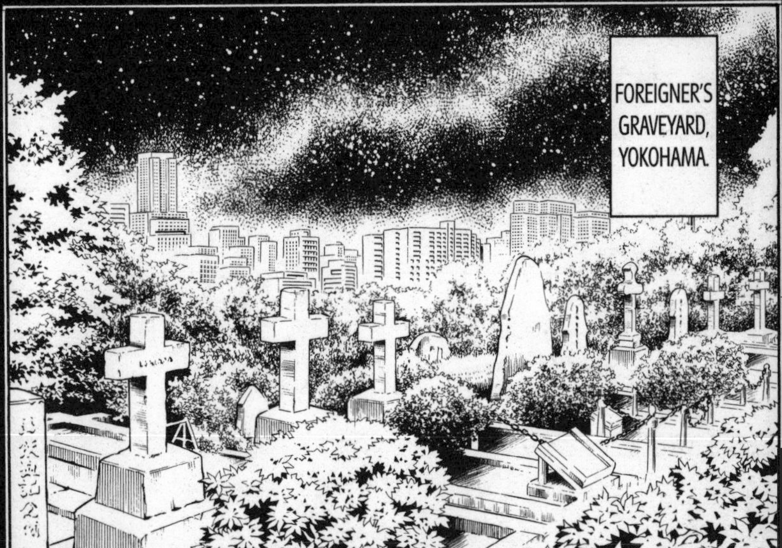
FOREIGNER'S GRAVEYARD, YOKOHAMA.

READ THIS WAY

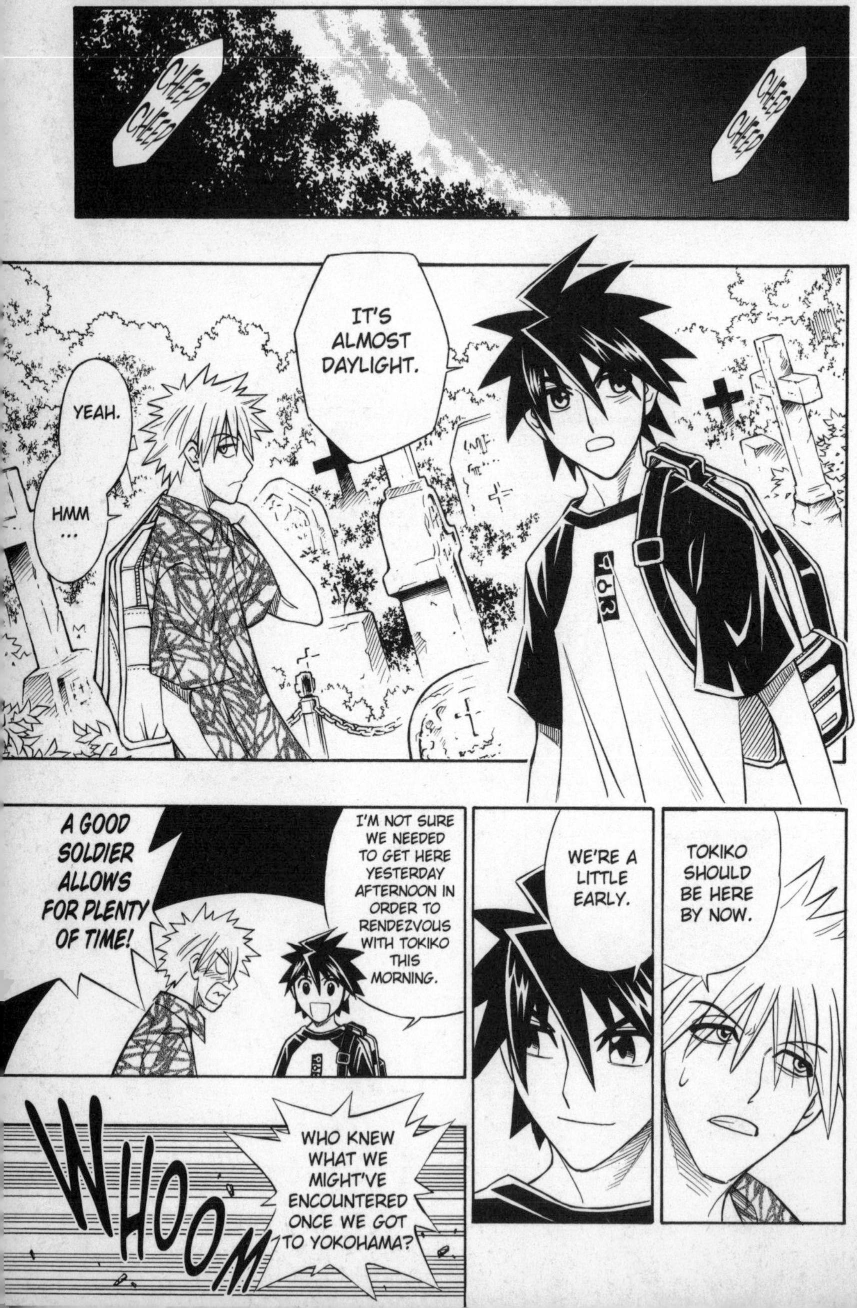
CHEEP CHEEP
CHEEP CHEEP
IT'S ALMOST DAYLIGHT.
YEAH.
HMM...
TOKIKO SHOULD BE HERE BY NOW.
WE'RE A LITTLE EARLY.
I'M NOT SURE WE NEEDED TO GET HERE YESTERDAY AFTERNOON IN ORDER TO RENDEZVOUS WITH TOKIKO THIS MORNING.
A GOOD SOLDIER ALLOWS FOR PLENTY OF TIME!
WHO KNEW WHAT WE MIGHT'VE ENCOUNTERED ONCE WE GOT TO YOKOHAMA?
WHOOM

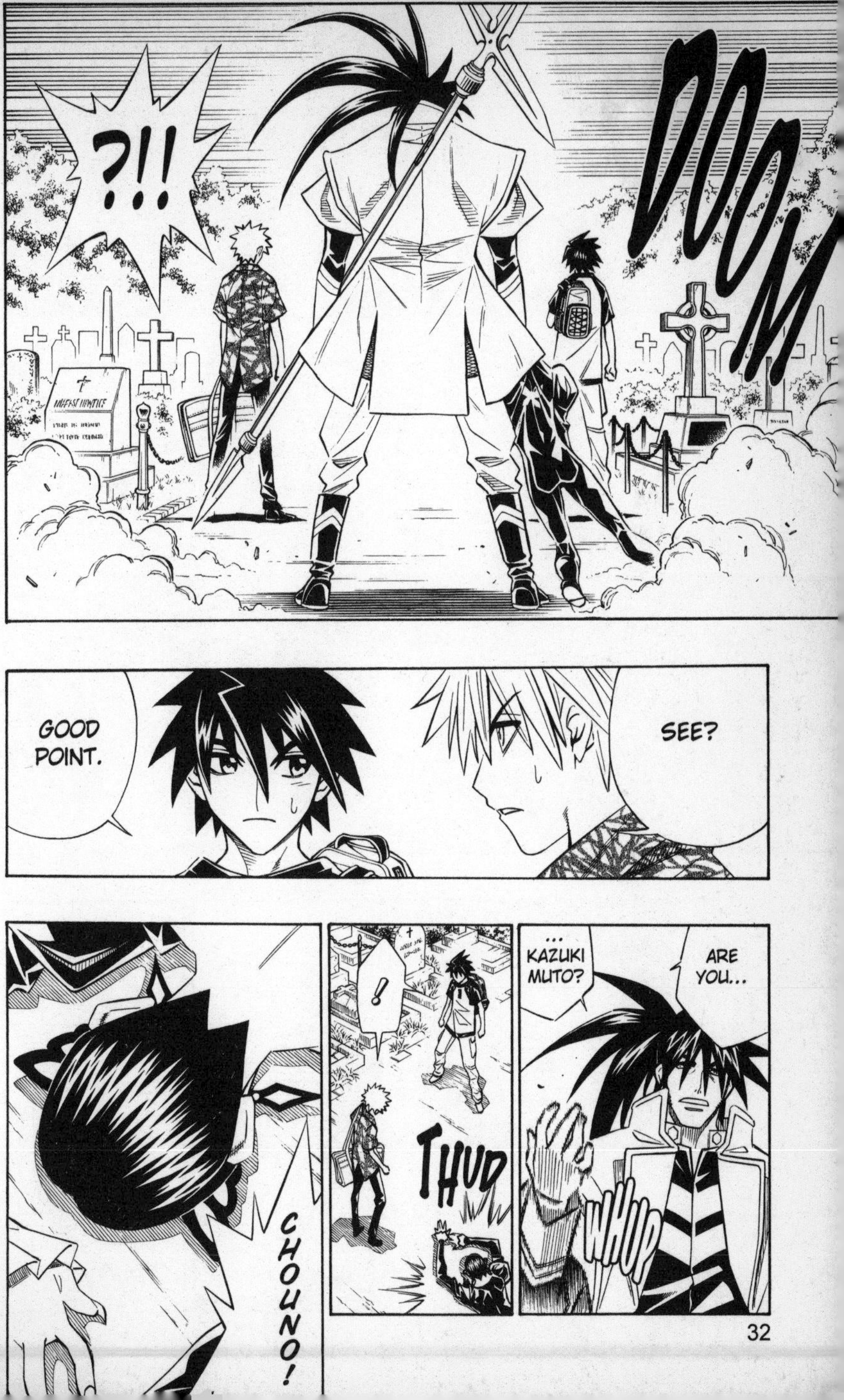
DOOM
?!!
SEE?
GOOD POINT.
ARE YOU...
...KAZUKI MUTO?
WHUP
!
THUD
CHOUNO!

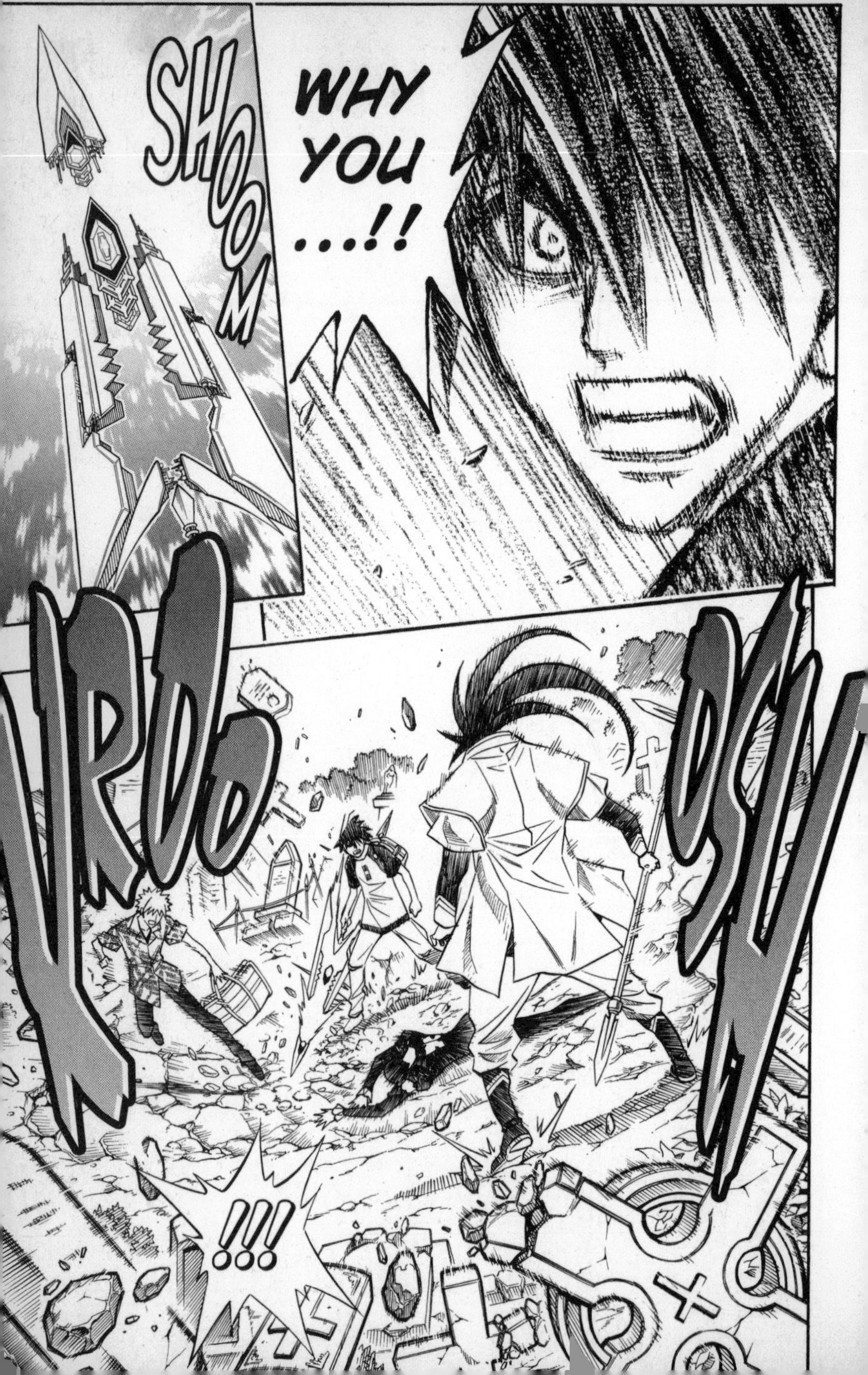
WHY YOU ...!!
SHOOOM
KROOOSH
!!!

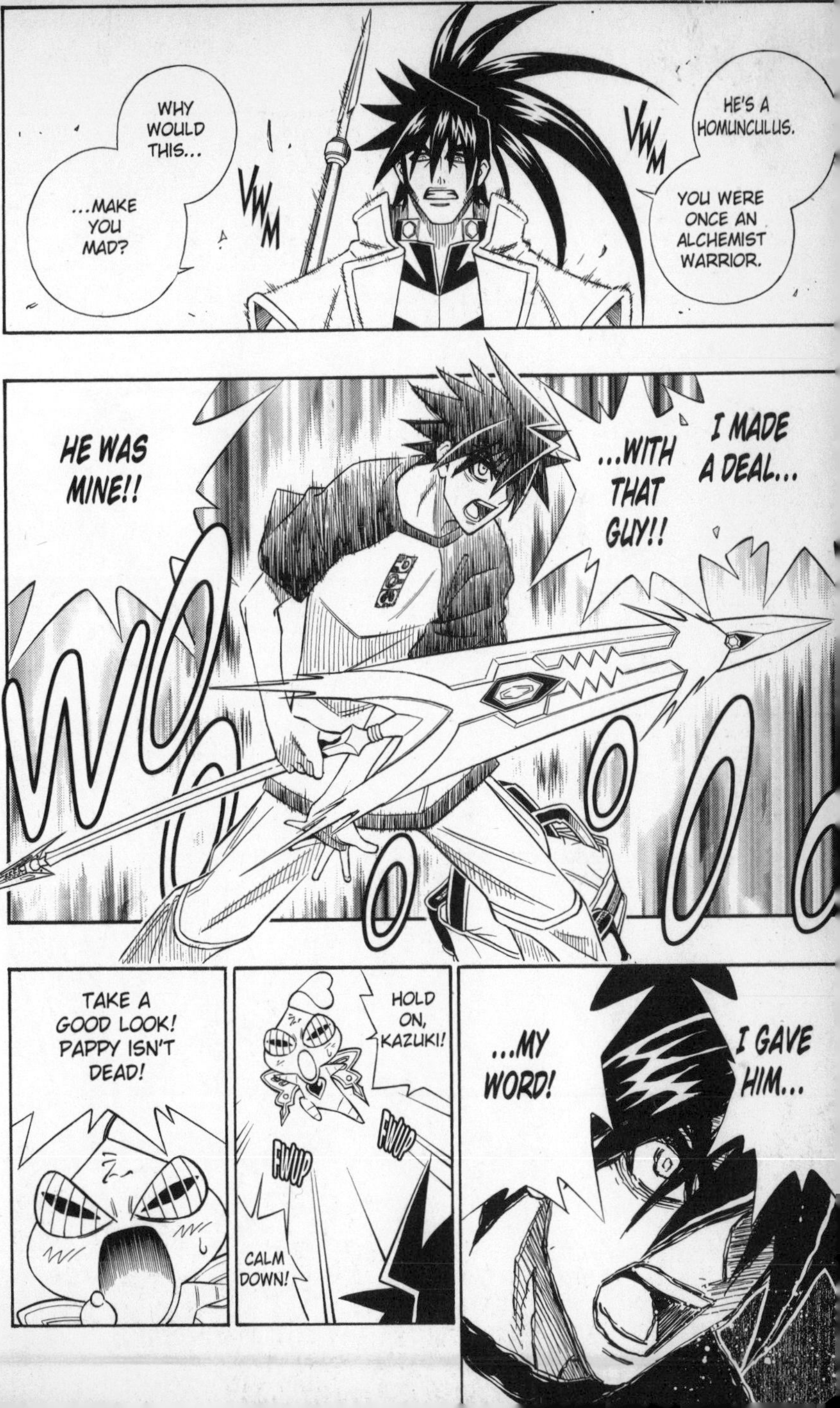
HE'S A HOMUNCULUS.
YOU WERE ONCE AN ALCHEMIST WARRIOR.
VWM
VWM
WHY WOULD THIS...
...MAKE YOU MAD?
I MADE A DEAL...
...WITH THAT GUY!!
HE WAS MINE!!
WOO
I GAVE HIM...
...MY WORD!
HOLD ON, KAZUKI!
FWUP
FWUP
CALM DOWN!
TAKE A GOOD LOOK! PAPPY ISN'T DEAD!

READ THIS WAY

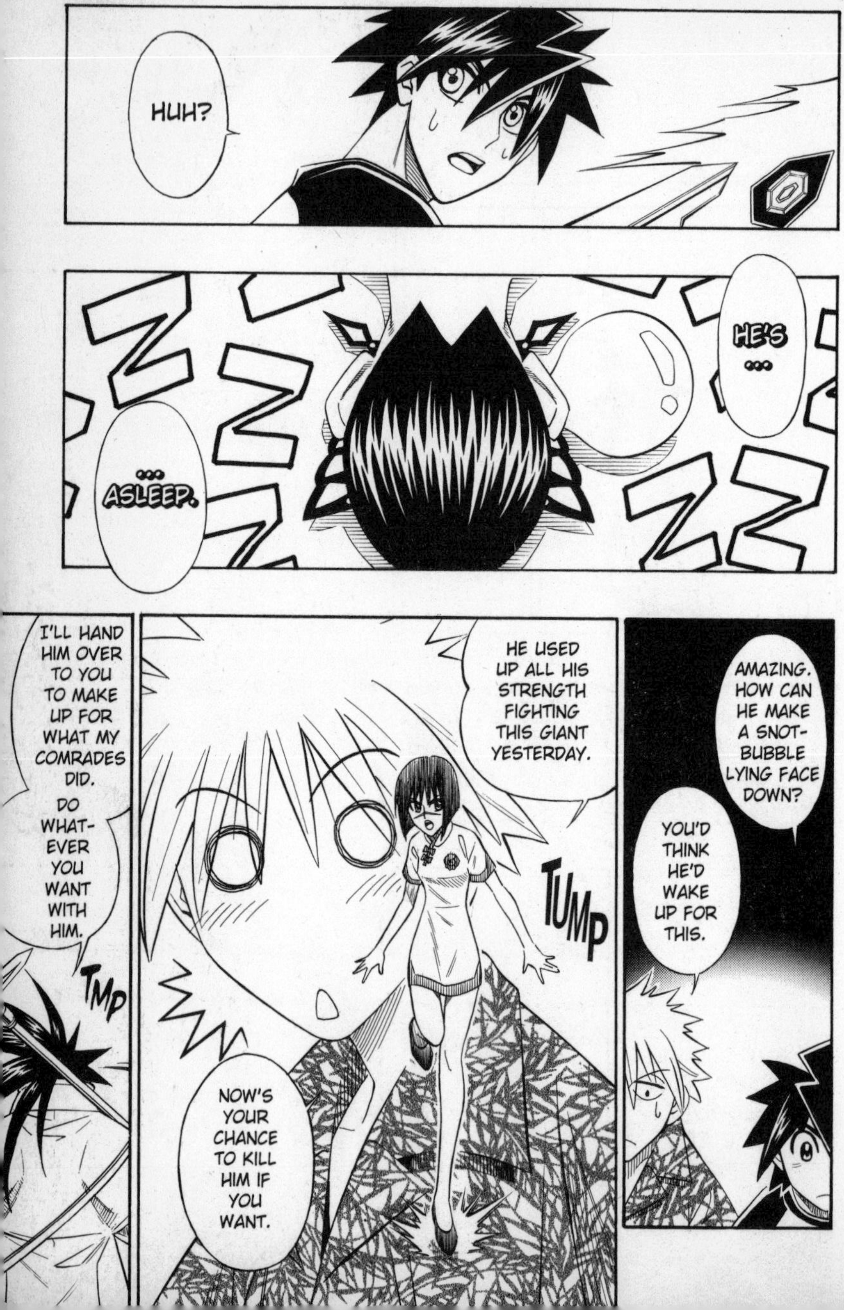
HUH?
HE'S...
...ASLEEP.
AMAZING. HOW CAN HE MAKE A SNOT-BUBBLE LYING FACE DOWN?
YOU'D THINK HE'D WAKE UP FOR THIS.
HE USED UP ALL HIS STRENGTH FIGHTING THIS GIANT YESTERDAY.
TUMP
NOW'S YOUR CHANCE TO KILL HIM IF YOU WANT.
I'LL HAND HIM OVER TO YOU TO MAKE UP FOR WHAT MY COMRADES DID.
DO WHAT-EVER YOU WANT WITH HIM.
TMP

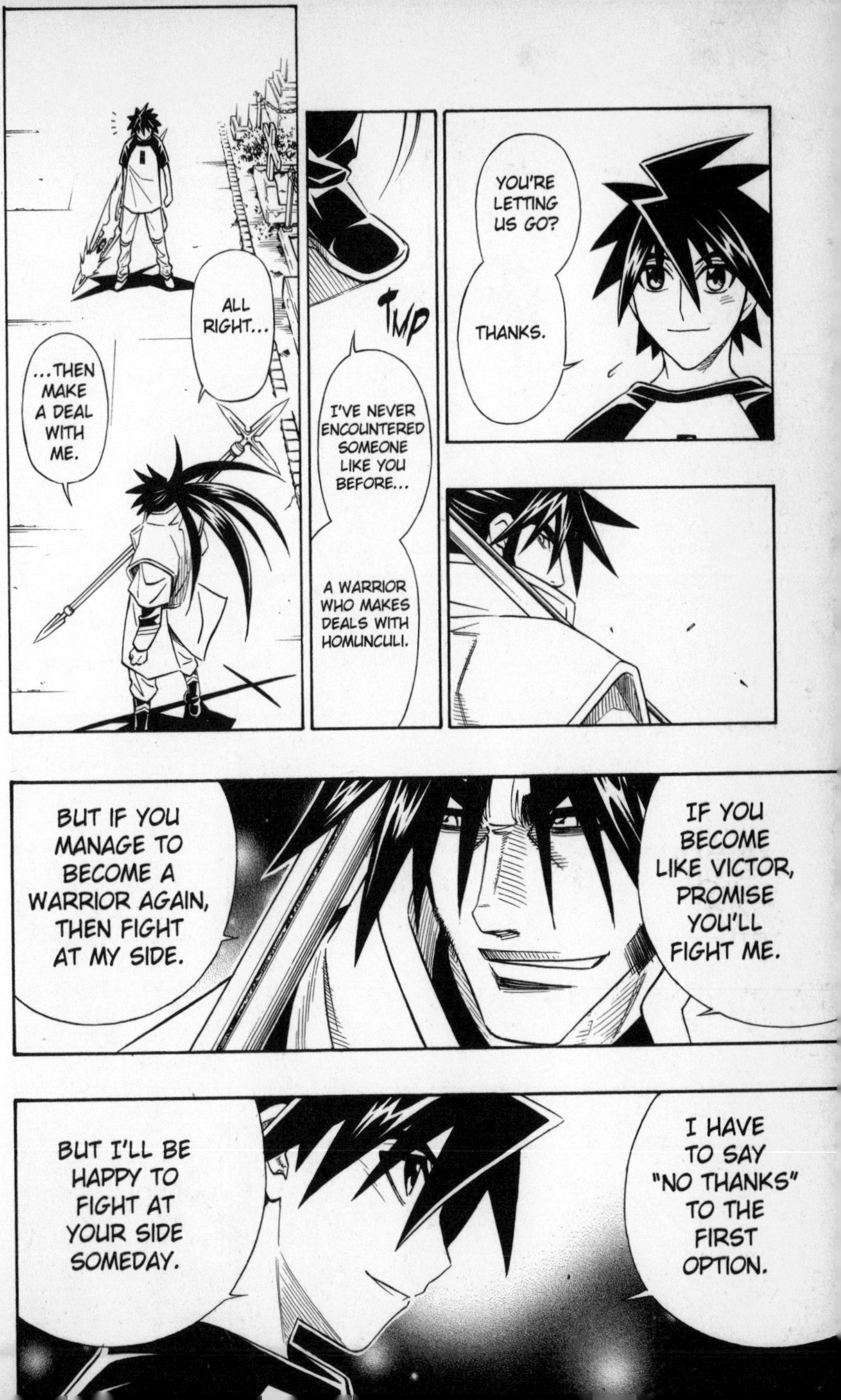
YOU'RE LETTING US GO?
THANKS.
TMP
I'VE NEVER ENCOUNTERED SOMEONE LIKE YOU BEFORE...
A WARRIOR WHO MAKES DEALS WITH HOMUNCULI.
ALL RIGHT...
...THEN MAKE A DEAL WITH ME.
IF YOU BECOME LIKE VICTOR, PROMISE YOU'LL FIGHT ME.
BUT IF YOU MANAGE TO BECOME A WARRIOR AGAIN, THEN FIGHT AT MY SIDE.
I HAVE TO SAY "NO THANKS" TO THE FIRST OPTION.
BUT I'LL BE HAPPY TO FIGHT AT YOUR SIDE SOMEDAY.

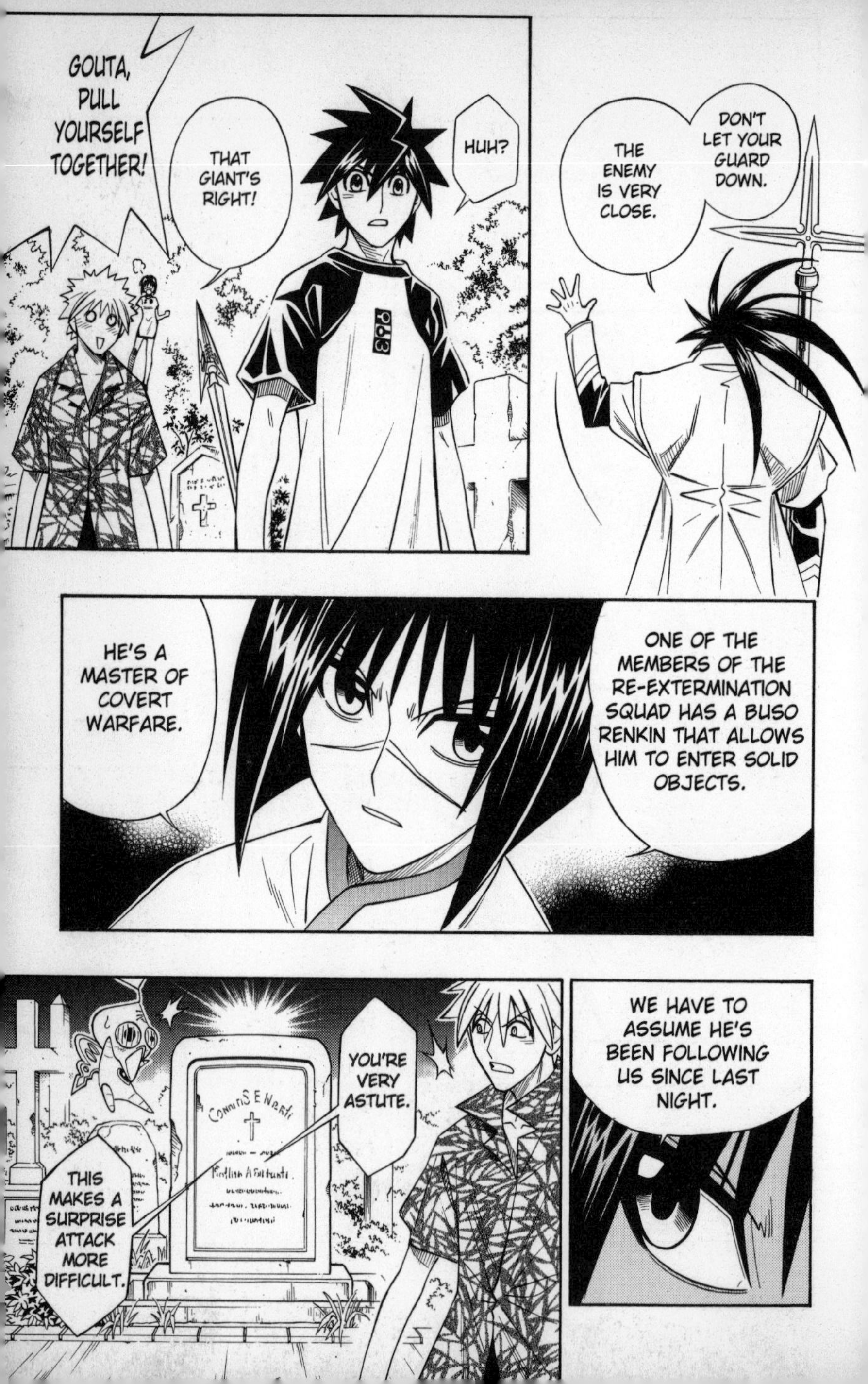
DON'T LET YOUR GUARD DOWN.
THE ENEMY IS VERY CLOSE.
HUH?
THAT GIANT'S RIGHT!
GOUTA, PULL YOURSELF TOGETHER!
ONE OF THE MEMBERS OF THE RE-EXTERMINATION SQUAD HAS A BUSO RENKIN THAT ALLOWS HIM TO ENTER SOLID OBJECTS.
HE'S A MASTER OF COVERT WARFARE.
WE HAVE TO ASSUME HE'S BEEN FOLLOWING US SINCE LAST NIGHT.
YOU'RE VERY ASTUTE.
THIS MAKES A SURPRISE ATTACK MORE DIFFICULT.

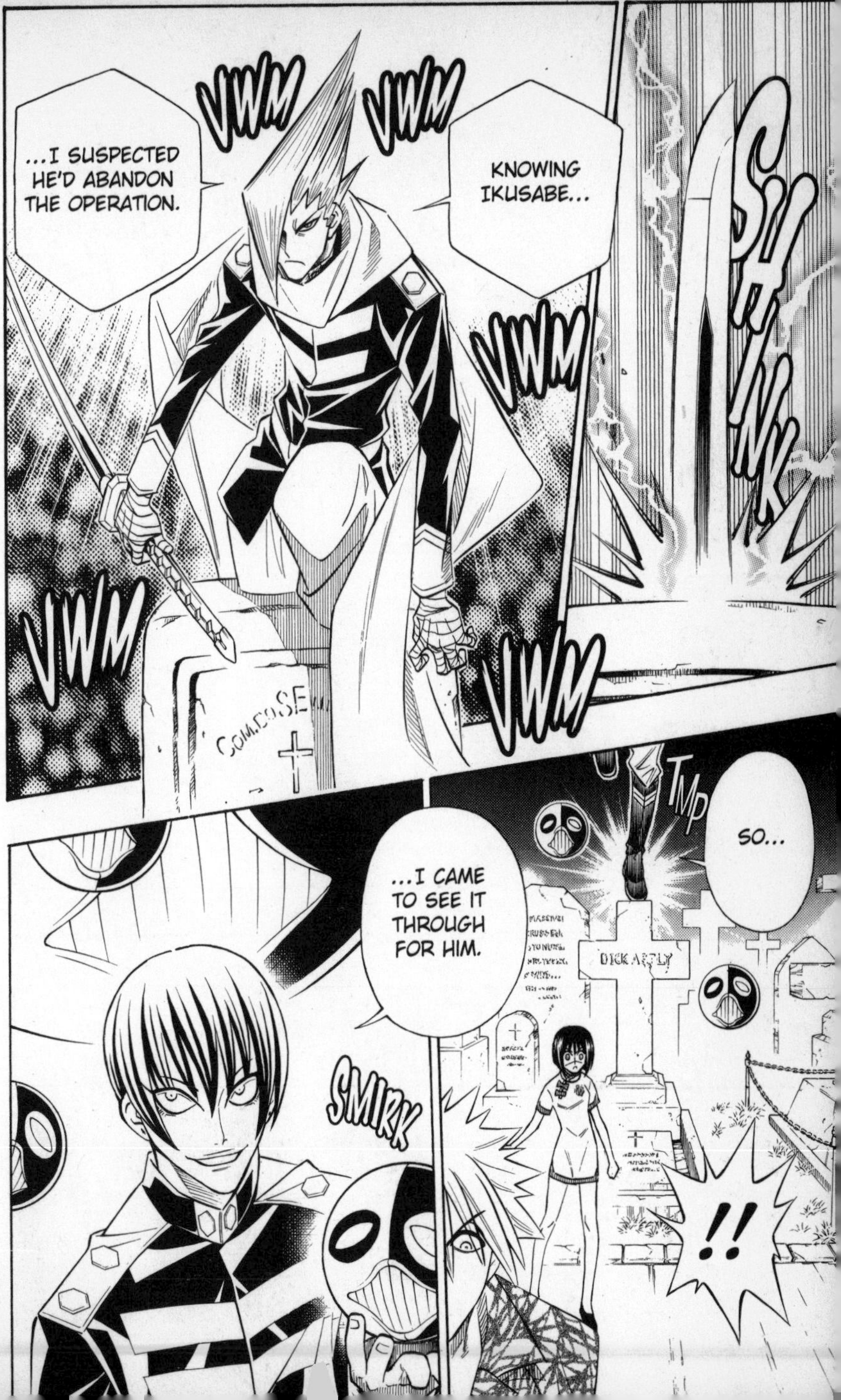
SHINK
VWM
VWM
KNOWING IKUSABE...
...I SUSPECTED HE'D ABANDON THE OPERATION.
VWM
VWM
VWM
TMP
SO...
!!
...I CAME TO SEE IT THROUGH FOR HIM.
SMIRK

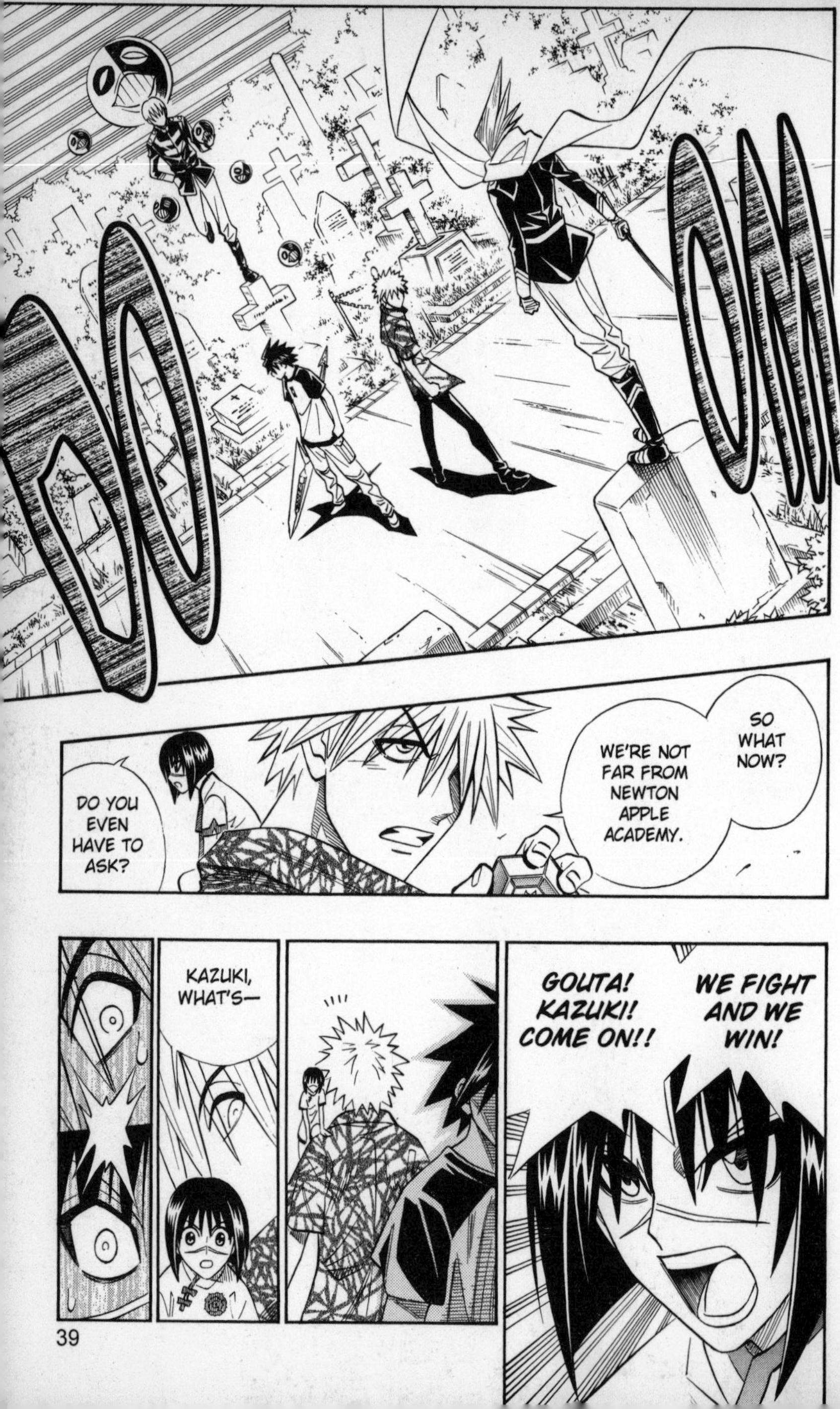
DOOM
SO WHAT NOW?
WE'RE NOT FAR FROM NEWTON APPLE ACADEMY.
DO YOU EVEN HAVE TO ASK?
WE FIGHT AND WE WIN!
GOUTA! KAZUKI! COME ON!!
KAZUKI, WHAT'S—

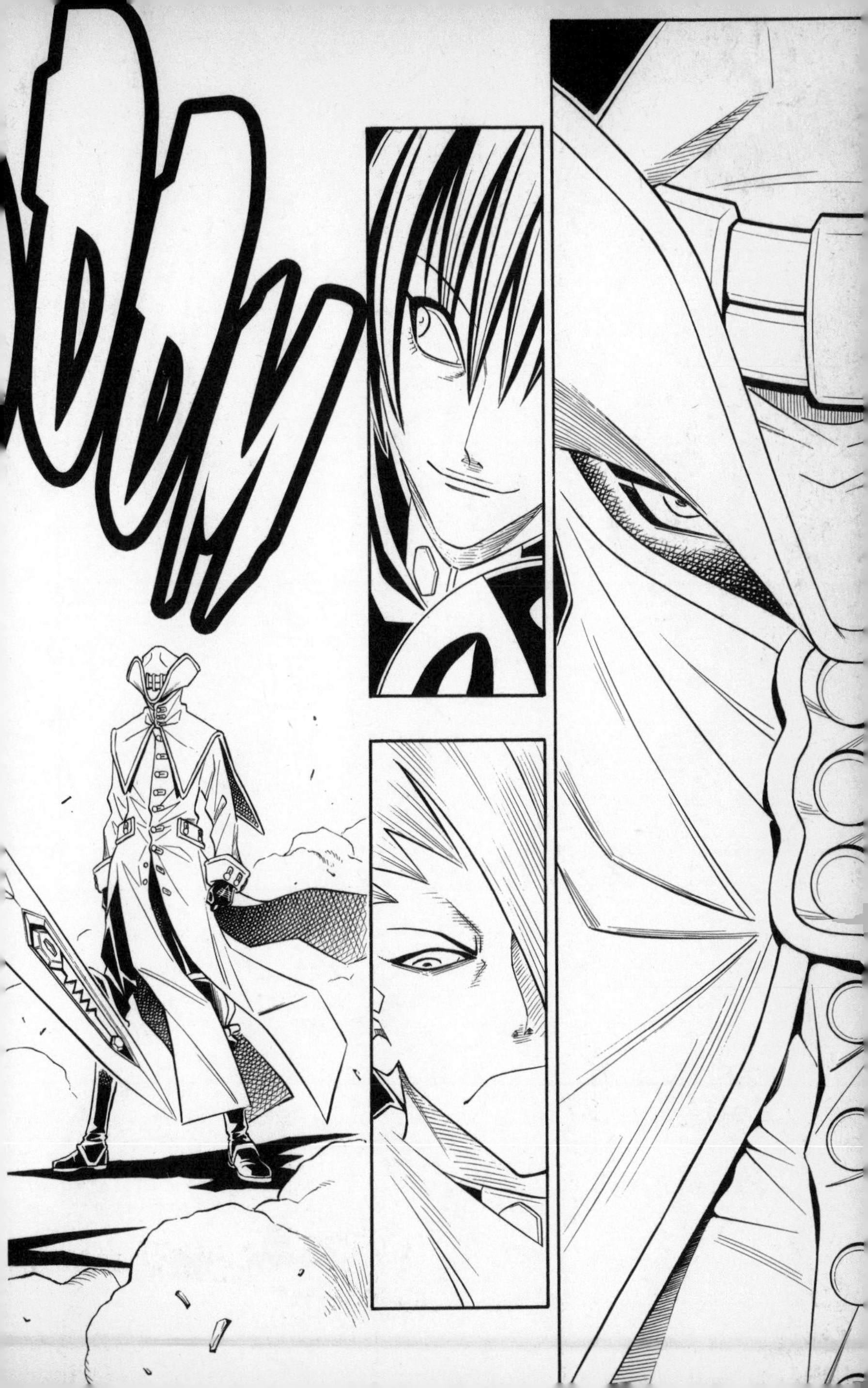

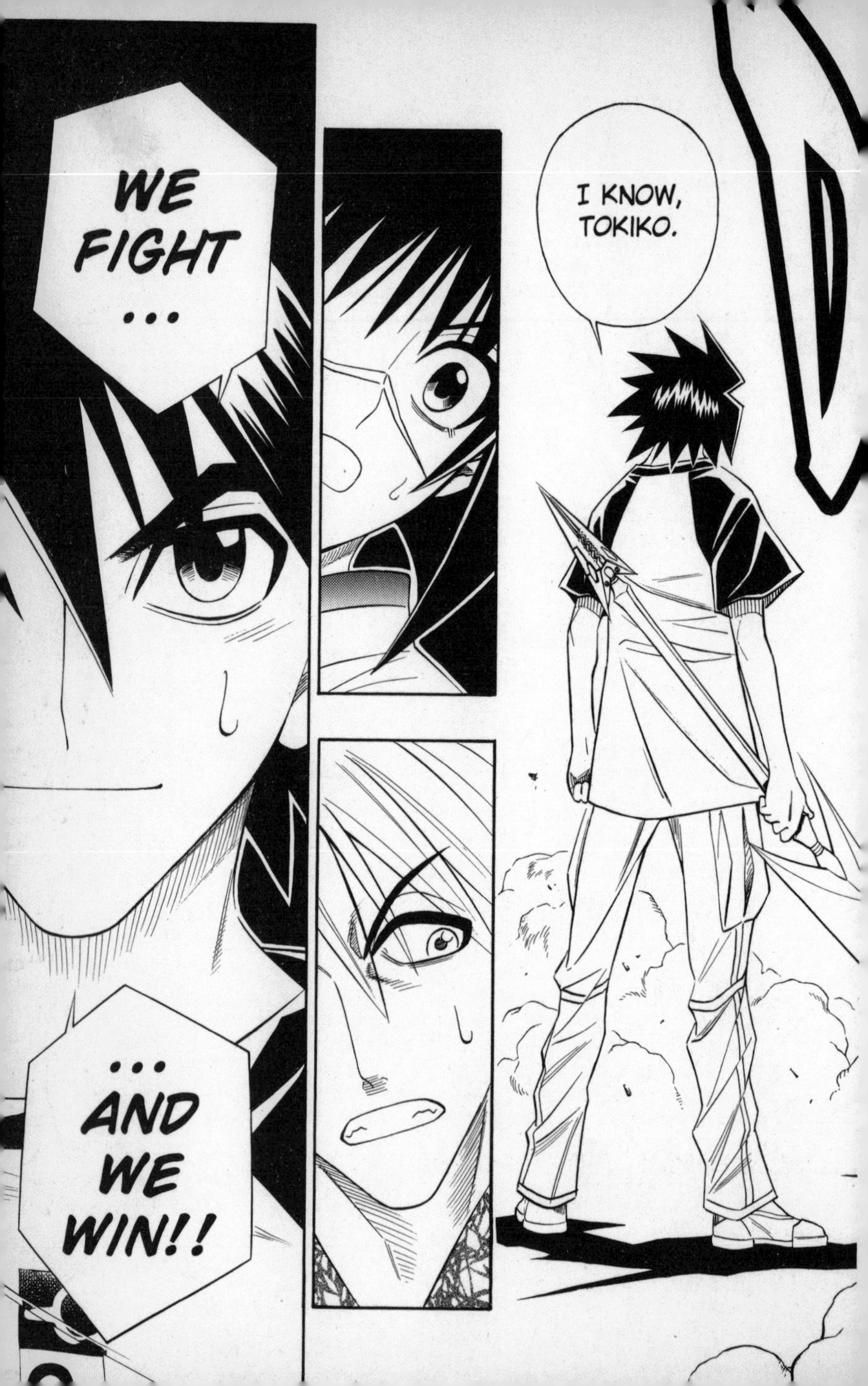
I KNOW, TOKIKO.
WE FIGHT ...
... AND WE WIN!!

· Height: 193 cm; Weight: 120 kg
· Born: July 27; Leo; Blood Type: B; Age: 27
· Likes: Winning battles, losing battles
· Dislikes: A peaceful life, sneak attacks, trickery
· Hobby: Studying military history
· Special Ability: Eating homunculi
· Affiliations: Alchemist Army, Re-Extermination Squad

Character File No. 29

GENJI IKUSABE

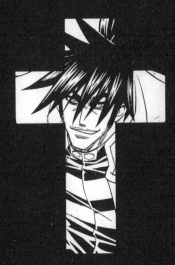

Author's Notes

· Ikusabe is the "Battle Maniac" that's a stock character in most action manga. But I wanted to make sure he didn't come across as someone who was actually insane, so maybe Ikusabe would be more correctly classified as a "Battle Enthusiast."

· Even before I became a manga artist, I had in mind a character whose strength was determined by how much he ate. I combined that with the ancient belief that a warrior could acquire the power of anything—or anyone—he ate, and the result was Ikusabe.

· I had a bunch of ideas for this character—like having his hair bristle when he got excited or having him laugh maniacally and run around like an anatomical model from a biology class whenever he regenerated—but I decided against them all in the end. Now that I think about it, since he ended up fighting Papillon, maybe I should've left them in.

· I wanted him to look like an extravagant sword master or feudal warlord with a Watsuki flavor, but he ended up looking more like Haohmaru from *Samurai Shodown*.

· He is one of my favorite Re-Extermination Squad characters. I'd like to use him again

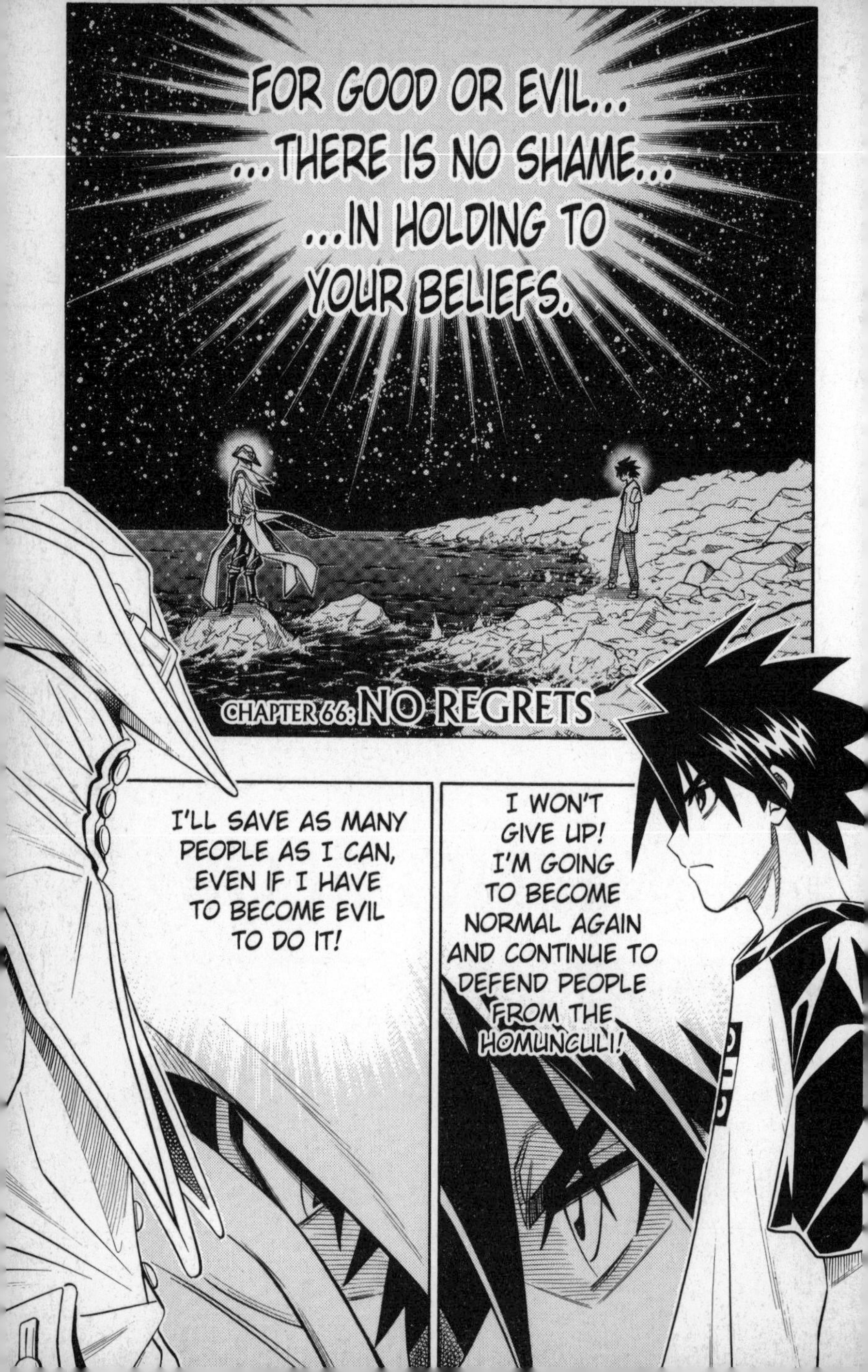
FOR GOOD OR EVIL...
...THERE IS NO SHAME...
...IN HOLDING TO YOUR BELIEFS.
CHAPTER 66: NO REGRETS
I WON'T GIVE UP! I'M GOING TO BECOME NORMAL AGAIN AND CONTINUE TO DEFEND PEOPLE FROM THE HOMUNCULI!
I'LL SAVE AS MANY PEOPLE AS I CAN, EVEN IF I HAVE TO BECOME EVIL TO DO IT!

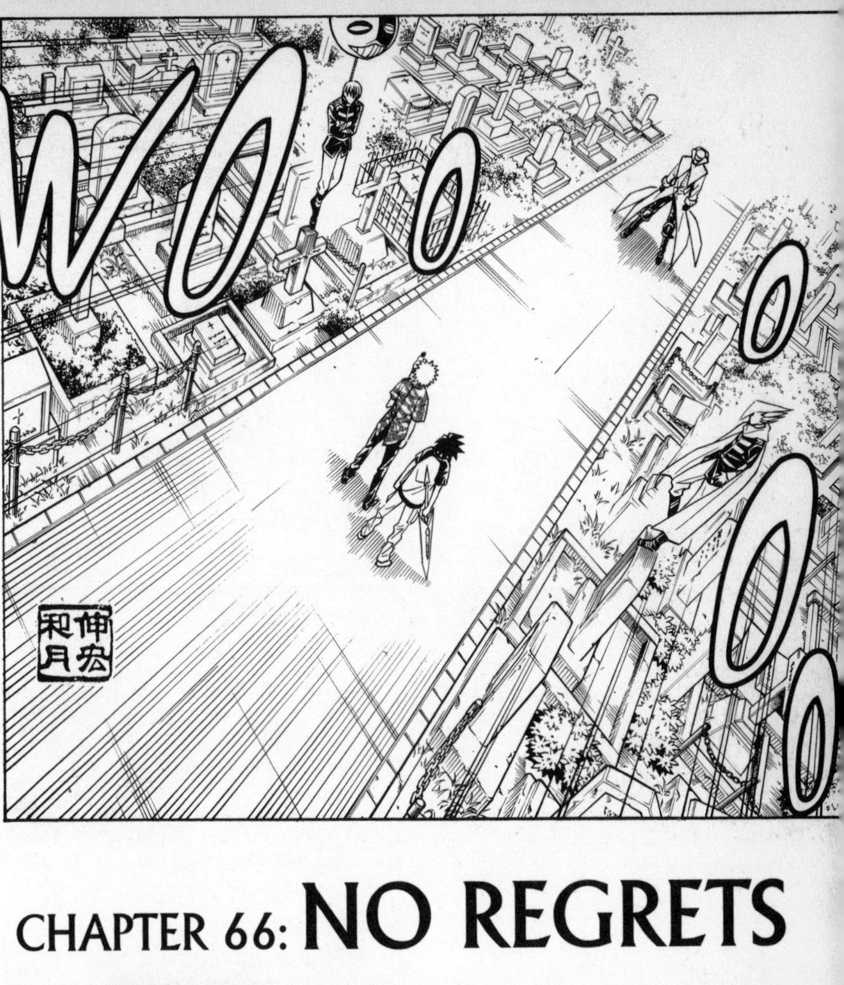
WOOOOOOO
和月伸宏

CHAPTER 66: NO REGRETS

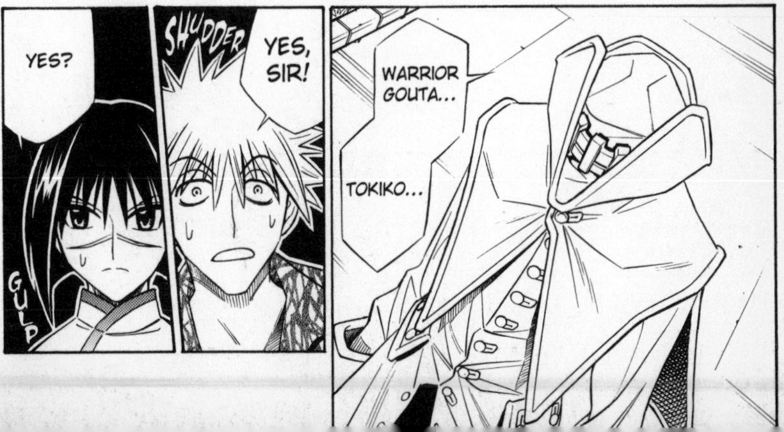
WARRIOR GOUTA...
TOKIKO...
SHUDDER
YES, SIR!
YES?
GULP

READ THIS WAY

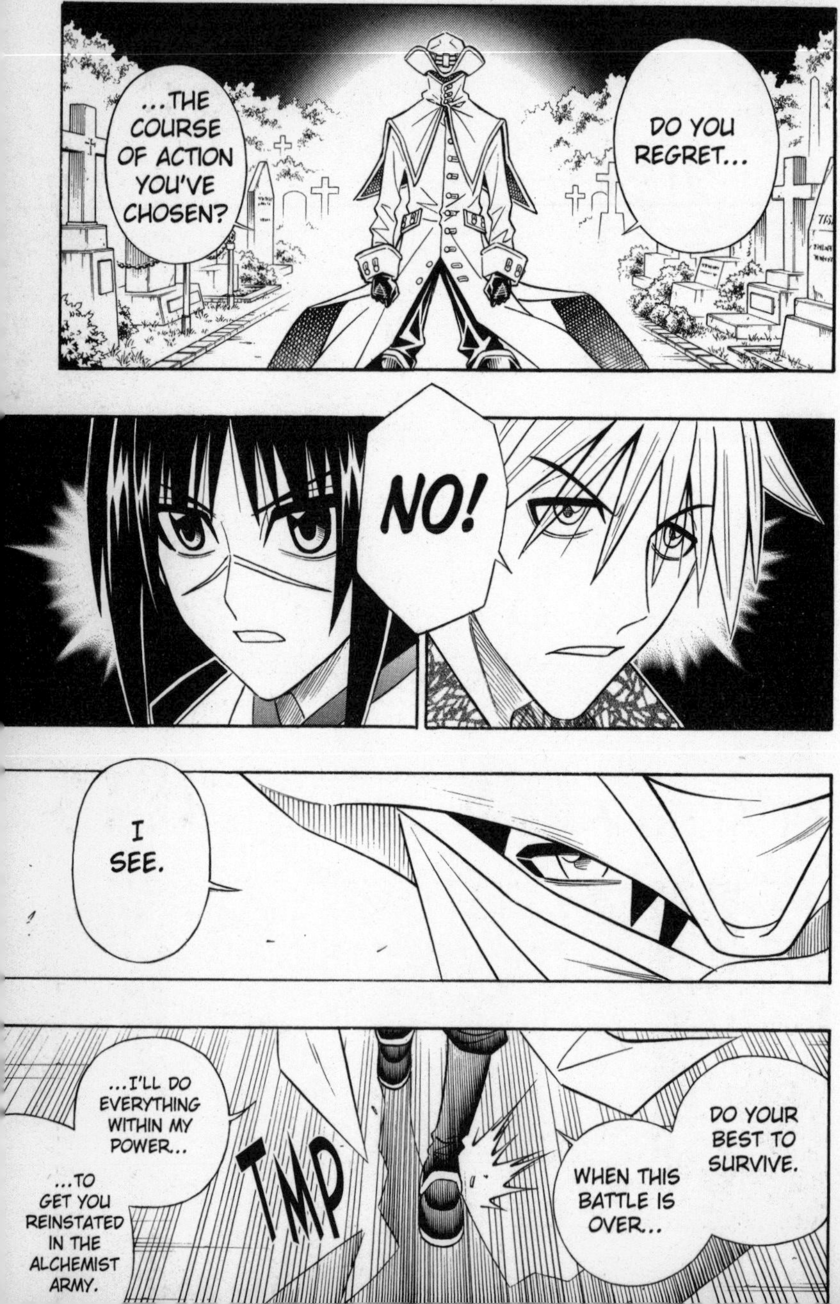
DO YOU REGRET...
...THE COURSE OF ACTION YOU'VE CHOSEN?
NO!
I SEE.
DO YOUR BEST TO SURVIVE.
WHEN THIS BATTLE IS OVER...
TMP
...I'LL DO EVERYTHING WITHIN MY POWER...
...TO GET YOU REINSTATED IN THE ALCHEMIST ARMY.

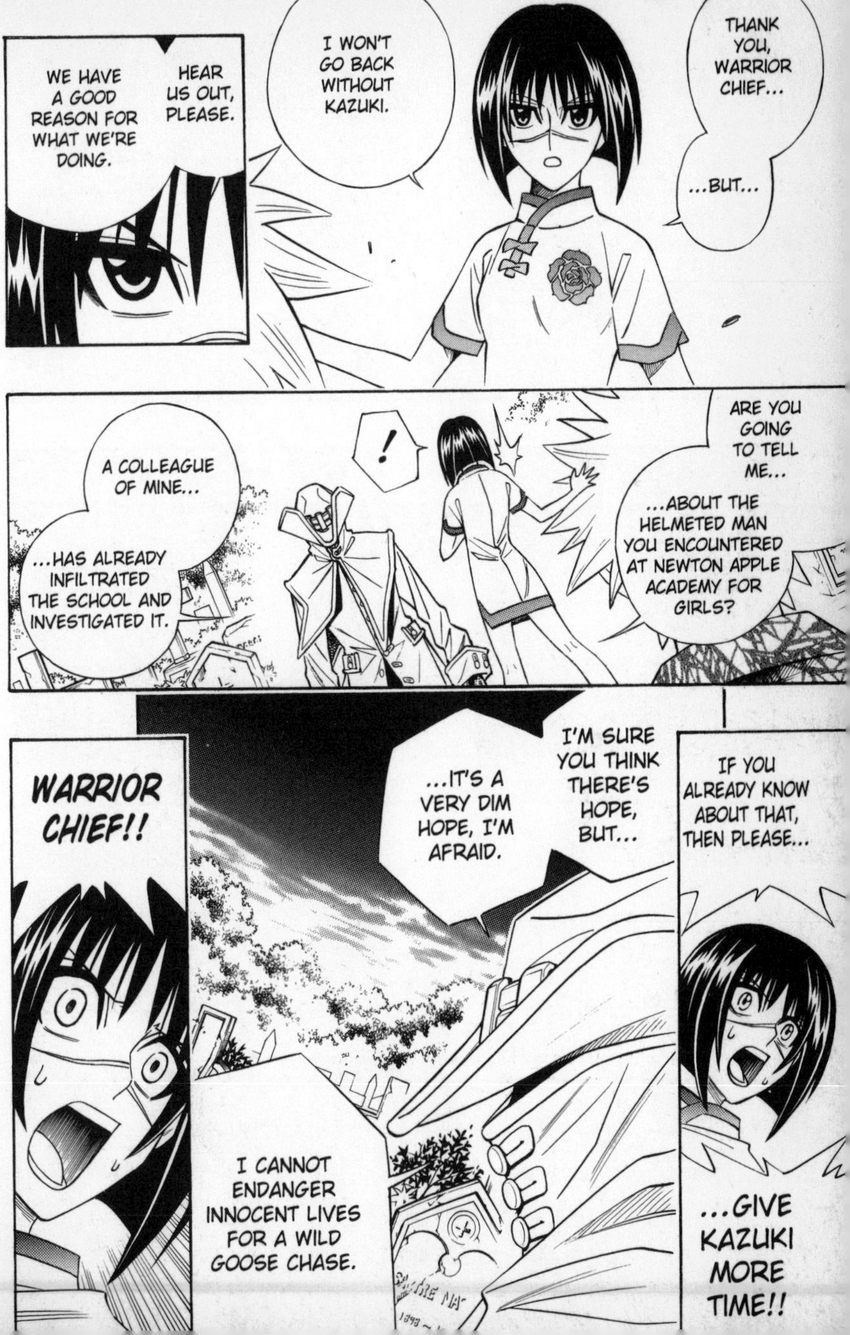
THANK YOU, WARRIOR CHIEF...
...BUT...
I WON'T GO BACK WITHOUT KAZUKI.
HEAR US OUT, PLEASE.
WE HAVE A GOOD REASON FOR WHAT WE'RE DOING.
ARE YOU GOING TO TELL ME...
...ABOUT THE HELMETED MAN YOU ENCOUNTERED AT NEWTON APPLE ACADEMY FOR GIRLS?
!
A COLLEAGUE OF MINE...
...HAS ALREADY INFILTRATED THE SCHOOL AND INVESTIGATED IT.
IF YOU ALREADY KNOW ABOUT THAT, THEN PLEASE...
...GIVE KAZUKI MORE TIME!!
I'M SURE YOU THINK THERE'S HOPE, BUT...
...IT'S A VERY DIM HOPE, I'M AFRAID.
I CANNOT ENDANGER INNOCENT LIVES FOR A WILD GOOSE CHASE.
WARRIOR CHIEF!!

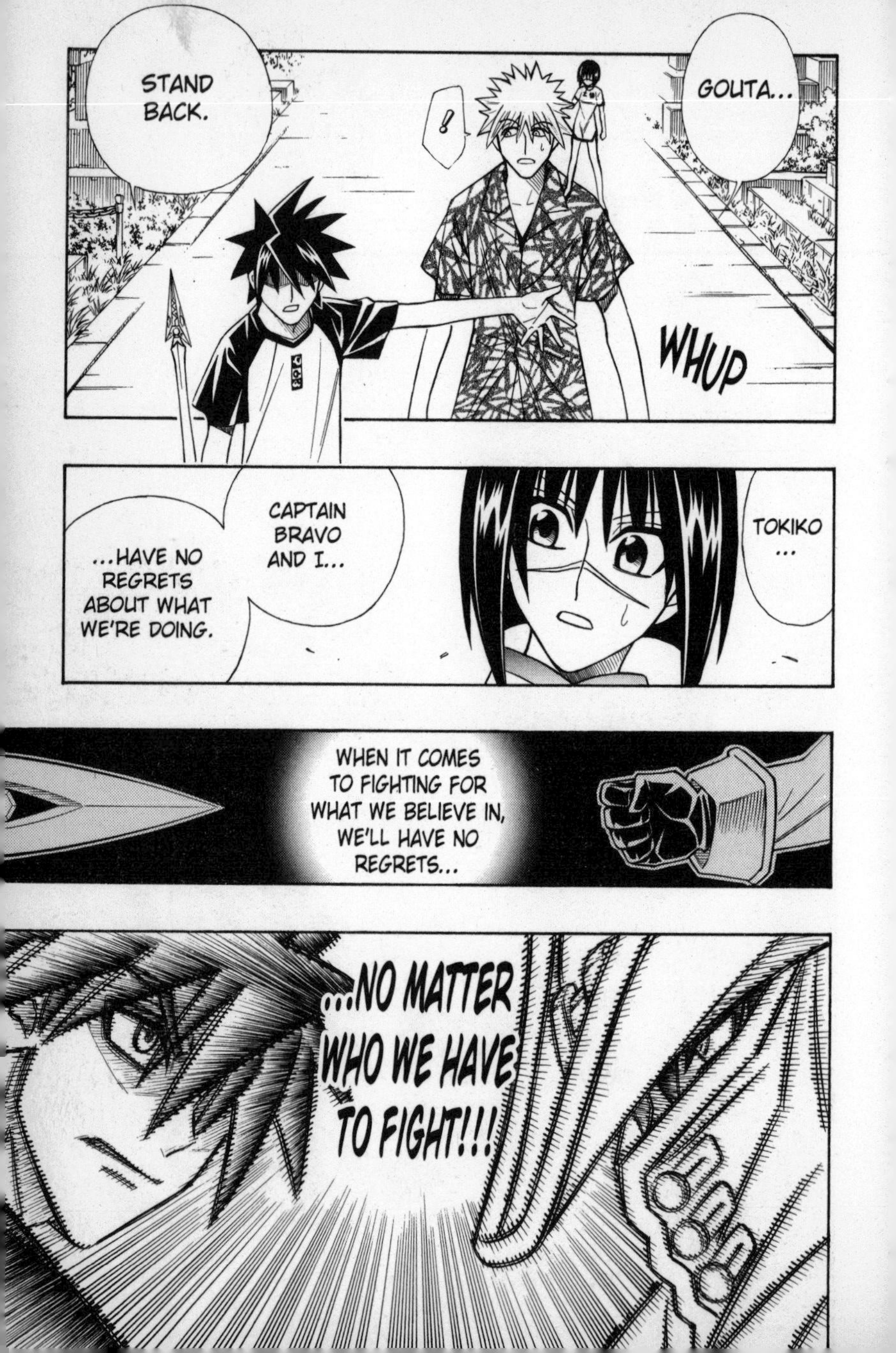
GOUTA...
!
STAND BACK.
WHUP
TOKIKO...
CAPTAIN BRAVO AND I...
...HAVE NO REGRETS ABOUT WHAT WE'RE DOING.
WHEN IT COMES TO FIGHTING FOR WHAT WE BELIEVE IN, WE'LL HAVE NO REGRETS...
...NO MATTER WHO WE HAVE TO FIGHT!!!

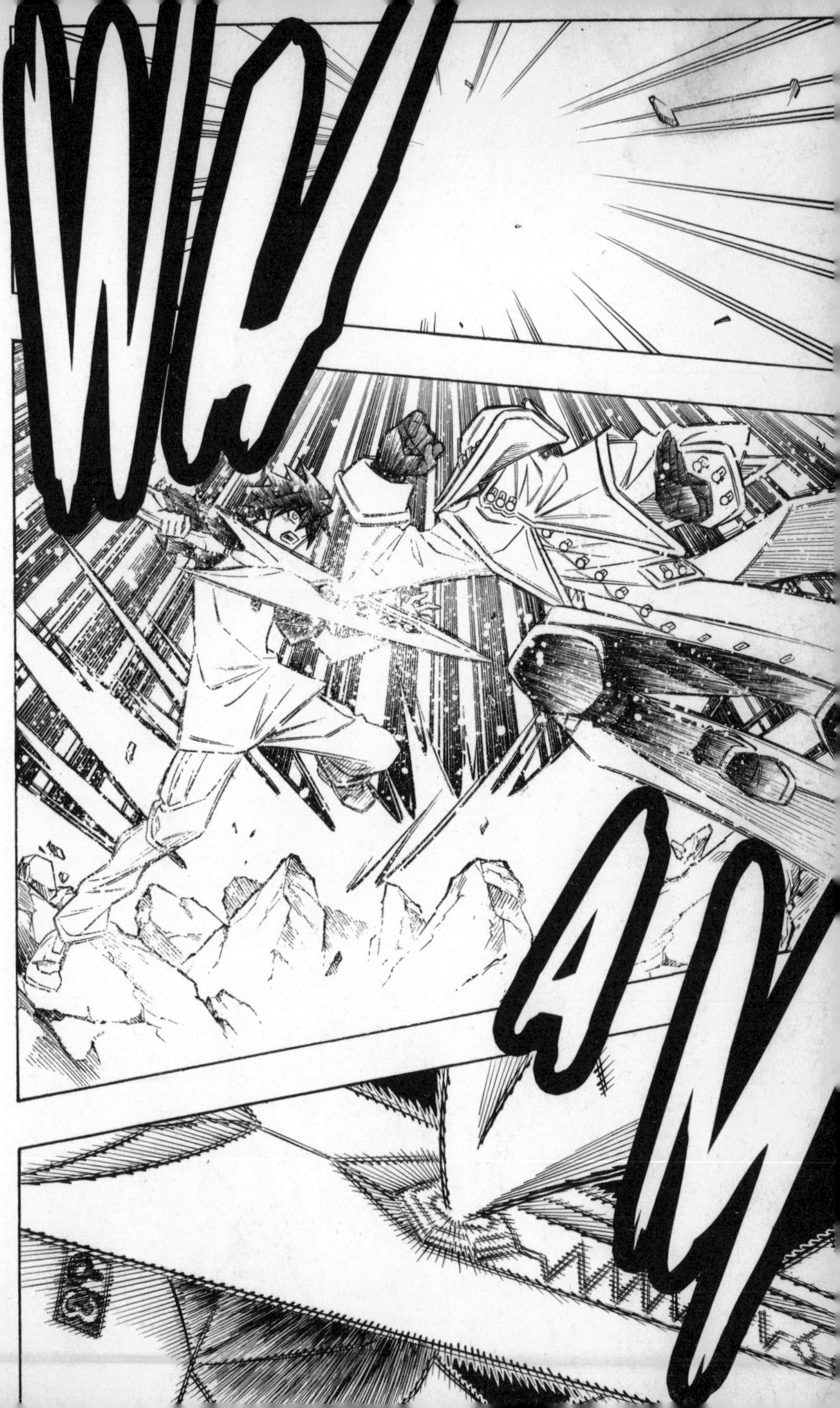

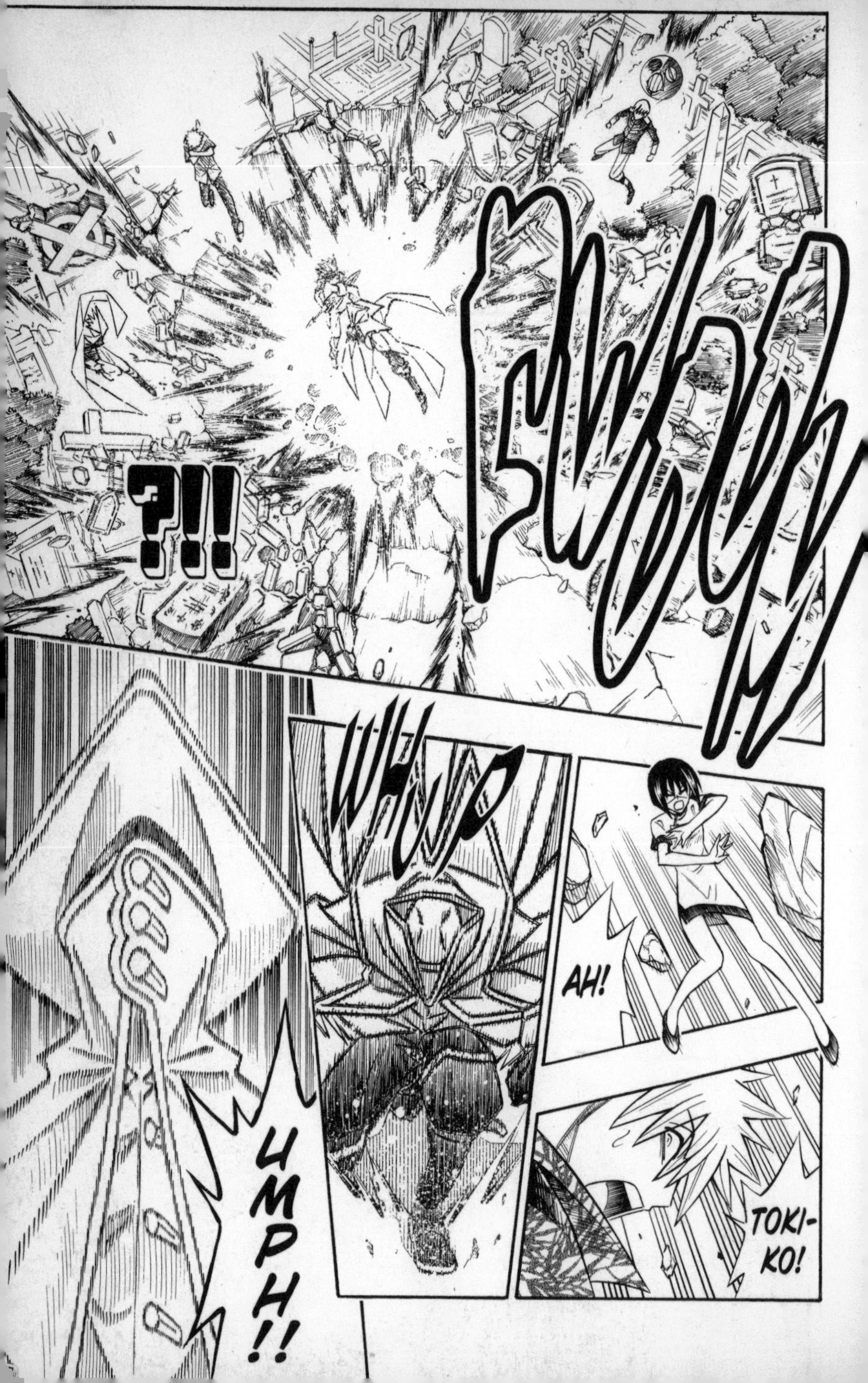
?!!
AH!
TOKI-
KO!
UMPH!!

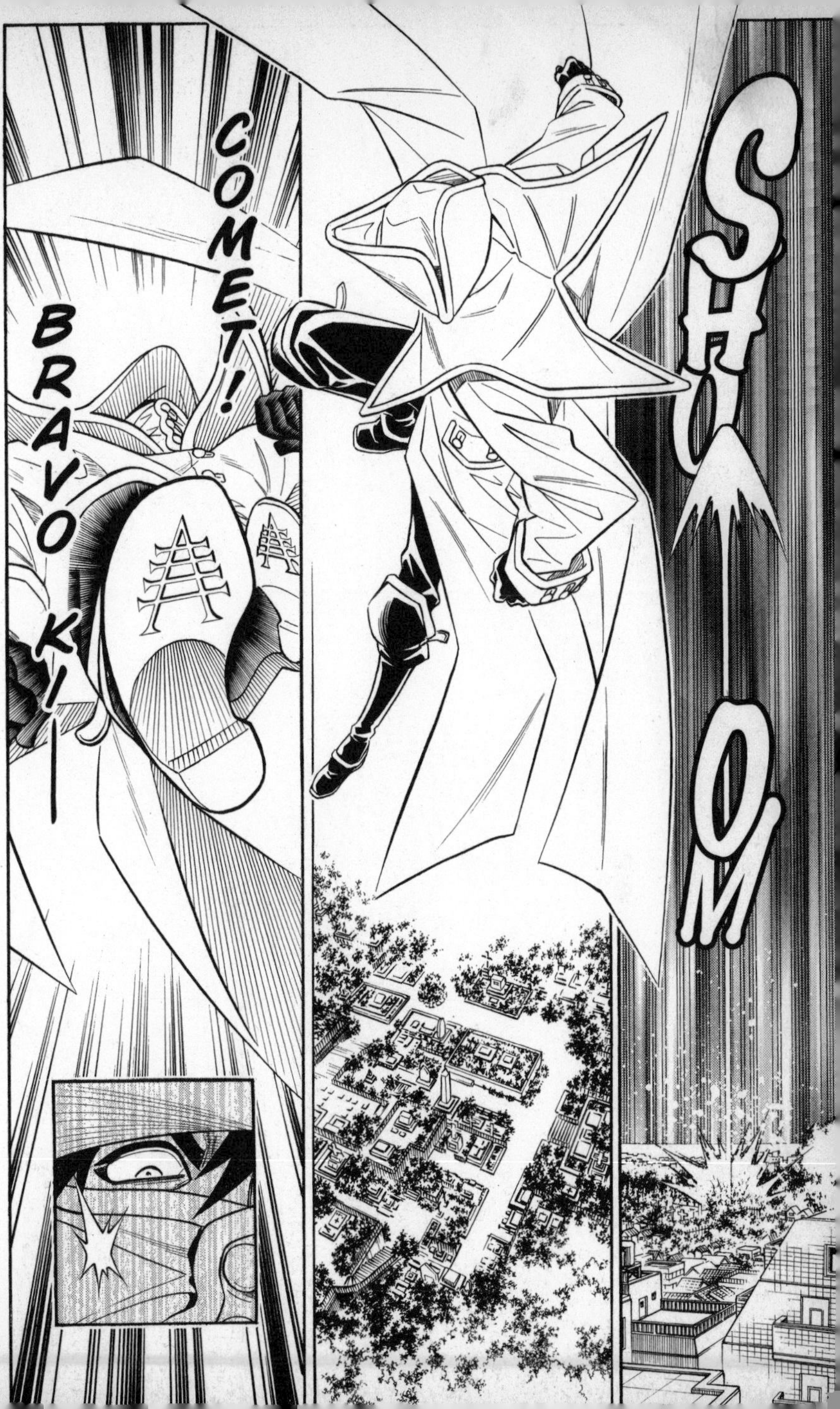
SHOOM
COMET!
BRAVO KI—

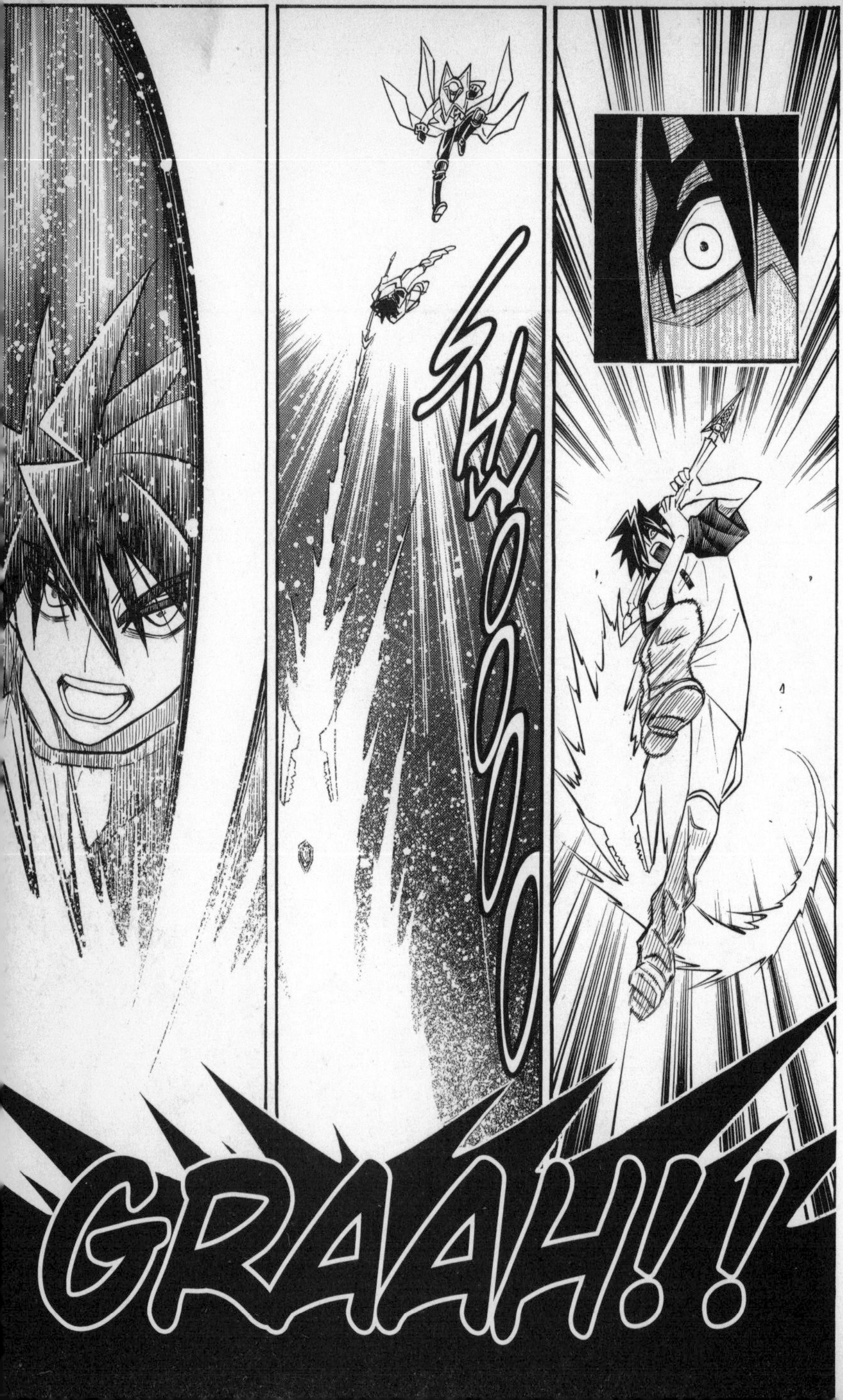
GRAAH!!!

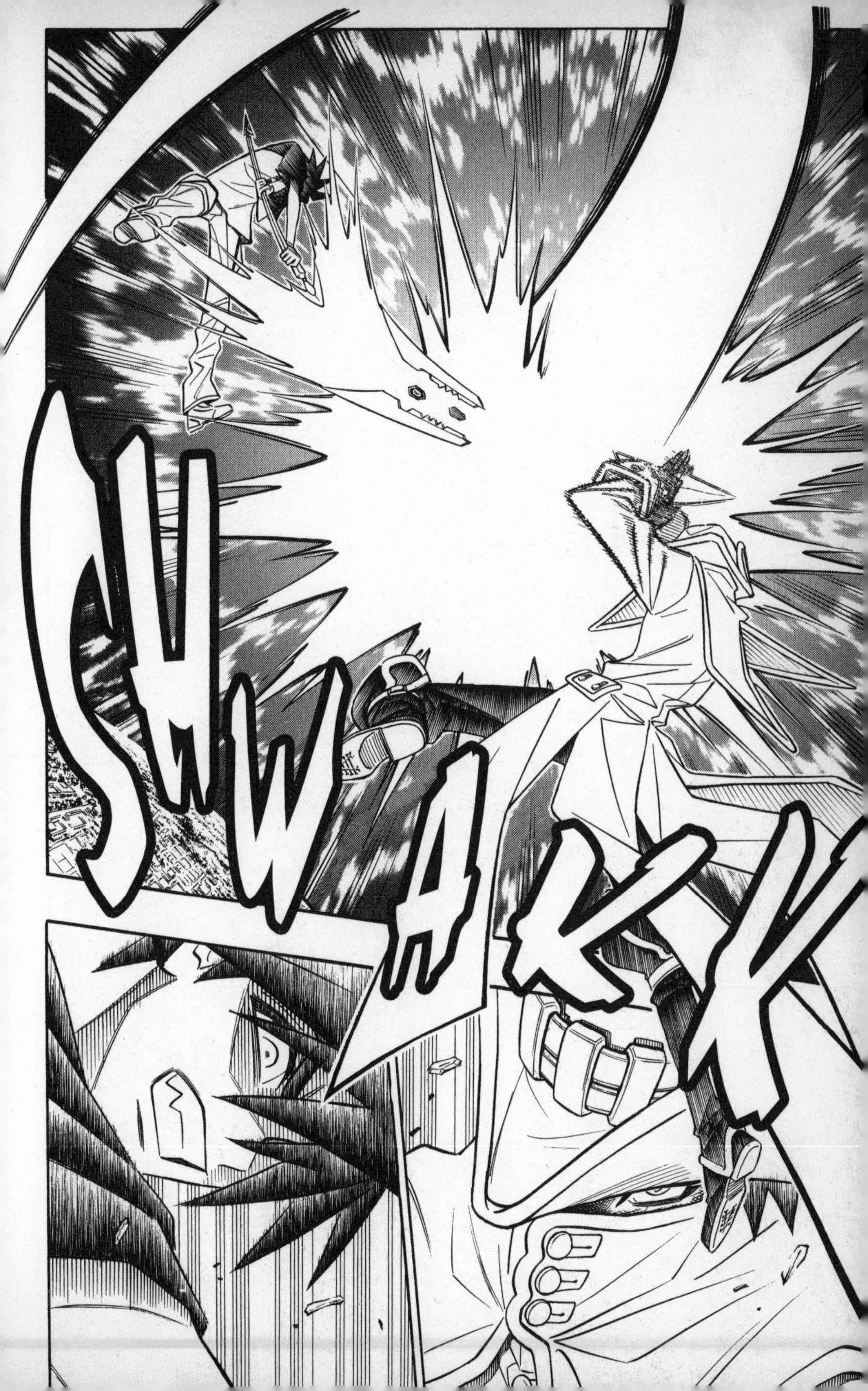
SWAKK

READ THIS WAY

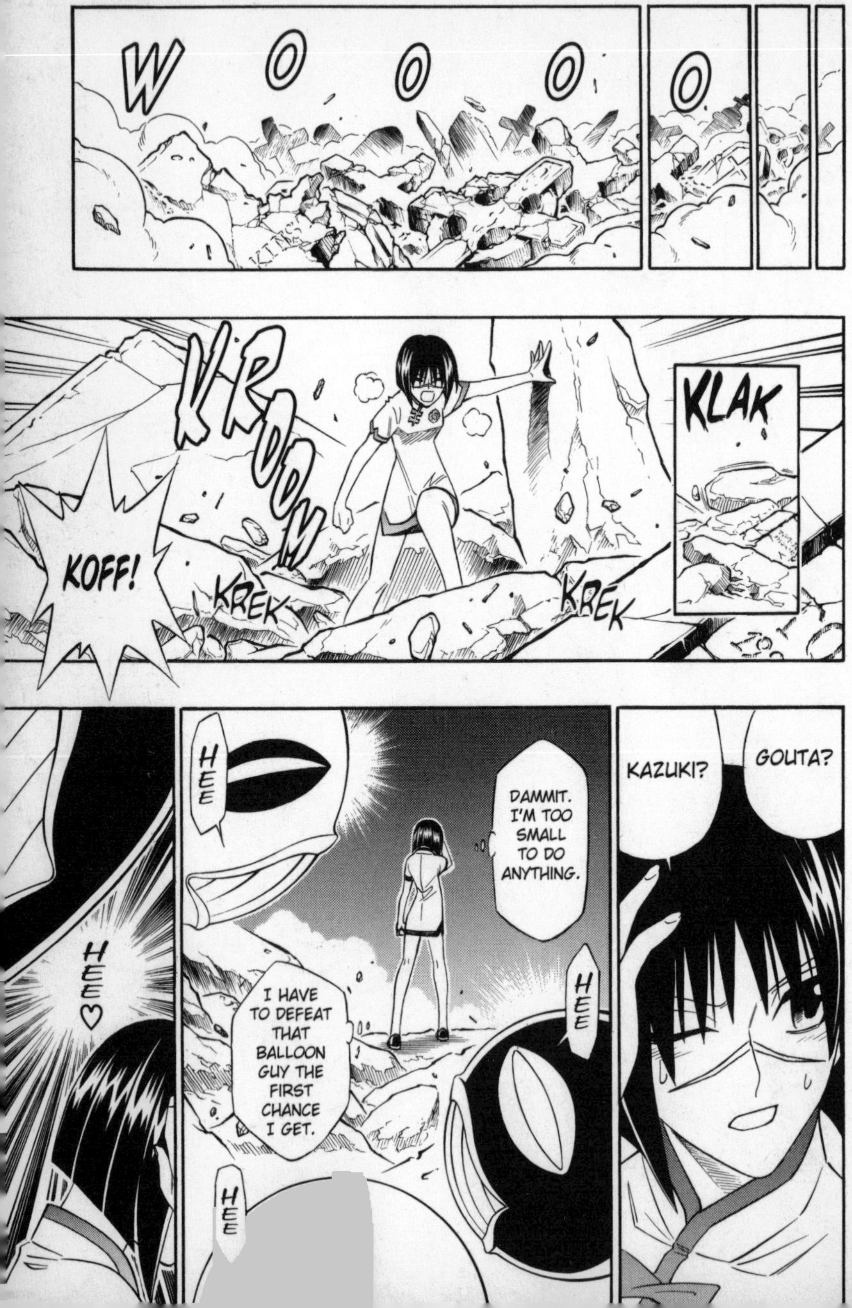
WOOOO
KLAK
KROOM
KREK
KREK
KOFF!
GOUTA?
KAZUKI?
DAMMIT. I'M TOO SMALL TO DO ANYTHING.
HEE
I HAVE TO DEFEAT THAT BALLOON GUY THE FIRST CHANCE I GET.
HEE
HEE
HEE♥
HEE

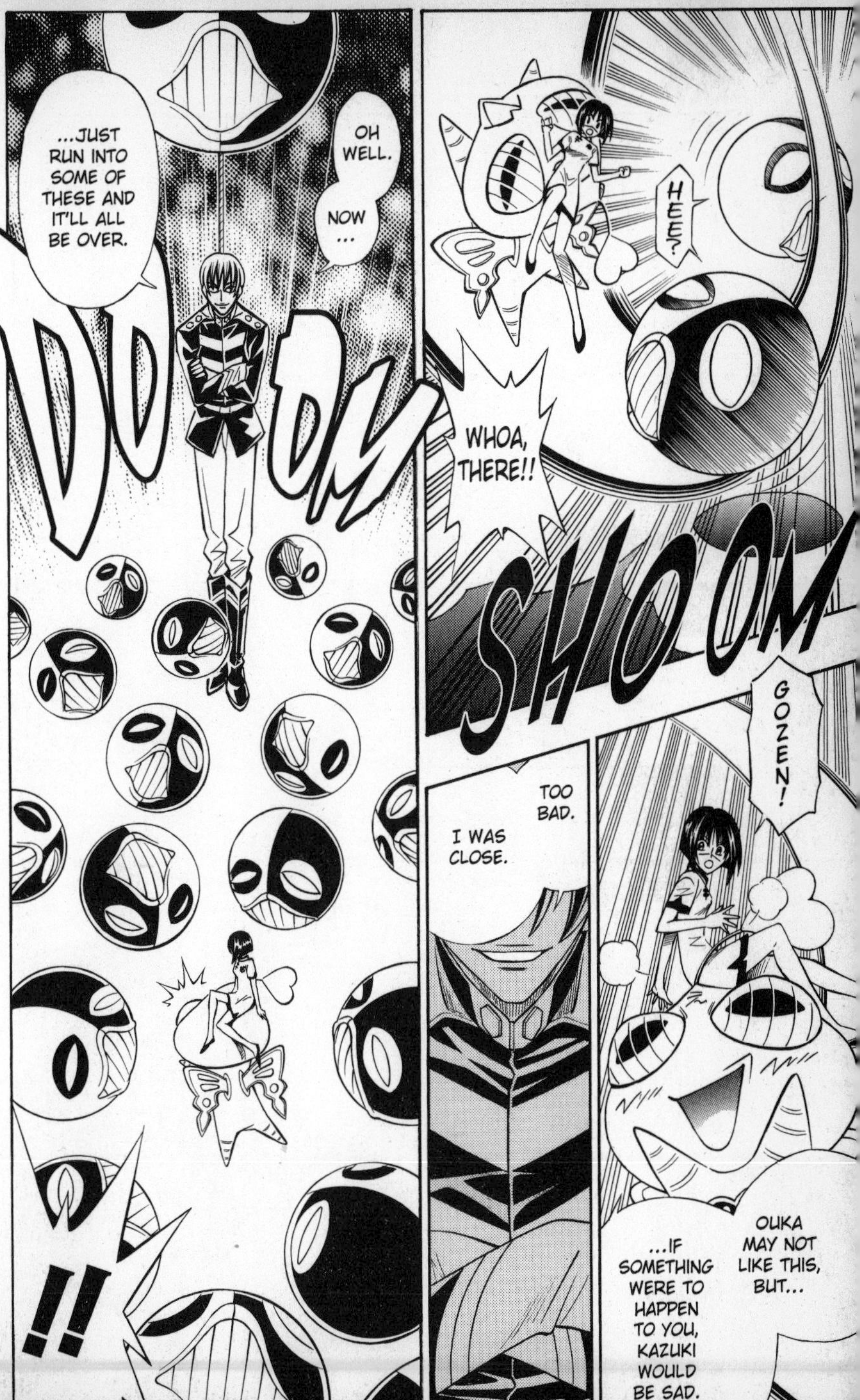
OH WELL.
NOW ...
...JUST RUN INTO SOME OF THESE AND IT'LL ALL BE OVER.
DOOM
!!
HEE?
WHOA, THERE!!
SHOOM
GOZEN!
OUKA MAY NOT LIKE THIS, BUT...
...IF SOMETHING WERE TO HAPPEN TO YOU, KAZUKI WOULD BE SAD.
TOO BAD.
I WAS CLOSE.

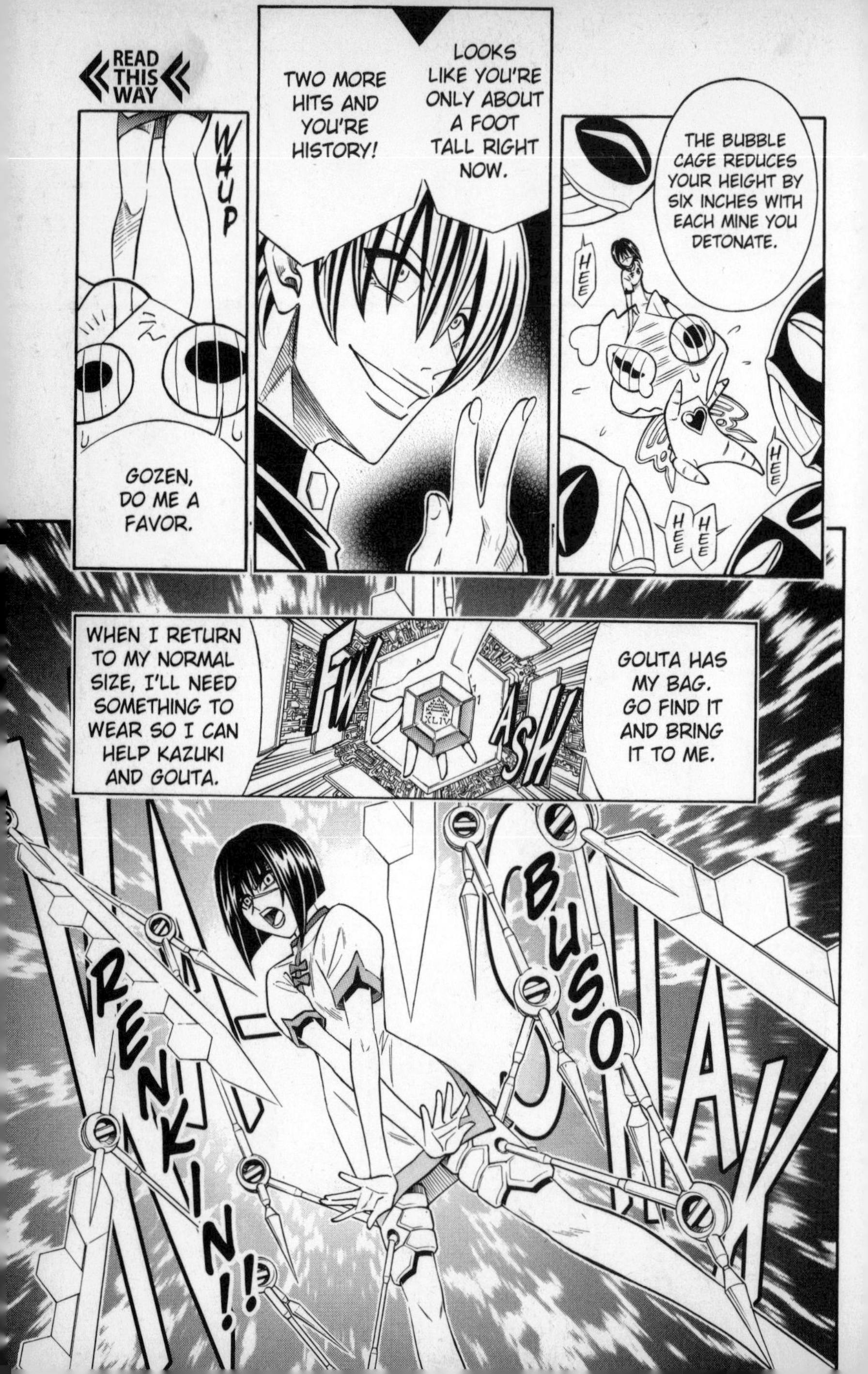
READ THIS WAY
THE BUBBLE CAGE REDUCES YOUR HEIGHT BY SIX INCHES WITH EACH MINE YOU DETONATE.
HEE
HEE
HEE HEE
LOOKS LIKE YOU'RE ONLY ABOUT A FOOT TALL RIGHT NOW.
TWO MORE HITS AND YOU'RE HISTORY!
WHUP
GOZEN, DO ME A FAVOR.
GOUTA HAS MY BAG. GO FIND IT AND BRING IT TO ME.
FWASH
XLIV
WHEN I RETURN TO MY NORMAL SIZE, I'LL NEED SOMETHING TO WEAR SO I CAN HELP KAZUKI AND GOUTA.
BUSO
RENKIN!!

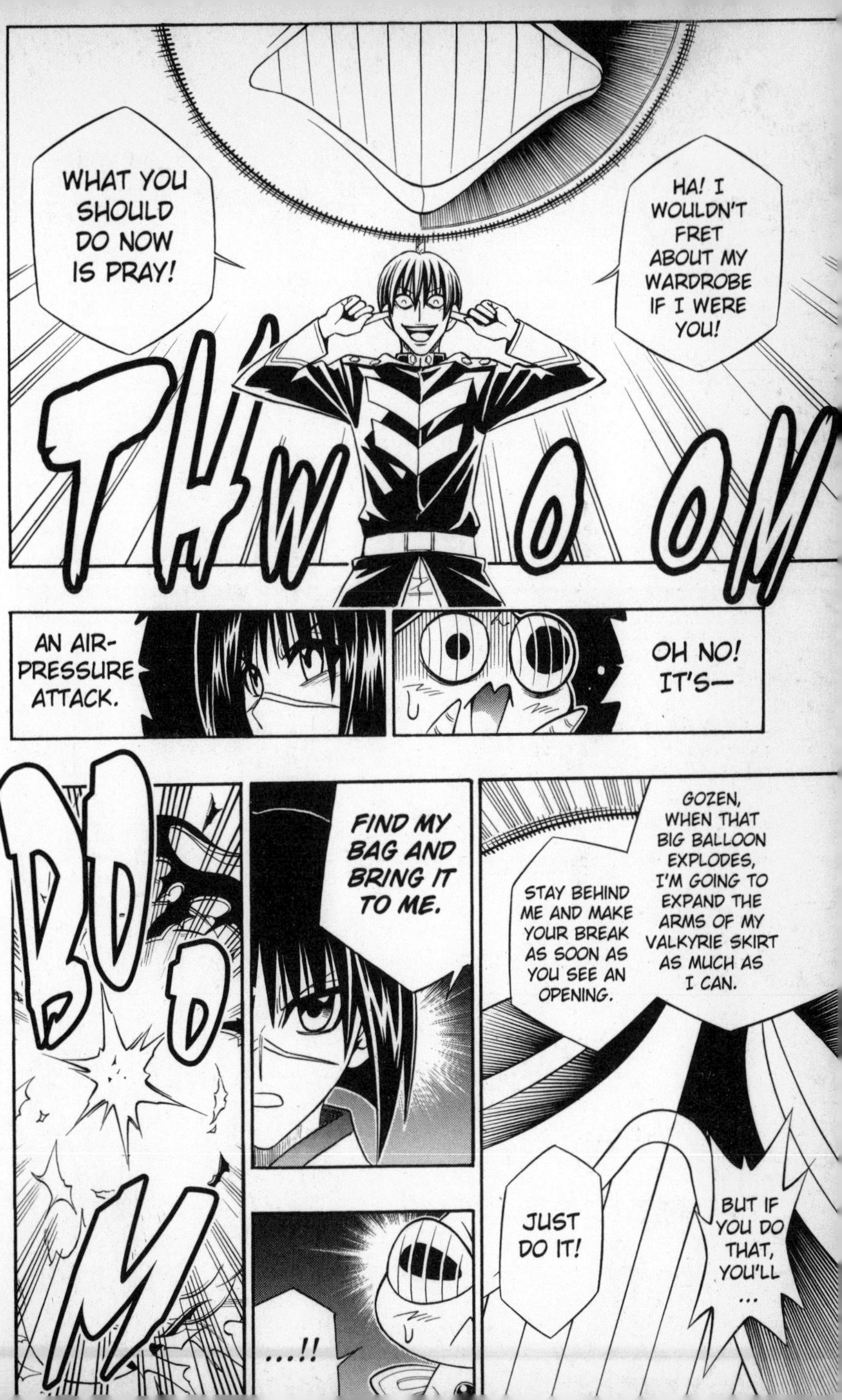
HA! I WOULDN'T FRET ABOUT MY WARDROBE IF I WERE YOU!
WHAT YOU SHOULD DO NOW IS PRAY!
THWOOM
OH NO! IT'S—
AN AIR-PRESSURE ATTACK.
GOZEN, WHEN THAT BIG BALLOON EXPLODES, I'M GOING TO EXPAND THE ARMS OF MY VALKYRIE SKIRT AS MUCH AS I CAN.
STAY BEHIND ME AND MAKE YOUR BREAK AS SOON AS YOU SEE AN OPENING.
BUT IF YOU DO THAT, YOU'LL ...
JUST DO IT!
FIND MY BAG AND BRING IT TO ME.
...!!
BOOM

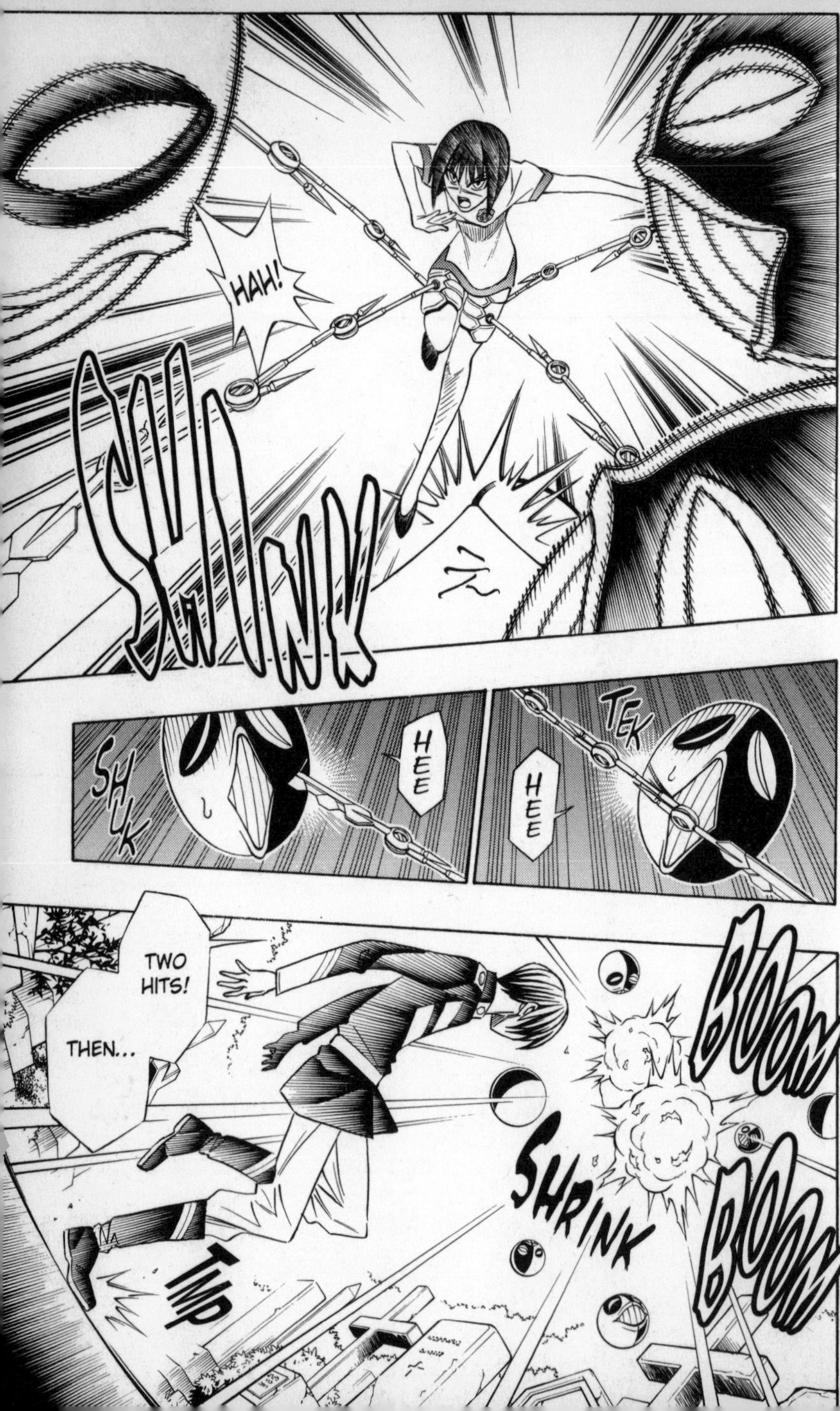
HAH!
SWINK
TEK
HEE
HEE
SHUK
BOOM
BOOM
SHRINK
TWO HITS!
THEN...
TMP

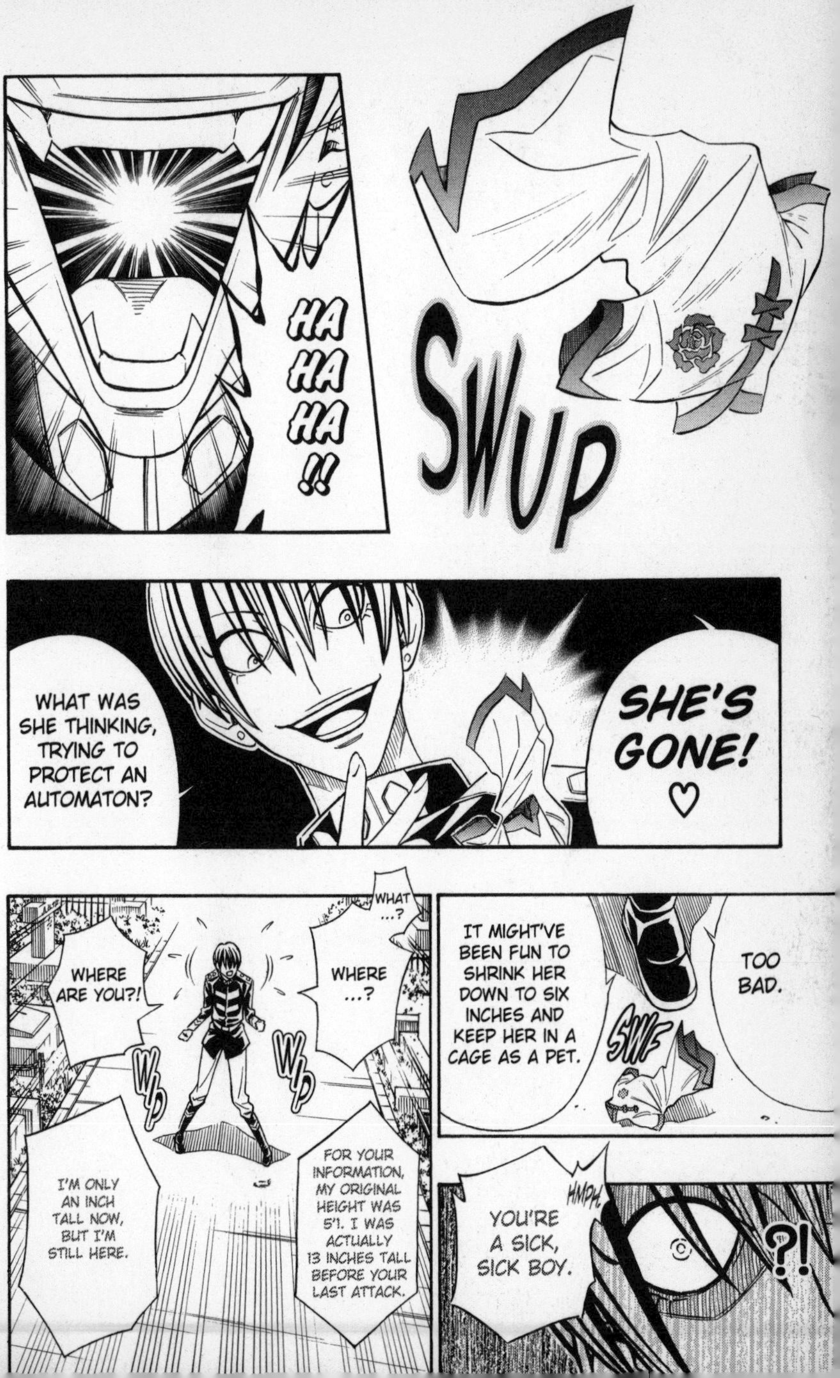
SWUP
HA HA HA!!
SHE'S GONE! ♡
WHAT WAS SHE THINKING, TRYING TO PROTECT AN AUTOMATON?
TOO BAD.
IT MIGHT'VE BEEN FUN TO SHRINK HER DOWN TO SIX INCHES AND KEEP HER IN A CAGE AS A PET.
SWF
?!
YOU'RE A SICK, SICK BOY.
HMPH
WHAT ...?
WHERE ...?
WHERE ARE YOU?!
WIP
WIP
FOR YOUR INFORMATION, MY ORIGINAL HEIGHT WAS 5'1. I WAS ACTUALLY 13 INCHES TALL BEFORE YOUR LAST ATTACK.
I'M ONLY AN INCH TALL NOW, BUT I'M STILL HERE.

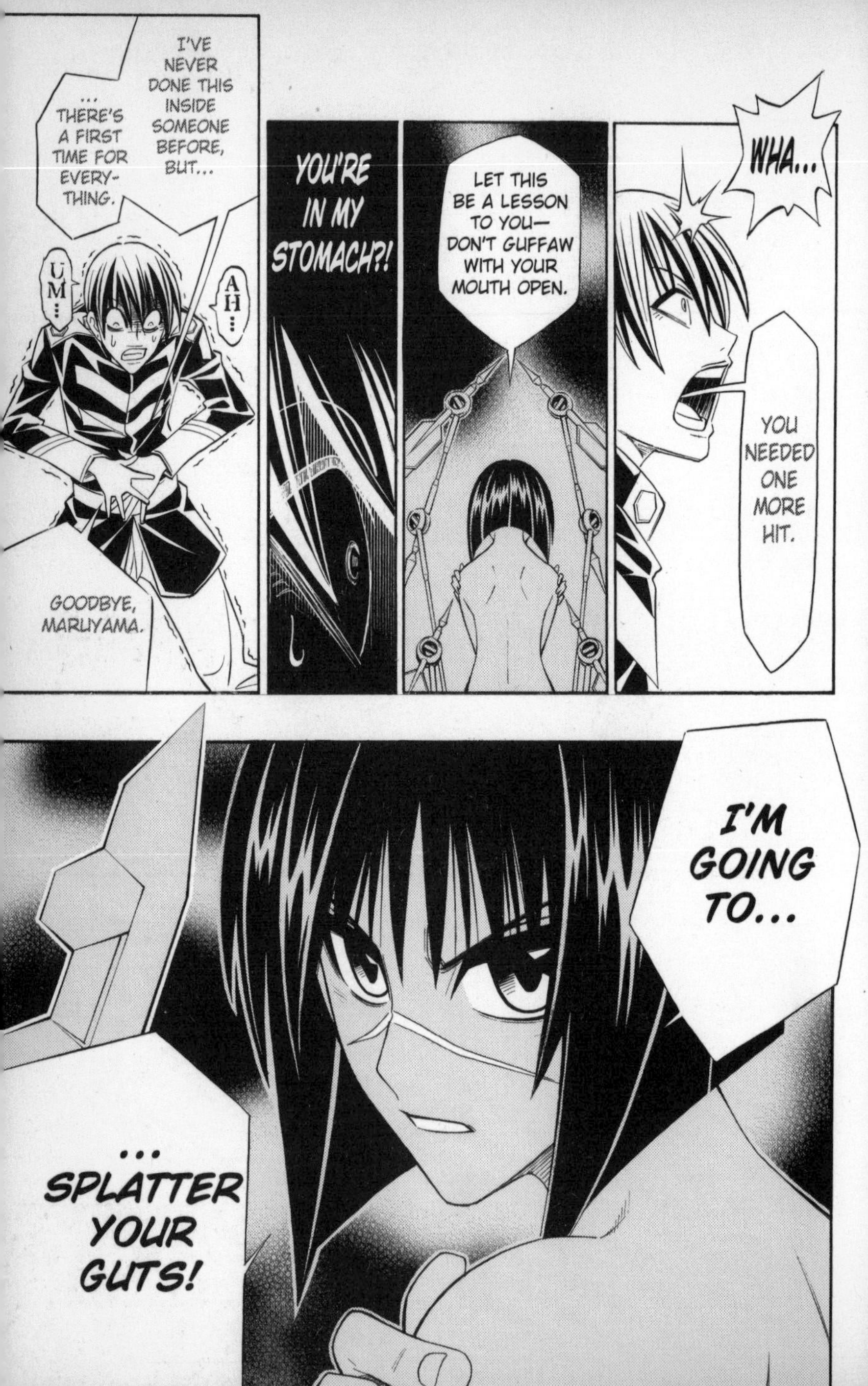
WHA...
YOU NEEDED ONE MORE HIT.
LET THIS BE A LESSON TO YOU—DON'T GUFFAW WITH YOUR MOUTH OPEN.
YOU'RE IN MY STOMACH?!
I'VE NEVER DONE THIS INSIDE SOMEONE BEFORE, BUT...
...THERE'S A FIRST TIME FOR EVERY-THING.
AH...
UM...
GOODBYE, MARUYAMA.
I'M GOING TO...
...SPLATTER YOUR GUTS!

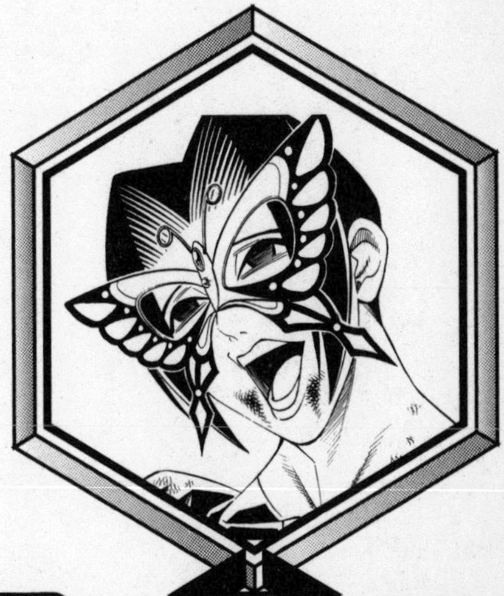

Buso Renkin

ブソウレンキン

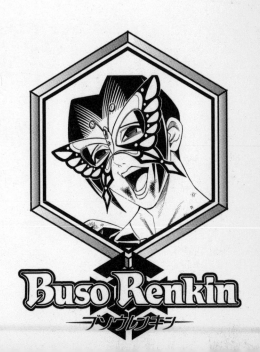

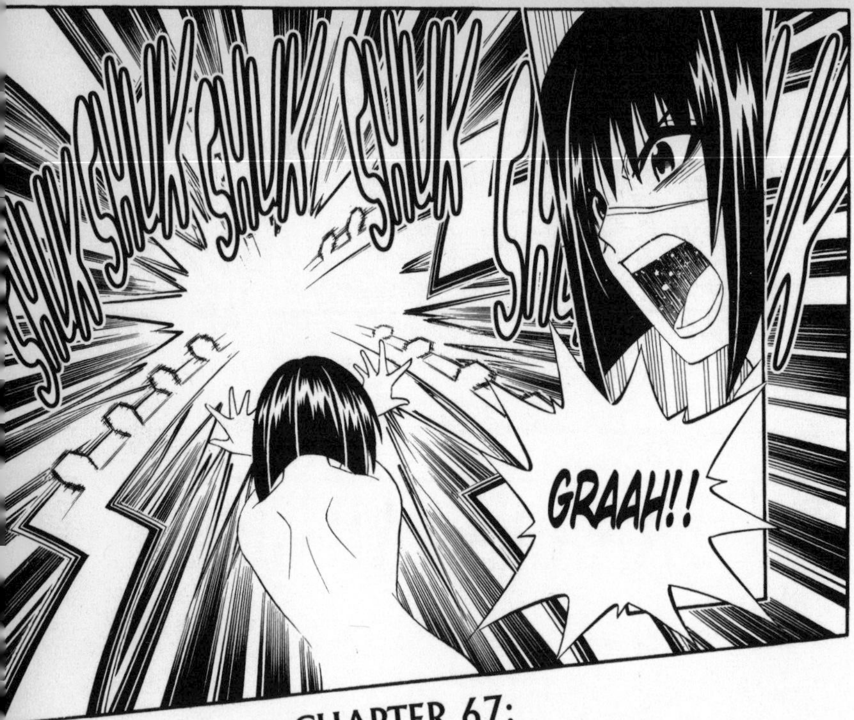
SHUK SHUK SHUK SHUK
GRAAH!!

CHAPTER 67:
SECRET PASSAGE OF SHADOWS

伸宏
和月

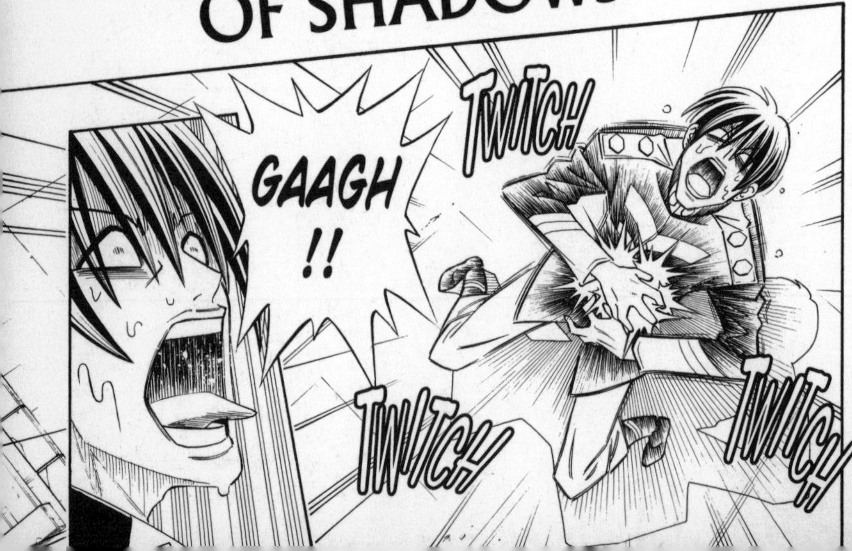
TWITCH
GAAGH !!
TWITCH
TWITCH

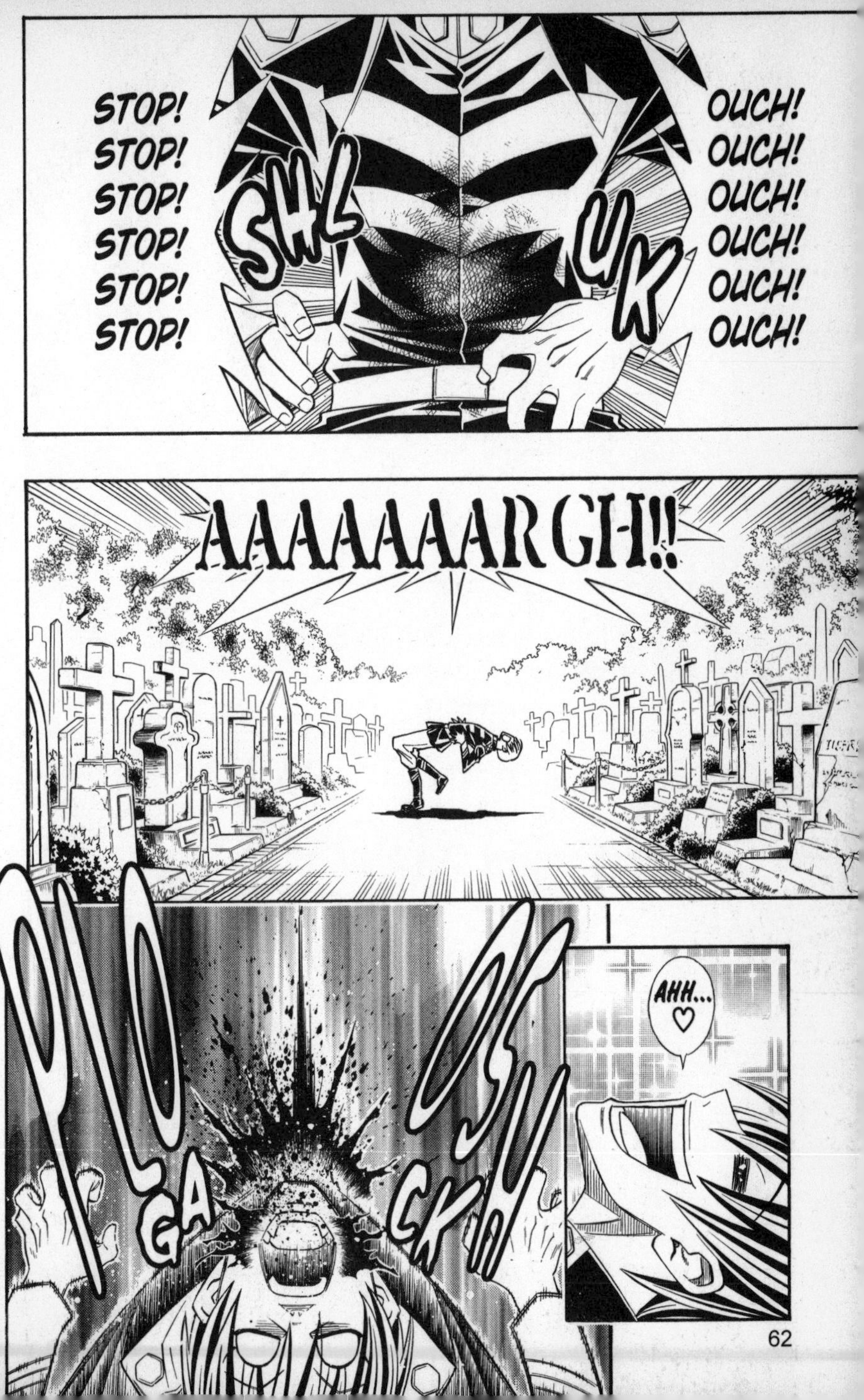
OUCH!
OUCH!
OUCH!
OUCH!
OUCH!
OUCH!
SHLUK
STOP!
STOP!
STOP!
STOP!
STOP!
STOP!
AAAAAAARGH!!
AHH... ♥
GA
CK

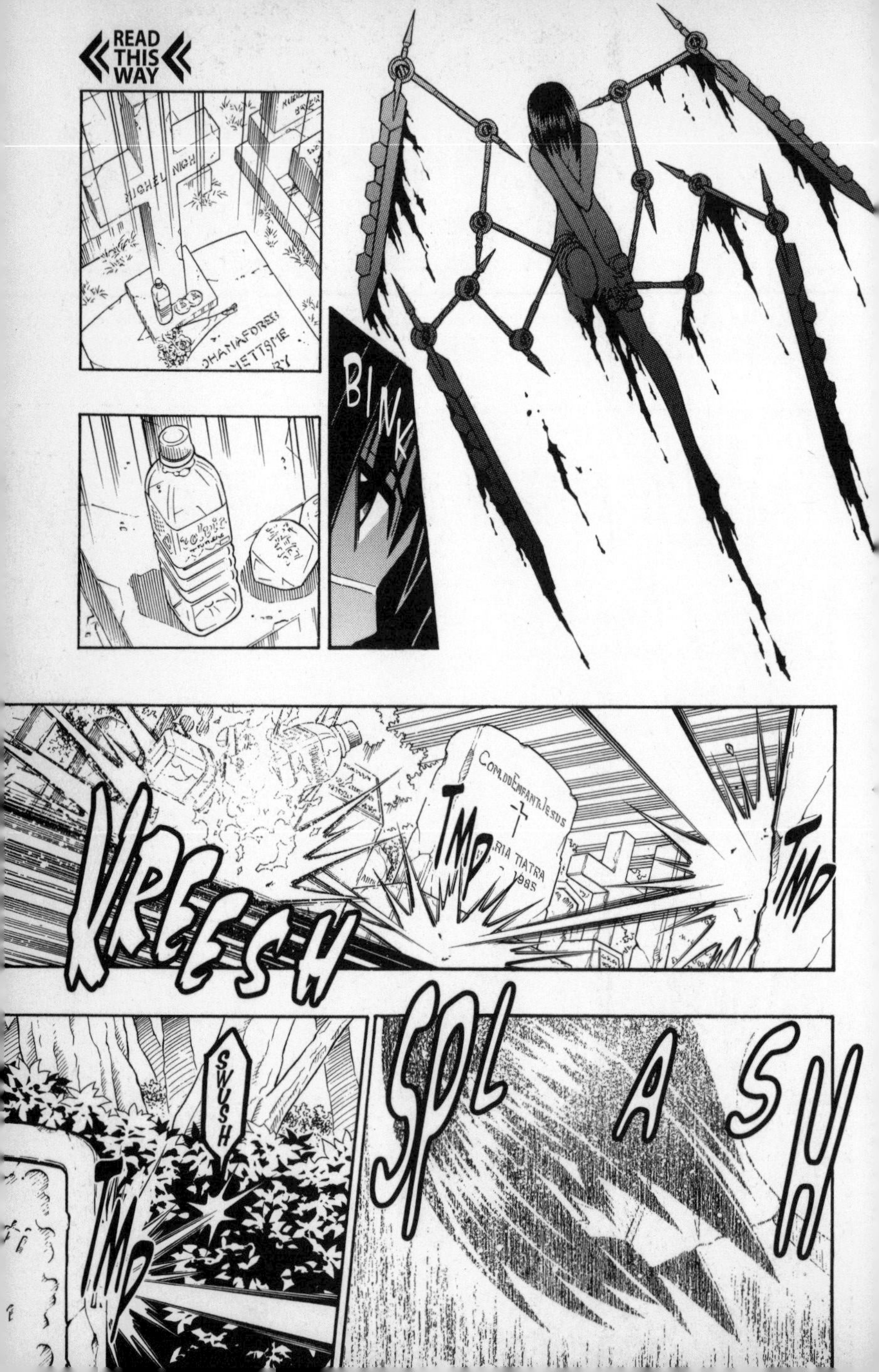
READ THIS WAY
MICHEL NIGH
BINK
CO.DOENFANTJESUS
TMP
TMP
VREESH
SPLASH
SWUSH
TMP

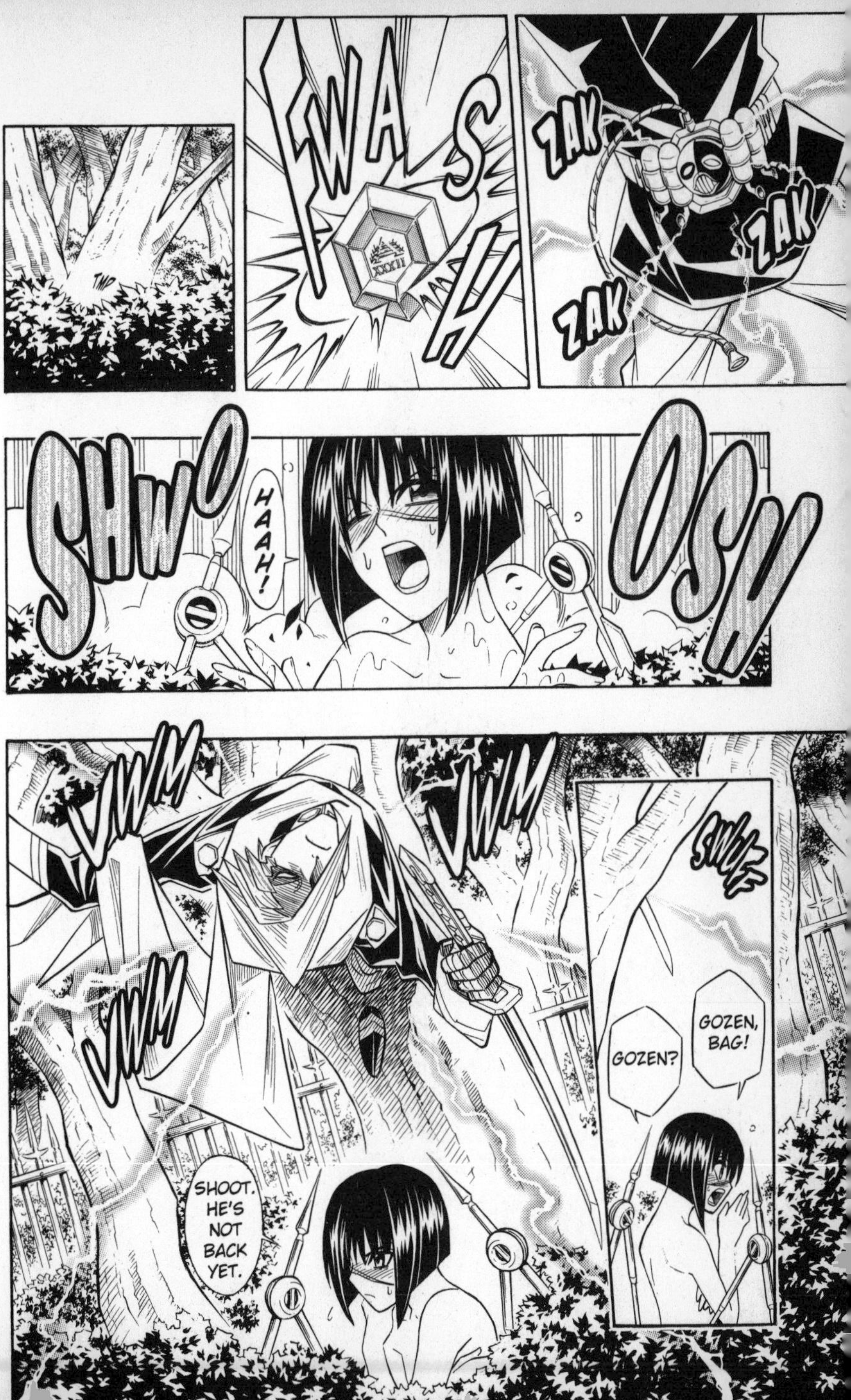
ZAK
ZAK
ZAK
FWASH
TMP
SHWOOSH
HAAAH!
GOZEN, BAG!
GOZEN?
VWM
VWM
VWM
SHOOT. HE'S NOT BACK YET.

READ THIS WAY

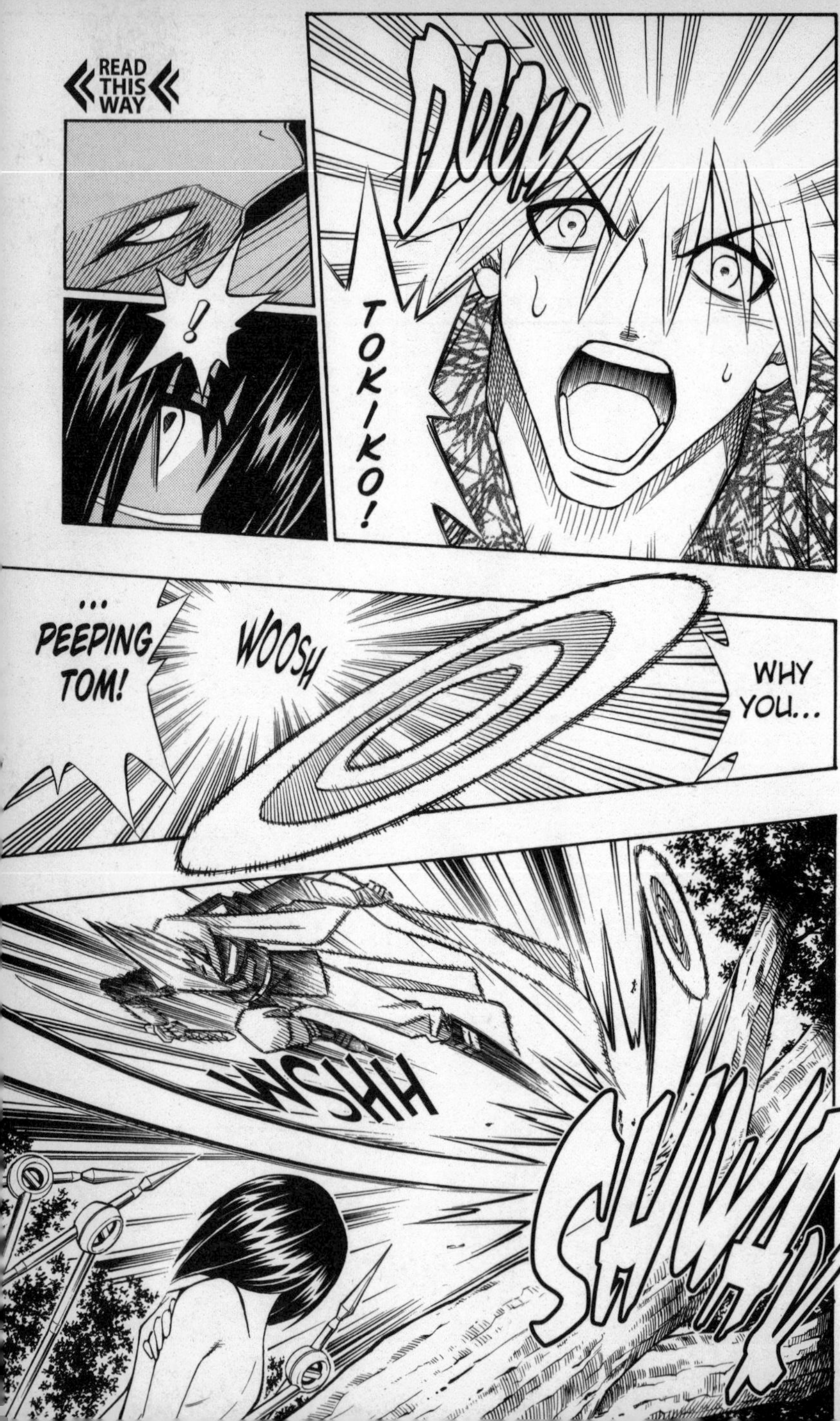
TOKIKO!
!
WHY YOU...
WOOSH
... PEEPING TOM!

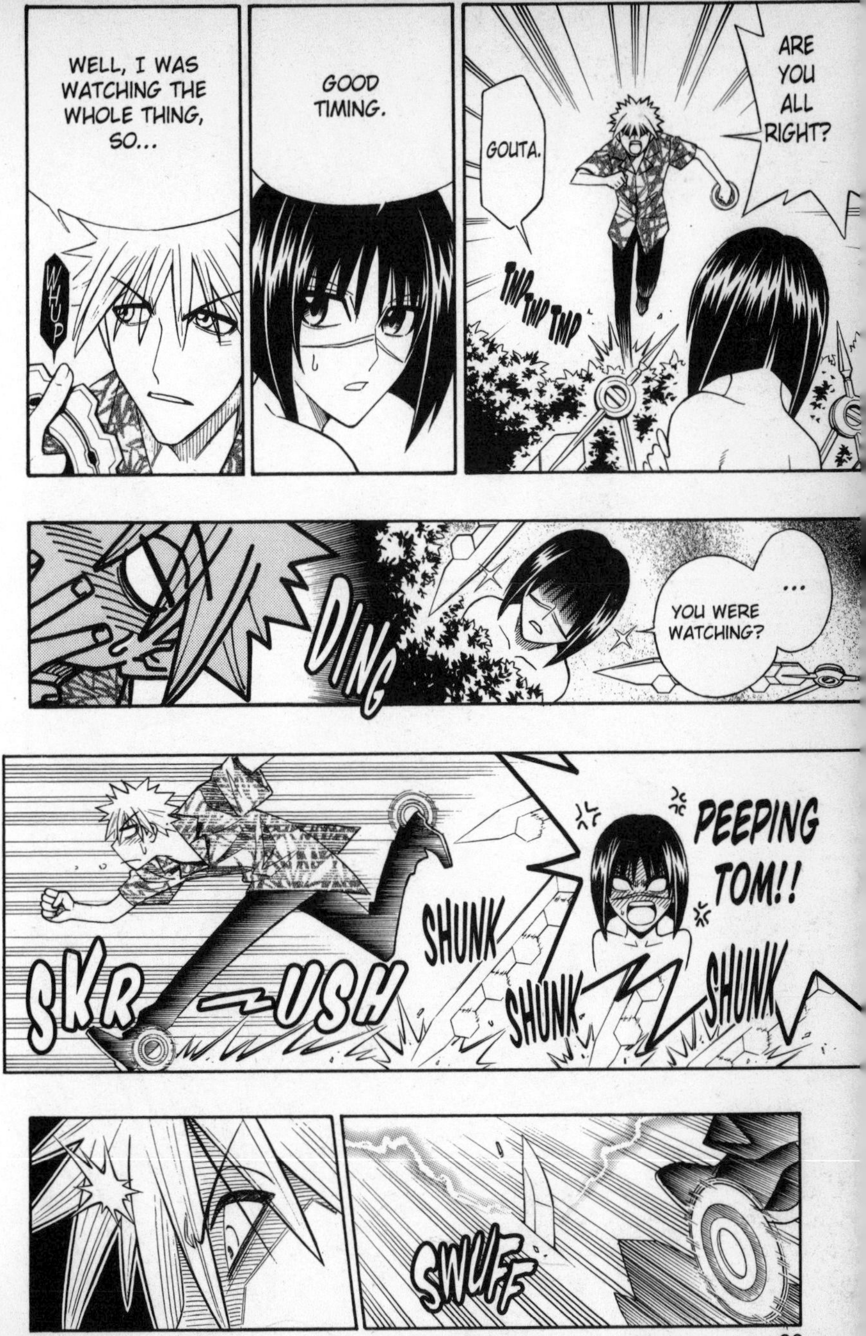
ARE YOU ALL RIGHT?
GOUTA.
TMP TMP TMP
GOOD TIMING.
WELL, I WAS WATCHING THE WHOLE THING, SO...
WHUP
...
YOU WERE WATCHING?
DING
PEEPING TOM!!
SHUNK
SHUNK
SHUNK
SKR-USH
SWUFF

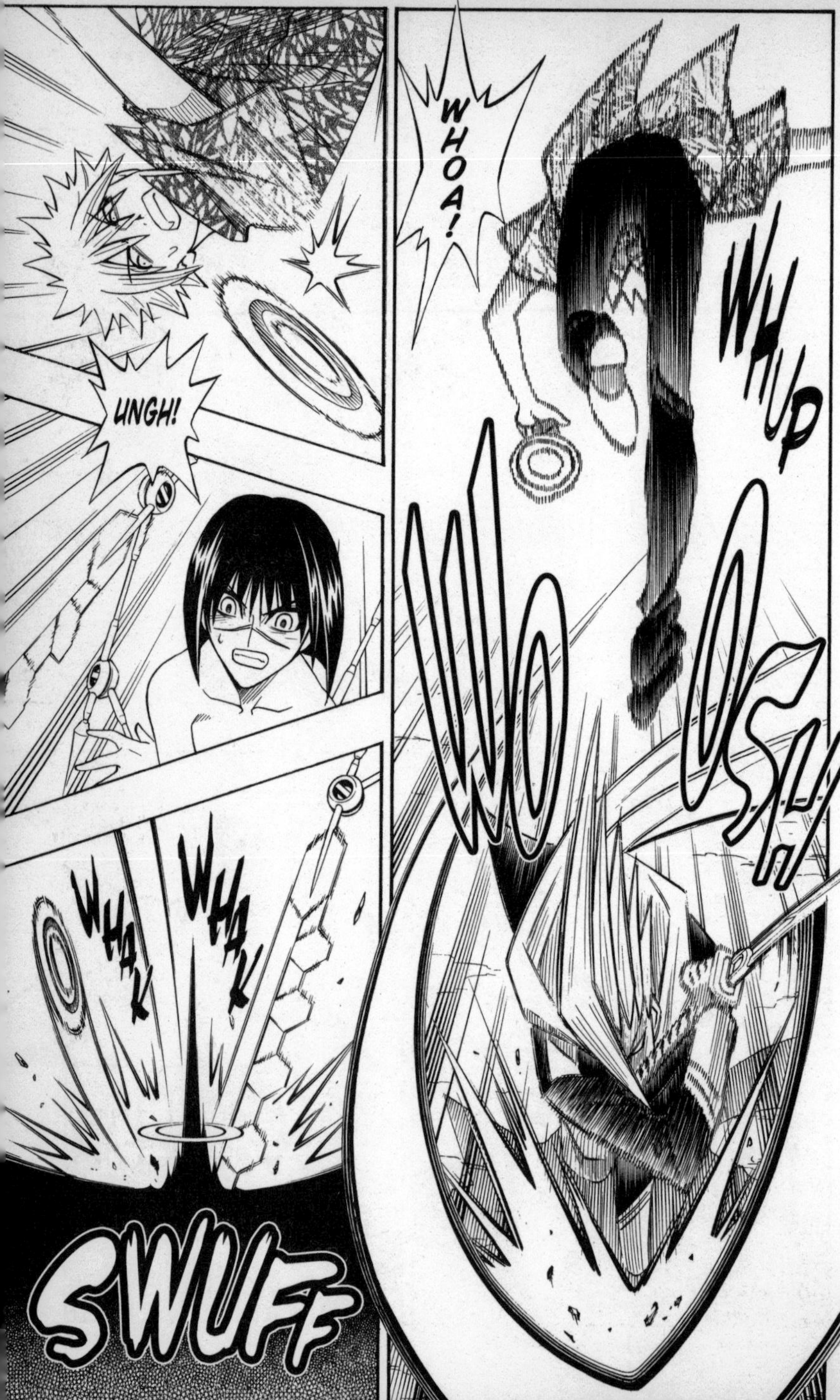
WHOA!
WHUP
WOOSH
UNGH!
WHAK
WHAK
SWUFF

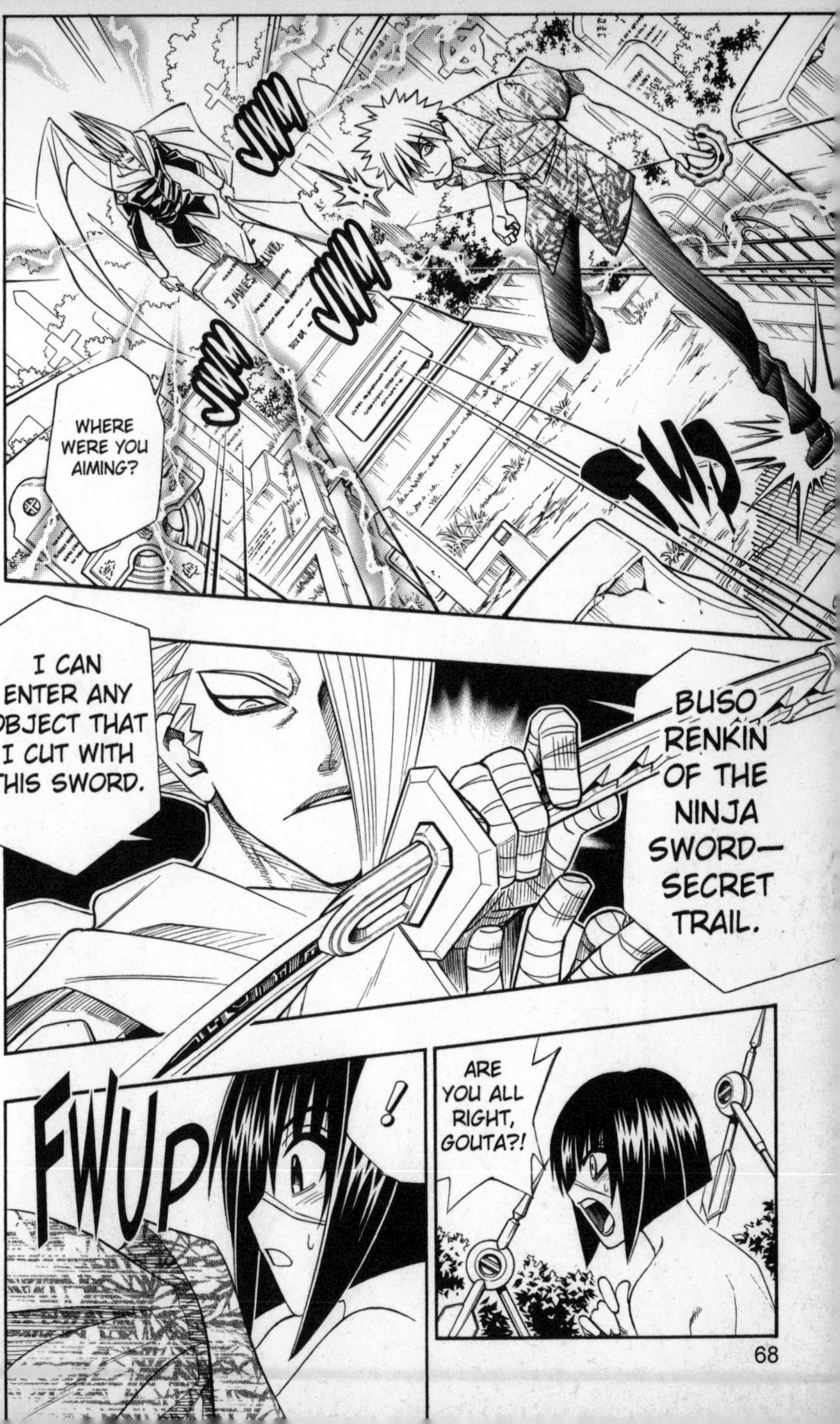
WHERE WERE YOU AIMING?
BUSO RENKIN OF THE NINJA SWORD— SECRET TRAIL.
I CAN ENTER ANY OBJECT THAT I CUT WITH THIS SWORD.
ARE YOU ALL RIGHT, GOUTA?!
!
FWUP

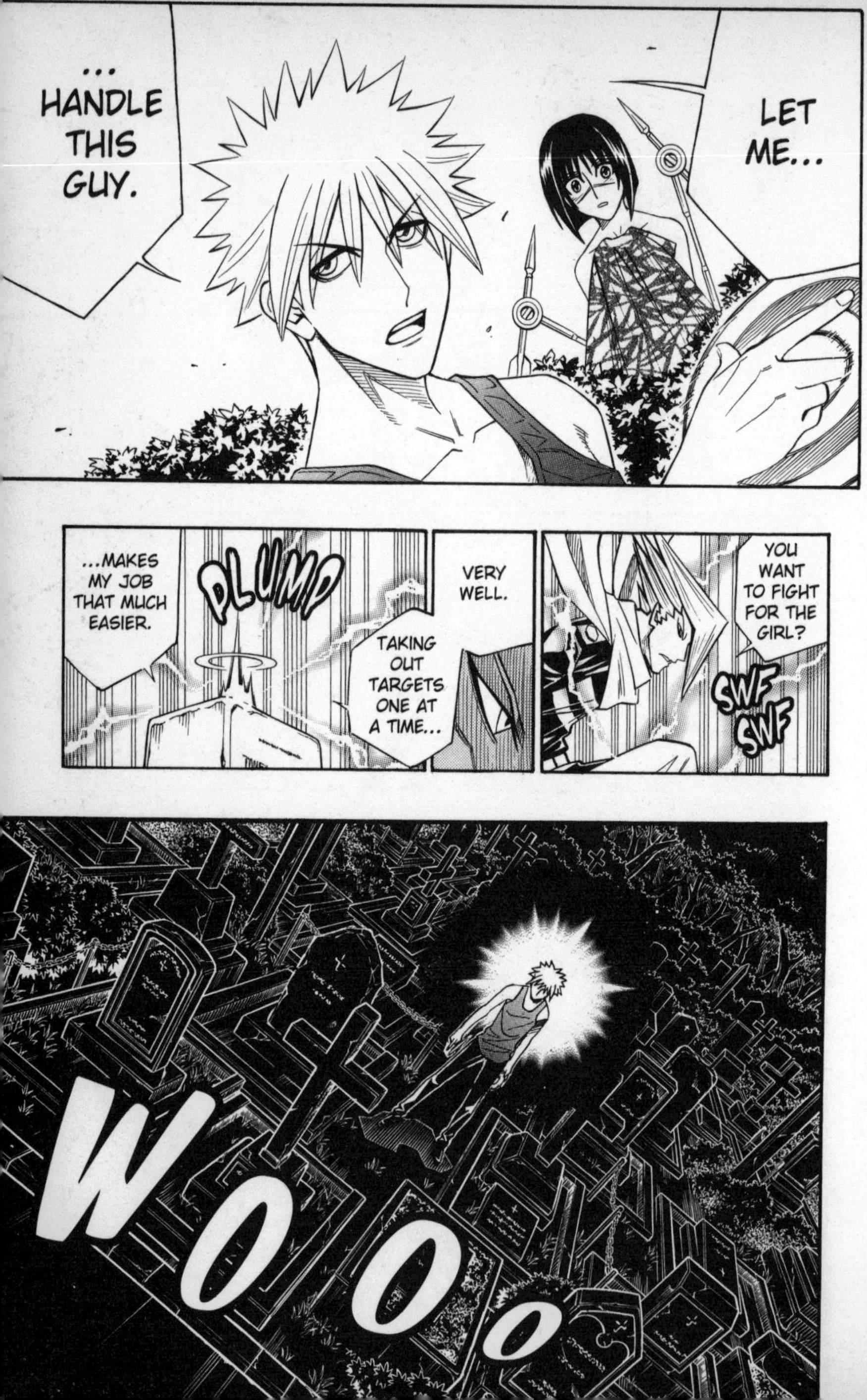
LET ME...
...HANDLE THIS GUY.
YOU WANT TO FIGHT FOR THE GIRL?
SWF SWF
VERY WELL.
TAKING OUT TARGETS ONE AT A TIME...
...MAKES MY JOB THAT MUCH EASIER.
PLUMP
WOOO

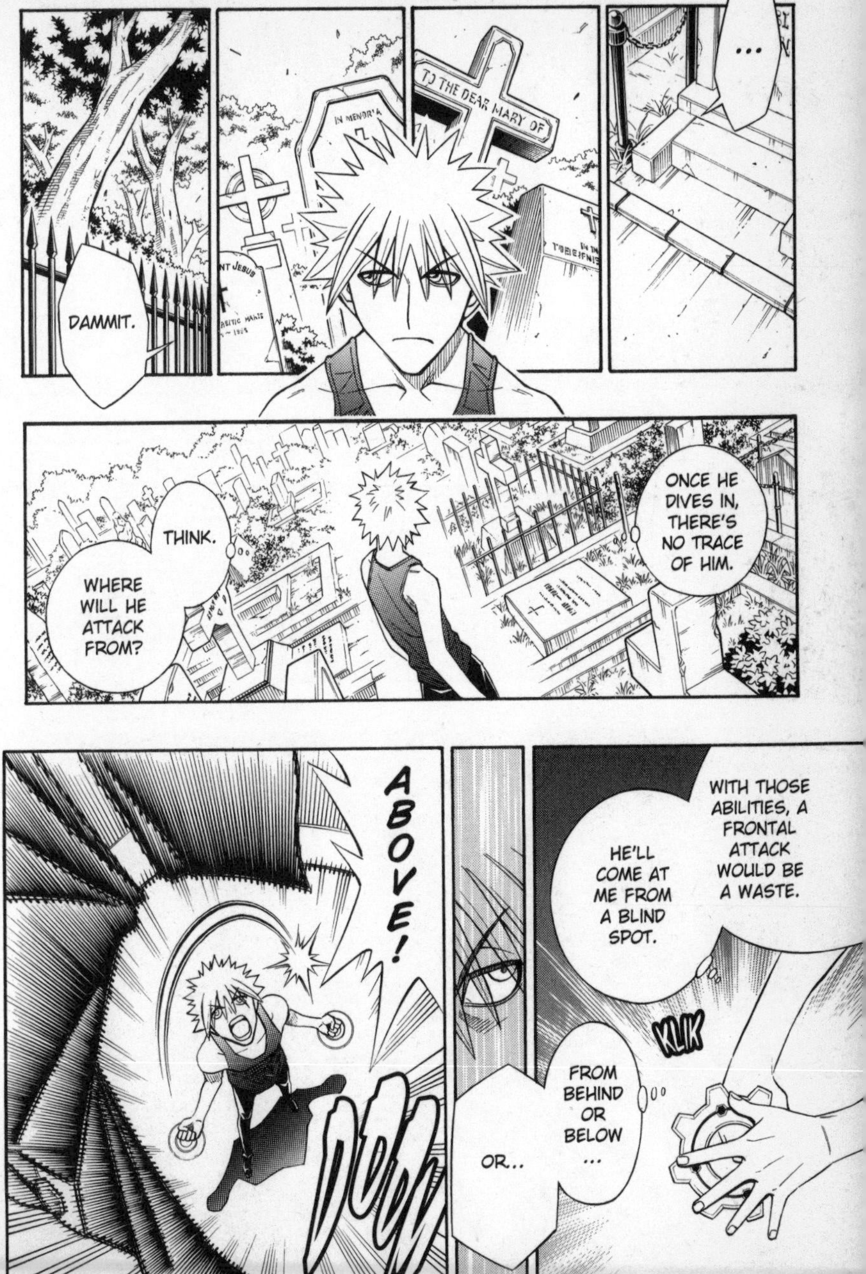
...
TO THE DEAR MARY OF
DAMMIT.
ONCE HE DIVES IN, THERE'S NO TRACE OF HIM.
THINK.
WHERE WILL HE ATTACK FROM?
WITH THOSE ABILITIES, A FRONTAL ATTACK WOULD BE A WASTE.
HE'LL COME AT ME FROM A BLIND SPOT.
KLIK
FROM BEHIND OR BELOW ...
OR...
ABOVE!

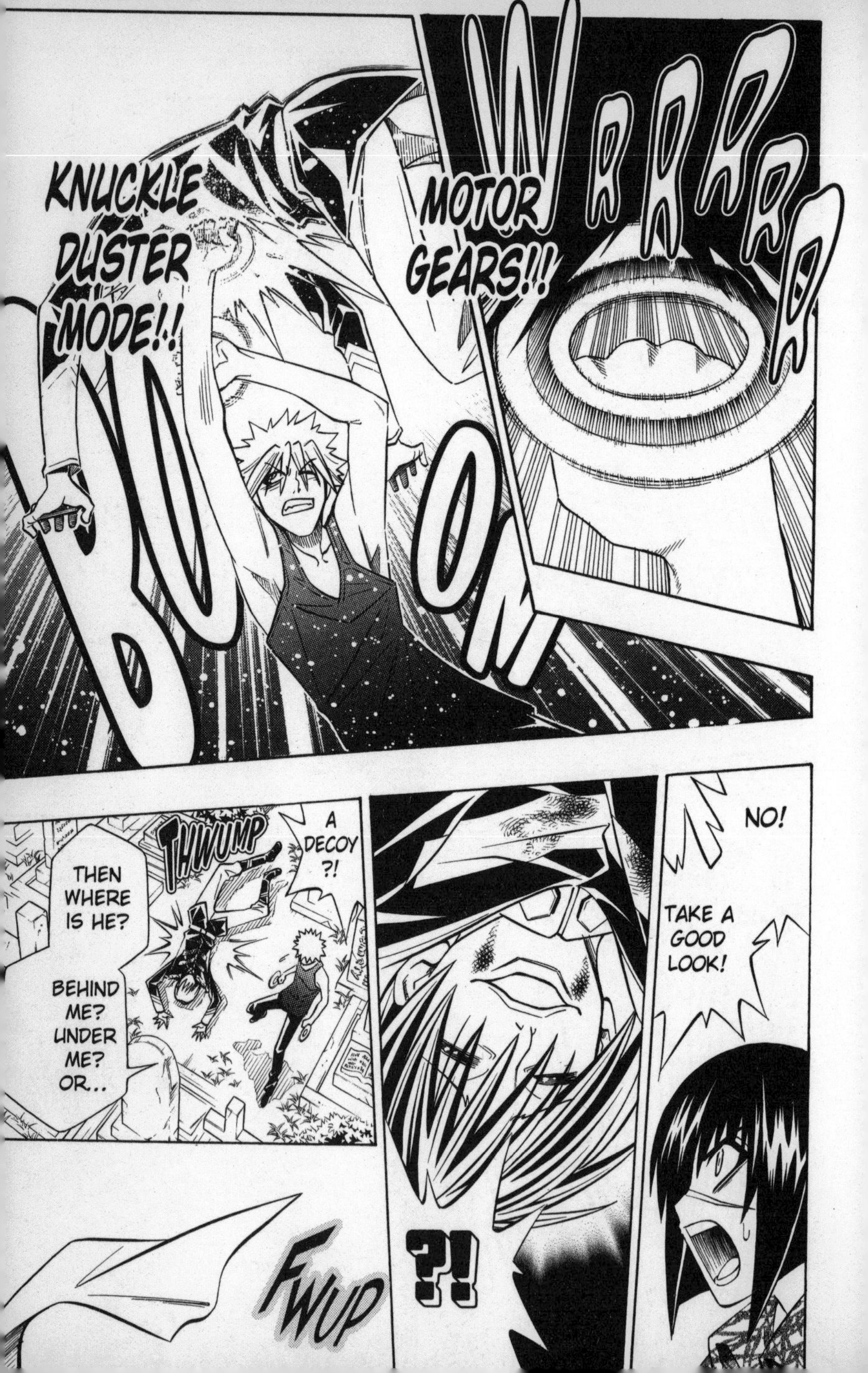
WRRRRR
MOTOR GEARS!!
KNUCKLE DUSTER MODE!!
BOOM
NO!
TAKE A GOOD LOOK!
?!
A DECOY ?!
THWUMP
THEN WHERE IS HE?
BEHIND ME? UNDER ME? OR...
FWUP

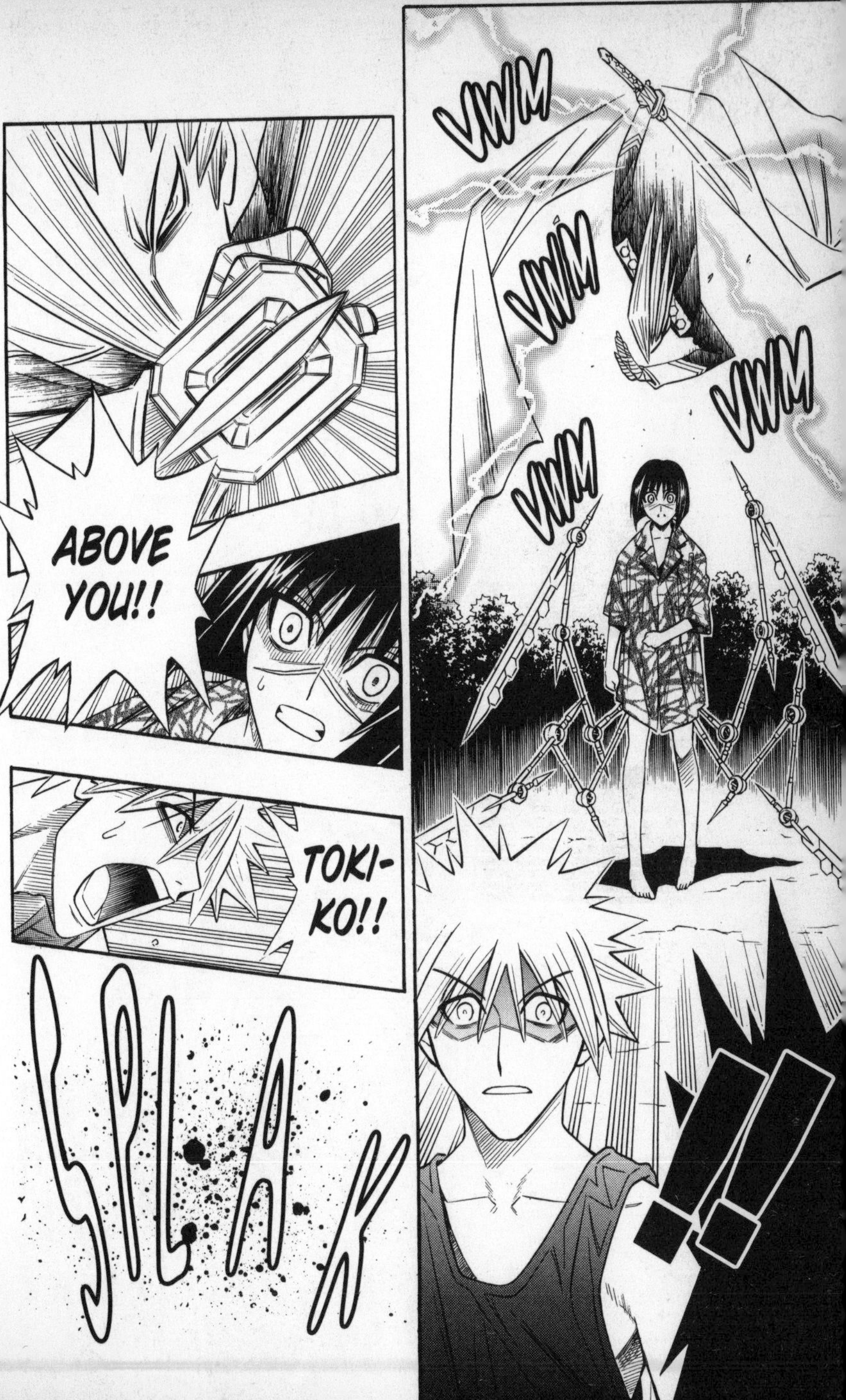
VWM
VWM
VWM
VWM
ABOVE YOU!!
TOKI-KO!!
SPLAK

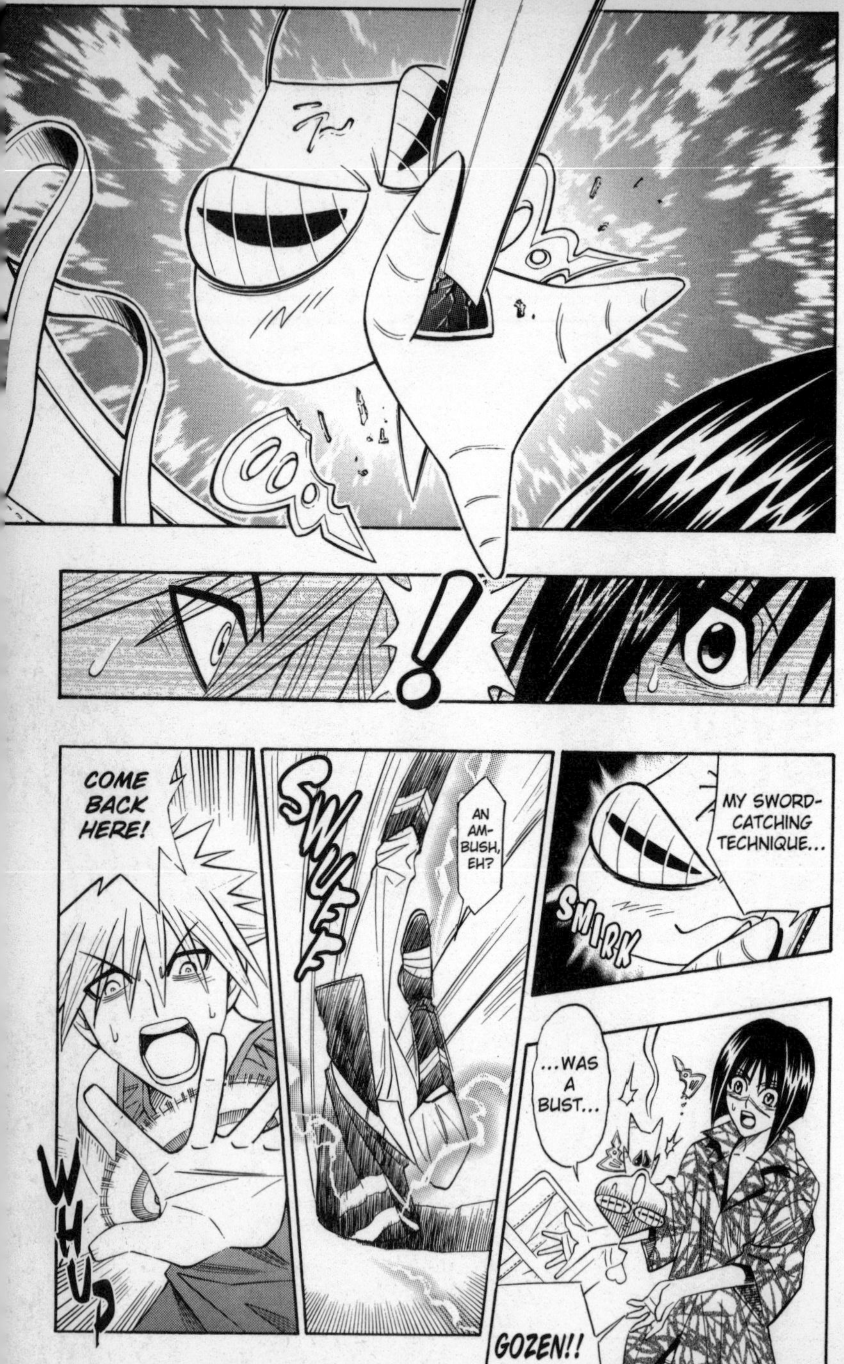
MY SWORD-CATCHING TECHNIQUE...
SMIRK
...WAS A BUST...
GOZEN!!
AN AMBUSH, EH?
COME BACK HERE!
WHUD

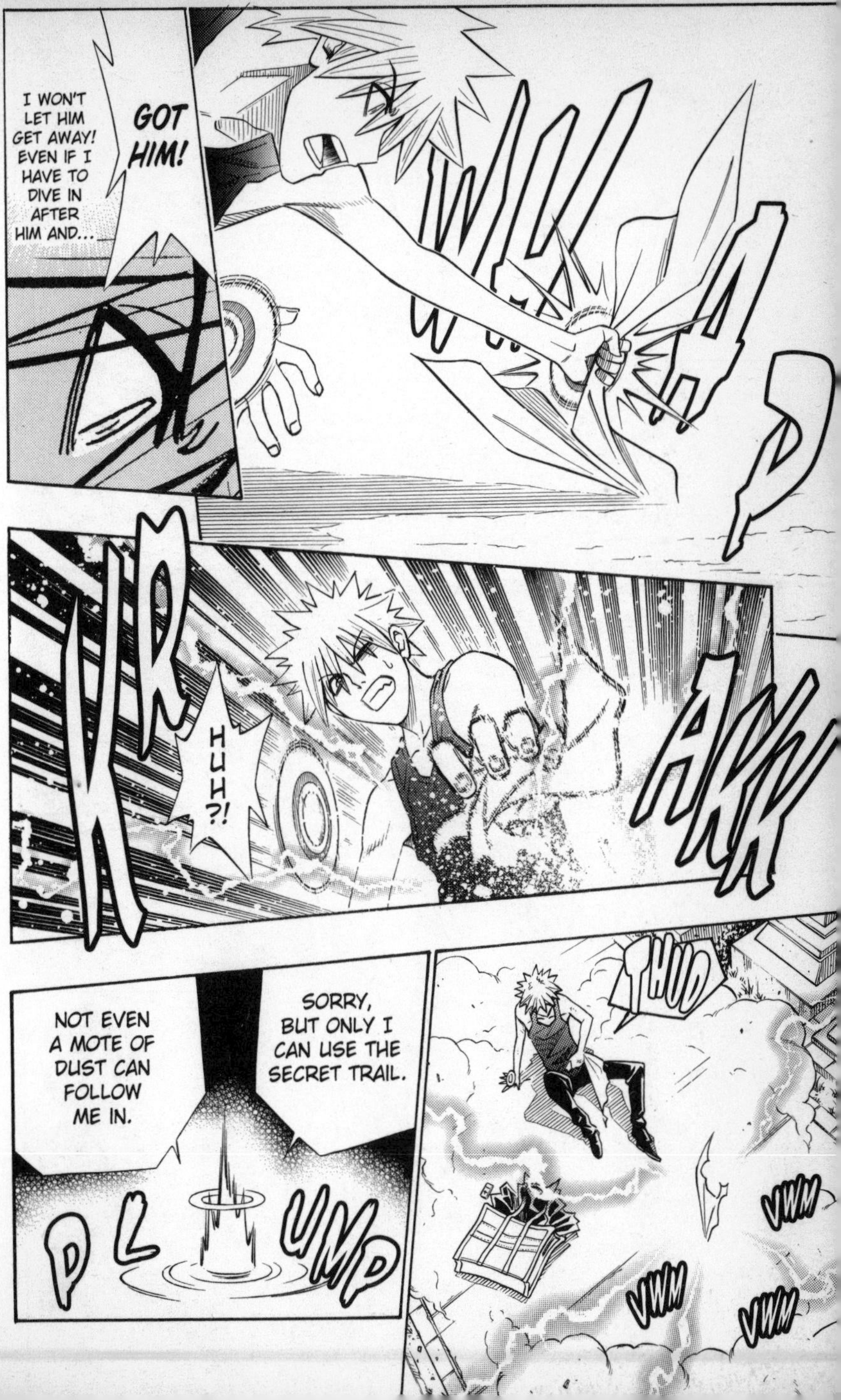
GOT HIM!
I WON'T LET HIM GET AWAY! EVEN IF I HAVE TO DIVE IN AFTER HIM AND...
HUH?!
THUD
VWM
VWM
VWM
SORRY, BUT ONLY I CAN USE THE SECRET TRAIL.
NOT EVEN A MOTE OF DUST CAN FOLLOW ME IN.

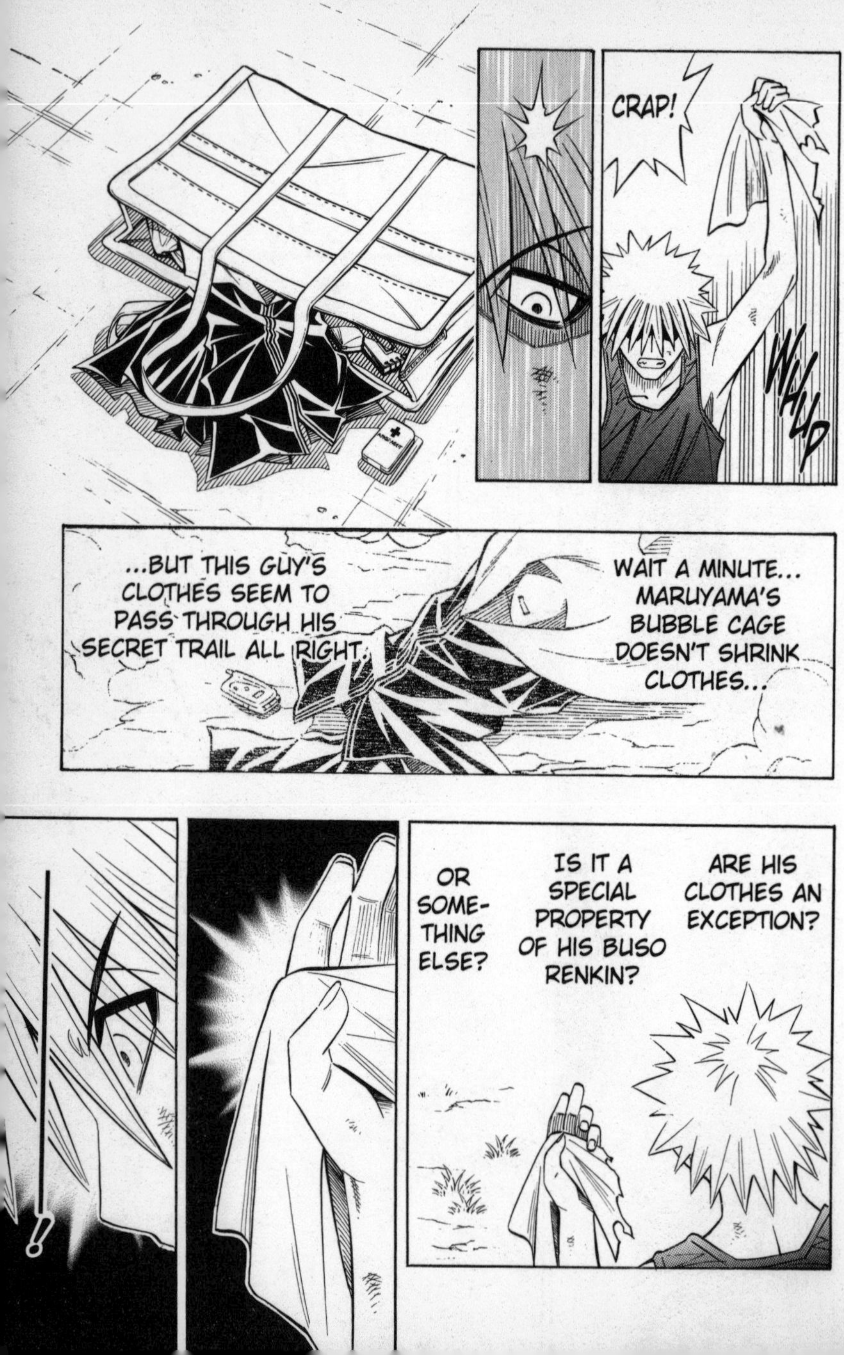
CRAP!
WHUP
WAIT A MINUTE... MARUYAMA'S BUBBLE CAGE DOESN'T SHRINK CLOTHES...
...BUT THIS GUY'S CLOTHES SEEM TO PASS THROUGH HIS SECRET TRAIL ALL RIGHT.
ARE HIS CLOTHES AN EXCEPTION?
IS IT A SPECIAL PROPERTY OF HIS BUSO RENKIN?
OR SOME-THING ELSE?
!

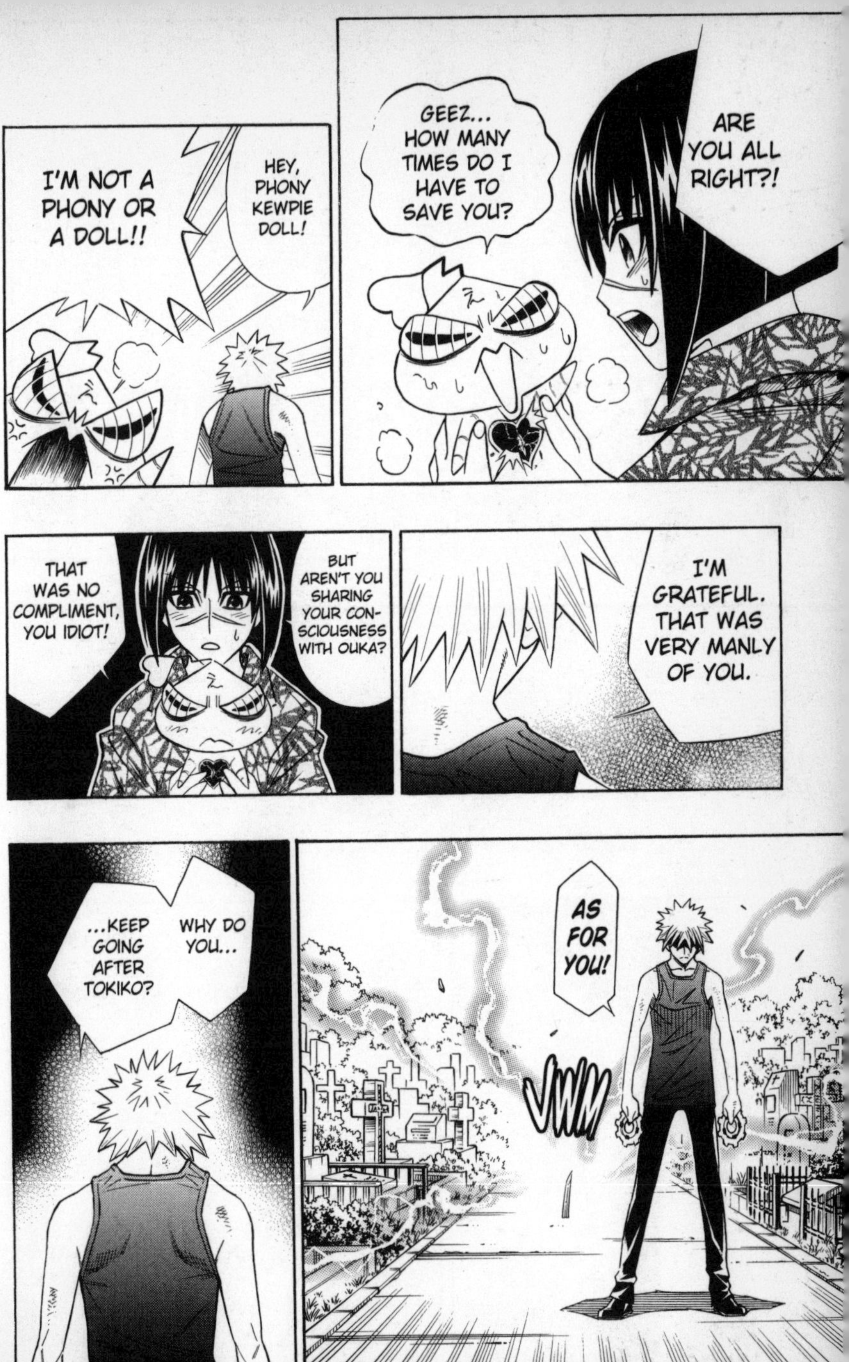
ARE YOU ALL RIGHT?!
GEEZ... HOW MANY TIMES DO I HAVE TO SAVE YOU?
HEY, PHONY KEWPIE DOLL!
I'M NOT A PHONY OR A DOLL!!
I'M GRATEFUL. THAT WAS VERY MANLY OF YOU.
BUT AREN'T YOU SHARING YOUR CON-SCIOUSNESS WITH OUKA?
THAT WAS NO COMPLIMENT, YOU IDIOT!
AS FOR YOU!
WHY DO YOU...
...KEEP GOING AFTER TOKIKO?

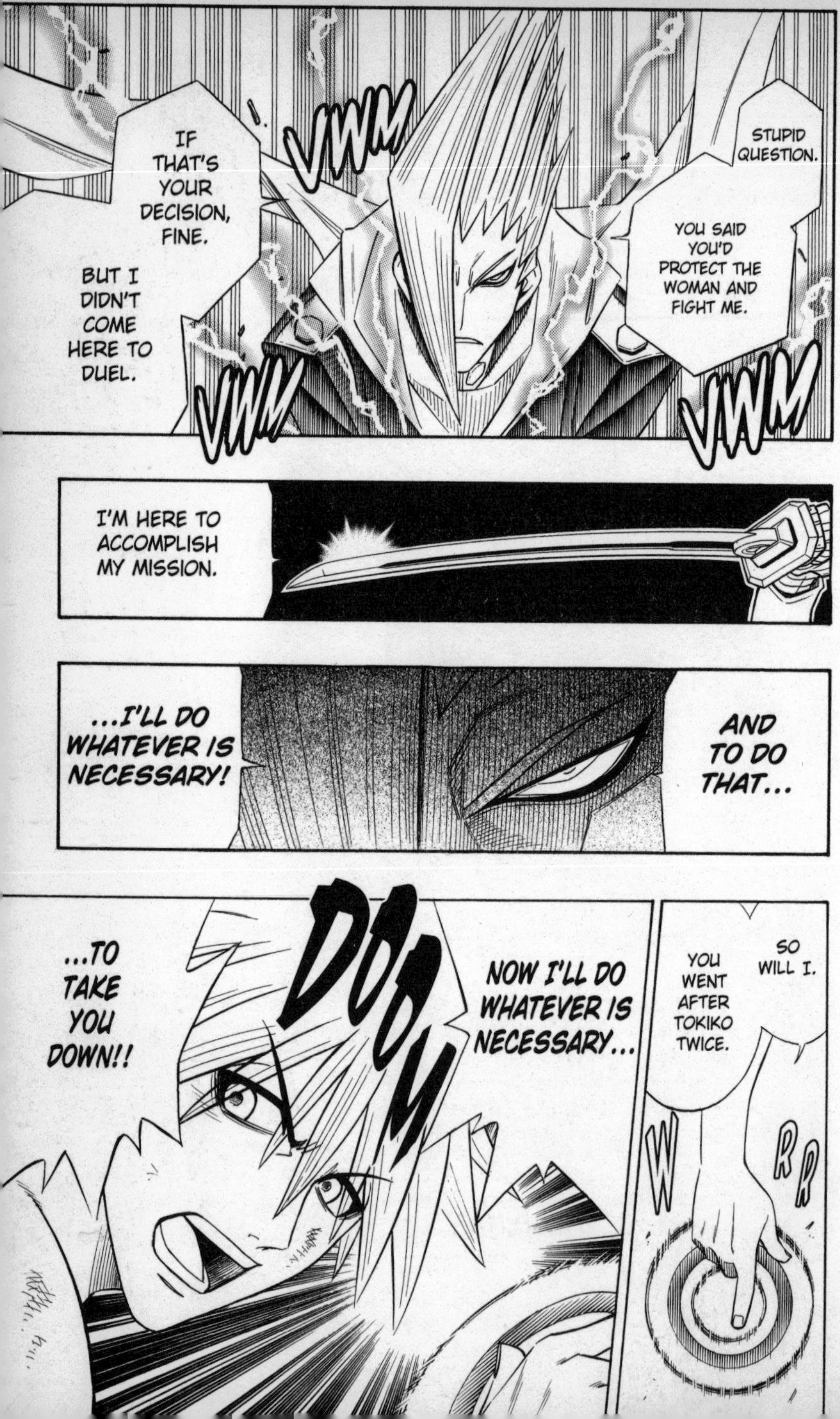
VWM
STUPID QUESTION.
YOU SAID YOU'D PROTECT THE WOMAN AND FIGHT ME.
IF THAT'S YOUR DECISION, FINE.
BUT I DIDN'T COME HERE TO DUEL.
VWM
VWM
I'M HERE TO ACCOMPLISH MY MISSION.
AND TO DO THAT...
...I'LL DO WHATEVER IS NECESSARY!
SO WILL I.
YOU WENT AFTER TOKIKO TWICE.
WRR
NOW I'LL DO WHATEVER IS NECESSARY...
DOOM
...TO TAKE YOU DOWN!!

- Height: 182 cm; Weight: 65 kg
- Born: April 4; Aries; Blood Type: AB; Age: 23
- Likes: Day spas, make-up, men
- Dislikes: Cleaning the toilet, taking out the trash, women
- Hobby: Collecting balloons
- Special Ability: The ability to draw a perfect circle without
  using a compass
- Affiliations: Alchemist Army, Re-Extermination Squad

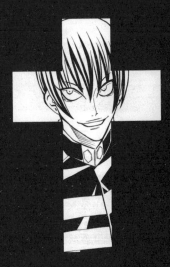

Character File No. 30
MADOKA MARUYAMA

Author's Notes
- In the beginning, I drew this character just to fill out the squad.
- When I got complaints that there were no good-looking guys in the Re-Extermination Squad, I redesigned this character right away.
- But he didn't seem quite right so I made him a little psychotic.
- That might've been hard to pull off in a weekly boy's magazine, so I made him kind of wimpy instead.
- As I went along, the character began to develop a personality, but I don't think this story was such a good vehicle for him.
- I wanted him to look a bit androgynous. If he'd shut up for a few minutes so that I could draw him carefully, he might've looked quite handsome.

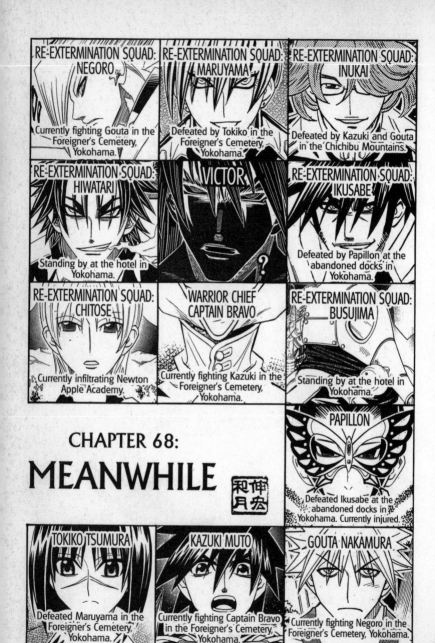

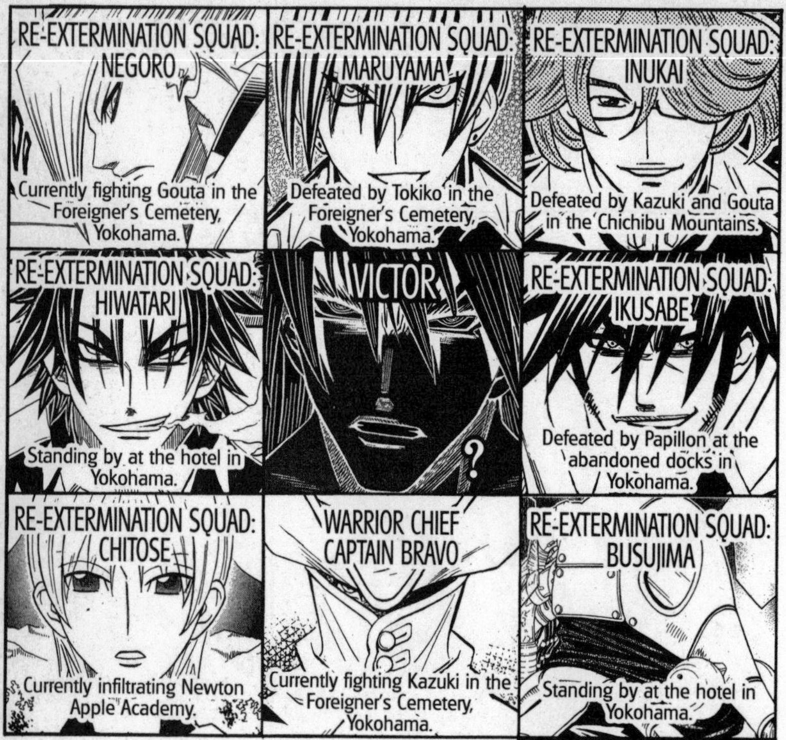
RE-EXTERMINATION SQUAD: INUKAI
Defeated by Kazuki and Gouta in the Chichibu Mountains.
RE-EXTERMINATION SQUAD: MARUYAMA
Defeated by Tokiko in the Foreigner's Cemetery, Yokohama.
RE-EXTERMINATION SQUAD: NEGORO
Currently fighting Gouta in the Foreigner's Cemetery, Yokohama.
RE-EXTERMINATION SQUAD: IKUSABE
Defeated by Papillon at the abandoned docks in Yokohama.
VICTOR
?
RE-EXTERMINATION SQUAD: HIWATARI
Standing by at the hotel in Yokohama.
RE-EXTERMINATION SQUAD: BUSUJIMA
Standing by at the hotel in Yokohama.
WARRIOR CHIEF CAPTAIN BRAVO
Currently fighting Kazuki in the Foreigner's Cemetery, Yokohama.
RE-EXTERMINATION SQUAD: CHITOSE
Currently infiltrating Newton Apple Academy.

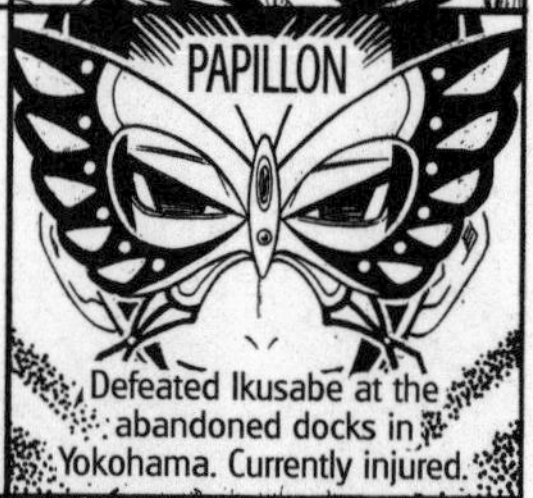
PAPILLON
Defeated Ikusabe at the abandoned docks in Yokohama. Currently injured.

CHAPTER 68:

MEANWHILE

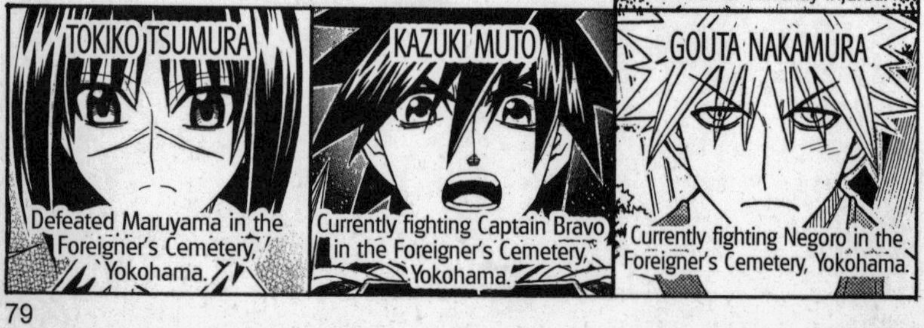
GOUTA NAKAMURA
Currently fighting Negoro in the Foreigner's Cemetery, Yokohama.
KAZUKI MUTO
Currently fighting Captain Bravo in the Foreigner's Cemetery, Yokohama.
TOKIKO TSUMURA
Defeated Maruyama in the Foreigner's Cemetery, Yokohama.

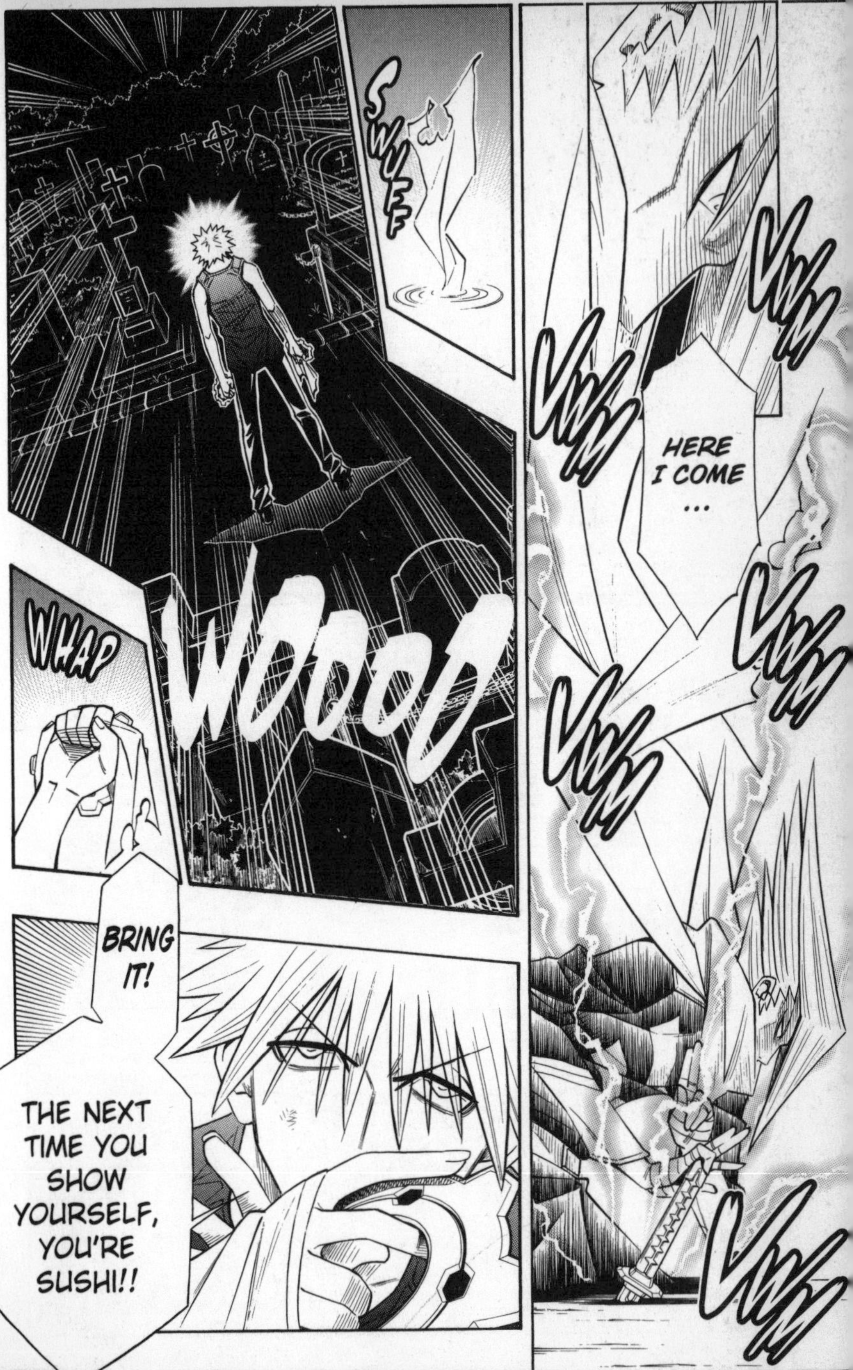
VWM
VWM
HERE I COME ...
VWM
VWM
VWM
SWIFF
WOOOO
WHAP
BRING IT!
THE NEXT TIME YOU SHOW YOURSELF, YOU'RE SUSHI!!

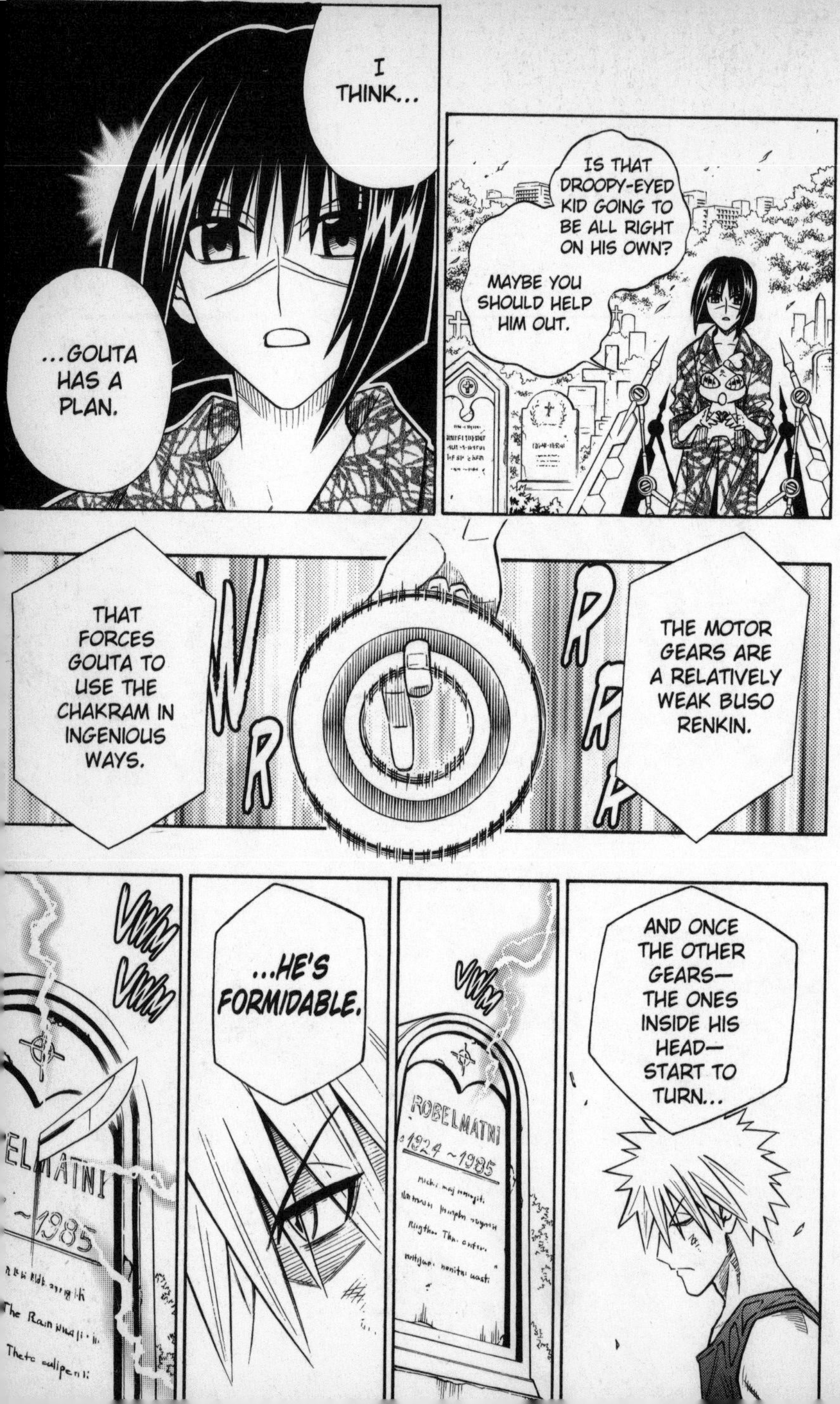
IS THAT DROOPY-EYED KID GOING TO BE ALL RIGHT ON HIS OWN?
MAYBE YOU SHOULD HELP HIM OUT.
I THINK...
...GOUTA HAS A PLAN.
RRRR
THE MOTOR GEARS ARE A RELATIVELY WEAK BUSO RENKIN.
WR
THAT FORCES GOUTA TO USE THE CHAKRAM IN INGENIOUS WAYS.
AND ONCE THE OTHER GEARS— THE ONES INSIDE HIS HEAD— START TO TURN...
VVVM
ROBELMATNI
1924 ~1985
...HE'S FORMIDABLE.
VVVM VVVM

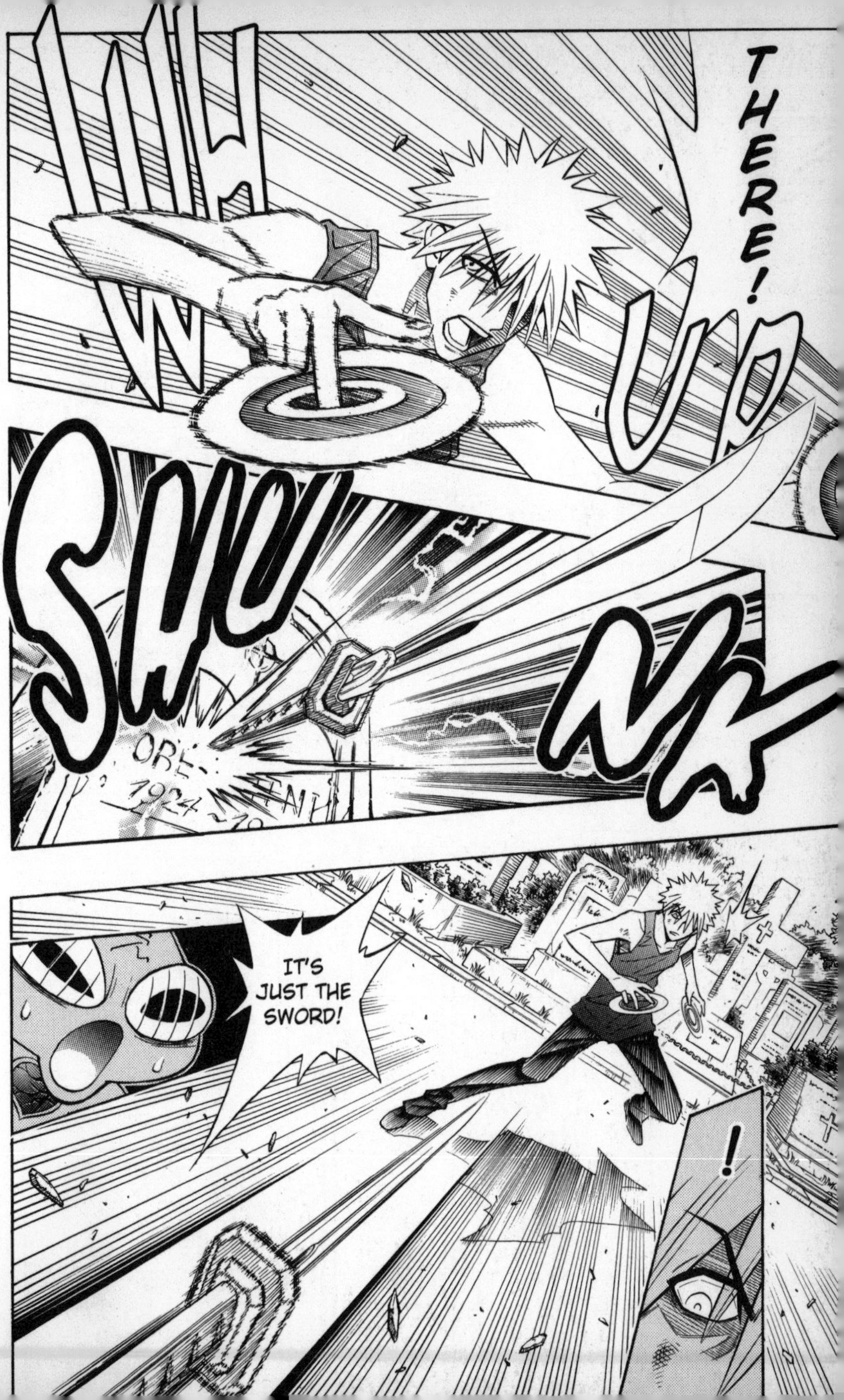
THERE!
IT'S JUST THE SWORD!
!

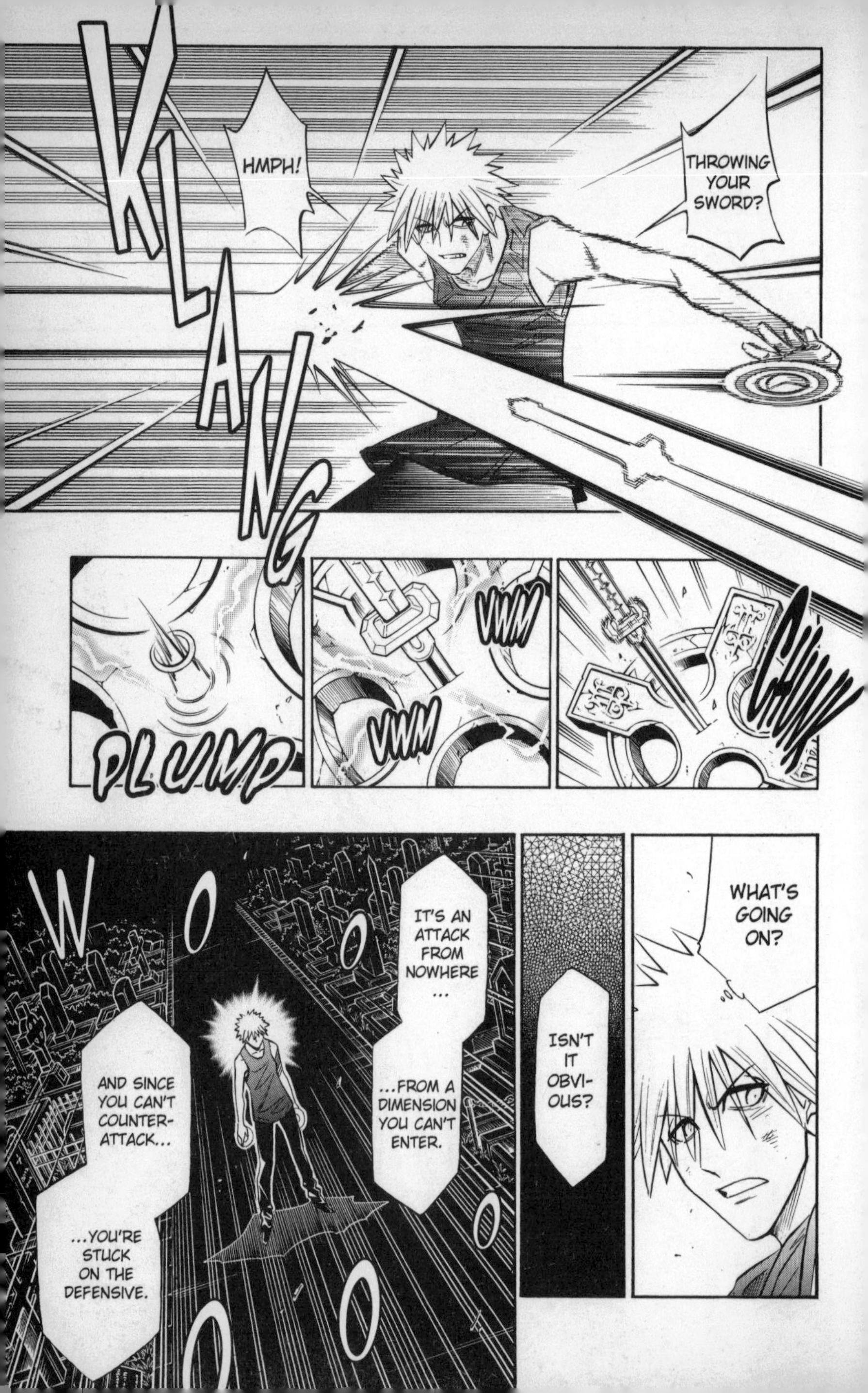
THROWING YOUR SWORD?
HMPH!
KLANG
CHINK
VWM
VWM
PLUMP
WHAT'S GOING ON?
ISN'T IT OBVIOUS?
IT'S AN ATTACK FROM NOWHERE...
...FROM A DIMENSION YOU CAN'T ENTER.
AND SINCE YOU CAN'T COUNTER-ATTACK...
...YOU'RE STUCK ON THE DEFENSIVE.
WOOOO

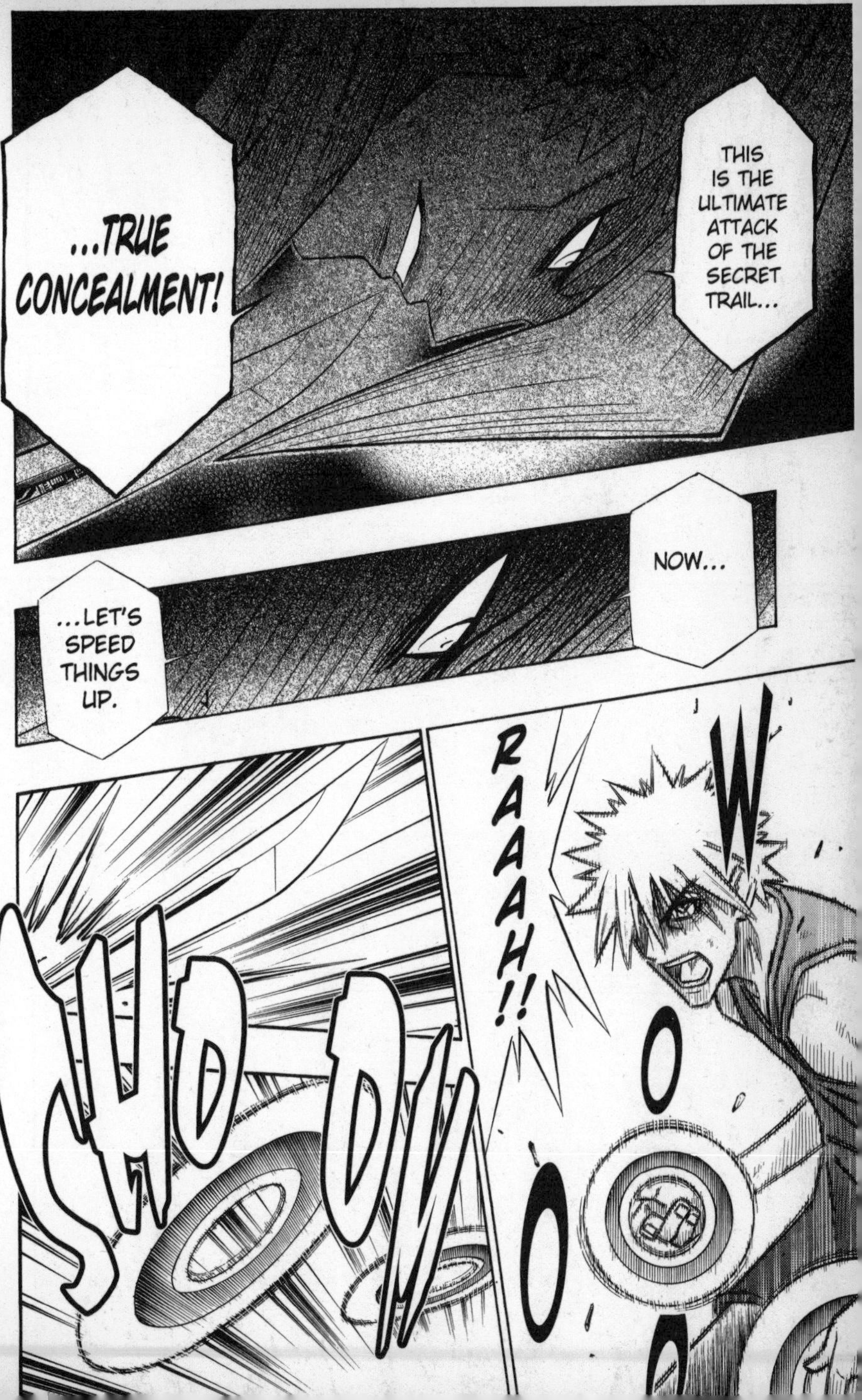
THIS IS THE ULTIMATE ATTACK OF THE SECRET TRAIL...
...TRUE CONCEALMENT!
NOW...
...LET'S SPEED THINGS UP.
W
RAAAAH!!
OOOO
SHOOM

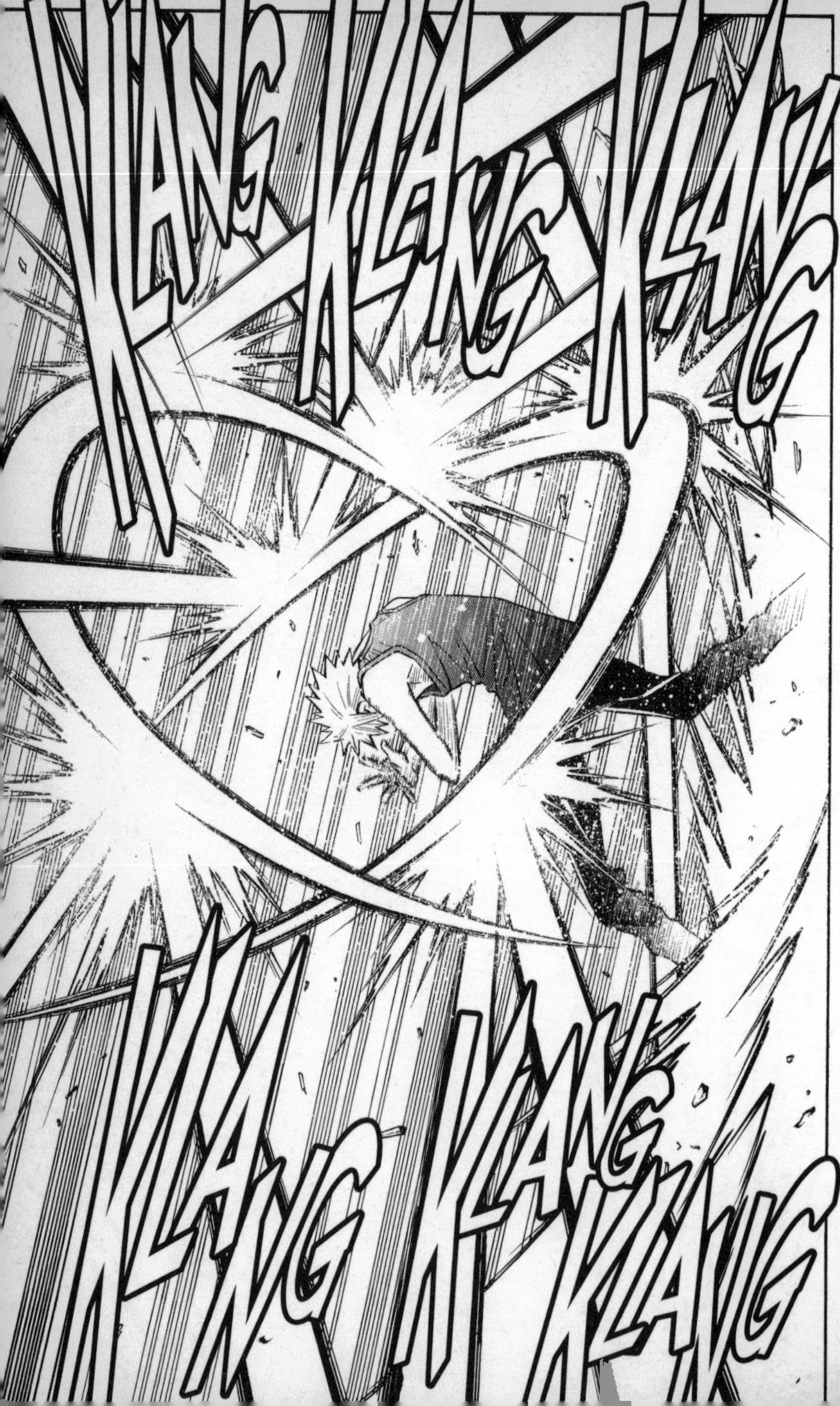
KLANG KLANG KLANG
KLANG KLANG KLANG KLANG

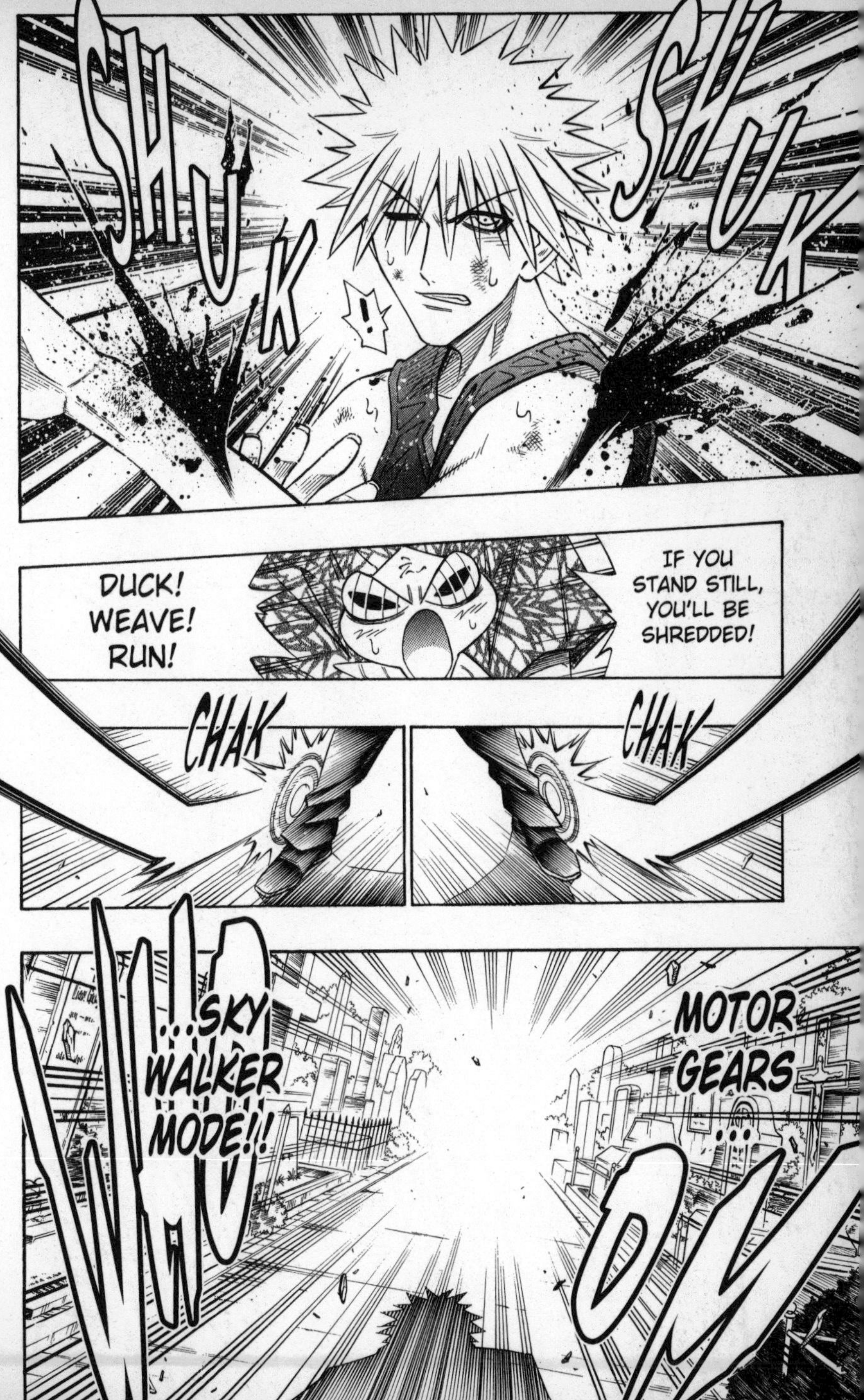
SHUK
SHUK
!
IF YOU STAND STILL, YOU'LL BE SHREDDED!
DUCK! WEAVE! RUN!
CHAK
CHAK
MOTOR GEARS...
...SKY WALKER MODE!!

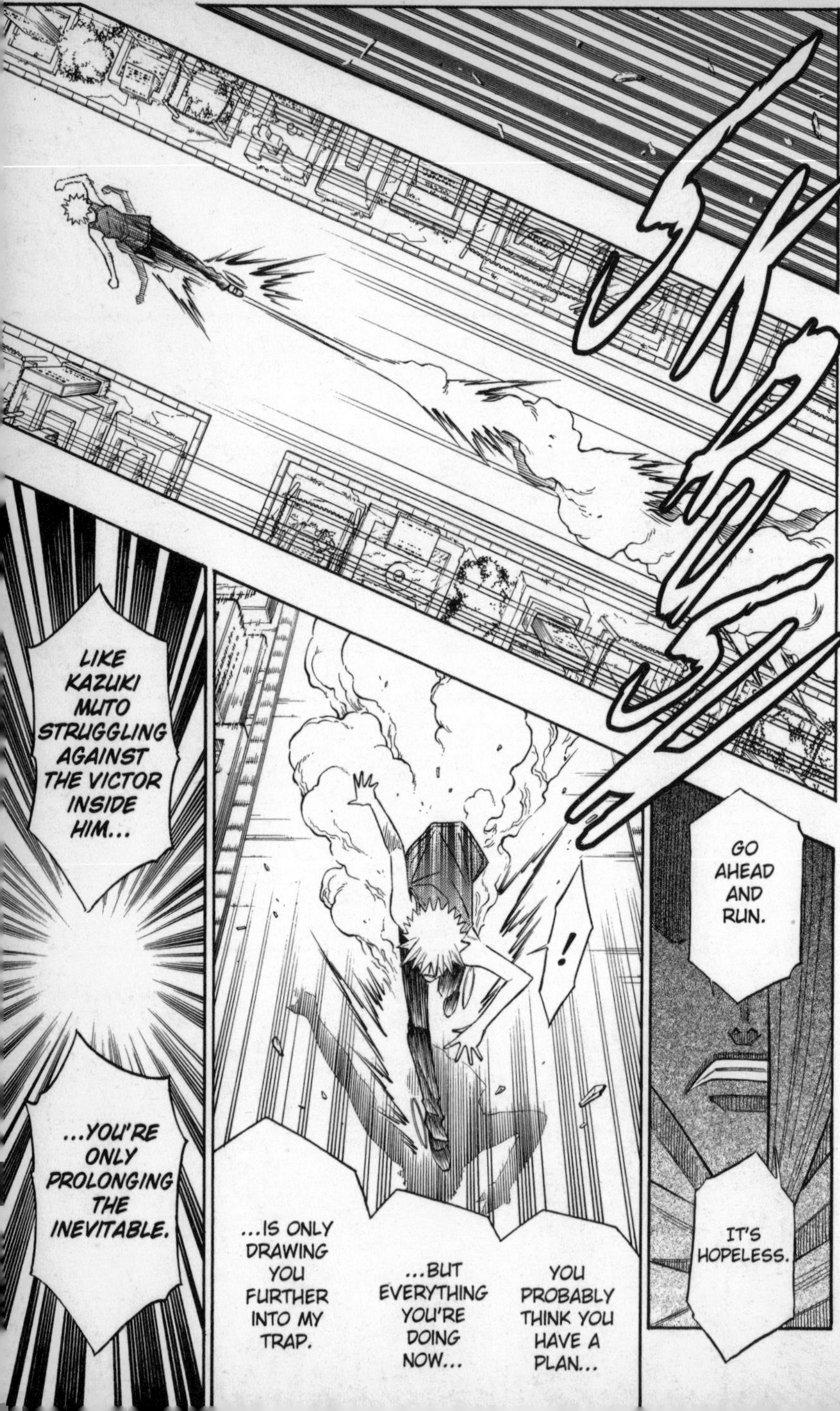
GO AHEAD AND RUN.
IT'S HOPELESS.
!
YOU PROBABLY THINK YOU HAVE A PLAN...
...BUT EVERYTHING YOU'RE DOING NOW...
...IS ONLY DRAWING YOU FURTHER INTO MY TRAP.
LIKE KAZUKI MUTO STRUGGLING AGAINST THE VICTOR INSIDE HIM...
...YOU'RE ONLY PROLONGING THE INEVITABLE.

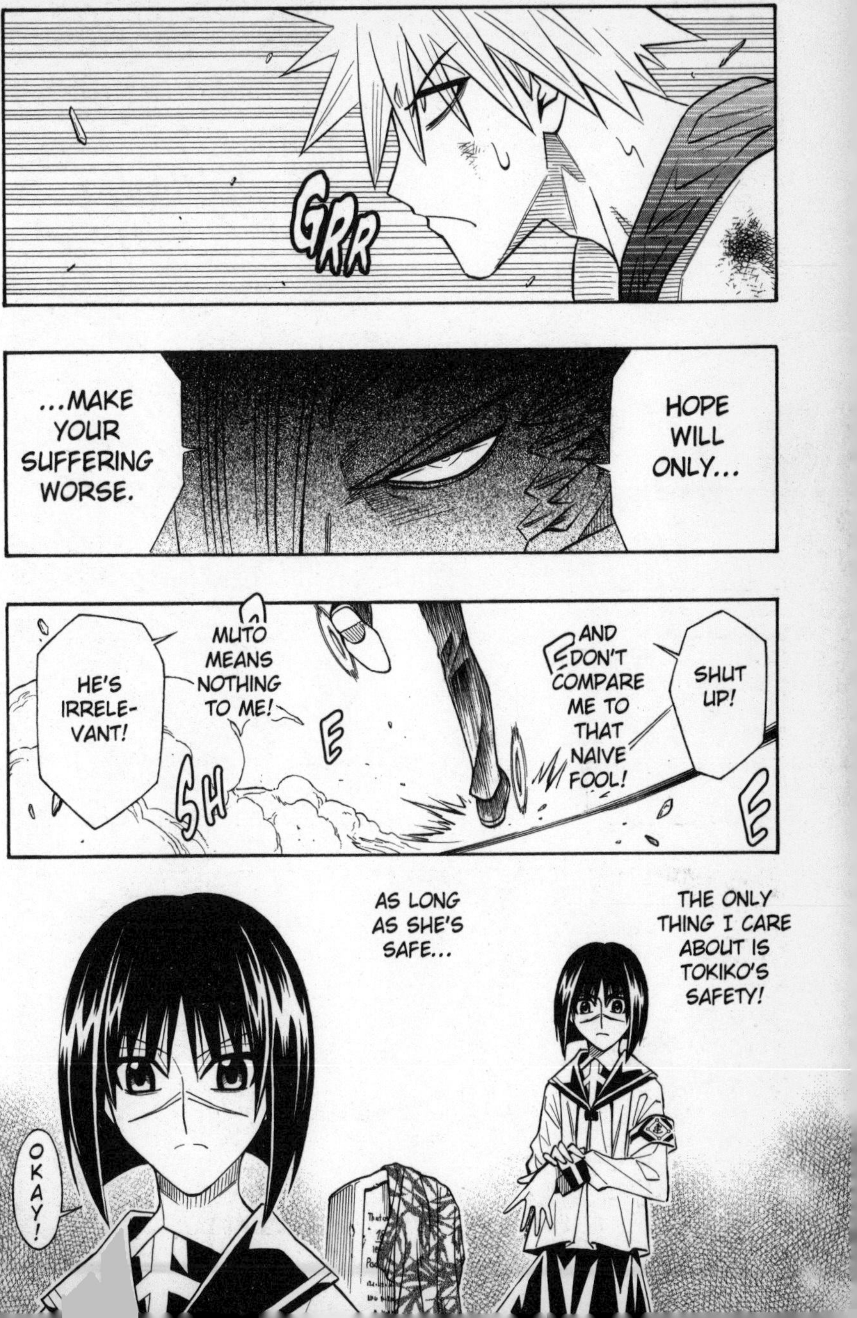
GRR
HOPE WILL ONLY...
...MAKE YOUR SUFFERING WORSE.
SHUT UP!
AND DON'T COMPARE ME TO THAT NAIVE FOOL!
MUTO MEANS NOTHING TO ME!
HE'S IRRELE-VANT!
THE ONLY THING I CARE ABOUT IS TOKIKO'S SAFETY!
AS LONG AS SHE'S SAFE...
OKAY!

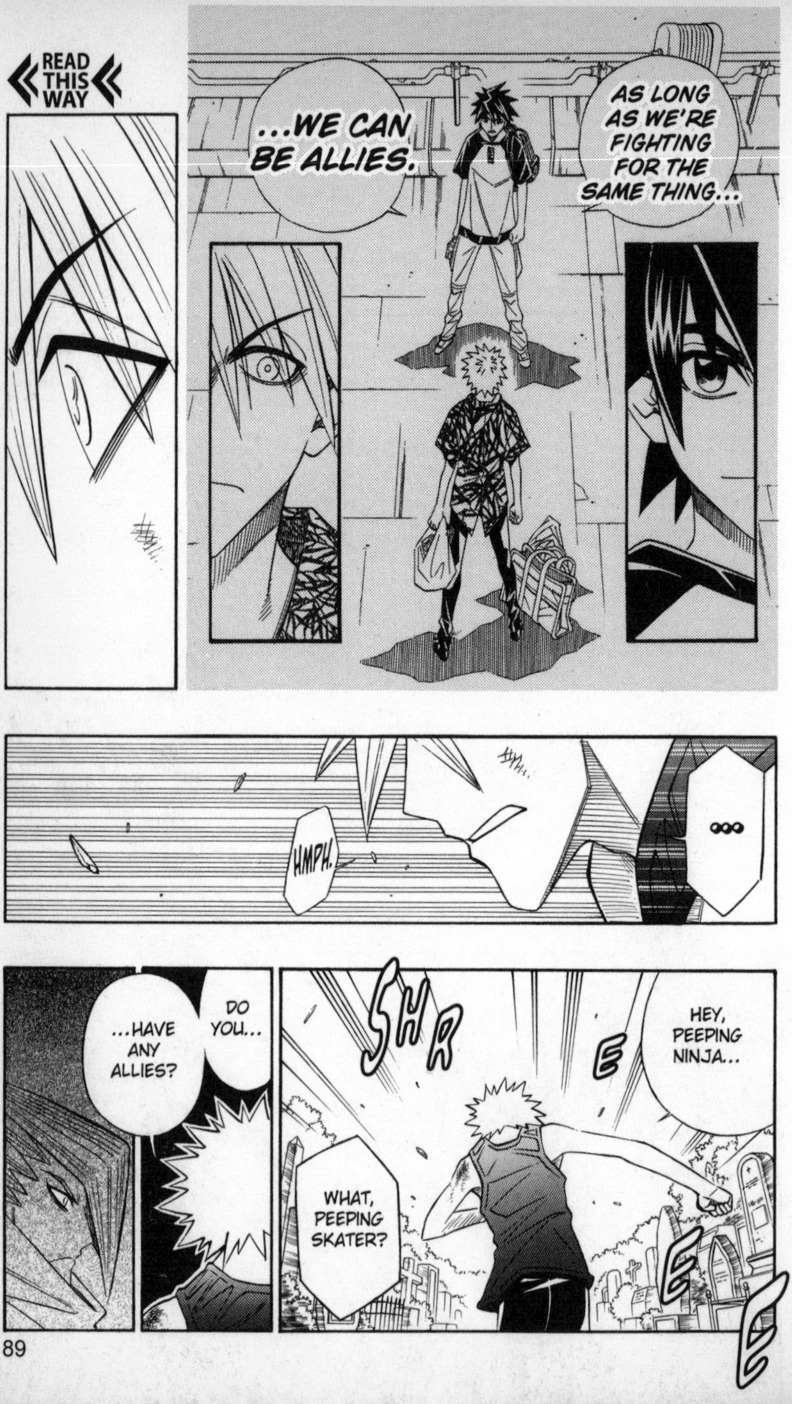
READ THIS WAY
AS LONG AS WE'RE FIGHTING FOR THE SAME THING...
...WE CAN BE ALLIES.
...
HMPH.
HEY, PEEPING NINJA...
SHREEEEE
WHAT, PEEPING SKATER?
DO YOU...
...HAVE ANY ALLIES?

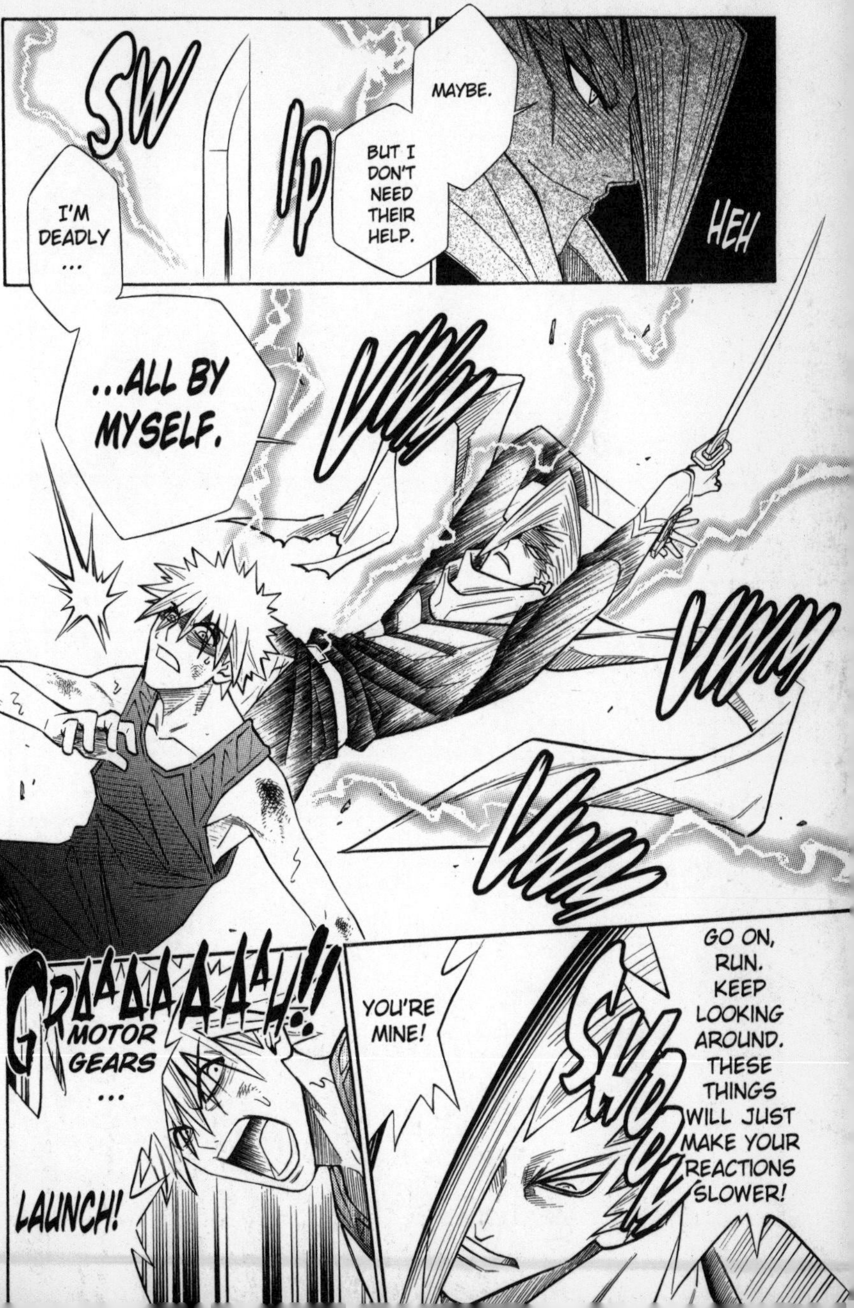
MAYBE.
BUT I DON'T NEED THEIR HELP.
HEH
SWIP
I'M DEADLY ...
...ALL BY MYSELF.
GO ON, RUN. KEEP LOOKING AROUND. THESE THINGS WILL JUST MAKE YOUR REACTIONS SLOWER!
YOU'RE MINE!
MOTOR GEARS ...
LAUNCH!

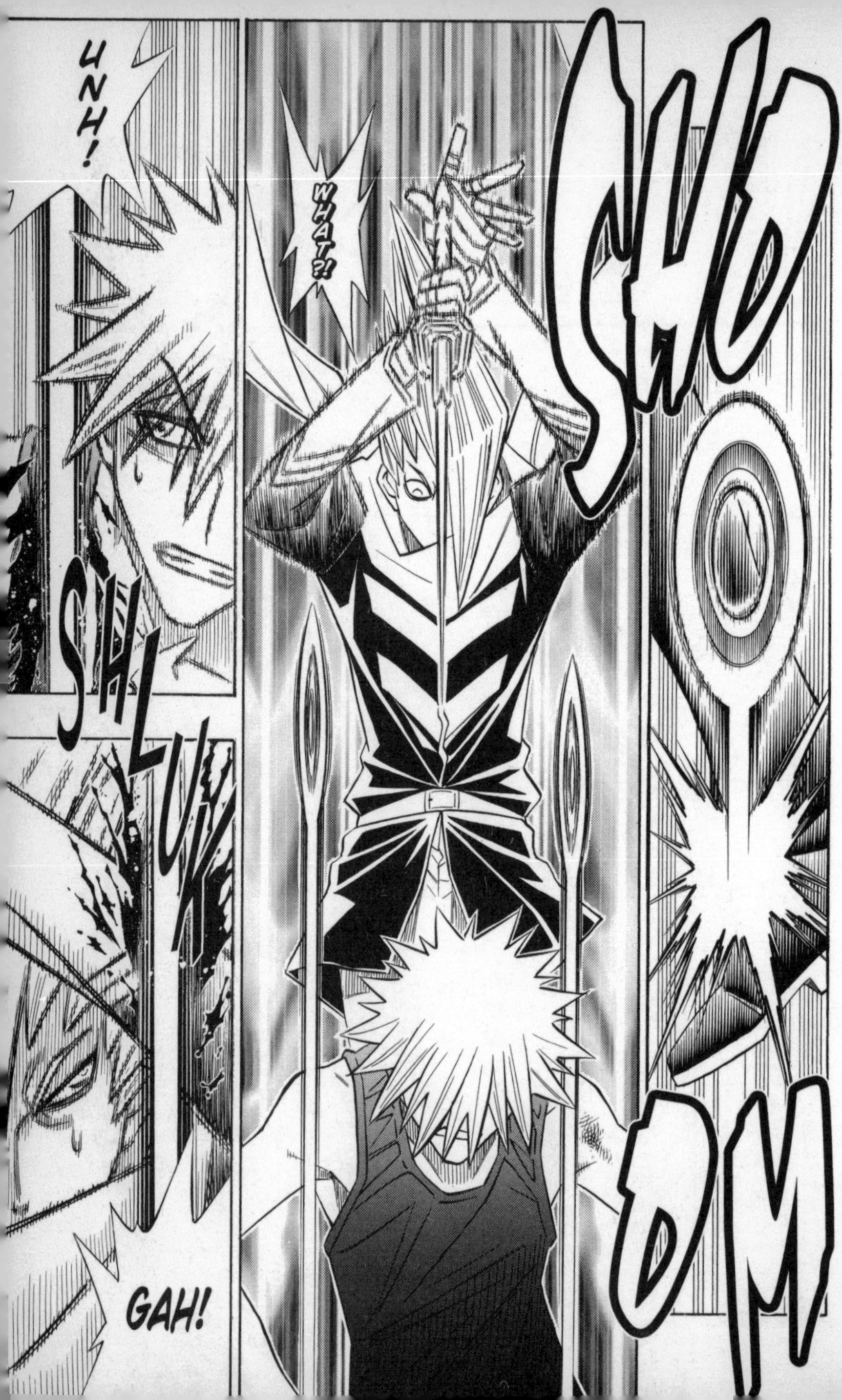
SHOOM
WHAT?!
UNH!
SHLUK
GAH!

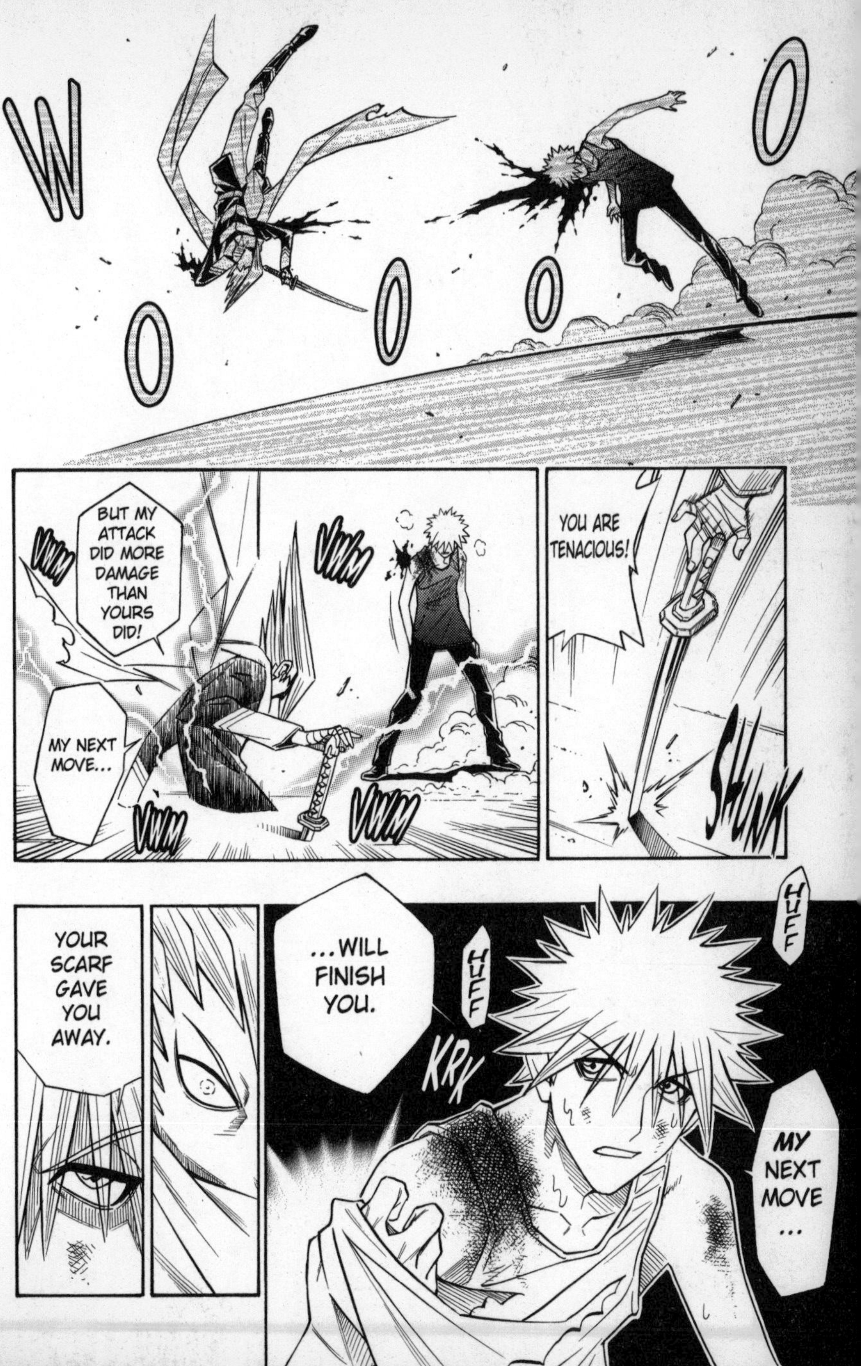
WOOOO
YOU ARE TENACIOUS!
SHUNK
VWM
VWM
BUT MY ATTACK DID MORE DAMAGE THAN YOURS DID!
MY NEXT MOVE...
VWM
VWM
HUFF
HUFF
...WILL FINISH YOU.
KRK
MY NEXT MOVE ...
YOUR SCARF GAVE YOU AWAY.

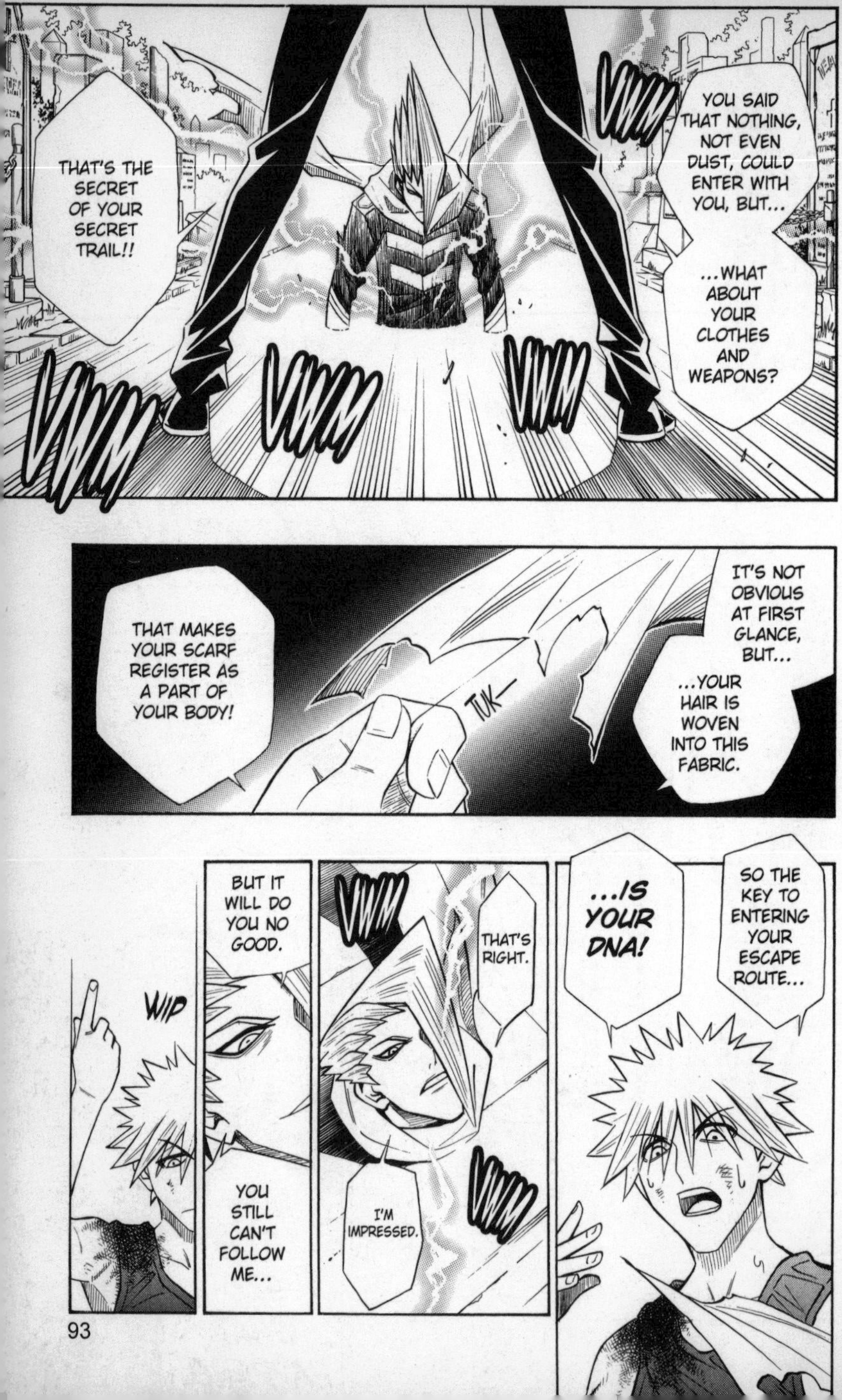

YOU SAID THAT NOTHING, NOT EVEN DUST, COULD ENTER WITH YOU, BUT...
...WHAT ABOUT YOUR CLOTHES AND WEAPONS?
VWM
THAT'S THE SECRET OF YOUR SECRET TRAIL!!
VWM
VWM
VWM
IT'S NOT OBVIOUS AT FIRST GLANCE, BUT...
...YOUR HAIR IS WOVEN INTO THIS FABRIC.
TUK—
THAT MAKES YOUR SCARF REGISTER AS A PART OF YOUR BODY!
SO THE KEY TO ENTERING YOUR ESCAPE ROUTE...
...IS YOUR DNA!
VWM
THAT'S RIGHT.
VWM
I'M IMPRESSED.
BUT IT WILL DO YOU NO GOOD.
YOU STILL CAN'T FOLLOW ME...
WIP

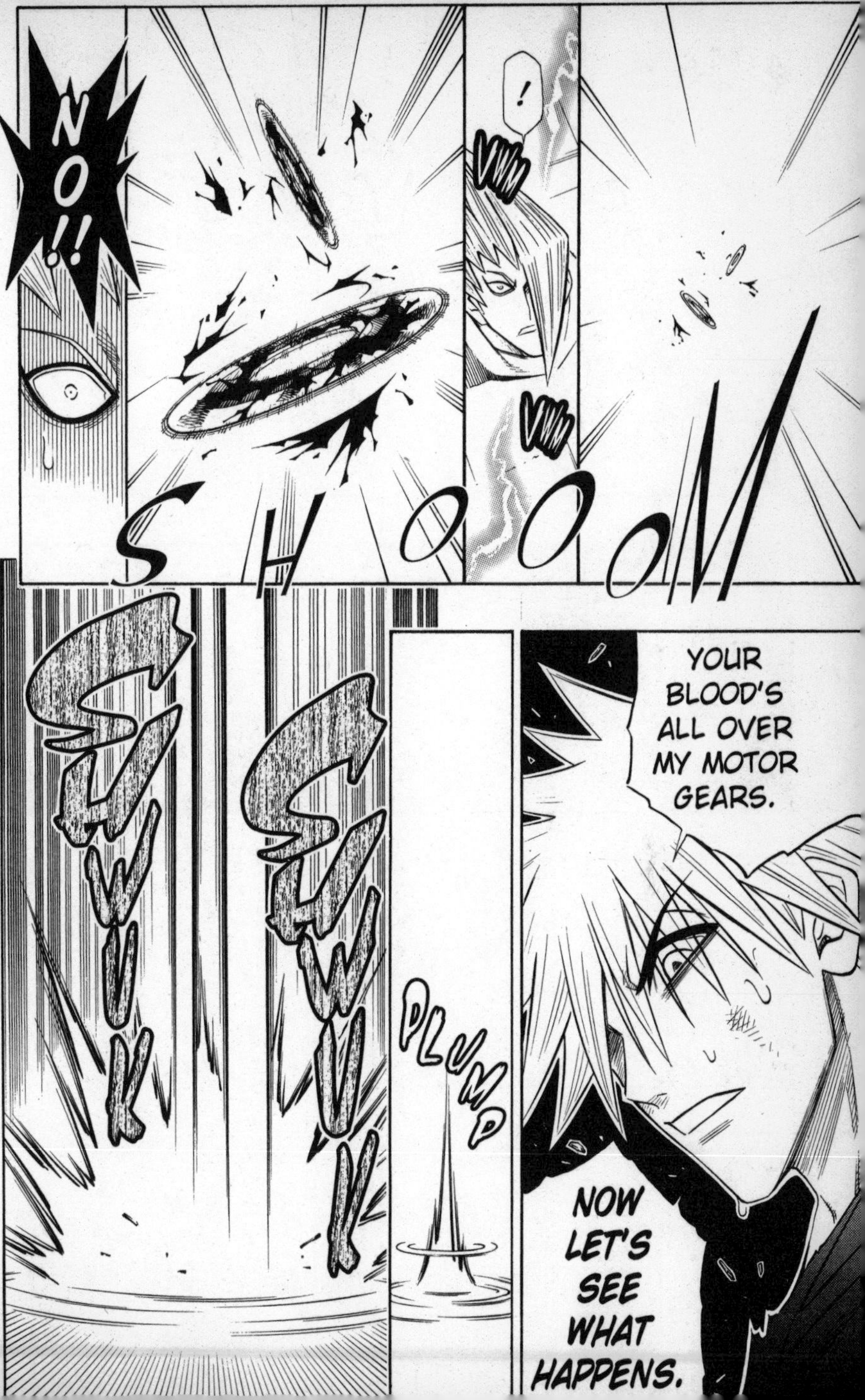
!
VWN
VWN
SHOOOM
NO!!
YOUR BLOOD'S ALL OVER MY MOTOR GEARS.
NOW LET'S SEE WHAT HAPPENS.
PLUMP
SWUK
SWUK

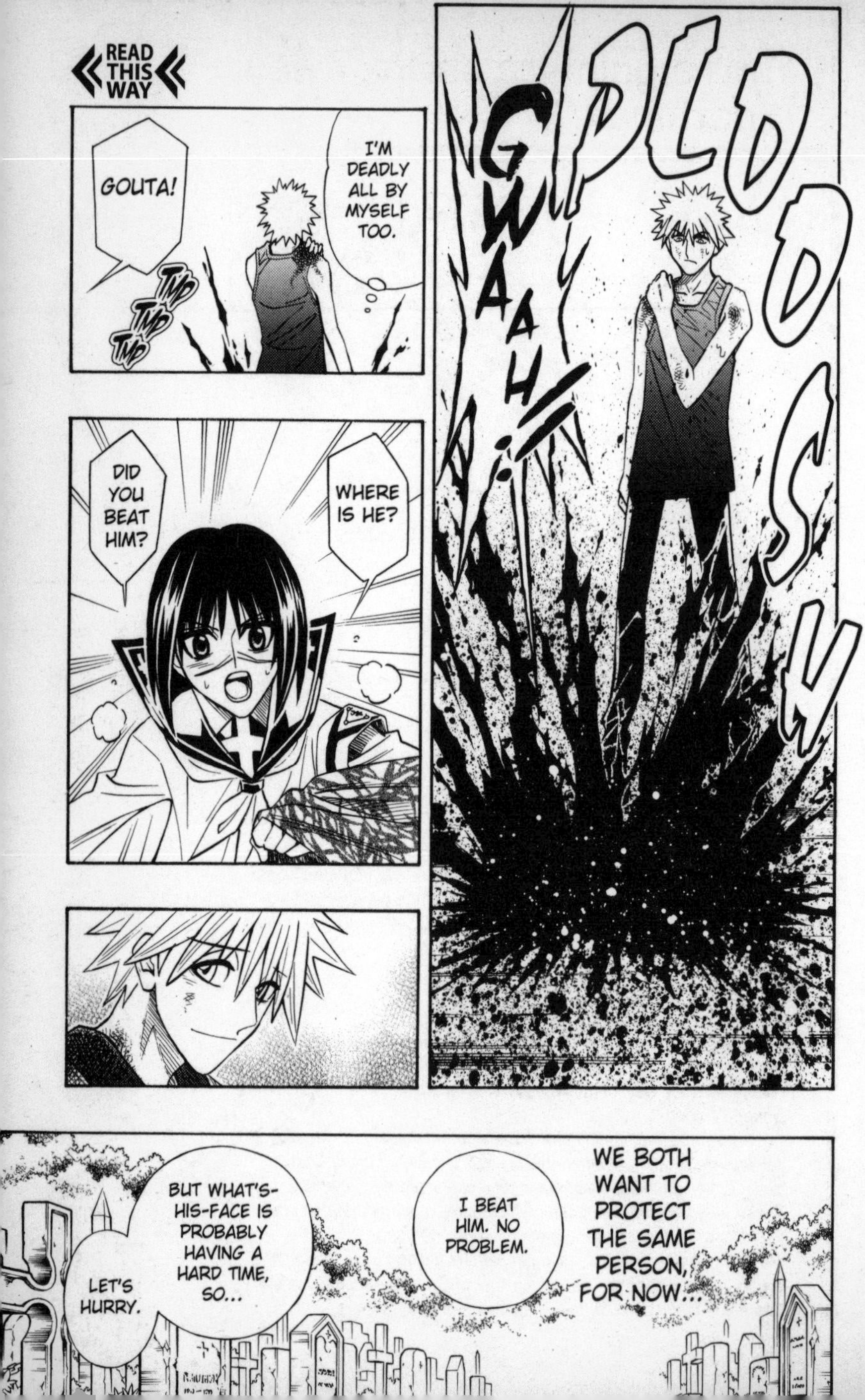
READ THIS WAY
PLOOSH
GWAAH!!
I'M DEADLY ALL BY MYSELF TOO.
GOUTA!
TMP TMP TMP
WHERE IS HE?
DID YOU BEAT HIM?
WE BOTH WANT TO PROTECT THE SAME PERSON, FOR NOW...
I BEAT HIM. NO PROBLEM.
BUT WHAT'S-HIS-FACE IS PROBABLY HAVING A HARD TIME, SO...
LET'S HURRY.

"You're going to shrink away to nothing." ♡

Buso Renkin File No. 15

バブル ケイジ
BUBBLE CAGE

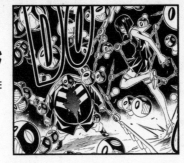

- ○ Kakugane Serial Number: XXXII (32)
- ○ Creator: Madoka Maruyama
- ○ Form: Floating Mine (Balloon Bombs)
- ○ Main Colors: Purple and Pink
- ○ Special Abilities: · The balloon bombs shrink whatever they hit by six inches.
- ○ Special Traits: · Able to position the balloons, albeit slowly, to surround the enemy.
  - · Able to over-inflate and burst a balloon at will as well as creating a gust of wind to propel the balloons toward the target. Only one balloon can be over-inflated at a time.
  - · Able to take to the air with the help of the balloons, but then he is at the mercy of the prevailing winds.
  - · Although they can be heard to say "Hee," the balloon mines are not sentient.

- ○ Author's Notes:
- · The design of this Buso Renkin was pretty simple. When I redesigned Maruyama, I used the original design for his head for the balloons.
- · I really liked the way all those weird, smiling, round faces fill the panels. It worked well.
- · I wanted to create a Buso Renkin that wouldn't cause any physical damage but would still diminish the target's ability to fight. Finally I decided that shrinking would be a good way to do that. The mini-Tokiko was a big hit with the fans, but I have to admit that this Buso Renkin's poor mobility made it hard to work with.
- · It might've been more interesting to use the Balloon Cage inside the school or the dormitory. Then again, that might've turned this manga into some kind of school-love-comedy-super-powers thing...

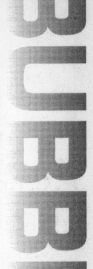

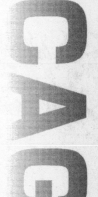

BUBBLE CAGE

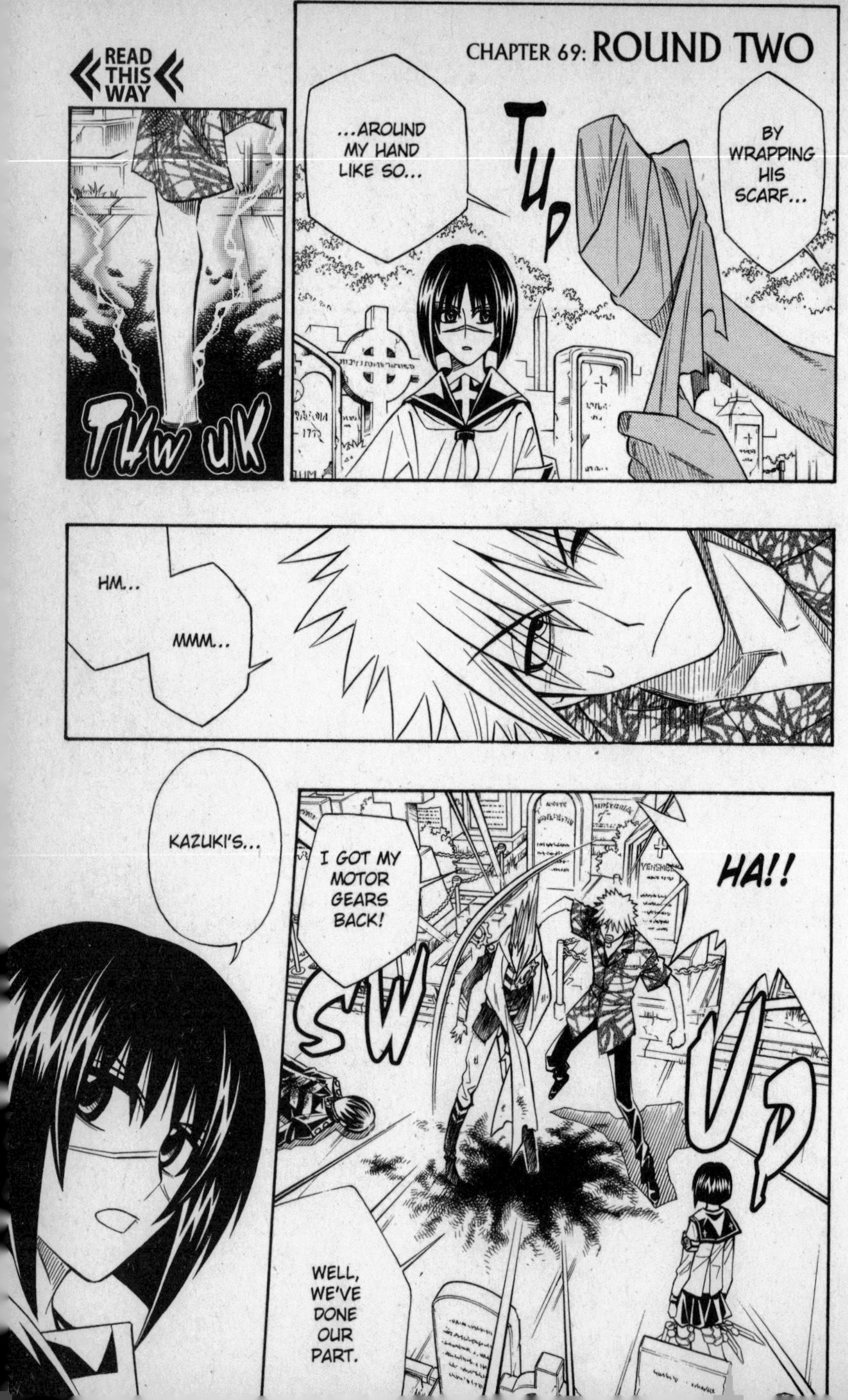
READ THIS WAY
CHAPTER 69: ROUND TWO
BY WRAPPING HIS SCARF...
TUP
...AROUND MY HAND LIKE SO...
THWUK
HM...
MMM...
HA!!
I GOT MY MOTOR GEARS BACK!
SW
UP
WELL, WE'VE DONE OUR PART.
KAZUKI'S...

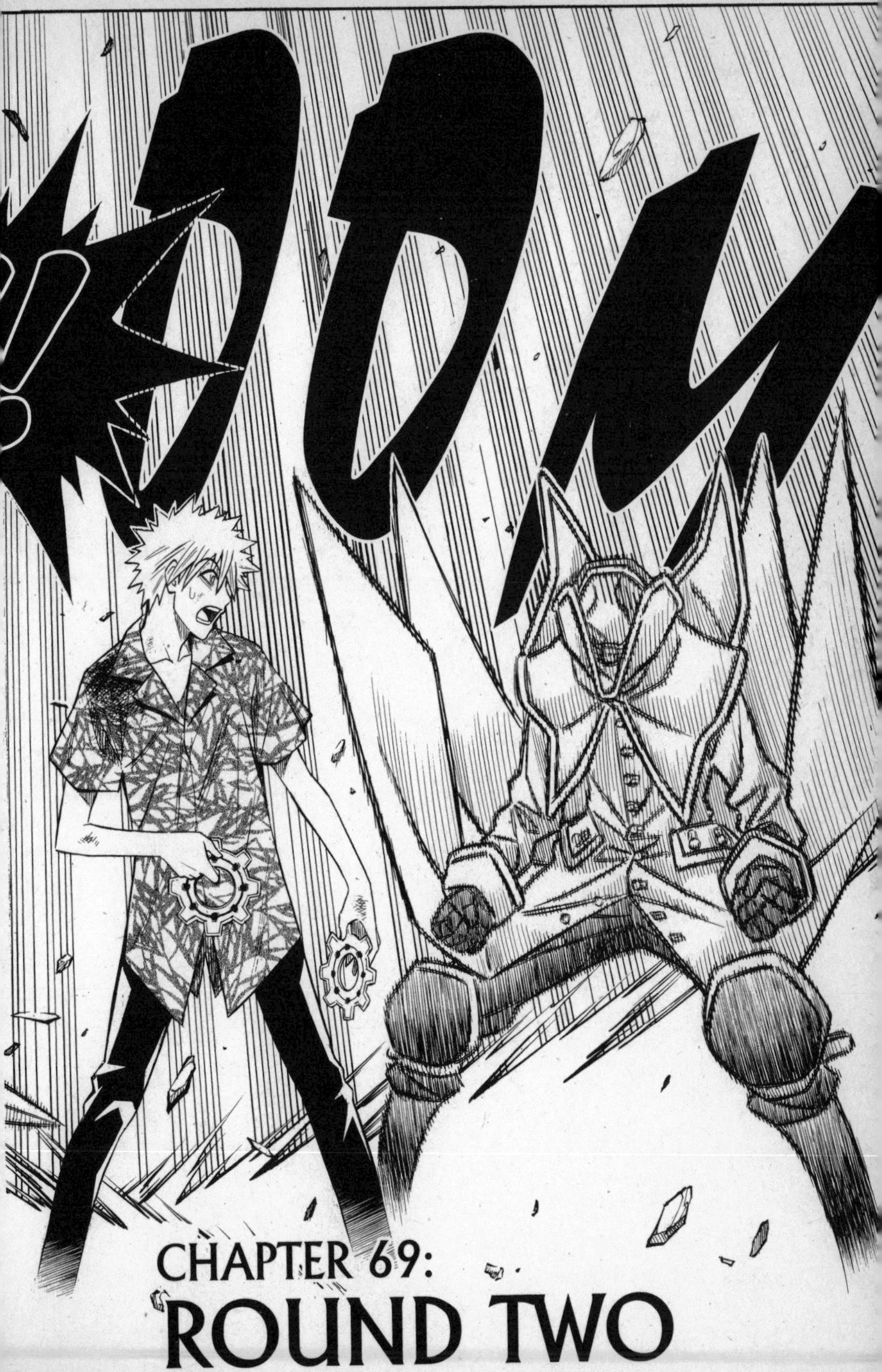

CHAPTER 69: ROUND TWO

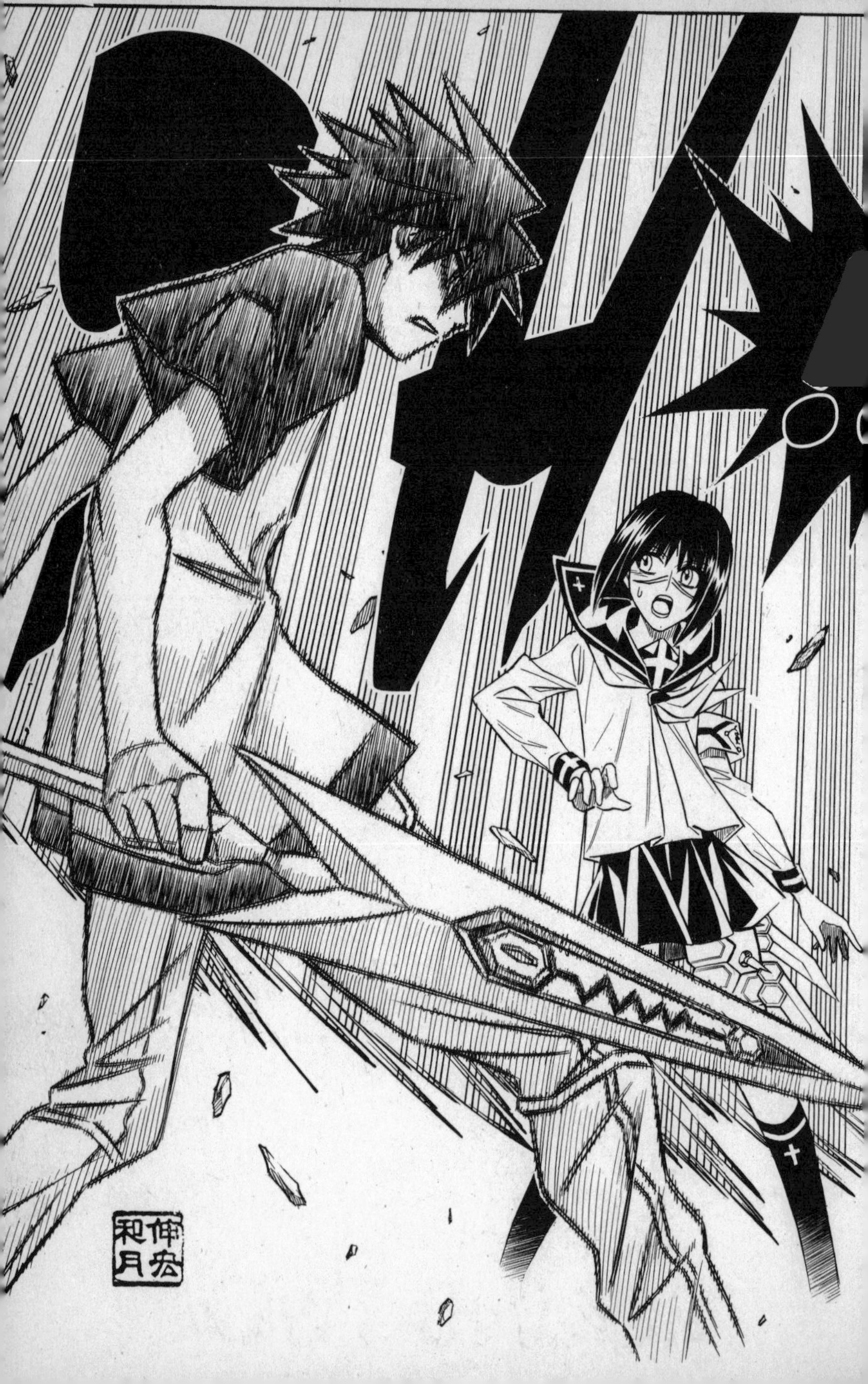

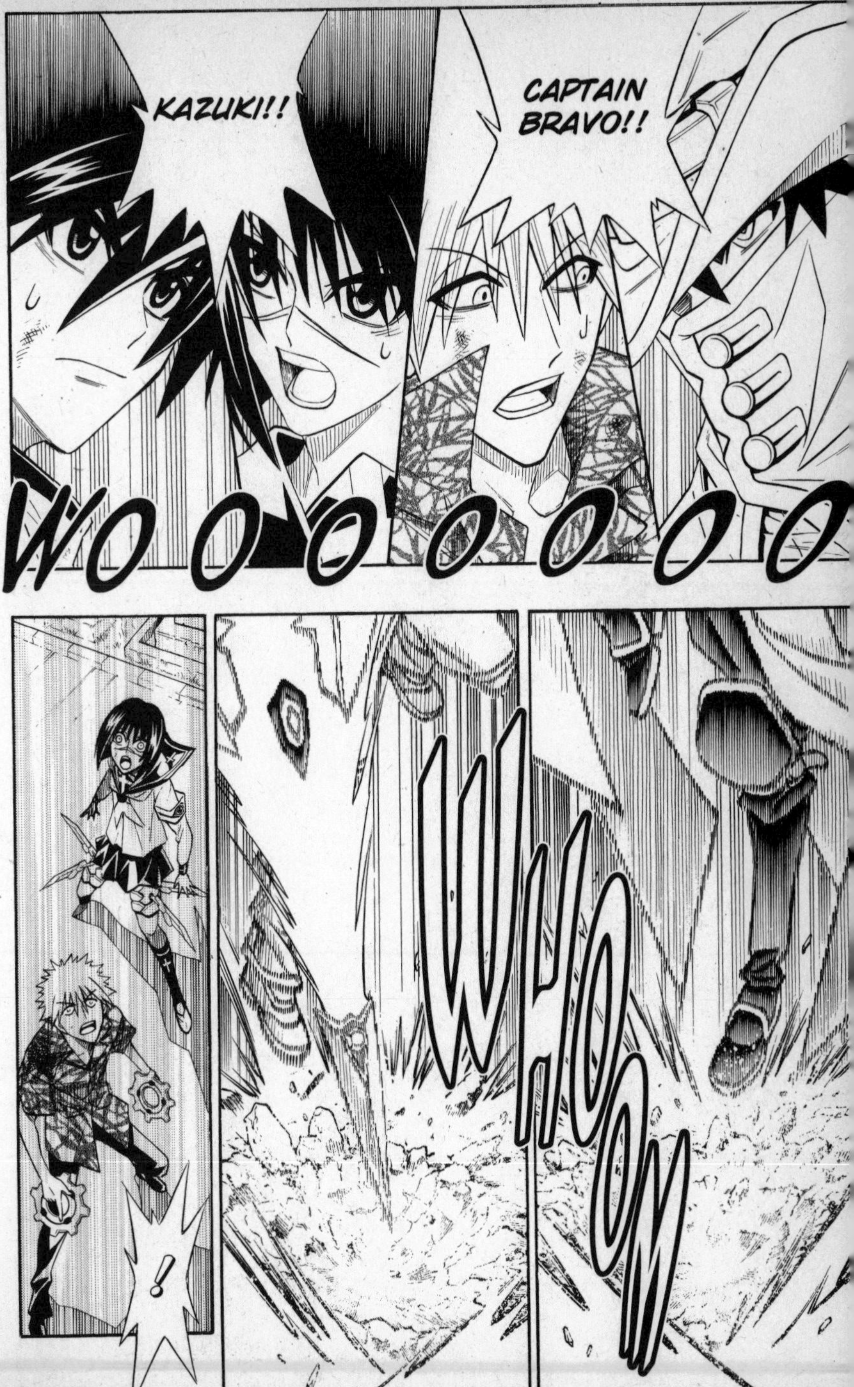
CAPTAIN BRAVO!!
KAZUKI!!
WOOOOOOOO
WHOOOM
!

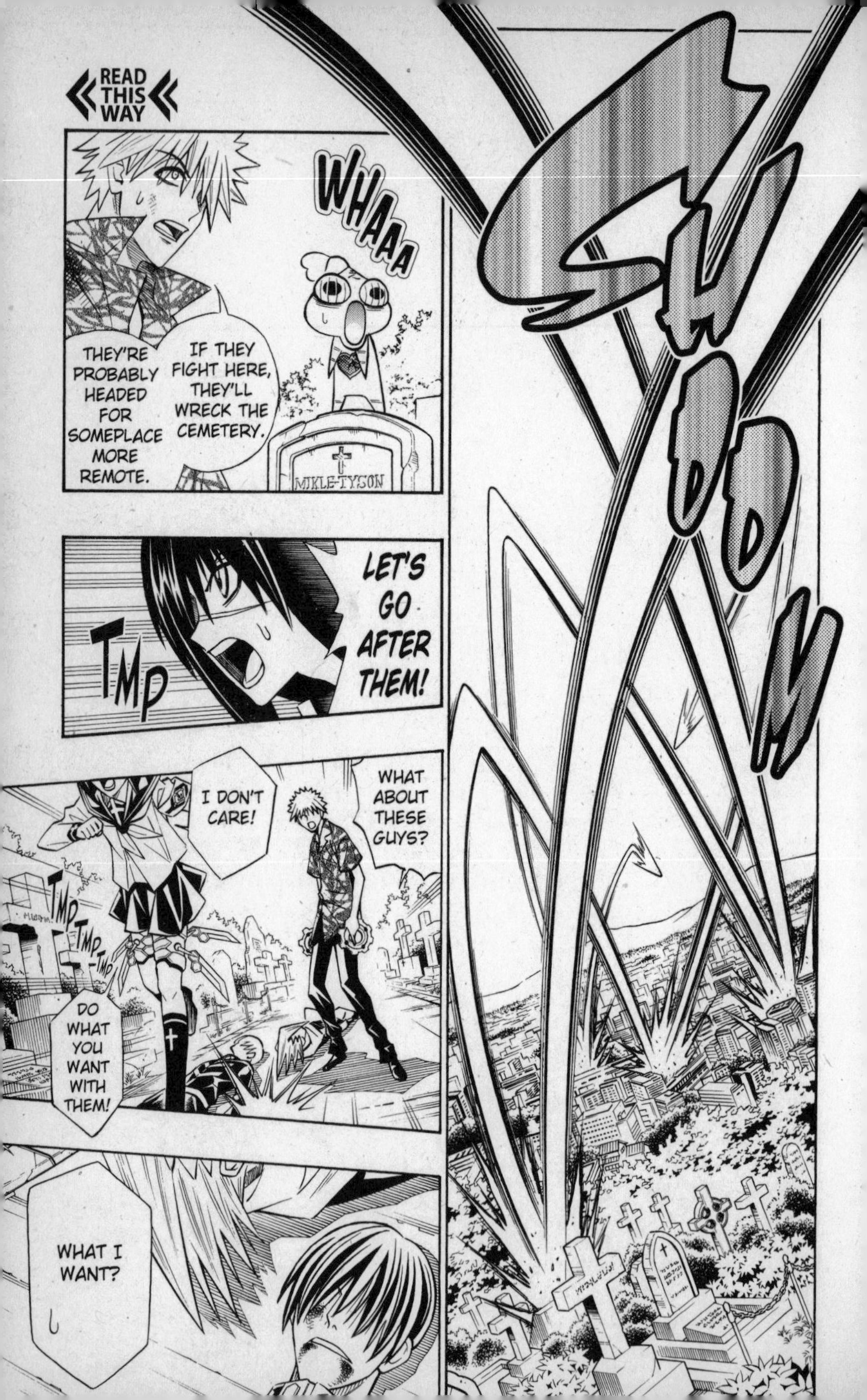
READ THIS WAY
WHAAAA
IF THEY FIGHT HERE, THEY'LL WRECK THE CEMETERY.
THEY'RE PROBABLY HEADED FOR SOMEPLACE MORE REMOTE.
MIKLE-TYSON
LET'S GO AFTER THEM!
TMP
WHAT ABOUT THESE GUYS?
I DON'T CARE!
TMP TMP TMP
DO WHAT YOU WANT WITH THEM!
WHAT I WANT?

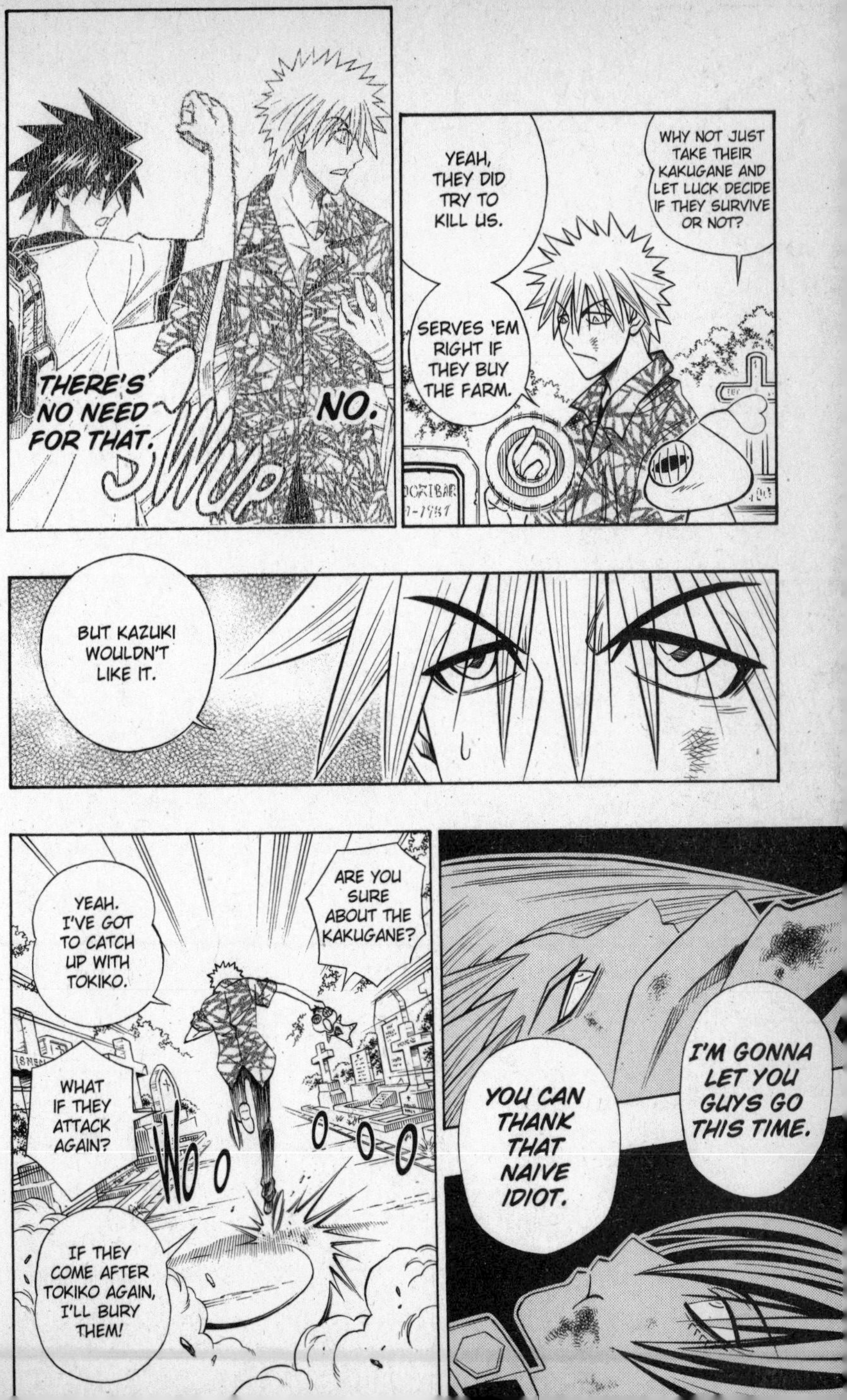
WHY NOT JUST TAKE THEIR KAKUGANE AND LET LUCK DECIDE IF THEY SURVIVE OR NOT?
YEAH, THEY DID TRY TO KILL US.
SERVES 'EM RIGHT IF THEY BUY THE FARM.
NO.
THERE'S NO NEED FOR THAT.
WUP
BUT KAZUKI WOULDN'T LIKE IT.
I'M GONNA LET YOU GUYS GO THIS TIME.
YOU CAN THANK THAT NAIVE IDIOT.
ARE YOU SURE ABOUT THE KAKUGANE?
YEAH. I'VE GOT TO CATCH UP WITH TOKIKO.
WHAT IF THEY ATTACK AGAIN?
WOO
IF THEY COME AFTER TOKIKO AGAIN, I'LL BURY THEM!

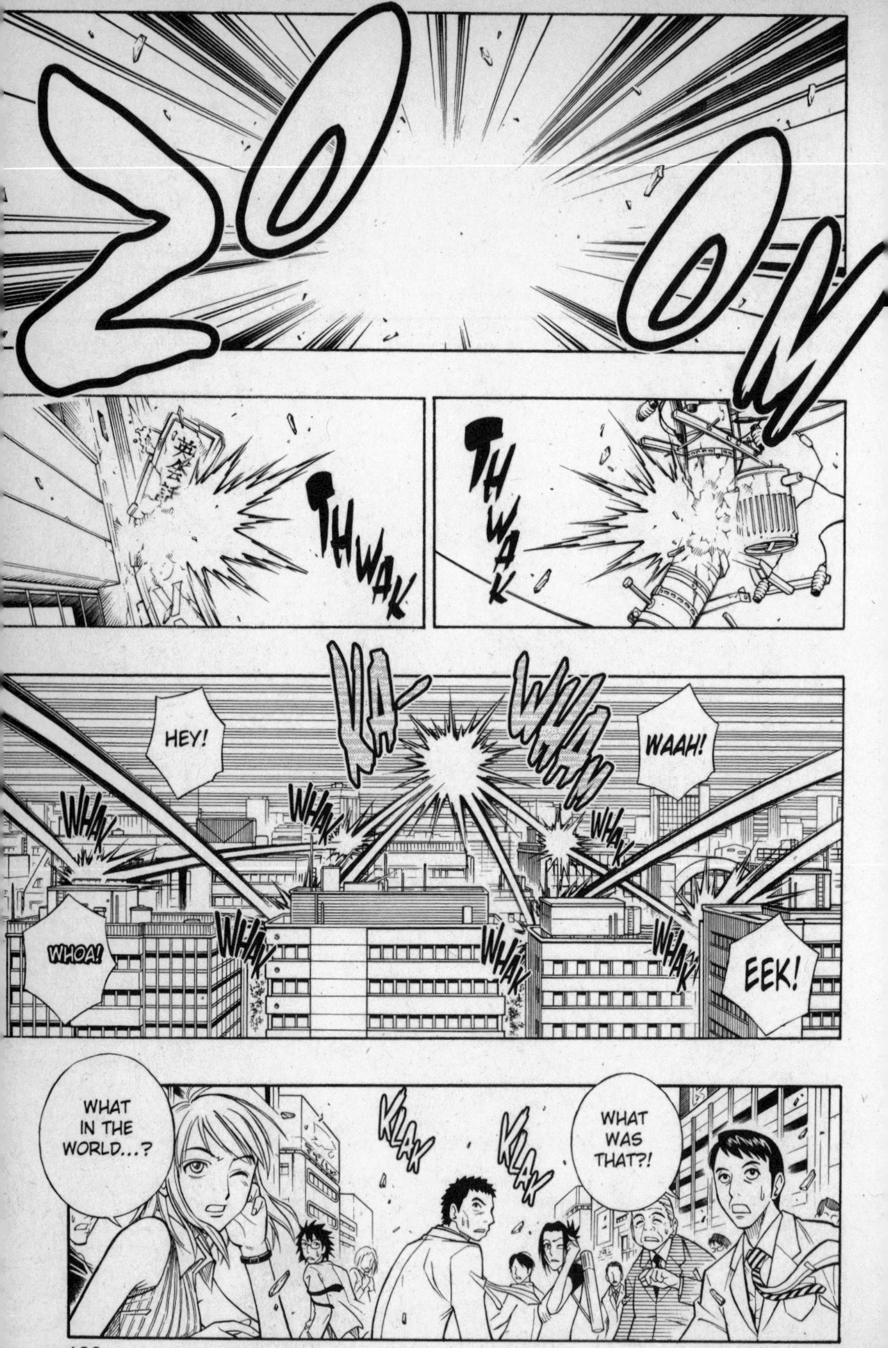
DOON
THWAK
THWAK
WAAH!
WHAN
VA-
HEY!
WHAK
WHAK
WHAK
WHAK
WHAK
WHAK
EEK!
WHOA!
WHAT WAS THAT?!
KLAK
KLAK
WHAT IN THE WORLD...?

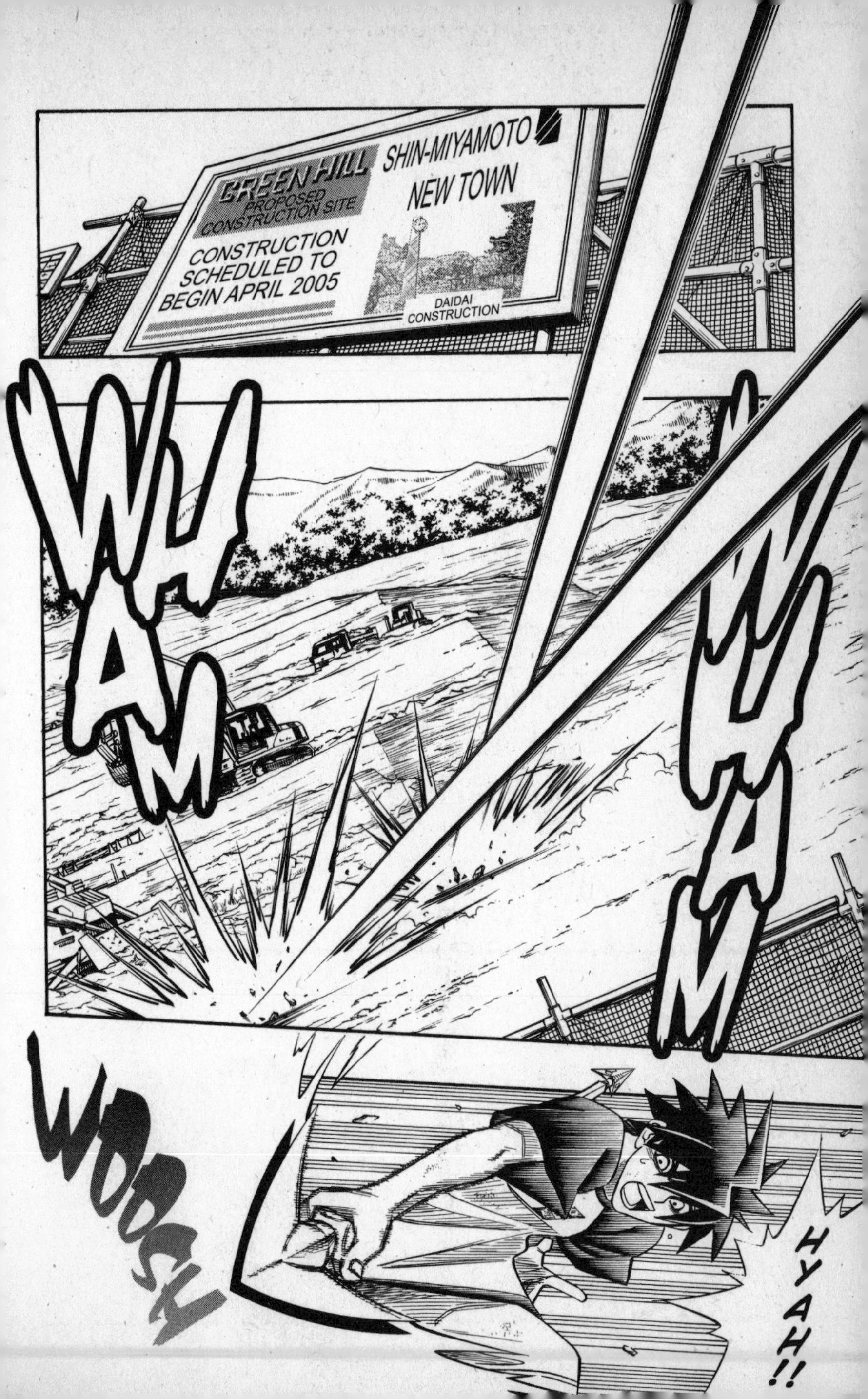
SHIN-MIYAMOTO
NEW TOWN
GREEN HILL
PROPOSED CONSTRUCTION SITE
CONSTRUCTION SCHEDULED TO BEGIN APRIL 2005
DAIDAI CONSTRUCTION
WHAM
WHAM
HYAH!!
WOOSH

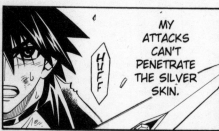

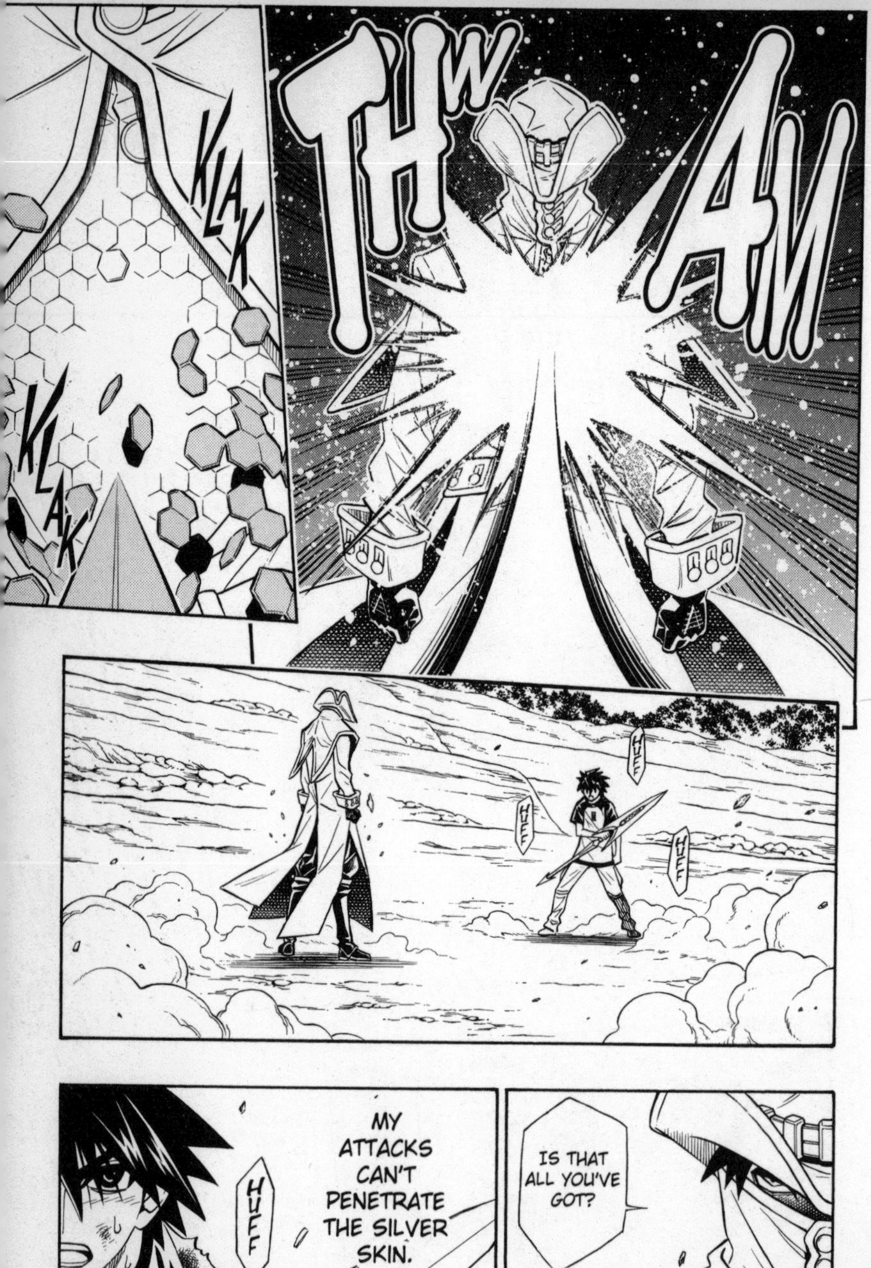
THWAM
KLAK
KLAK
HUFF
HUFF
HUFF
IS THAT ALL YOU'VE GOT?
HUFF HUFF
MY ATTACKS CAN'T PENETRATE THE SILVER SKIN.

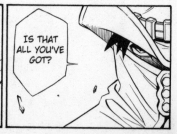

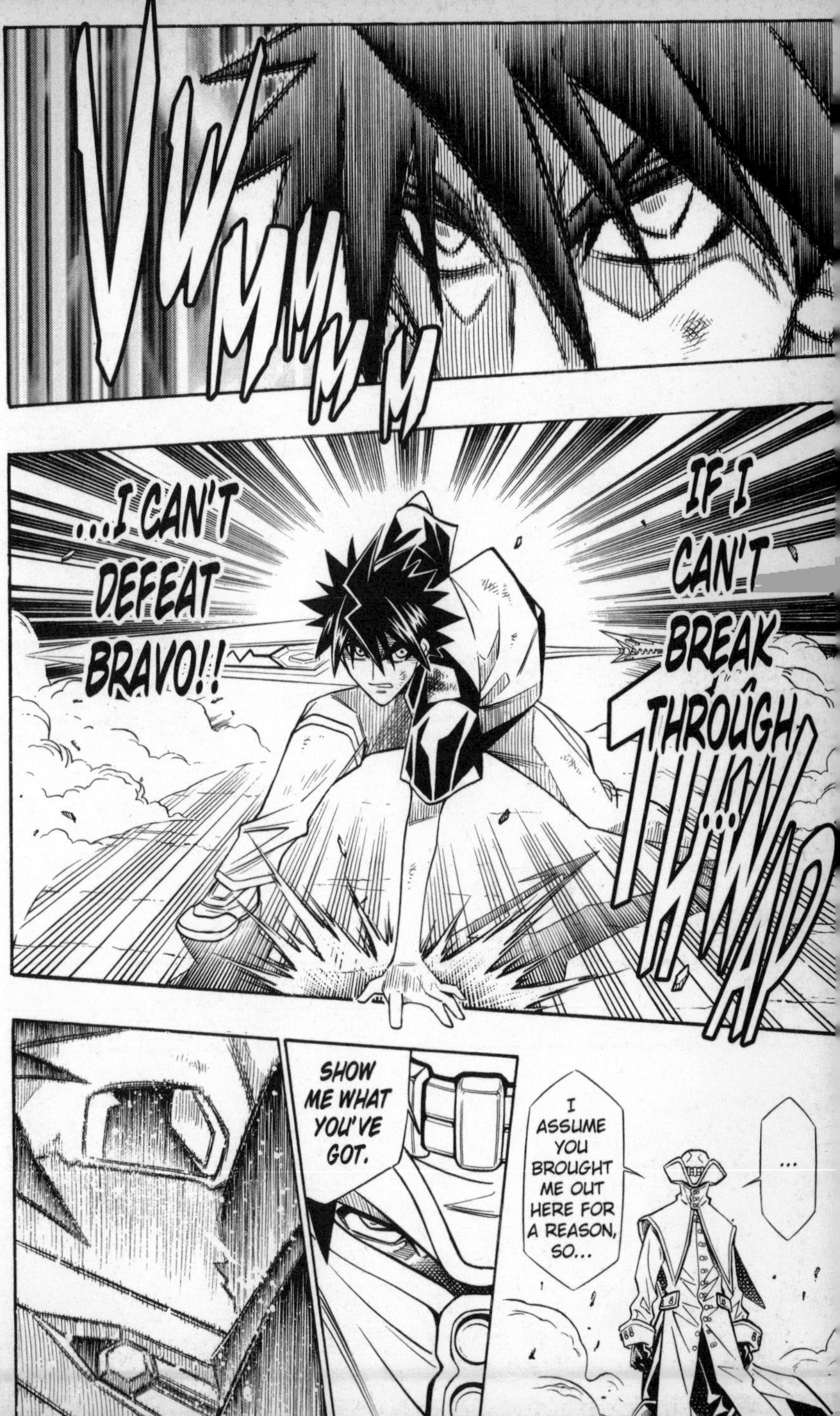
VWMMMMMM
IF I CAN'T BREAK THROUGH...
...I CAN'T DEFEAT BRAVO!!
THWAP
...
I ASSUME YOU BROUGHT ME OUT HERE FOR A REASON, SO...
SHOW ME WHAT YOU'VE GOT.

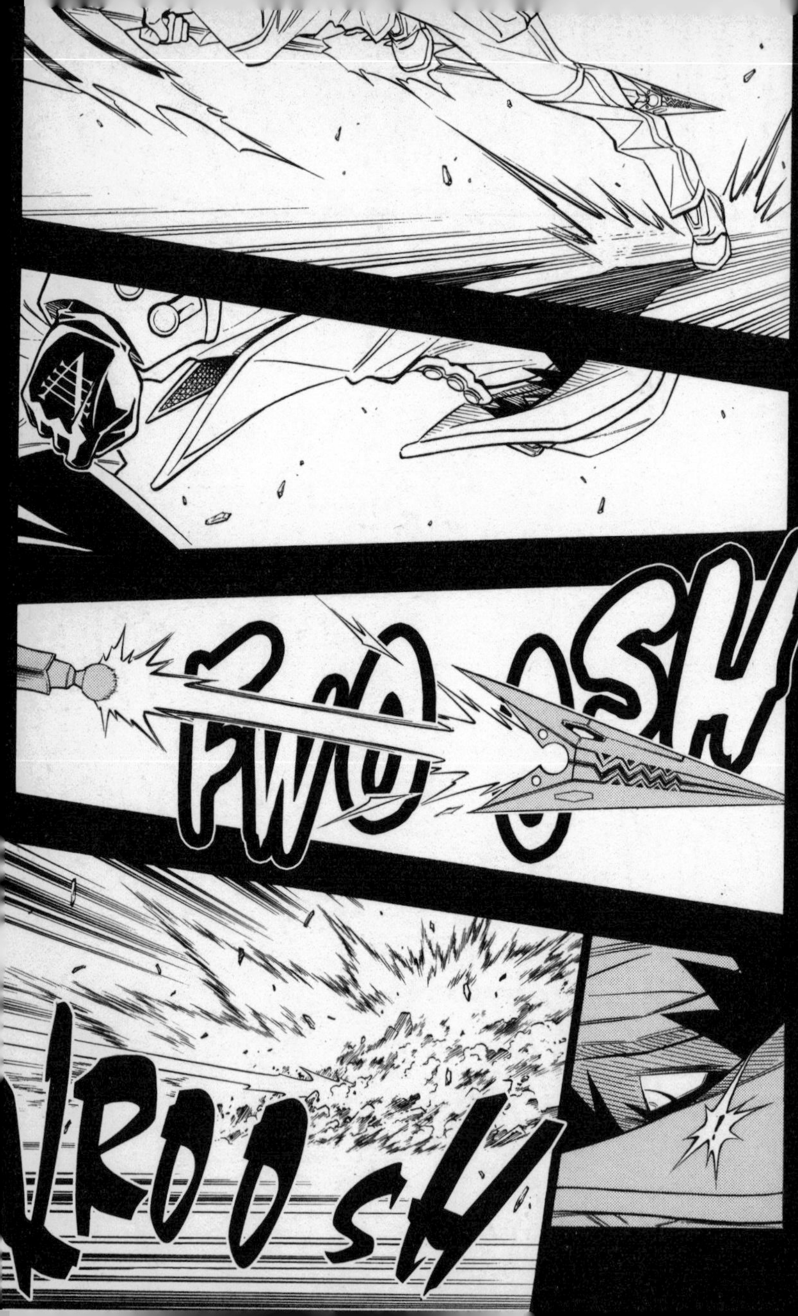
PWOOSH
ROOSH

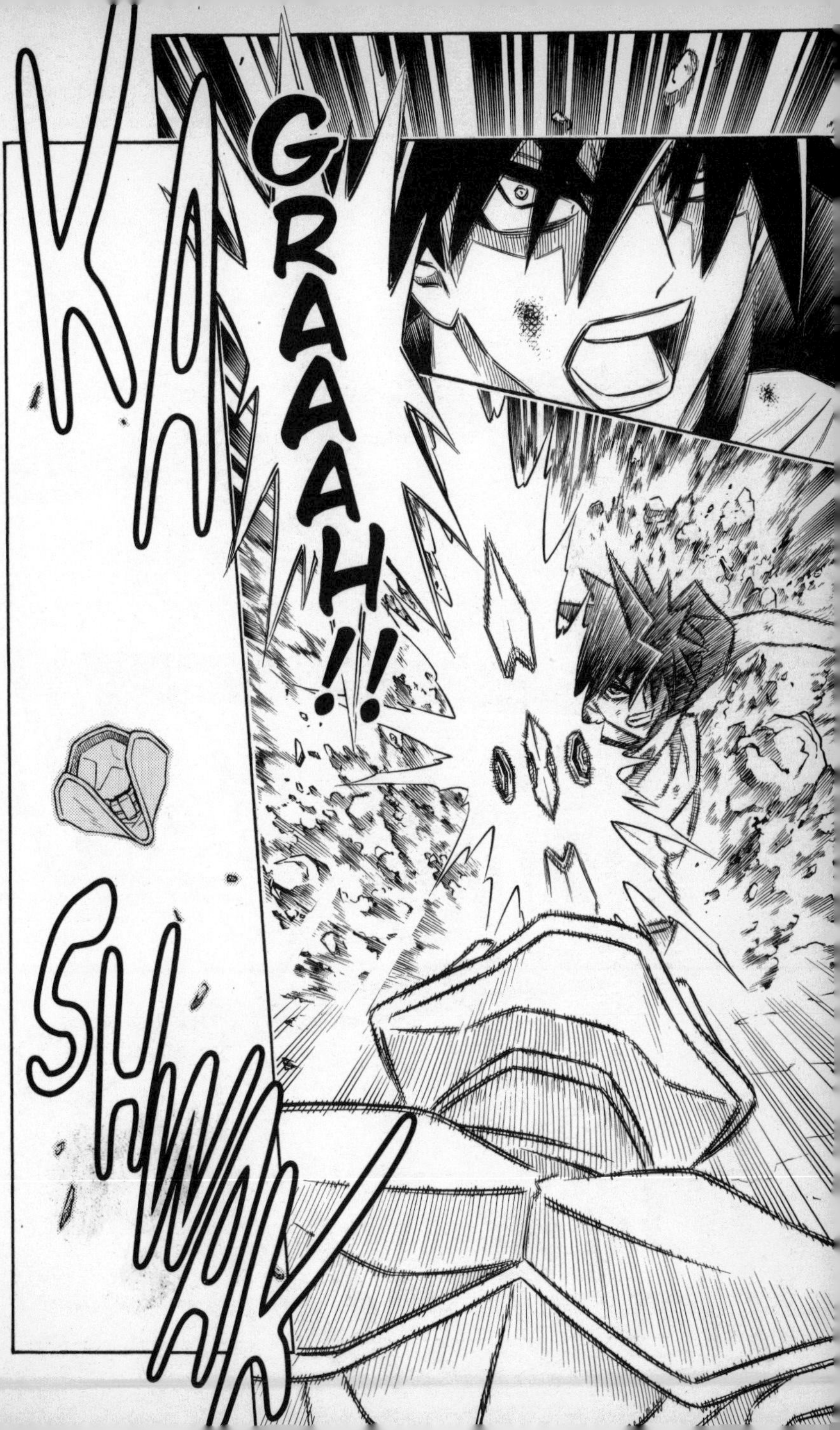
GRAAAH!!
KAH
SHNAK

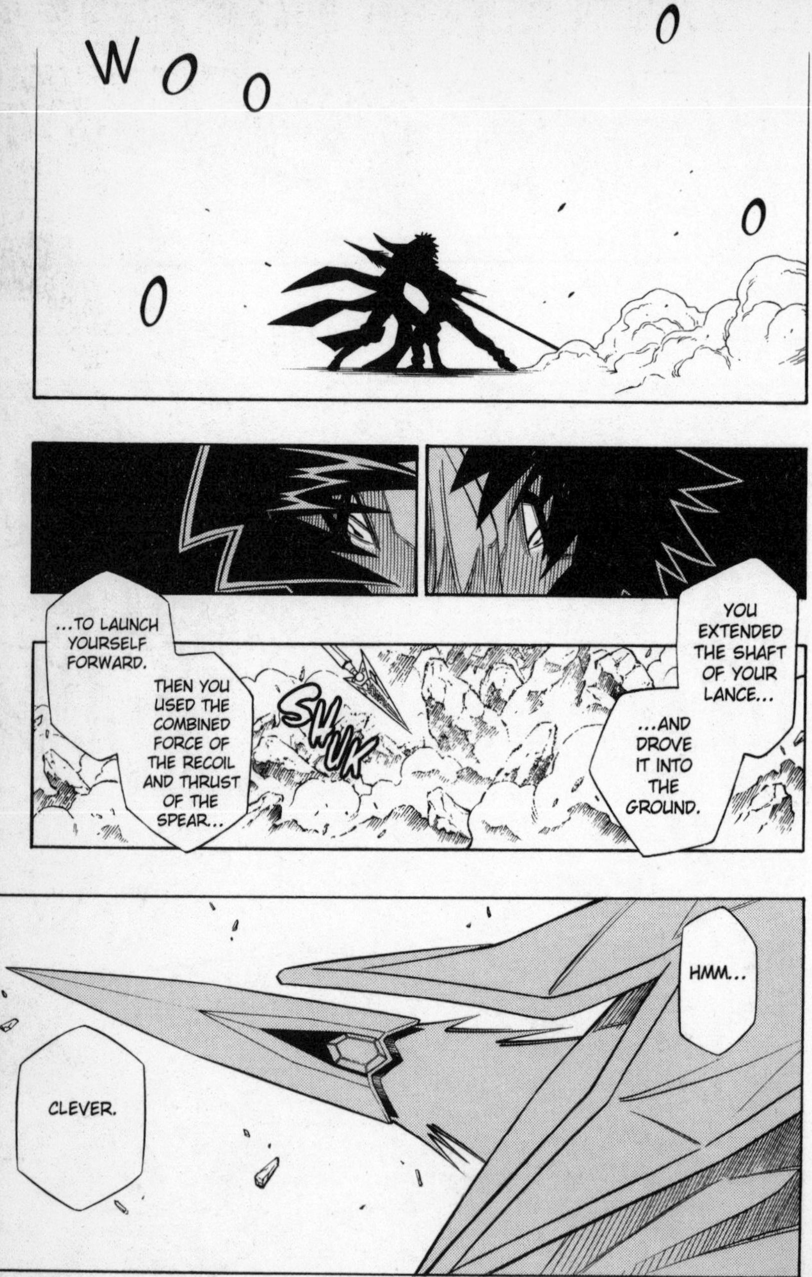
WOOOOO
YOU EXTENDED THE SHAFT OF YOUR LANCE...
...AND DROVE IT INTO THE GROUND.
SHUK
THEN YOU USED THE COMBINED FORCE OF THE RECOIL AND THRUST OF THE SPEAR...
...TO LAUNCH YOURSELF FORWARD.
HMM...
CLEVER.

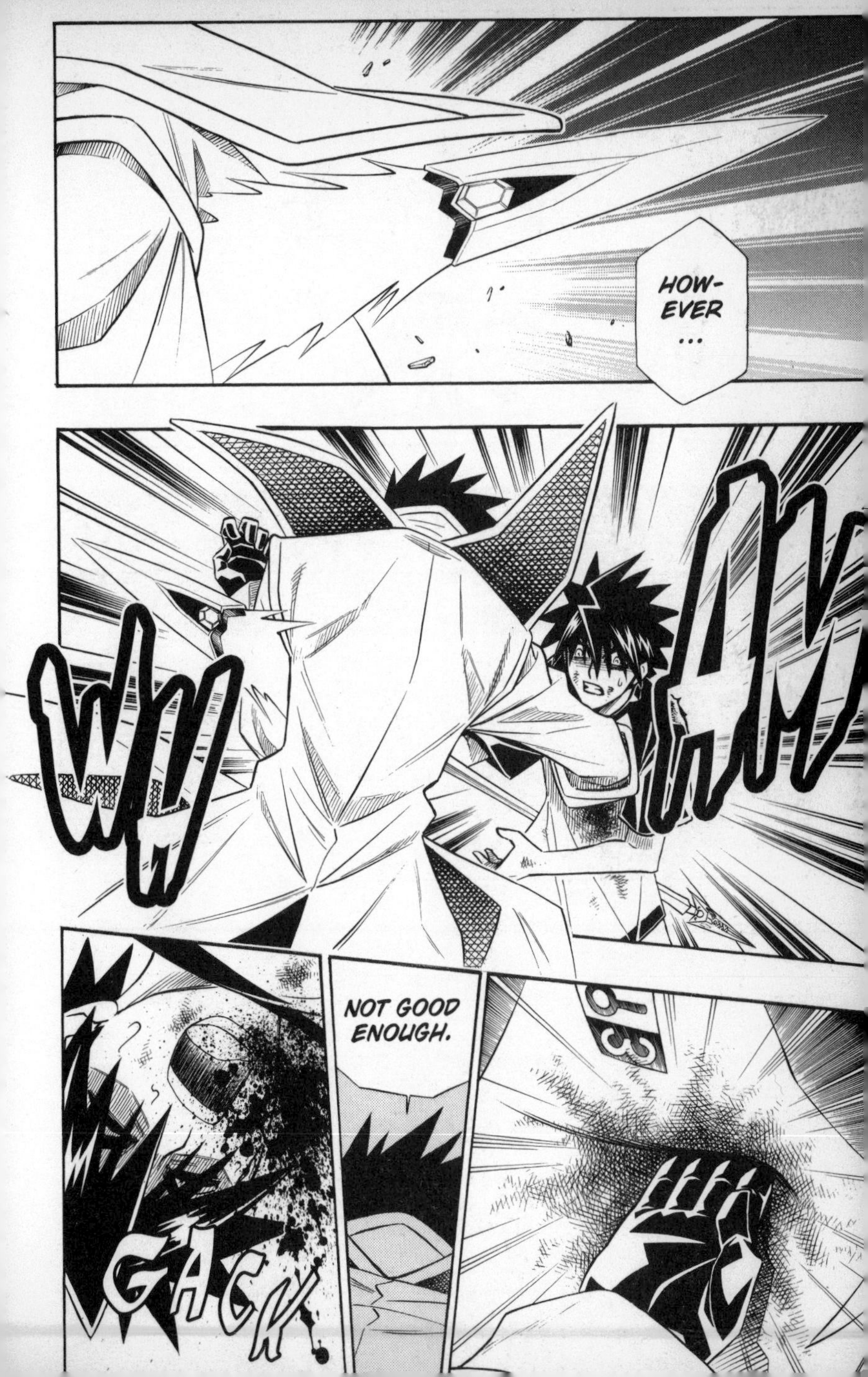
HOW-
EVER
...
WHAM
NOT GOOD
ENOUGH.
GACK

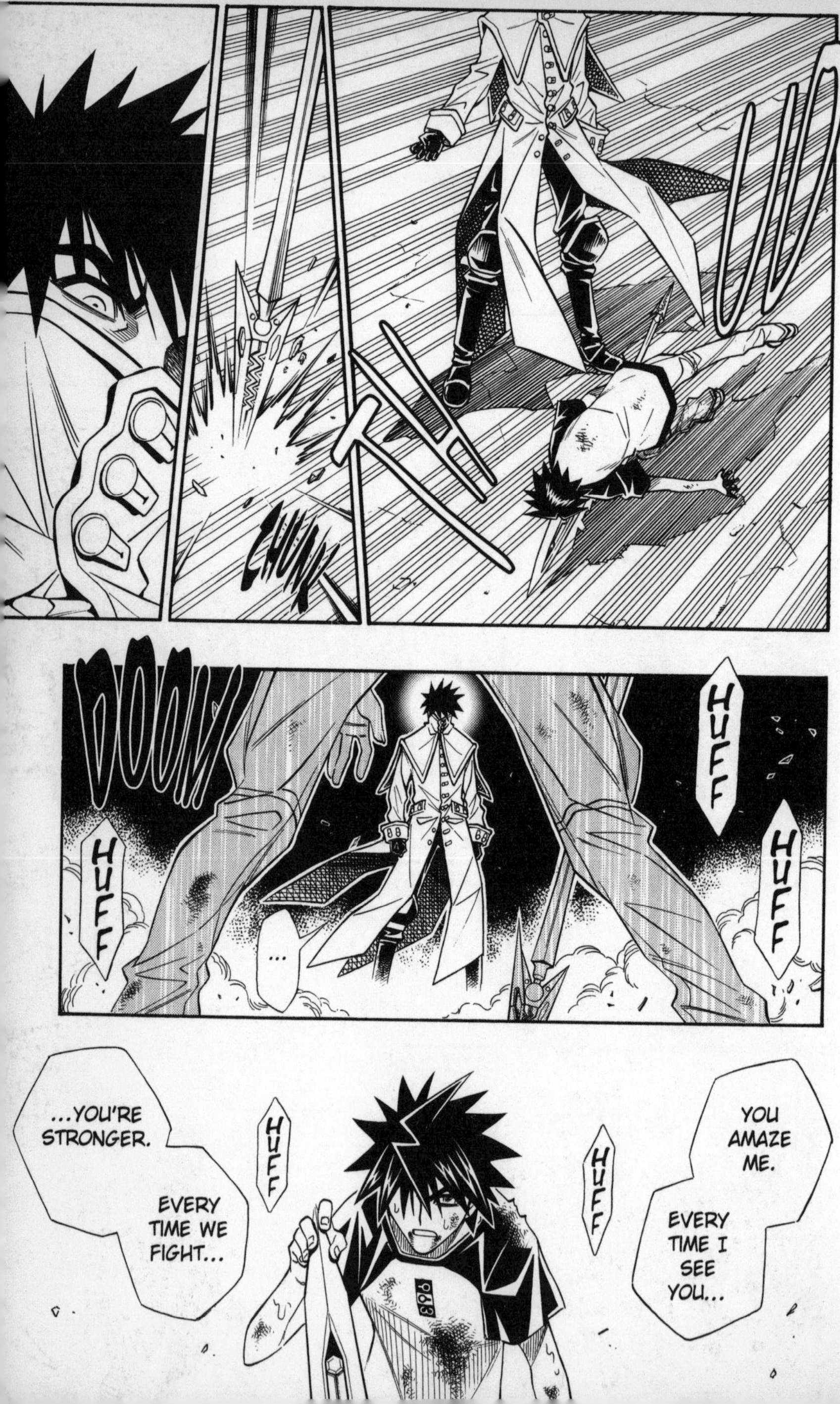
CHUNK
HUFF HUFF
HUFF HUFF
...
HUFF HUFF
DOOM
YOU AMAZE ME.
EVERY TIME I SEE YOU...
HUFF HUFF
HUFF HUFF
...YOU'RE STRONGER.
EVERY TIME WE FIGHT...

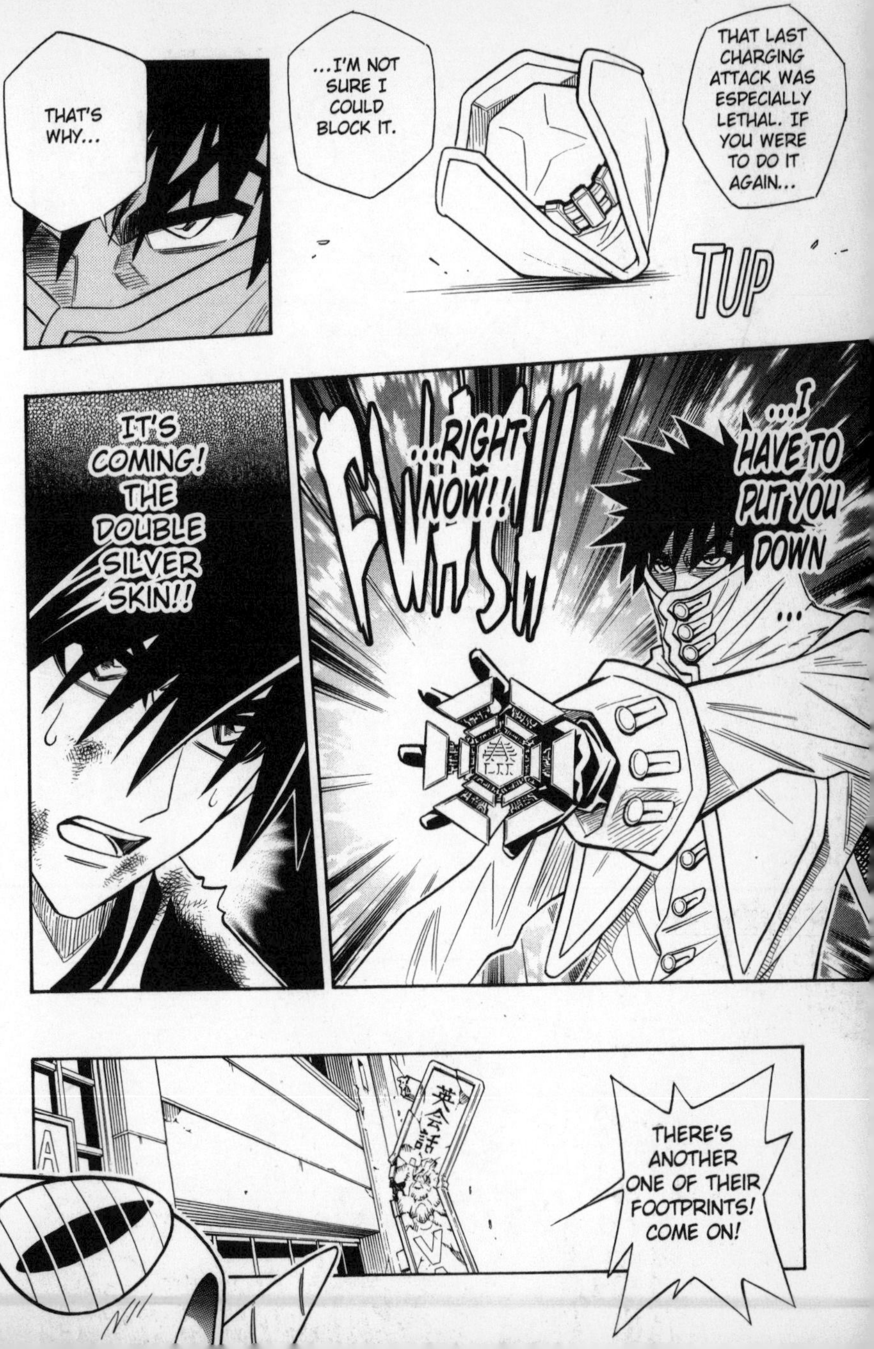
THAT LAST CHARGING ATTACK WAS ESPECIALLY LETHAL. IF YOU WERE TO DO IT AGAIN...
TUP
...I'M NOT SURE I COULD BLOCK IT.
THAT'S WHY...
...I HAVE TO PUT YOU DOWN ...
...RIGHT NOW!!
IT'S COMING! THE DOUBLE SILVER SKIN!!
THERE'S ANOTHER ONE OF THEIR FOOTPRINTS! COME ON!

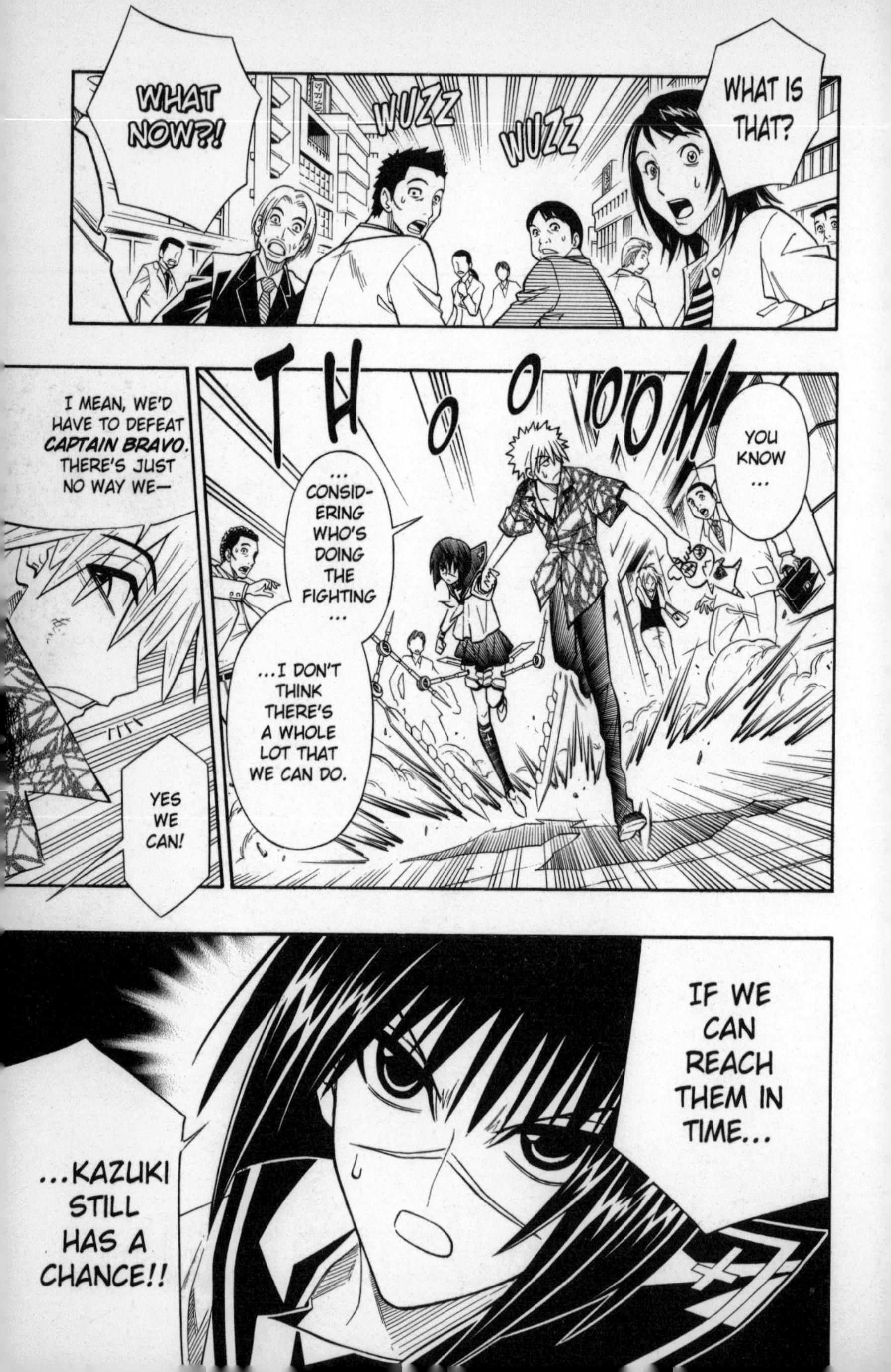
WHAT IS THAT?
WUZZ
WUZZ
WHAT NOW?!
THOOOM
YOU KNOW...
...CONSIDERING WHO'S DOING THE FIGHTING...
...I DON'T THINK THERE'S A WHOLE LOT THAT WE CAN DO.
I MEAN, WE'D HAVE TO DEFEAT CAPTAIN BRAVO. THERE'S JUST NO WAY WE—
YES WE CAN!
IF WE CAN REACH THEM IN TIME...
...KAZUKI STILL HAS A CHANCE!!

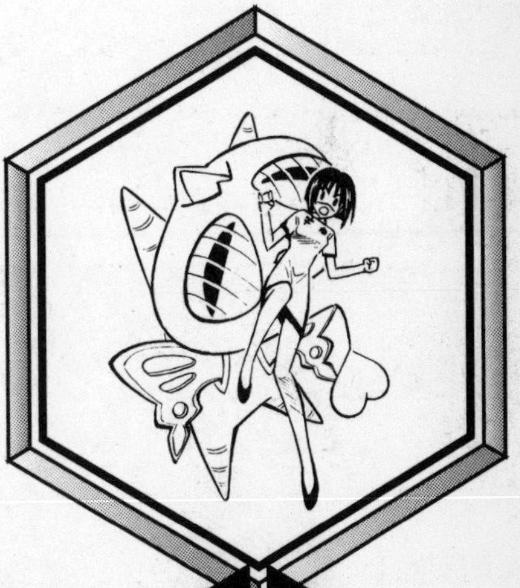

Buso Renkin
ブソウレンキン

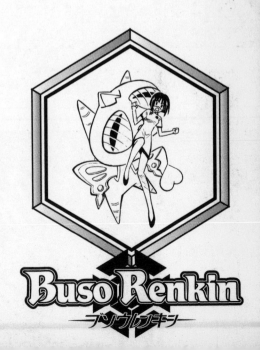

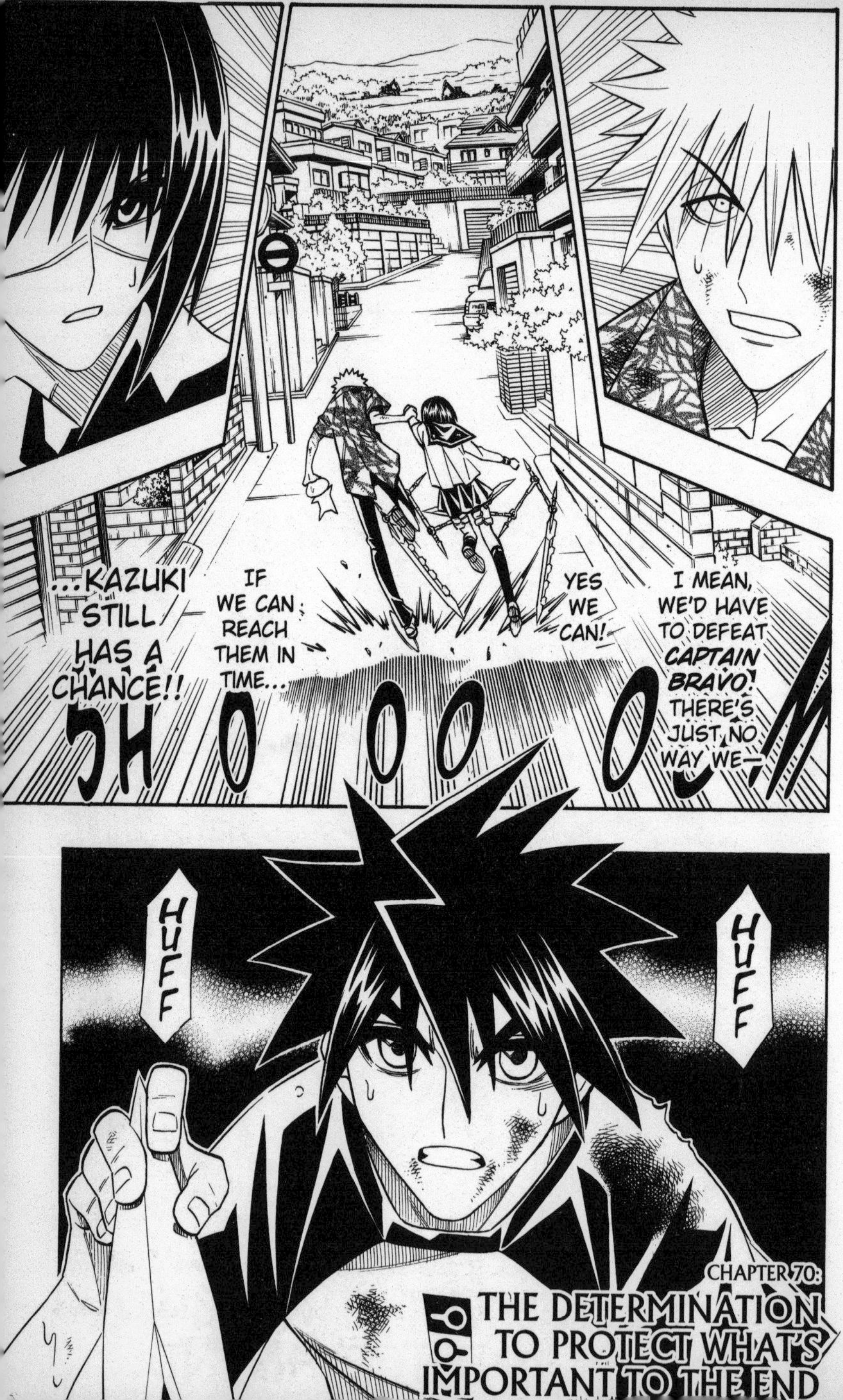
I MEAN, WE'D HAVE TO DEFEAT CAPTAIN BRAVO. THERE'S JUST NO WAY WE—
YES WE CAN!
IF WE CAN REACH THEM IN TIME...
...KAZUKI STILL HAS A CHANCE!!
SHOOOOM
HUFF
HUFF
CHAPTER 70:
THE DETERMINATION TO PROTECT WHAT'S IMPORTANT TO THE END

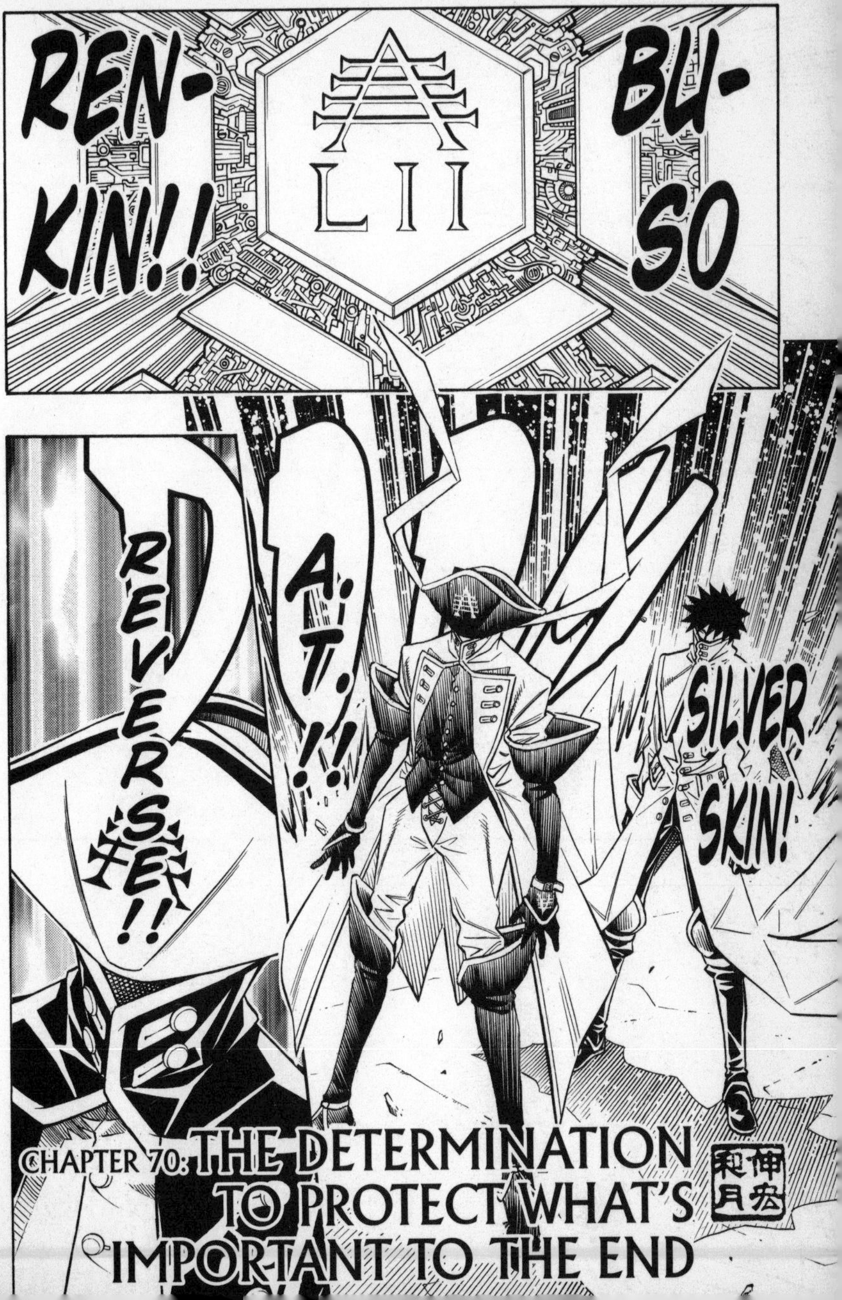
BU-SO
LII
REN-KIN!!
SILVER SKIN!
A.T.!!!
REVERSE!!

CHAPTER 70: THE DETERMINATION TO PROTECT WHAT'S IMPORTANT TO THE END

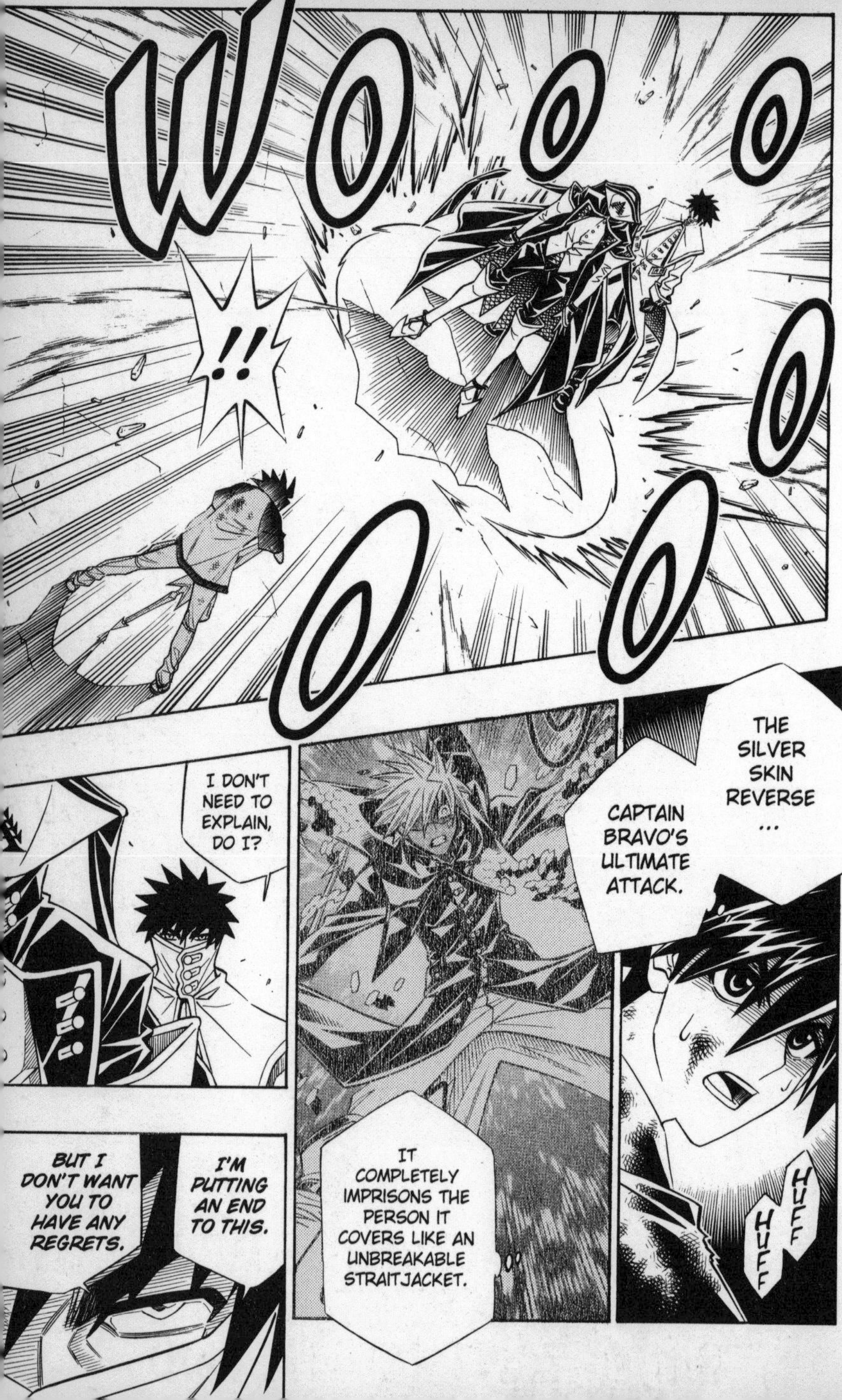
WOOOOOO
!!
THE SILVER SKIN REVERSE ...
CAPTAIN BRAVO'S ULTIMATE ATTACK.
HUFF HUFF
IT COMPLETELY IMPRISONS THE PERSON IT COVERS LIKE AN UNBREAKABLE STRAITJACKET.
I DON'T NEED TO EXPLAIN, DO I?
I'M PUTTING AN END TO THIS.
BUT I DON'T WANT YOU TO HAVE ANY REGRETS.

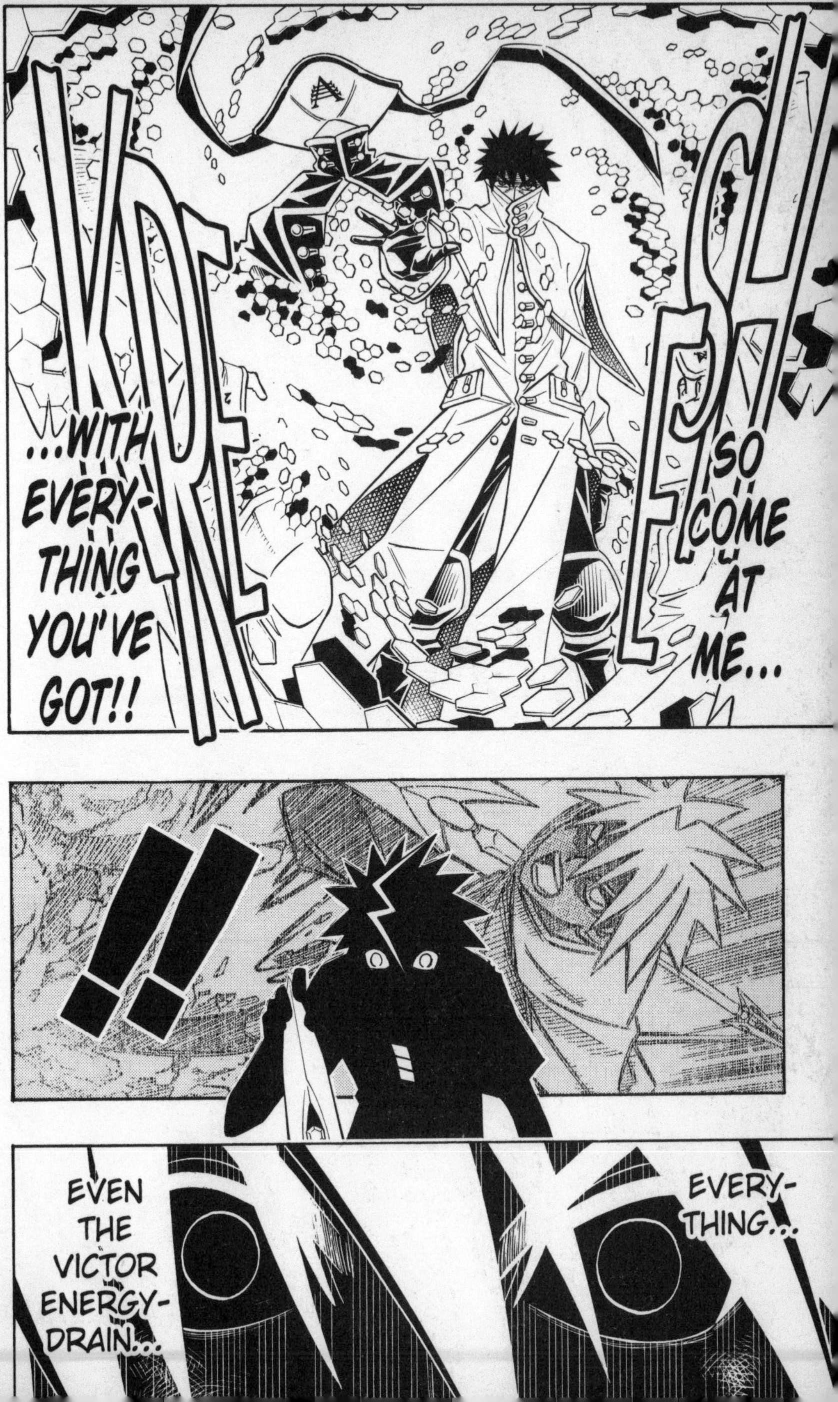
SO COME AT ME...
...WITH EVERY-THING YOU'VE GOT!!
!!
EVERY-THING...
EVEN THE VICTOR ENERGY-DRAIN...

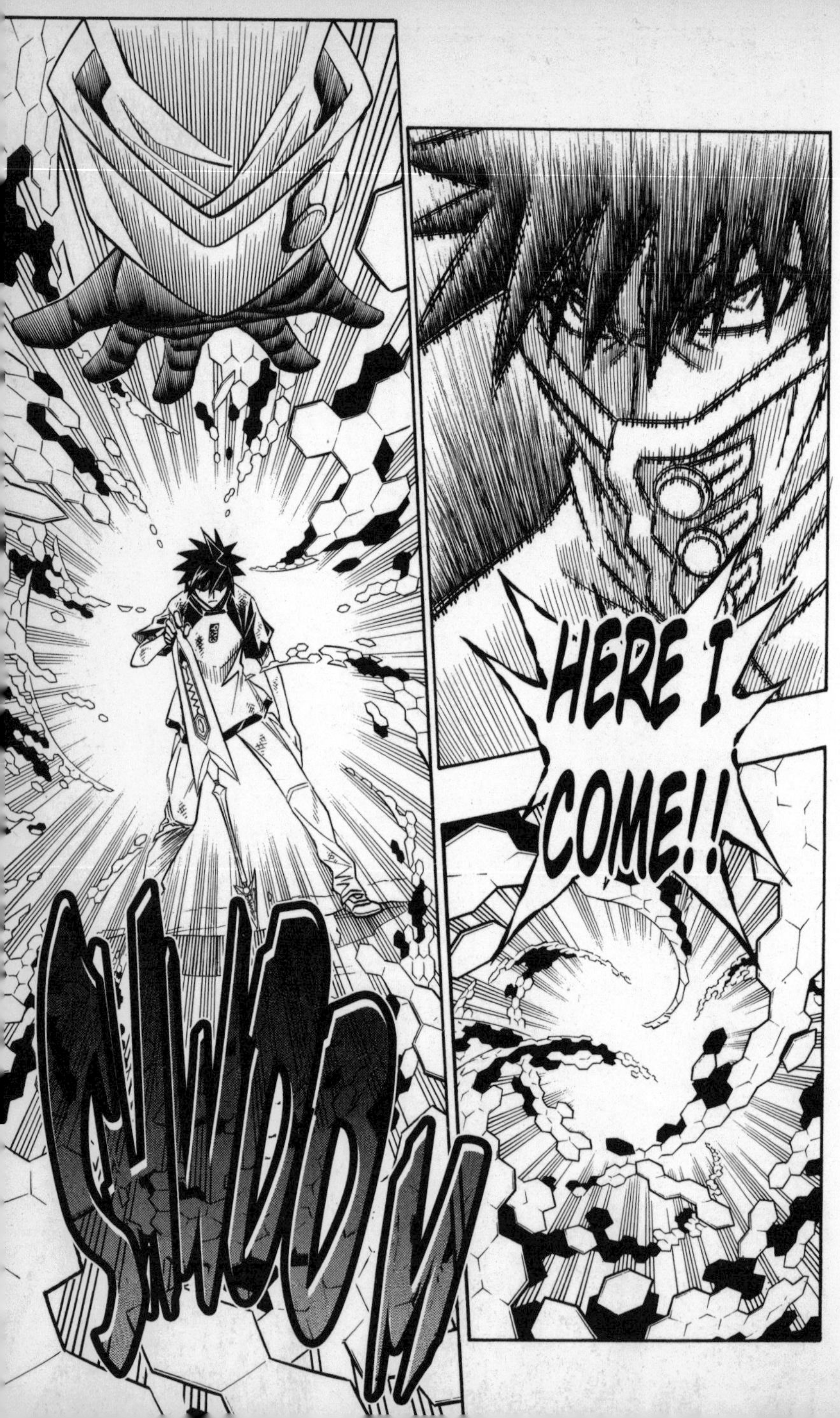
HERE I COME!!

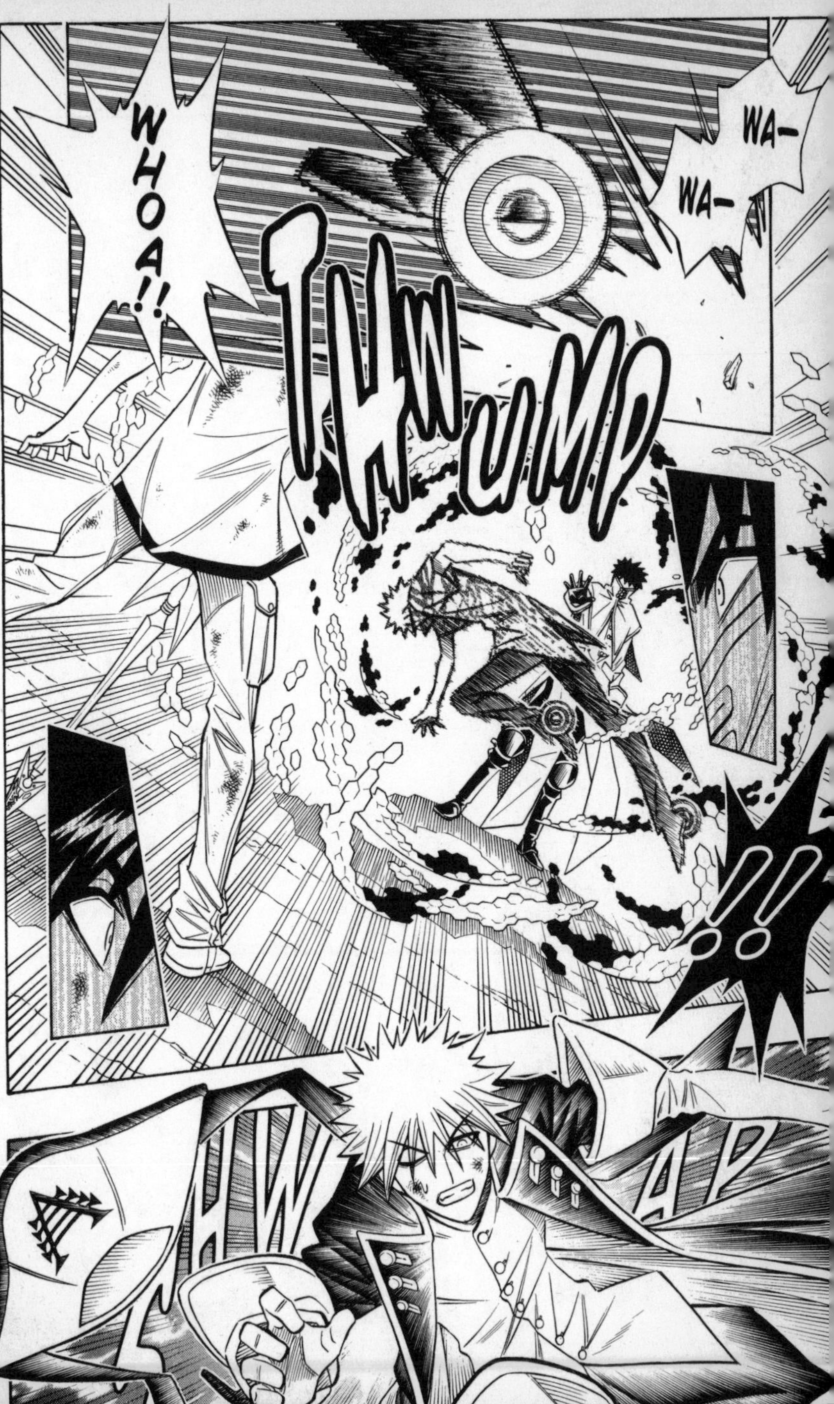
WA-
WA-
THWUMP
WHOA!!
!!

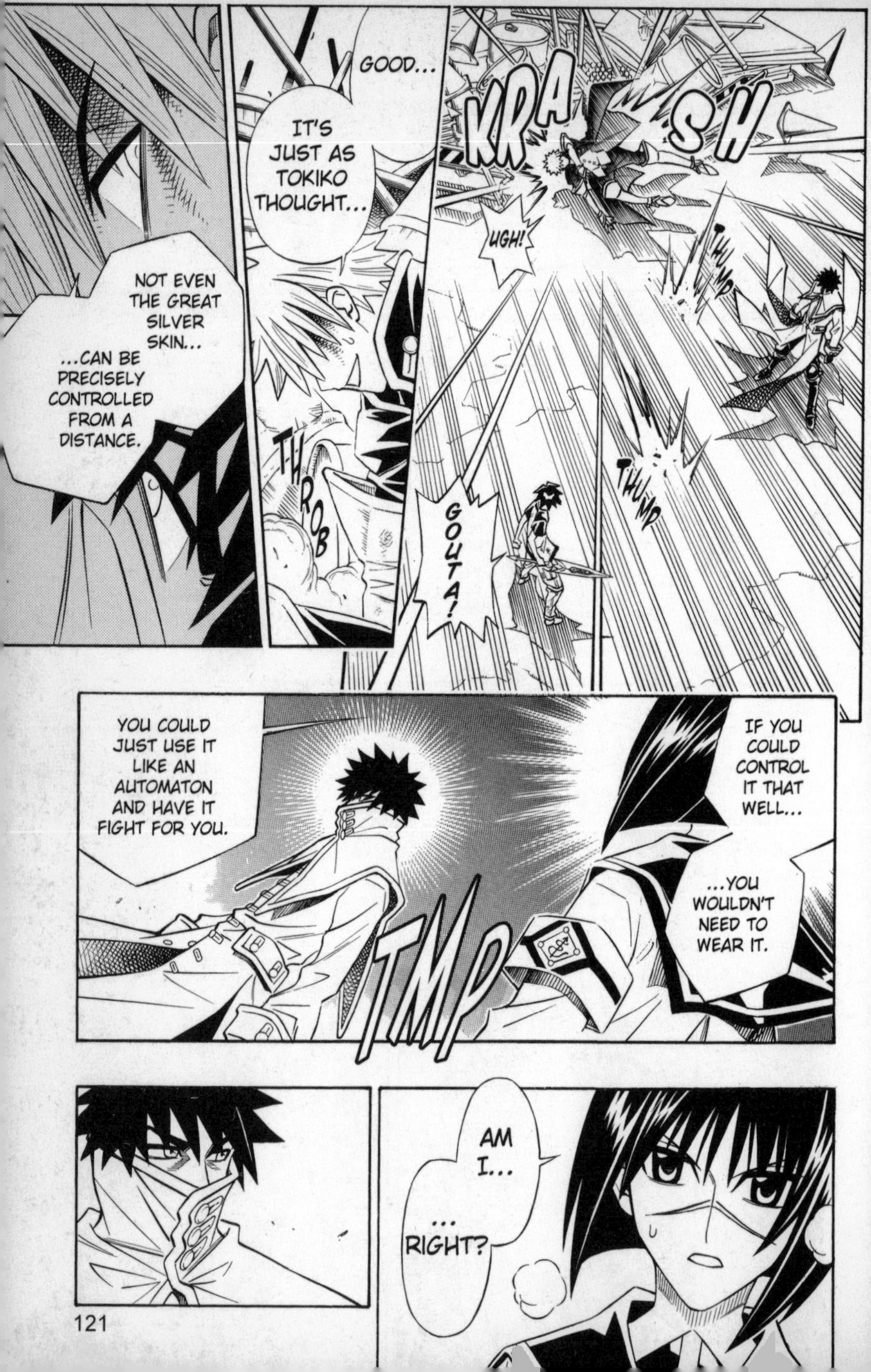
KRASH
UGH!
THUMP
THUMP
GOUTA!
GOOD...
IT'S JUST AS TOKIKO THOUGHT...
THROB
NOT EVEN THE GREAT SILVER SKIN...
...CAN BE PRECISELY CONTROLLED FROM A DISTANCE.
IF YOU COULD CONTROL IT THAT WELL...
...YOU WOULDN'T NEED TO WEAR IT.
YOU COULD JUST USE IT LIKE AN AUTOMATON AND HAVE IT FIGHT FOR YOU.
TMP
AM I...
...RIGHT?

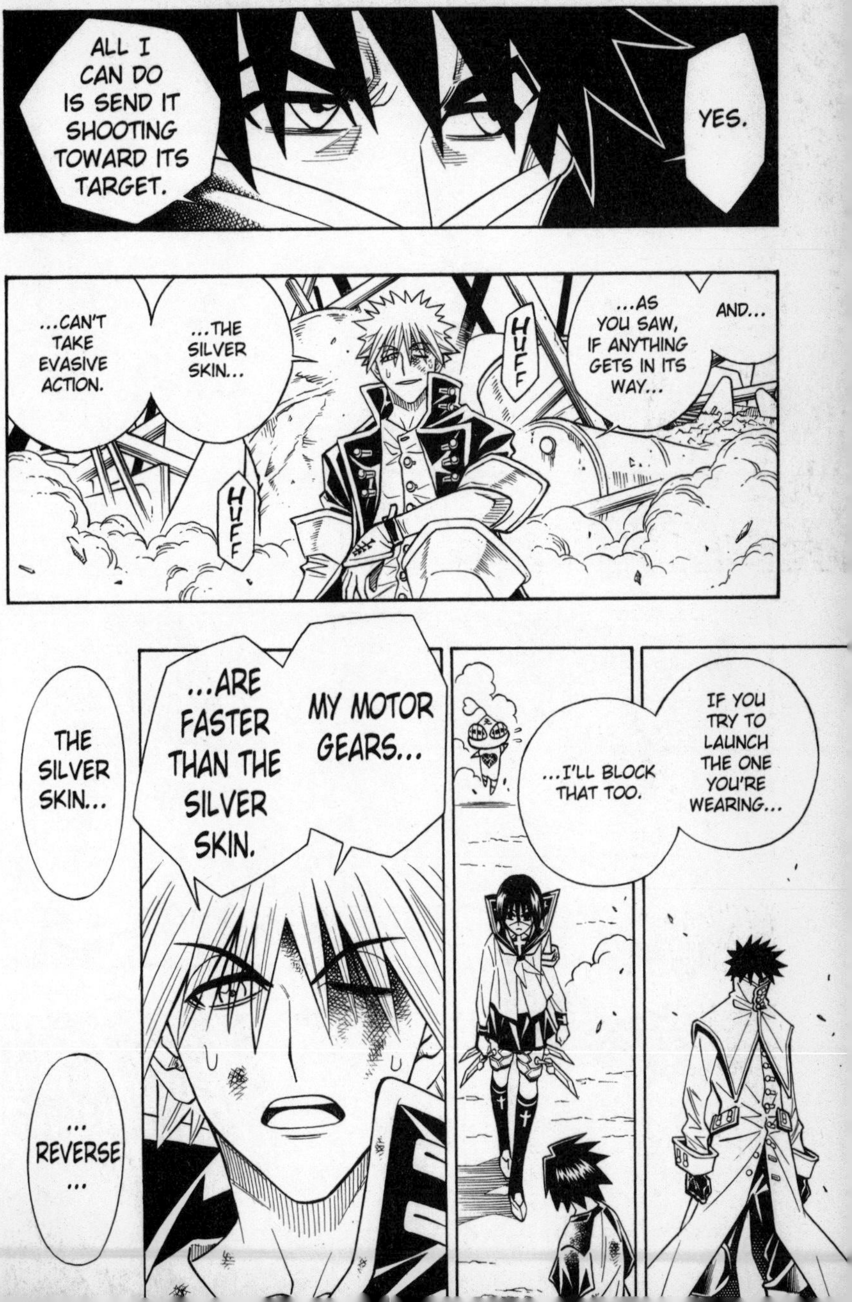
YES.
ALL I CAN DO IS SEND IT SHOOTING TOWARD ITS TARGET.
AND...
...AS YOU SAW, IF ANYTHING GETS IN ITS WAY...
HUFF
...THE SILVER SKIN...
...CAN'T TAKE EVASIVE ACTION.
HUFF
IF YOU TRY TO LAUNCH THE ONE YOU'RE WEARING...
...I'LL BLOCK THAT TOO.
MY MOTOR GEARS...
...ARE FASTER THAN THE SILVER SKIN.
THE SILVER SKIN...
...REVERSE...

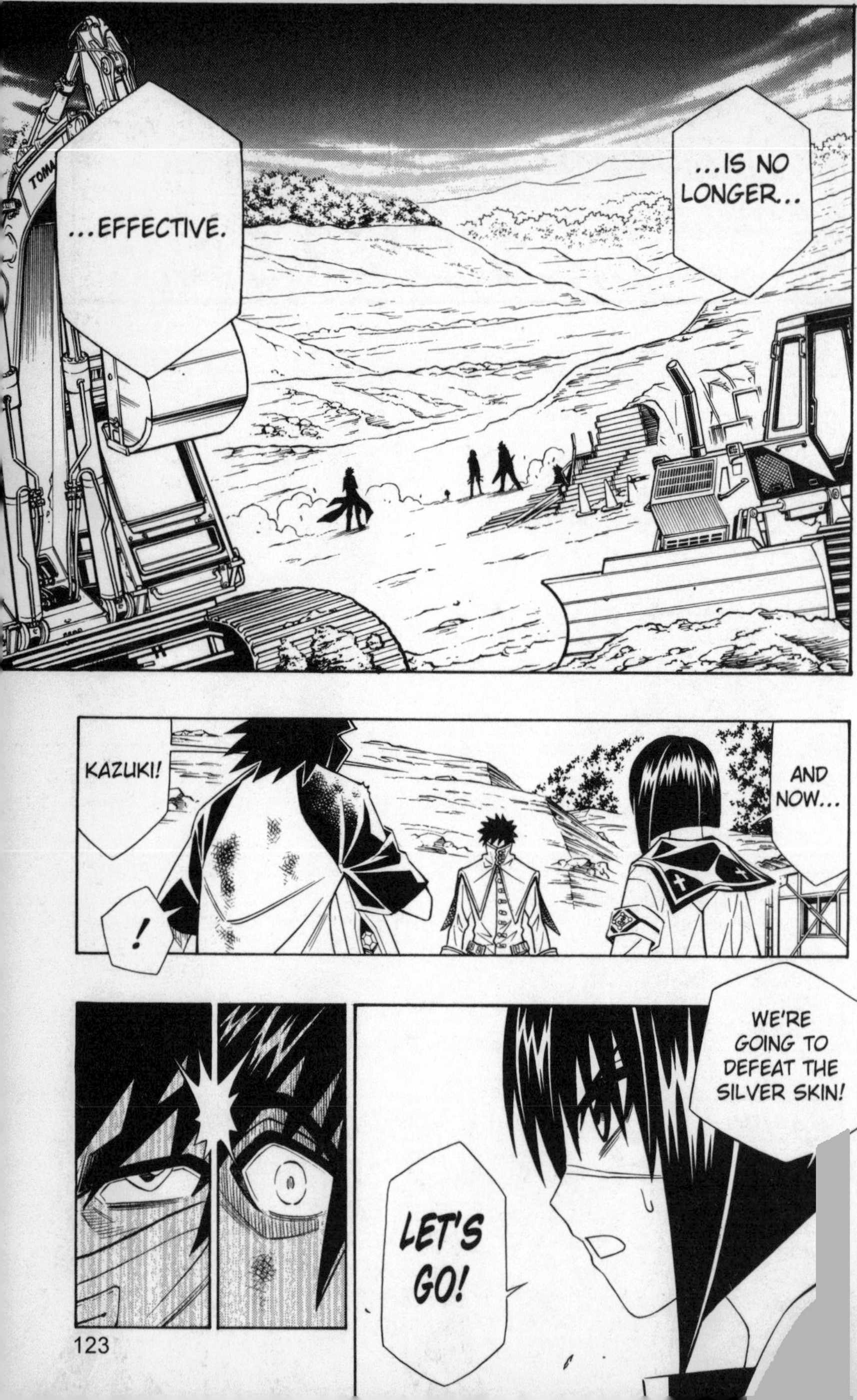
...IS NO LONGER...
...EFFECTIVE.
AND NOW...
KAZUKI!
!
WE'RE GOING TO DEFEAT THE SILVER SKIN!
LET'S GO!

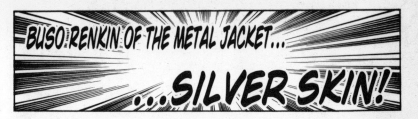

BUSO RENKIN OF THE METAL JACKET...
...SILVER SKIN!
IT HAS THE GREATEST DEFENSIVE ABILITIES OF ANY BUSO RENKIN.
IT'S VIRTUALLY INDESTRUCTIBLE.
BUT TWICE NOW...
...ONCE WHEN HE WAS BEING EVALUATED AS A WARRIOR AND THE SECOND TIME DURING THE BATTLE AT THE BEACH... KAZUKI HAS MANAGED TO PIERCE IT.
BY DELIVERING A STRONG ENOUGH BLOW, IT IS POSSIBLE TO BREAK THROUGH THE SILVER SKIN!
STILL, ITS INCREDIBLY FAST SELF-REPAIRING ABILITY RESTORES IT BEFORE THE OPENING CAN BE EXPLOITED, MAKING IT ALMOST UNBEATABLE!
BUT...
...IF HE CAN STRIKE AGAIN BEFORE IT CAN REPAIR ITSELF...
SWASH
KAZUKI, USE THIS!

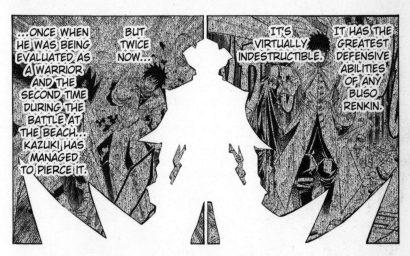

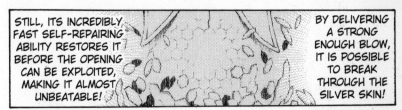

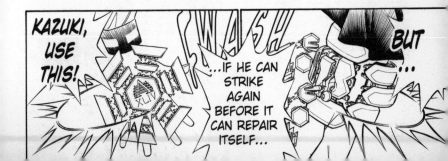

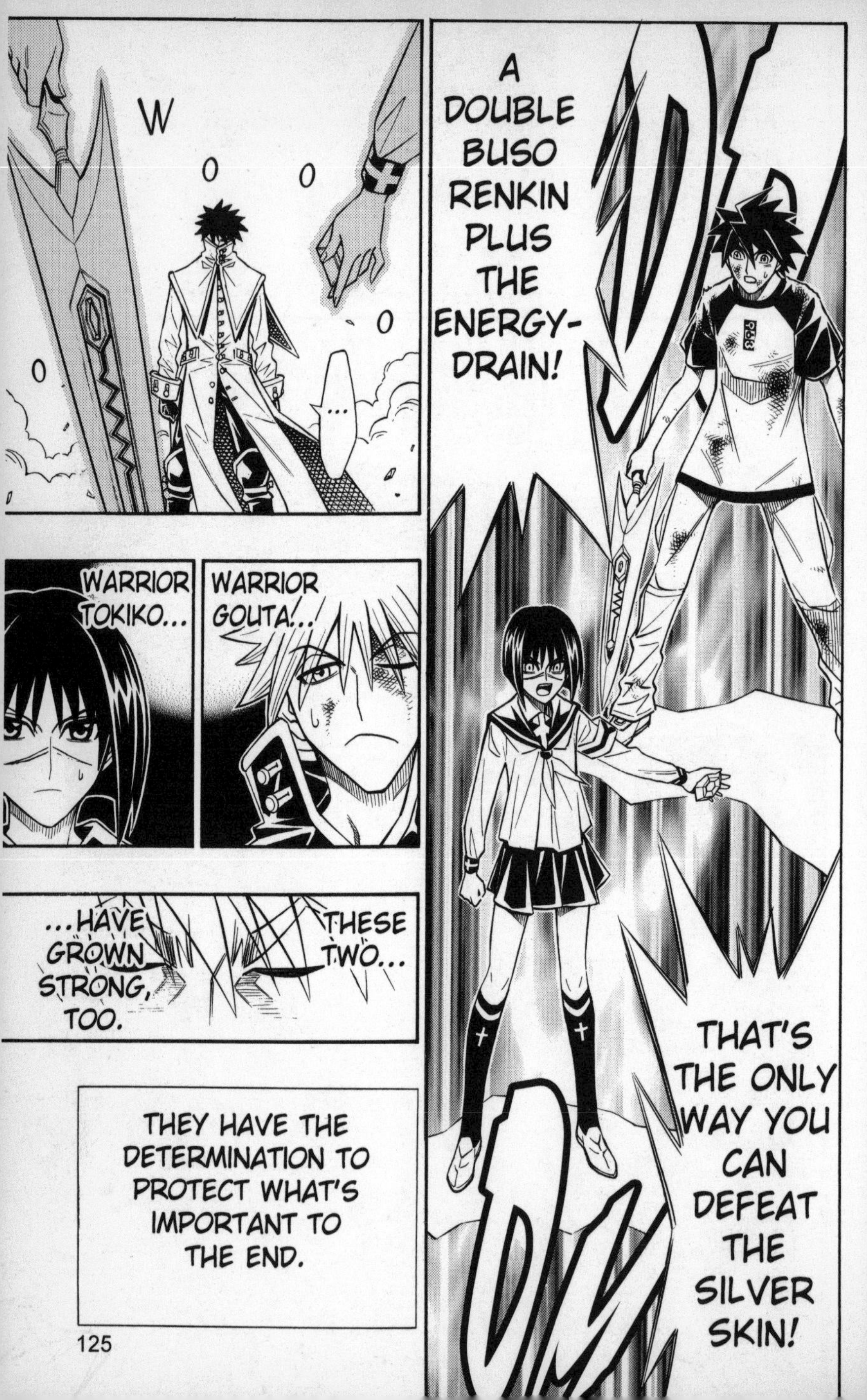
A DOUBLE BUSO RENKIN PLUS THE ENERGY-DRAIN!
THAT'S THE ONLY WAY YOU CAN DEFEAT THE SILVER SKIN!
W O O O O
...
WARRIOR GOUTA!...
WARRIOR TOKIKO...
THESE TWO...
...HAVE GROWN STRONG, TOO.
THEY HAVE THE DETERMINATION TO PROTECT WHAT'S IMPORTANT TO THE END.

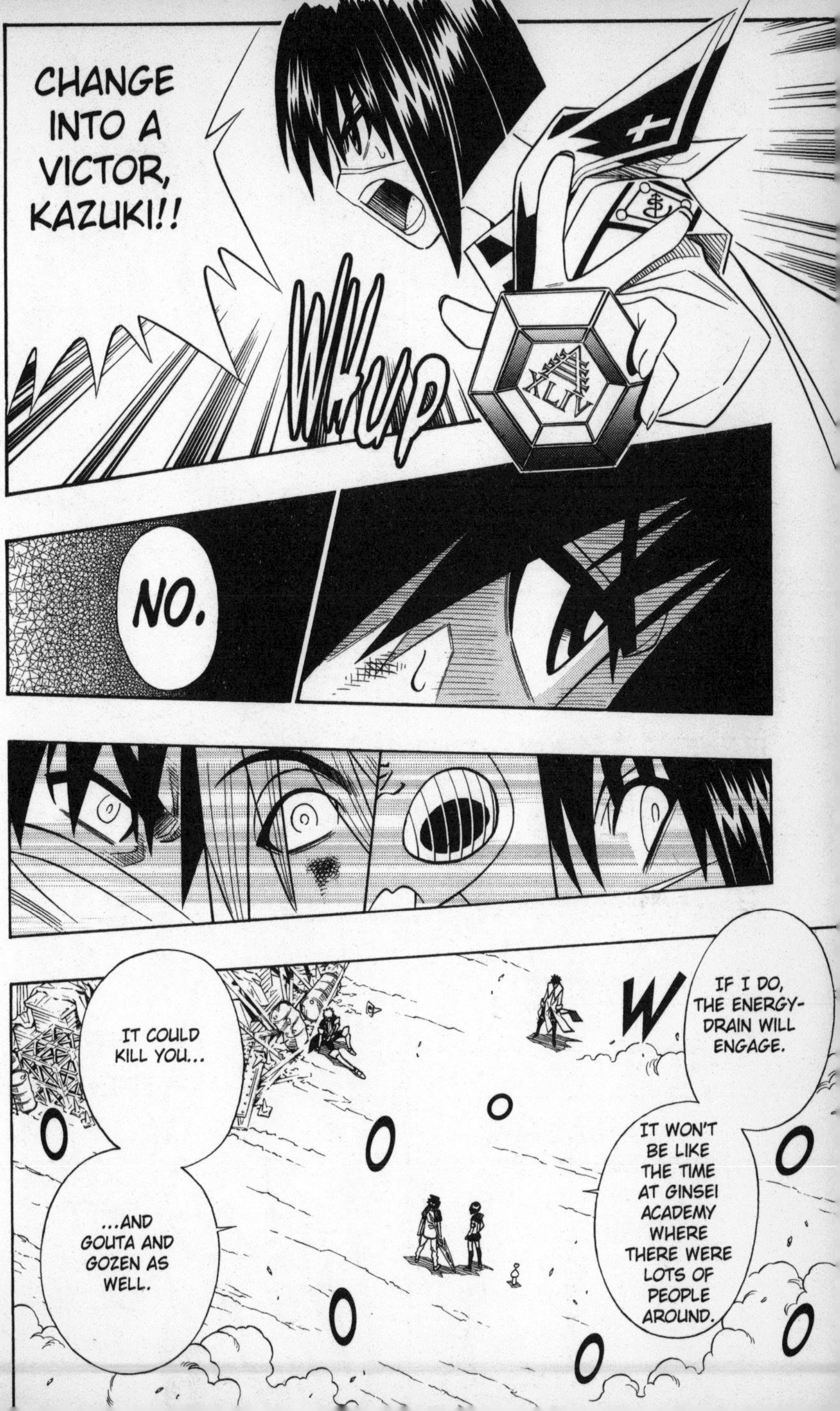
CHANGE INTO A VICTOR, KAZUKI!!
WHUP
NO.
IF I DO, THE ENERGY-DRAIN WILL ENGAGE.
IT WON'T BE LIKE THE TIME AT GINSEI ACADEMY WHERE THERE WERE LOTS OF PEOPLE AROUND.
IT COULD KILL YOU...
...AND GOUTA AND GOZEN AS WELL.

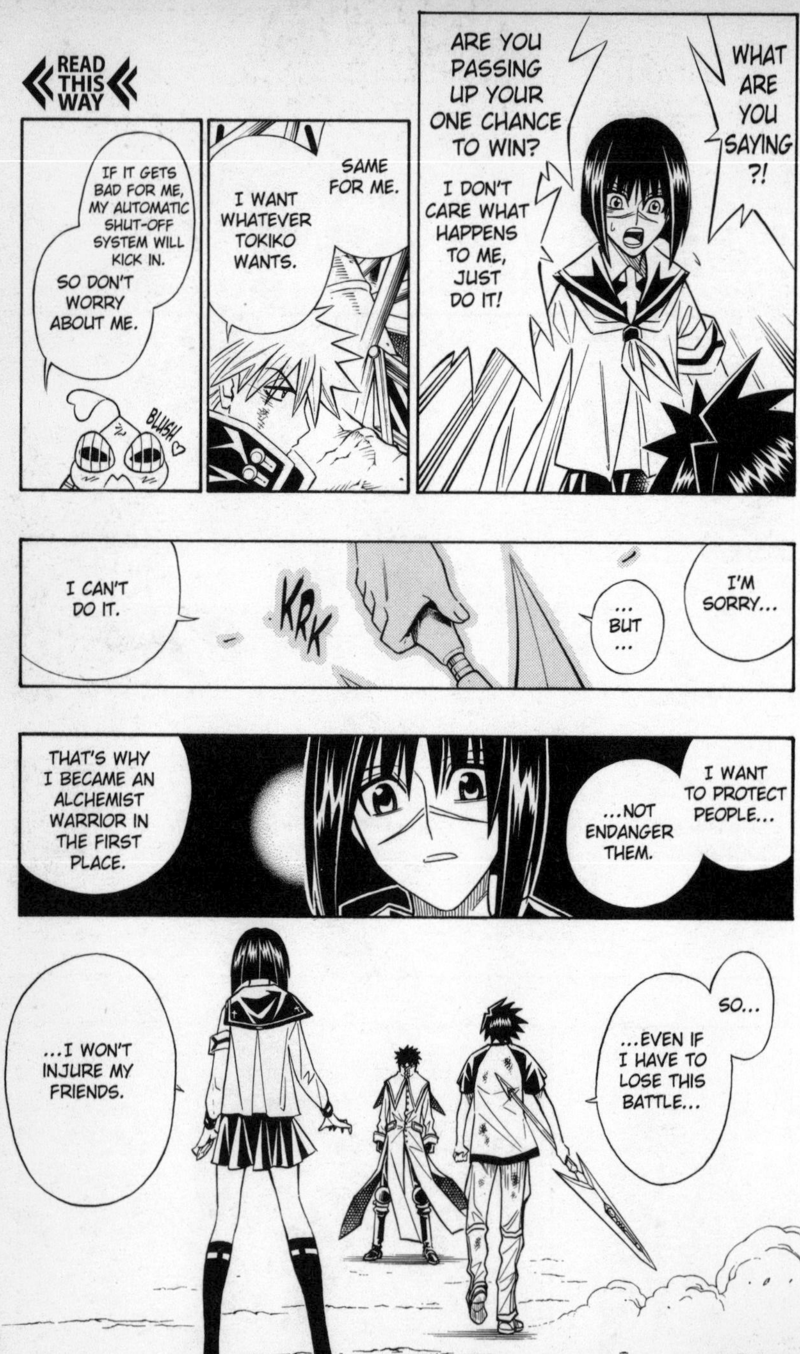
READ THIS WAY
WHAT ARE YOU SAYING?!
ARE YOU PASSING UP YOUR ONE CHANCE TO WIN?
I DON'T CARE WHAT HAPPENS TO ME, JUST DO IT!
SAME FOR ME.
I WANT WHATEVER TOKIKO WANTS.
IF IT GETS BAD FOR ME, MY AUTOMATIC SHUT-OFF SYSTEM WILL KICK IN.
SO DON'T WORRY ABOUT ME.
BLUSH
I'M SORRY...
...BUT...
KRK
I CAN'T DO IT.
I WANT TO PROTECT PEOPLE...
...NOT ENDANGER THEM.
THAT'S WHY I BECAME AN ALCHEMIST WARRIOR IN THE FIRST PLACE.
SO...
...EVEN IF I HAVE TO LOSE THIS BATTLE...
...I WON'T INJURE MY FRIENDS.

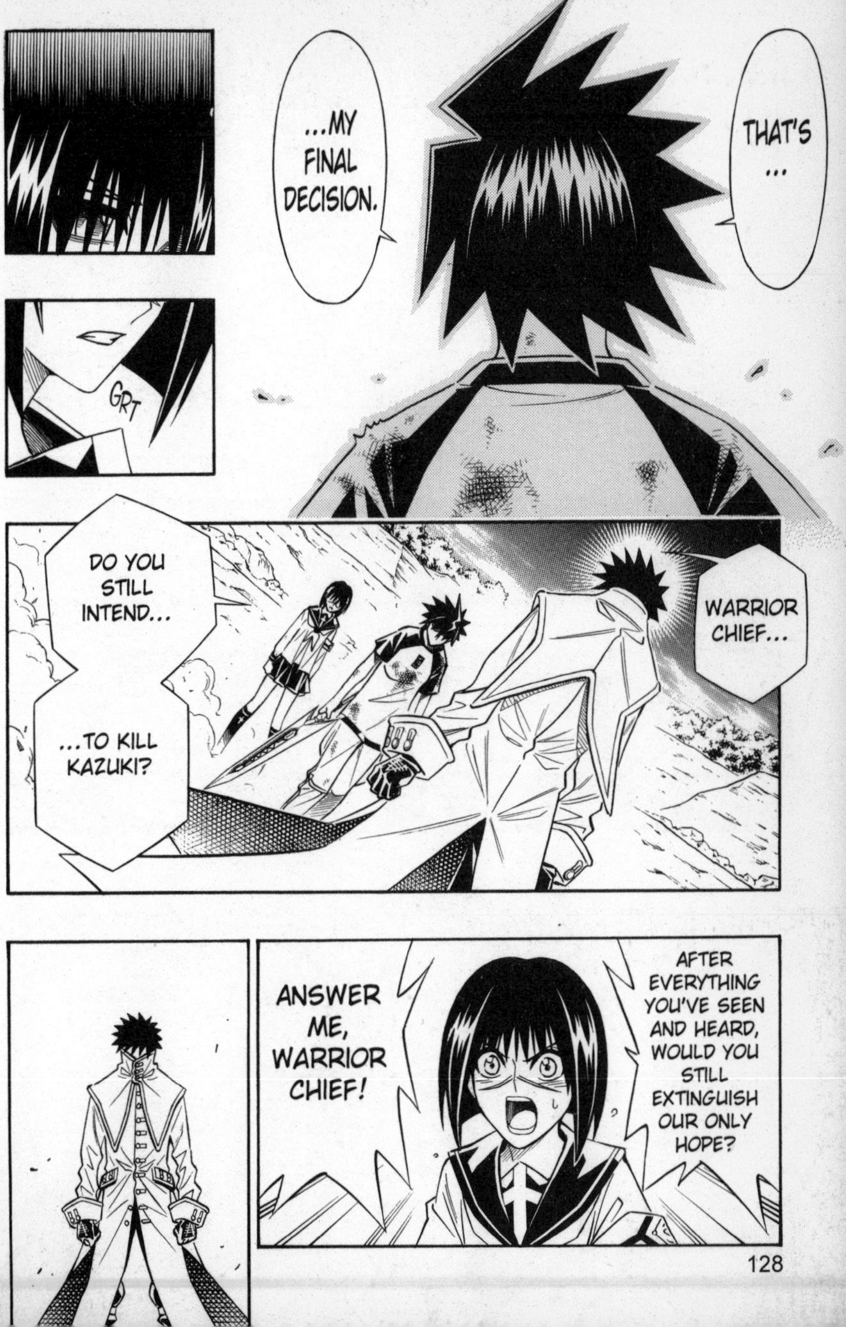
THAT'S...
...MY FINAL DECISION.
GRT
WARRIOR CHIEF...
DO YOU STILL INTEND...
...TO KILL KAZUKI?
AFTER EVERYTHING YOU'VE SEEN AND HEARD, WOULD YOU STILL EXTINGUISH OUR ONLY HOPE?
ANSWER ME, WARRIOR CHIEF!

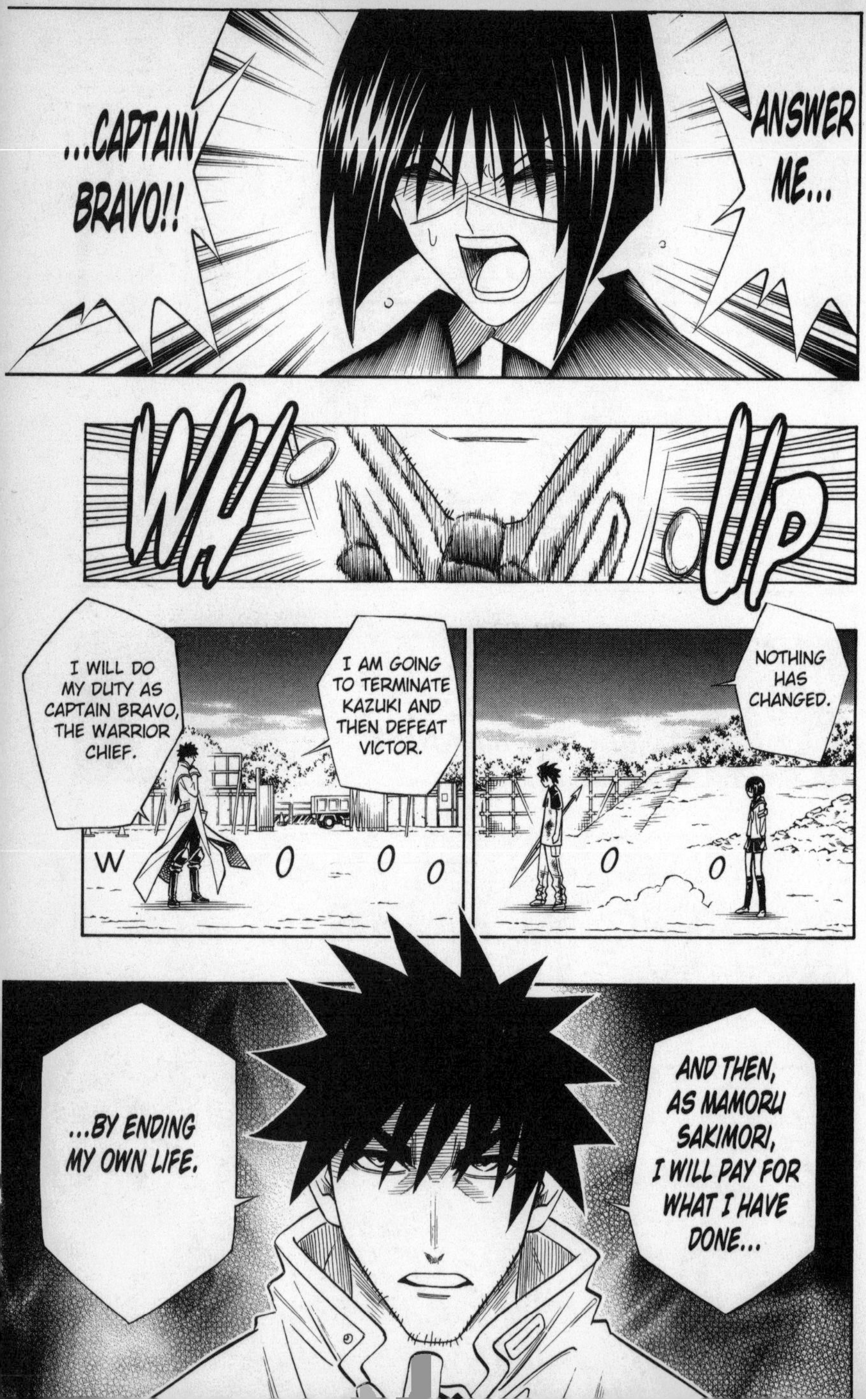
ANSWER ME...
...CAPTAIN BRAVO!!
WHUP
NOTHING HAS CHANGED.
W O O O O O
I AM GOING TO TERMINATE KAZUKI AND THEN DEFEAT VICTOR.
I WILL DO MY DUTY AS CAPTAIN BRAVO, THE WARRIOR CHIEF.
AND THEN, AS MAMORU SAKIMORI, I WILL PAY FOR WHAT I HAVE DONE...
...BY ENDING MY OWN LIFE.

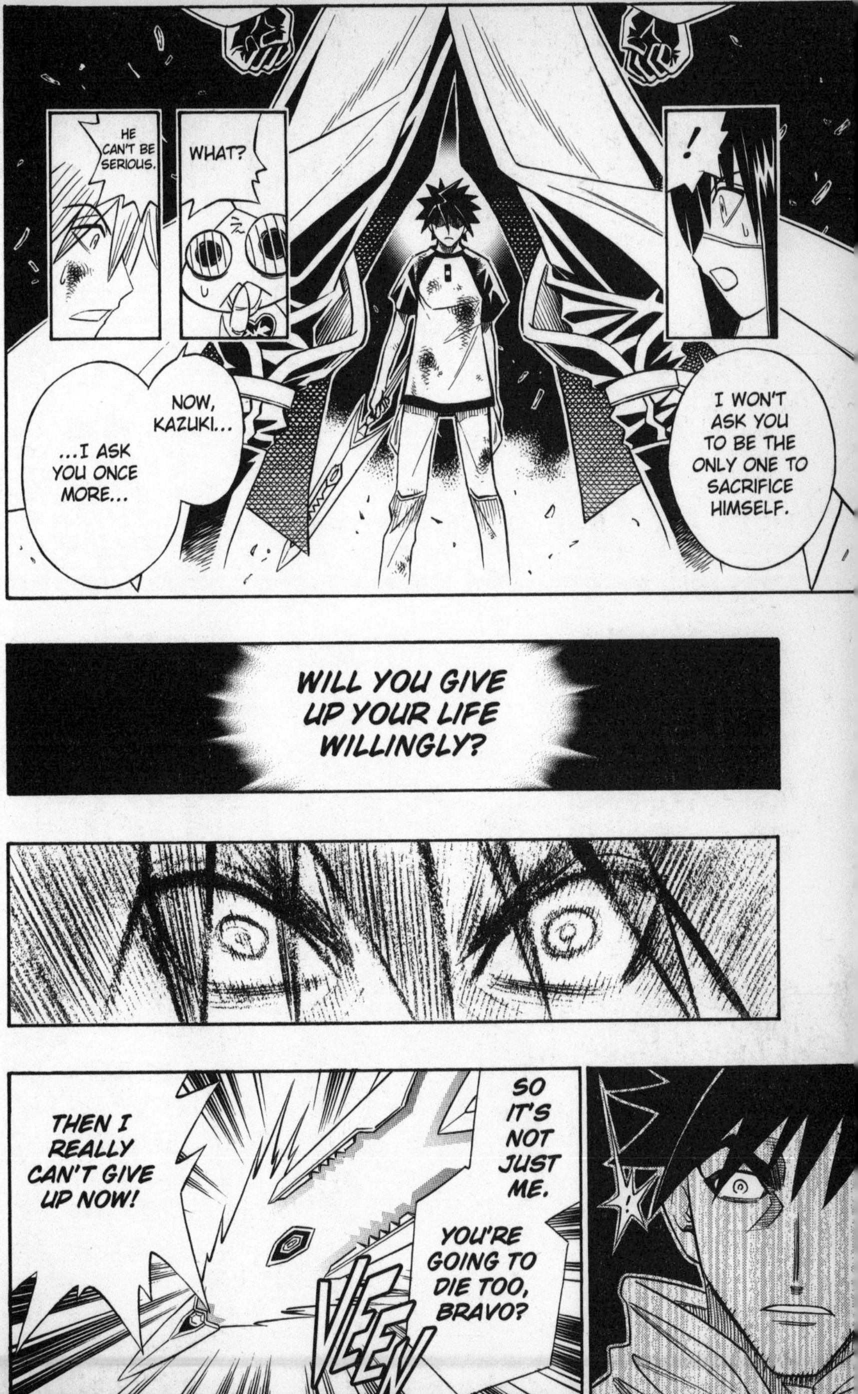
!
WHAT?
HE CAN'T BE SERIOUS.
I WON'T ASK YOU TO BE THE ONLY ONE TO SACRIFICE HIMSELF.
NOW, KAZUKI...
...I ASK YOU ONCE MORE...
WILL YOU GIVE UP YOUR LIFE WILLINGLY?
SO IT'S NOT JUST ME.
YOU'RE GOING TO DIE TOO, BRAVO?
THEN I REALLY CAN'T GIVE UP NOW!
VEEN

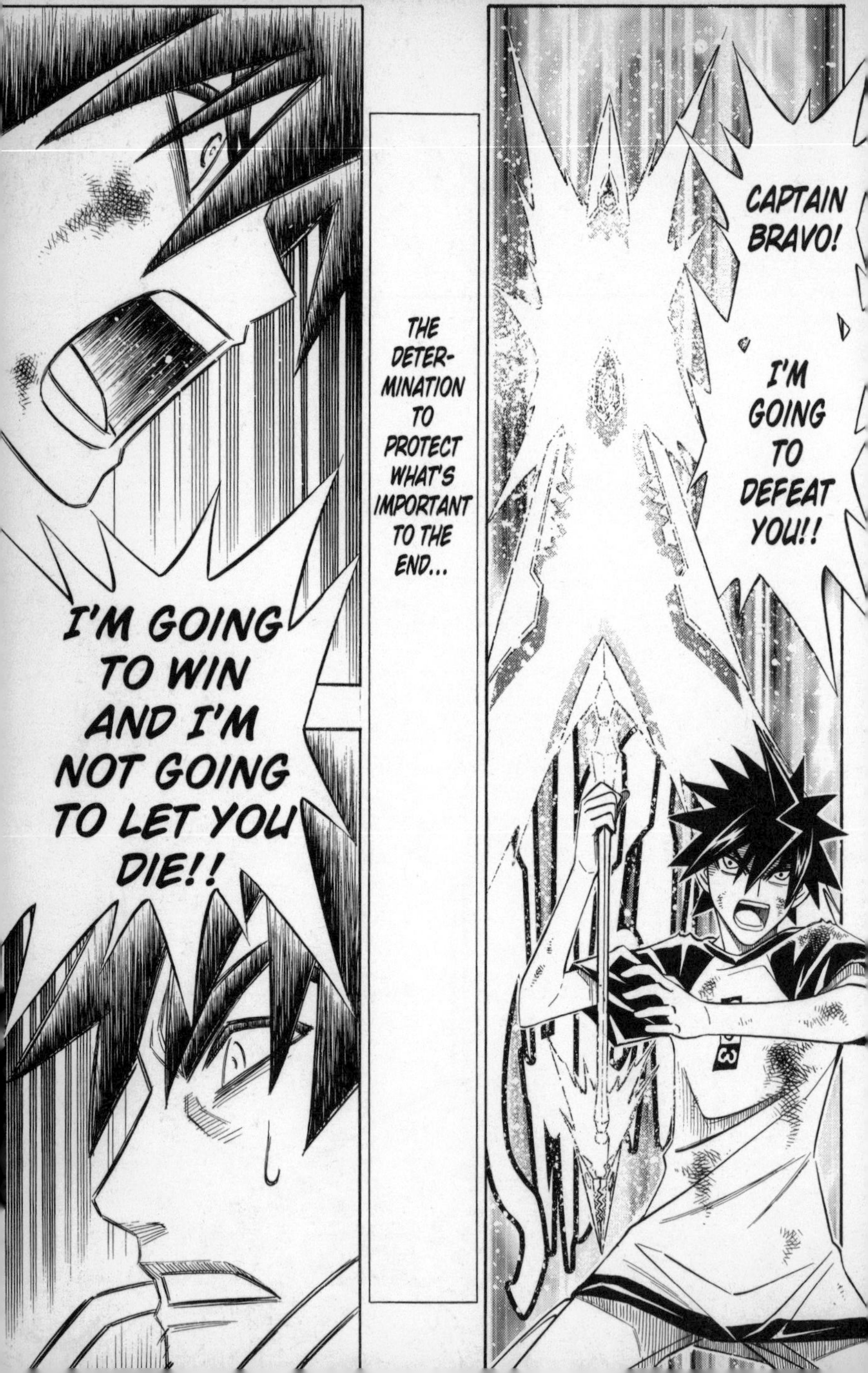
CAPTAIN BRAVO!
I'M GOING TO DEFEAT YOU!!
THE DETERMINATION TO PROTECT WHAT'S IMPORTANT TO THE END...
I'M GOING TO WIN AND I'M NOT GOING TO LET YOU DIE!!

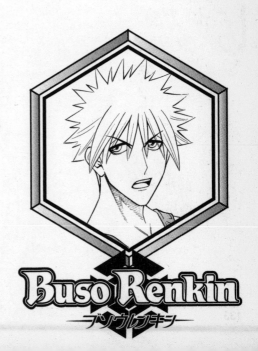

Buso Renkin
ブソウレンキン

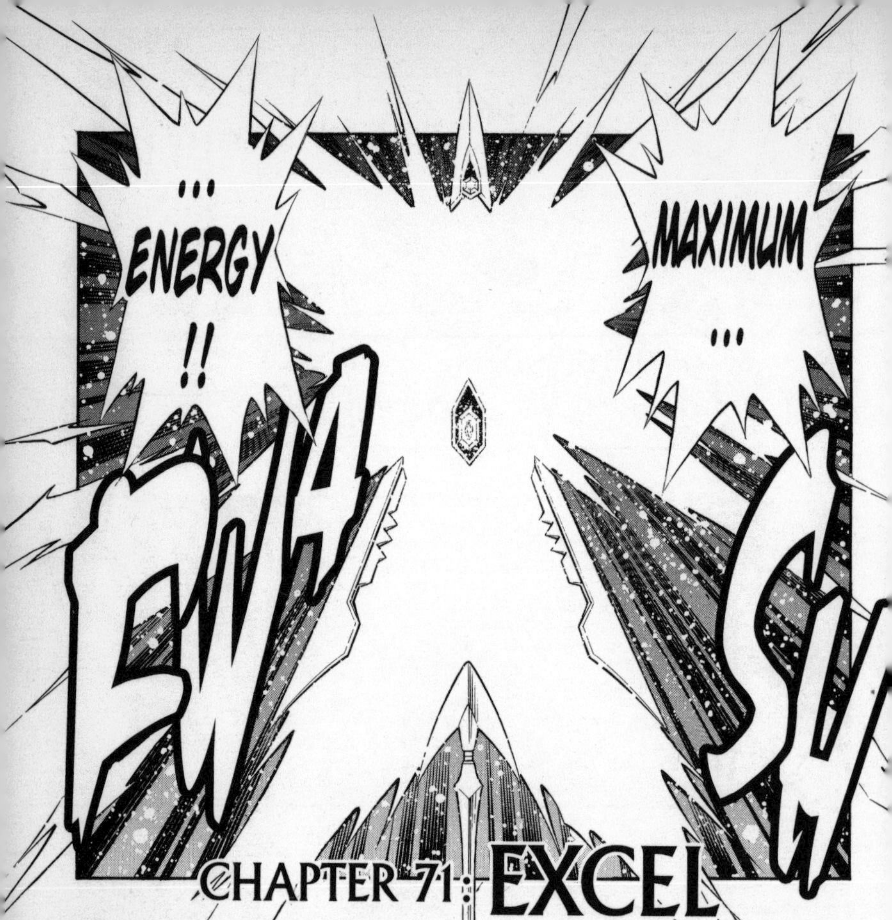
MAXIMUM ...
... ENERGY !!

CHAPTER 71: EXCEL

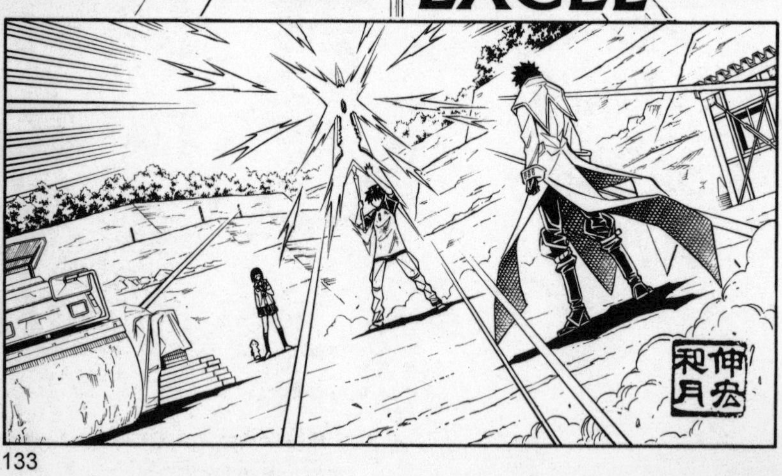
和月伸宏

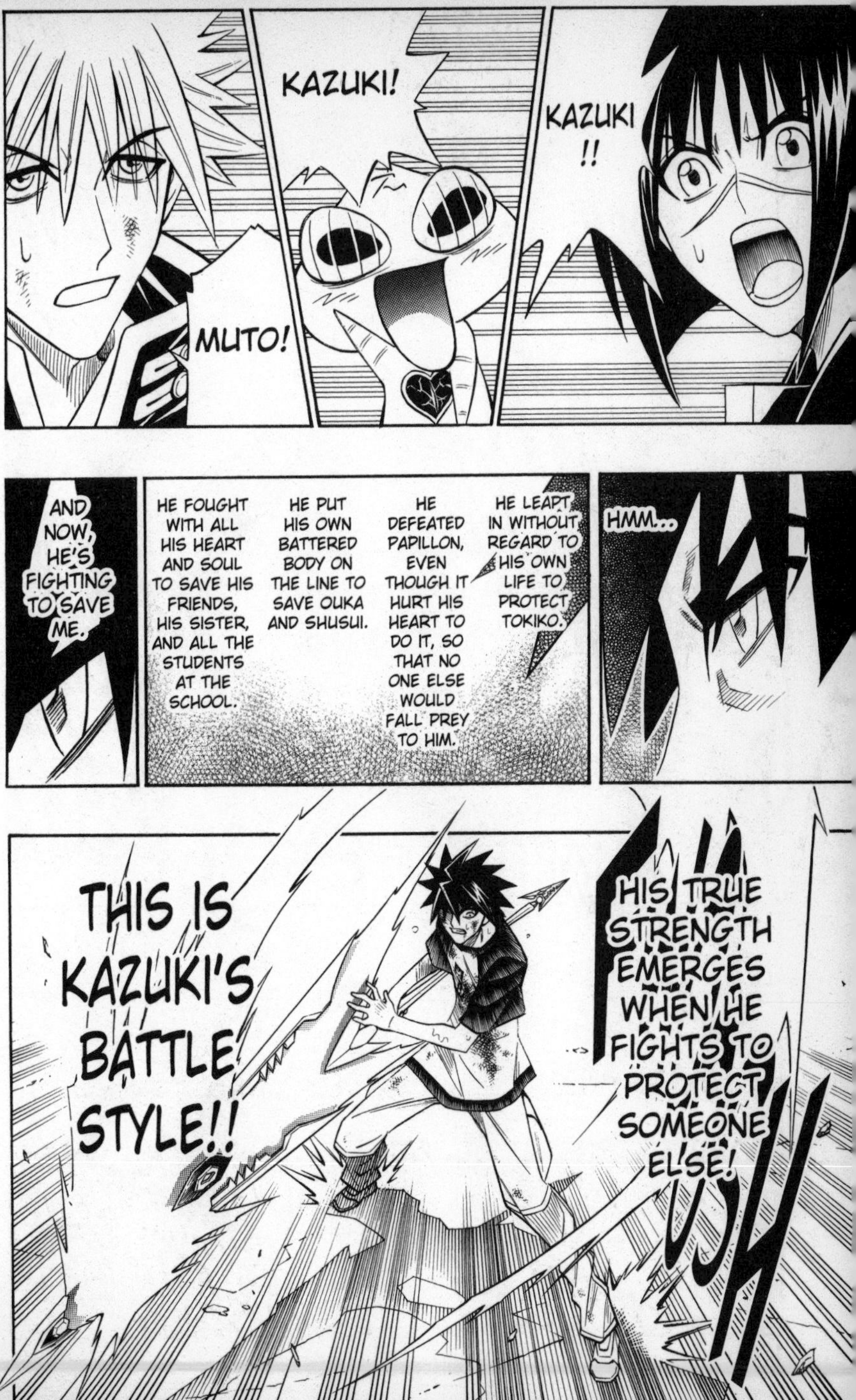
KAZUKI !!
KAZUKI!
MUTO!
HMM...
HE LEAPT IN WITHOUT REGARD TO HIS OWN LIFE TO PROTECT TOKIKO.
HE DEFEATED PAPILLON, EVEN THOUGH IT HURT HIS HEART TO DO IT, SO THAT NO ONE ELSE WOULD FALL PREY TO HIM.
HE PUT HIS OWN BATTERED BODY ON THE LINE TO SAVE OUKA AND SHUSUI.
HE FOUGHT WITH ALL HIS HEART AND SOUL TO SAVE HIS FRIENDS, HIS SISTER, AND ALL THE STUDENTS AT THE SCHOOL.
AND NOW, HE'S FIGHTING TO SAVE ME.
HIS TRUE STRENGTH EMERGES WHEN HE FIGHTS TO PROTECT SOMEONE ELSE!
THIS IS KAZUKI'S BATTLE STYLE!!

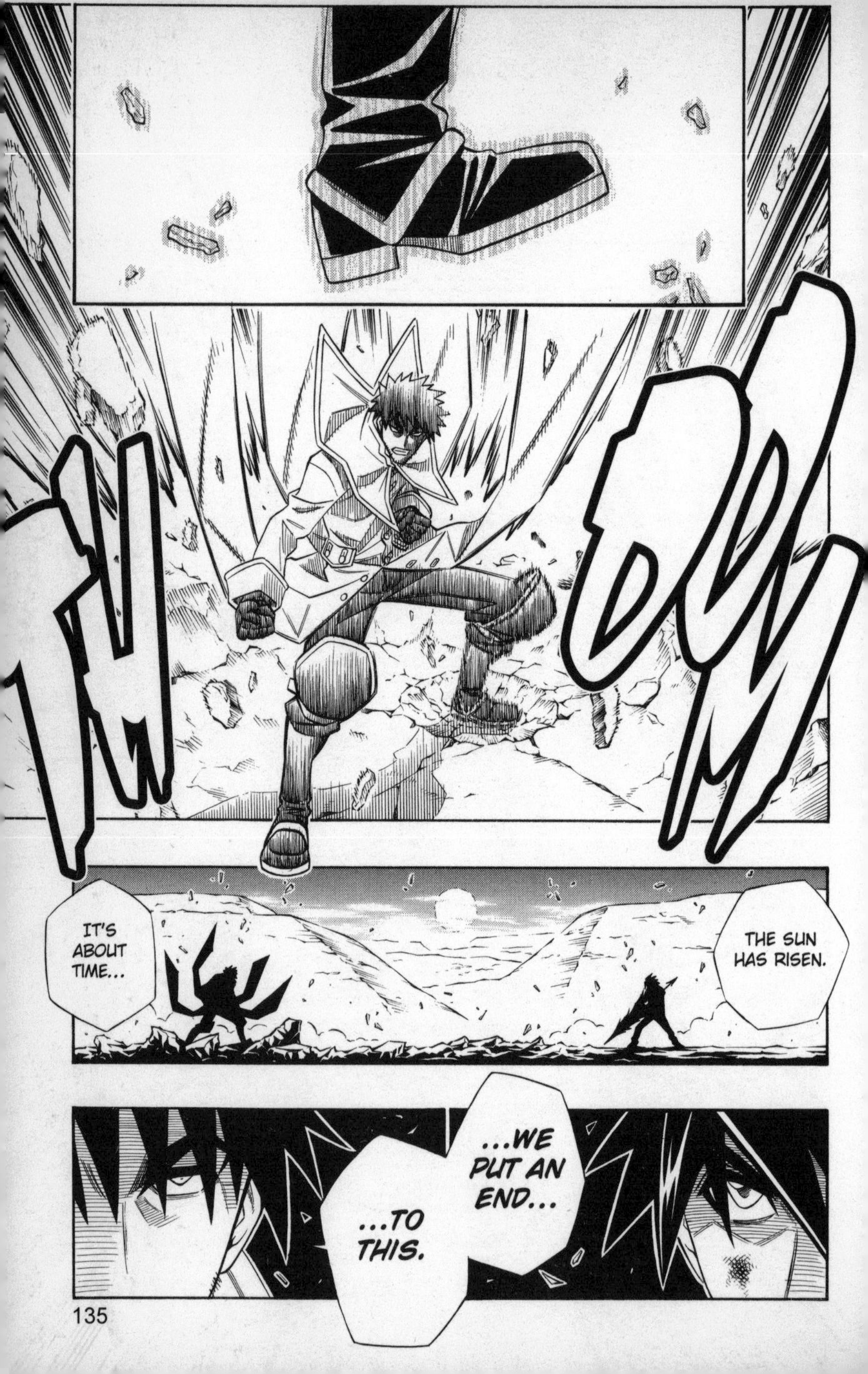
THE SUN HAS RISEN.
IT'S ABOUT TIME...
...WE PUT AN END...
...TO THIS.

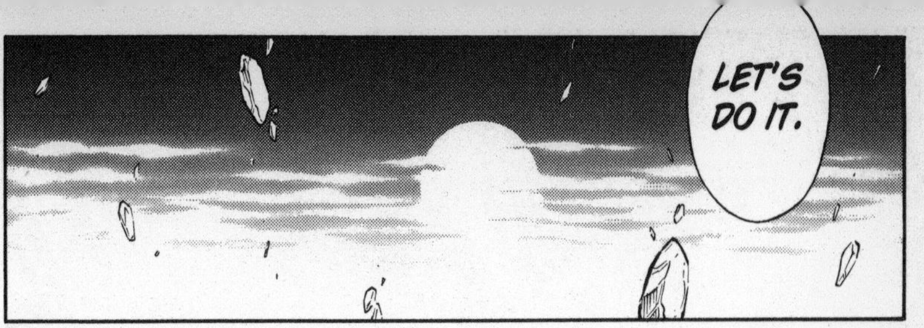
LET'S DO IT.
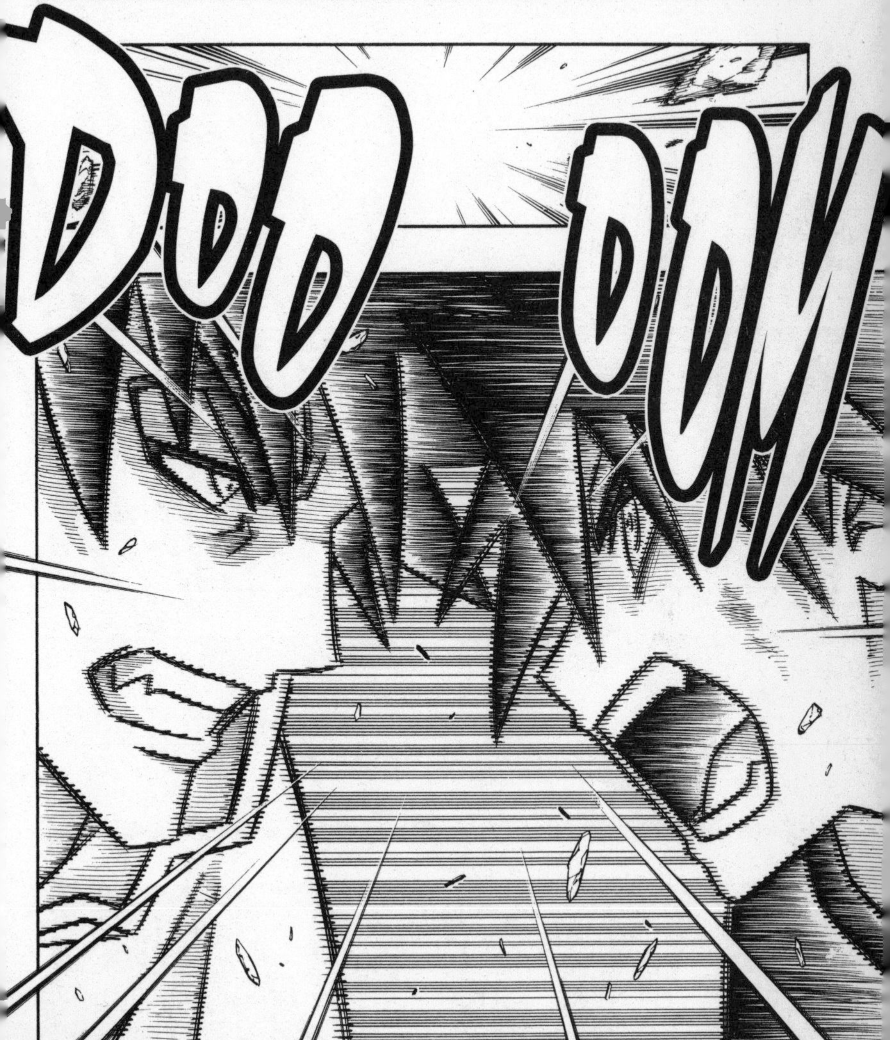
DOOO DOOM

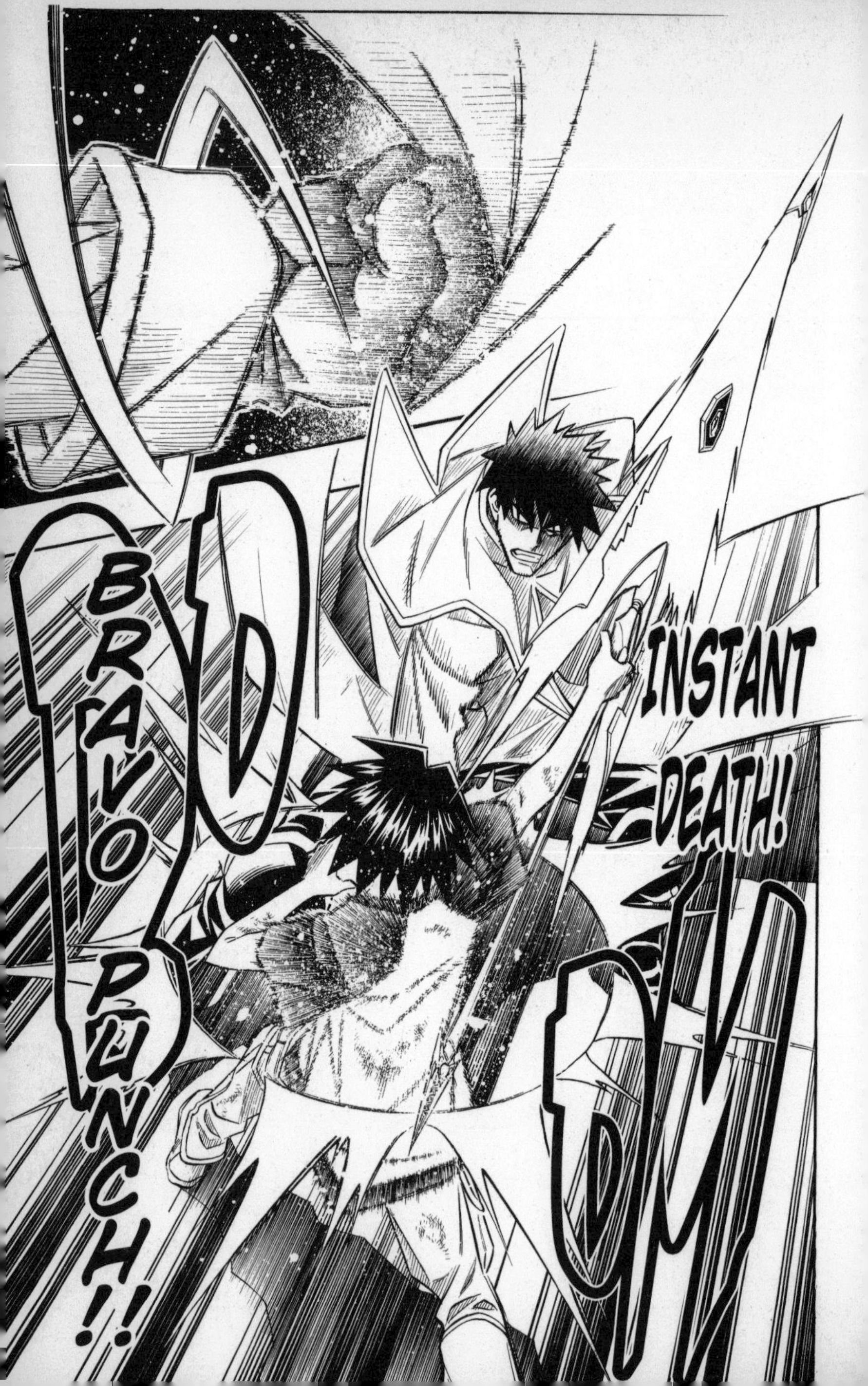
INSTANT DEATH!
BRAVO PUNCH!!

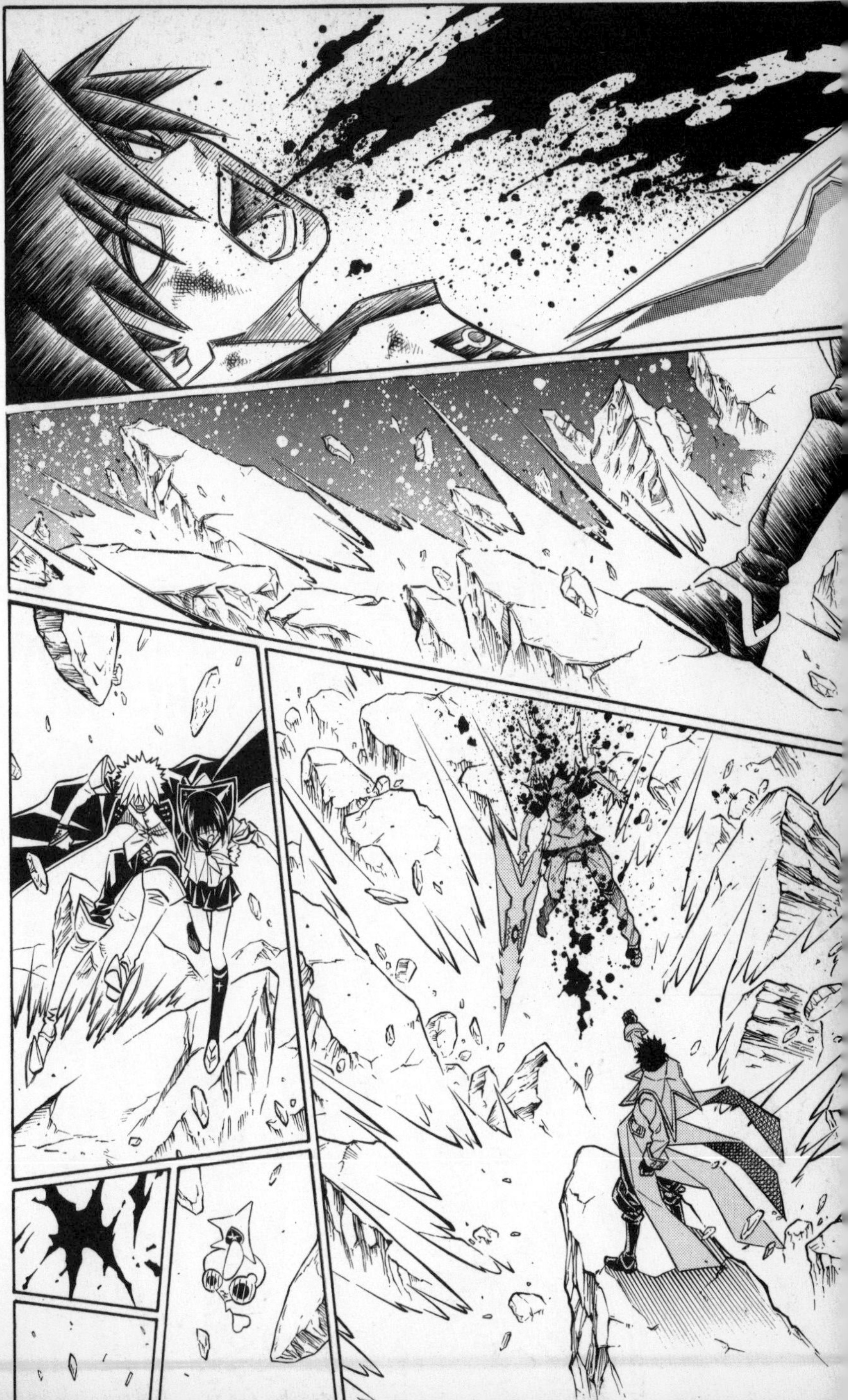

READ THIS WAY

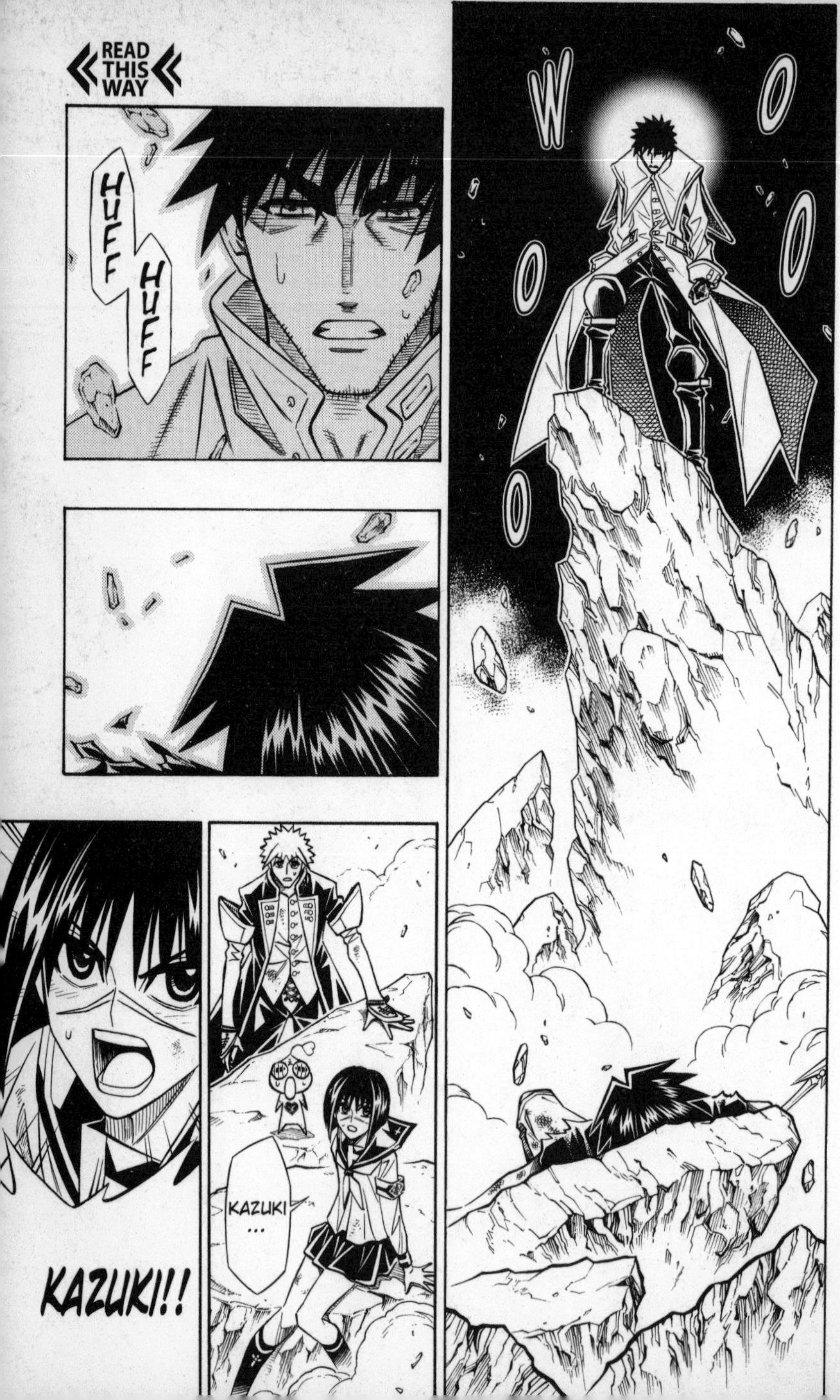
WOOOO
HUFF HUFF
KAZUKI ...
KAZUKI!!

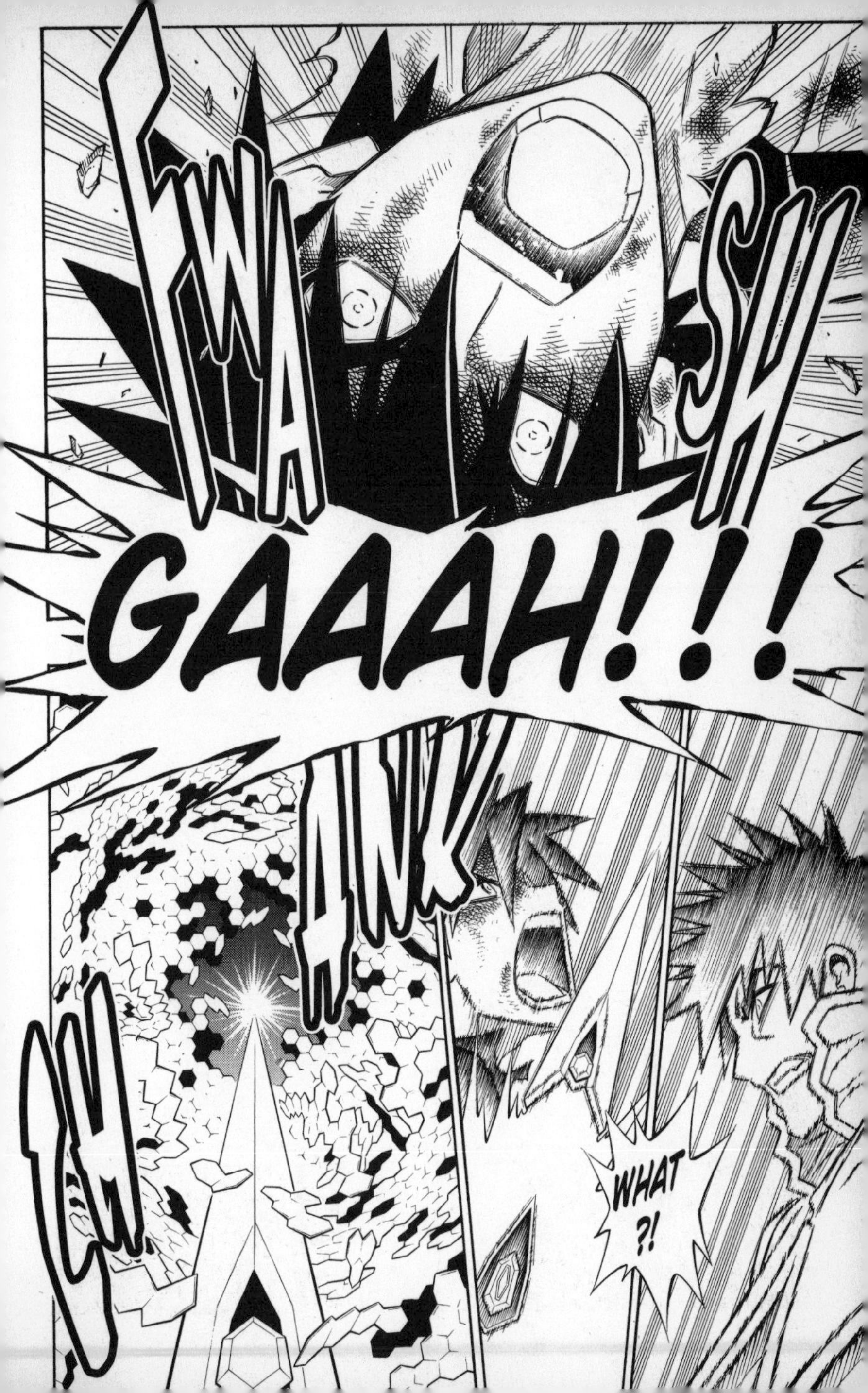
TWASH
GAAAH!!!
CHANK
WHAT ?!

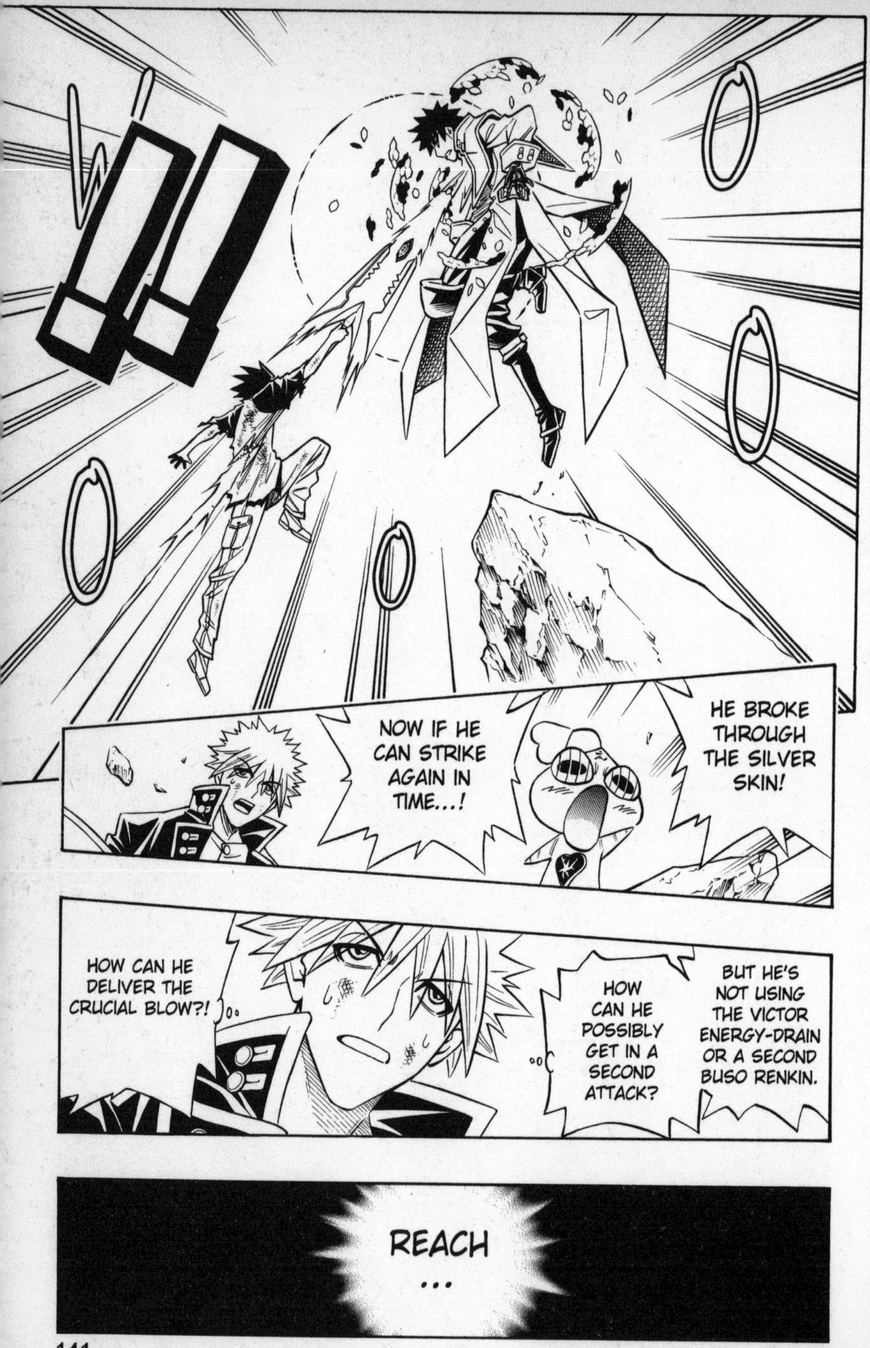
!!
HE BROKE THROUGH THE SILVER SKIN!
NOW IF HE CAN STRIKE AGAIN IN TIME...!
BUT HE'S NOT USING THE VICTOR ENERGY-DRAIN OR A SECOND BUSO RENKIN.
HOW CAN HE POSSIBLY GET IN A SECOND ATTACK?
HOW CAN HE DELIVER THE CRUCIAL BLOW?!
REACH
...

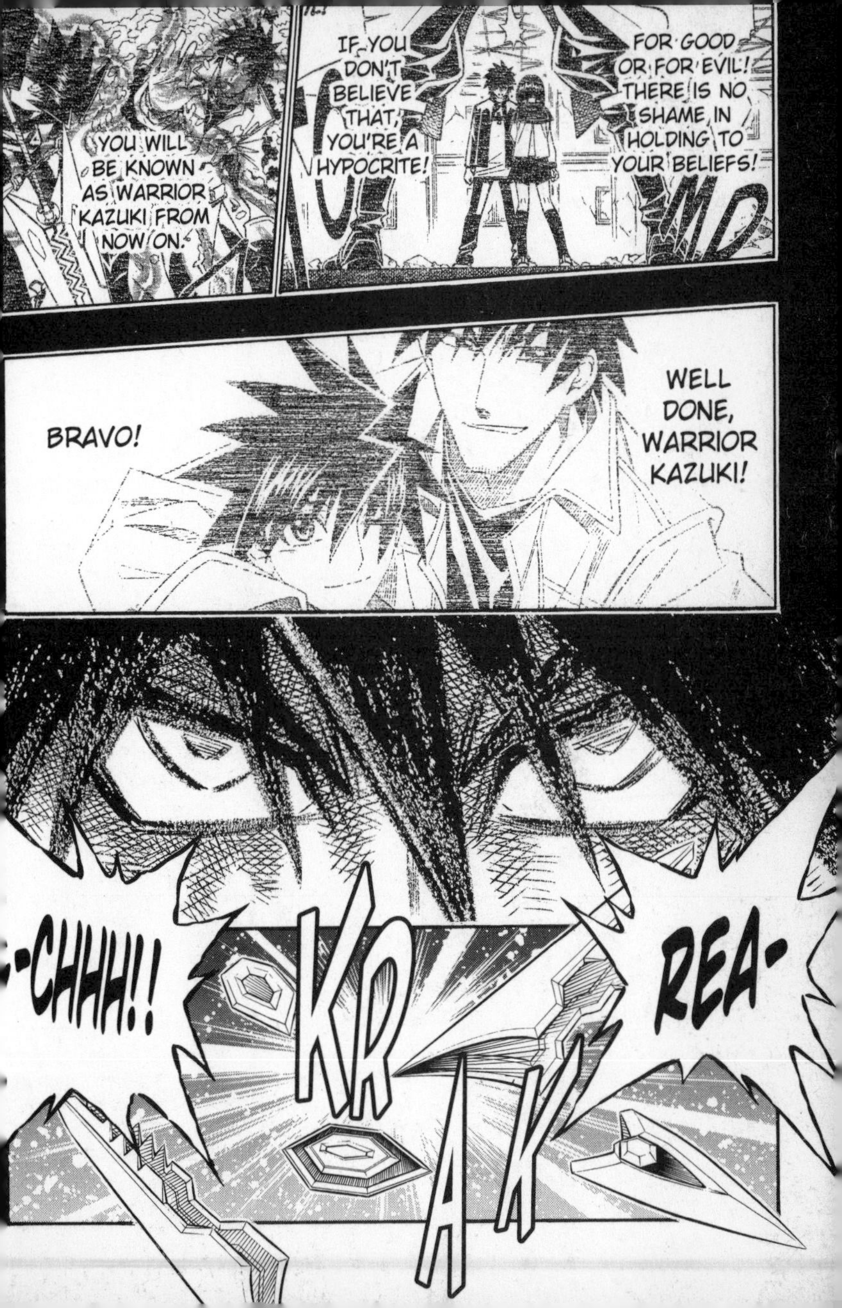
FOR GOOD OR FOR EVIL! THERE IS NO SHAME IN HOLDING TO YOUR BELIEFS!
IF YOU DON'T BELIEVE THAT, YOU'RE A HYPOCRITE!
YOU WILL BE KNOWN AS WARRIOR KAZUKI FROM NOW ON.
WELL DONE, WARRIOR KAZUKI!
BRAVO!
REA-
KRAAK
-CHHH!!

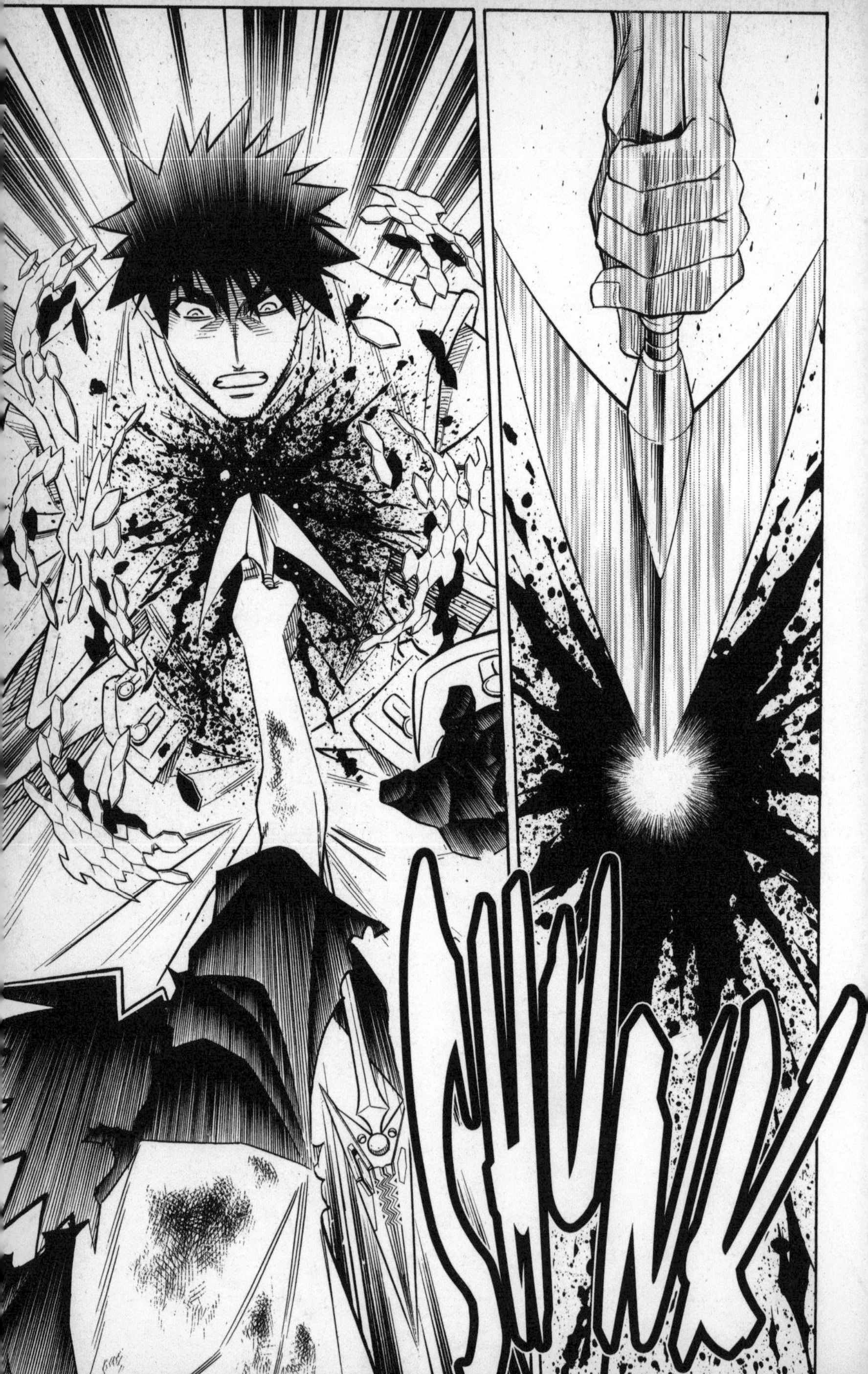
SHUNK

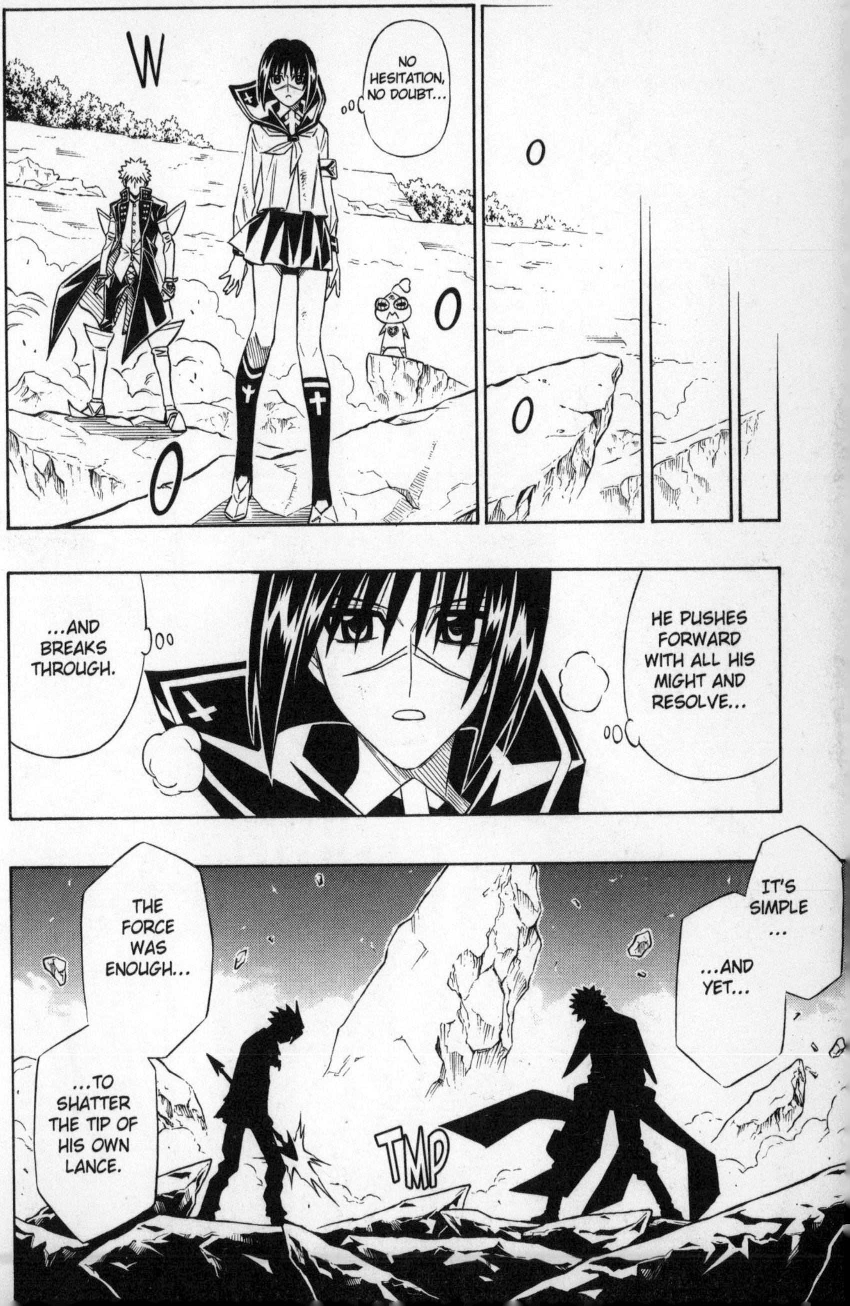
NO HESITATION, NO DOUBT...
WOOOO
HE PUSHES FORWARD WITH ALL HIS MIGHT AND RESOLVE...
...AND BREAKS THROUGH.
IT'S SIMPLE ...
...AND YET...
THE FORCE WAS ENOUGH...
...TO SHATTER THE TIP OF HIS OWN LANCE.
TMP

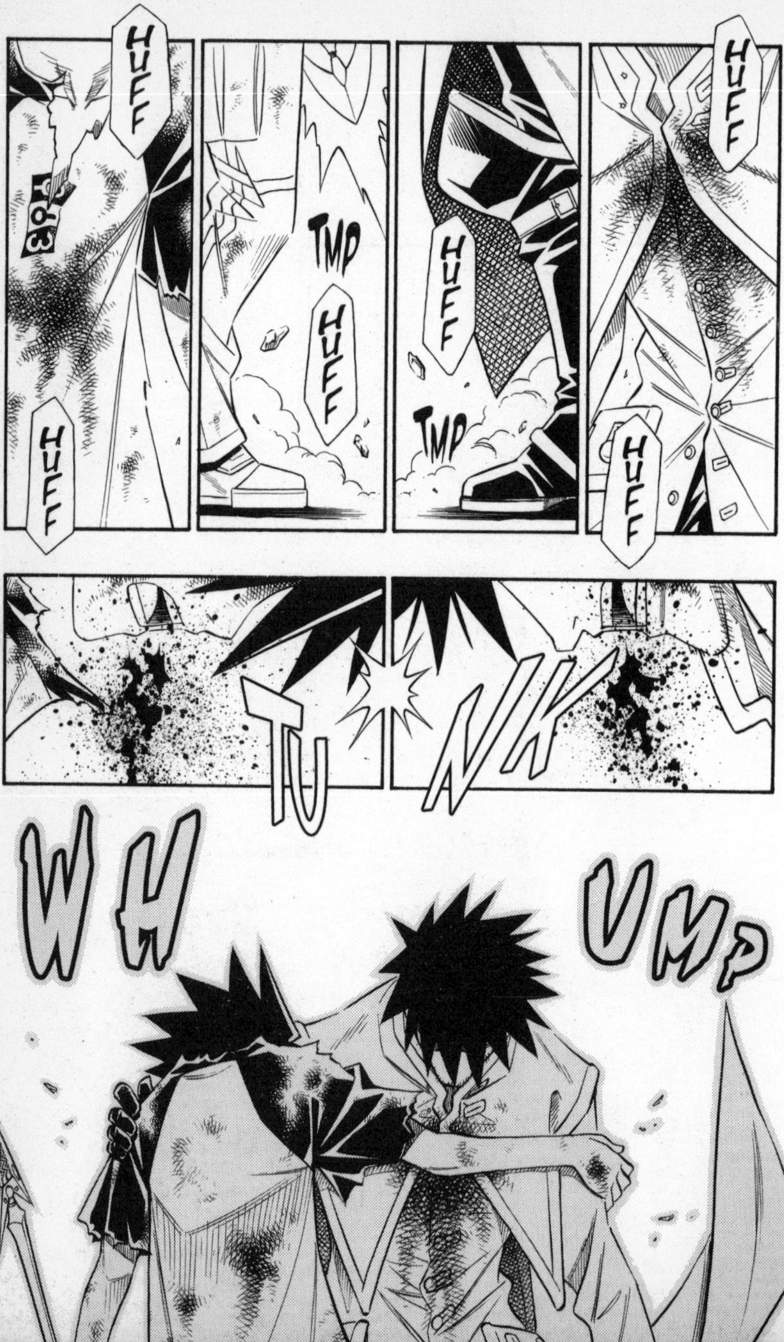
HUFF
HUFF
HUFF
TMP
TMP
HUFF
HUFF
HUFF
TUNK
WHUMP

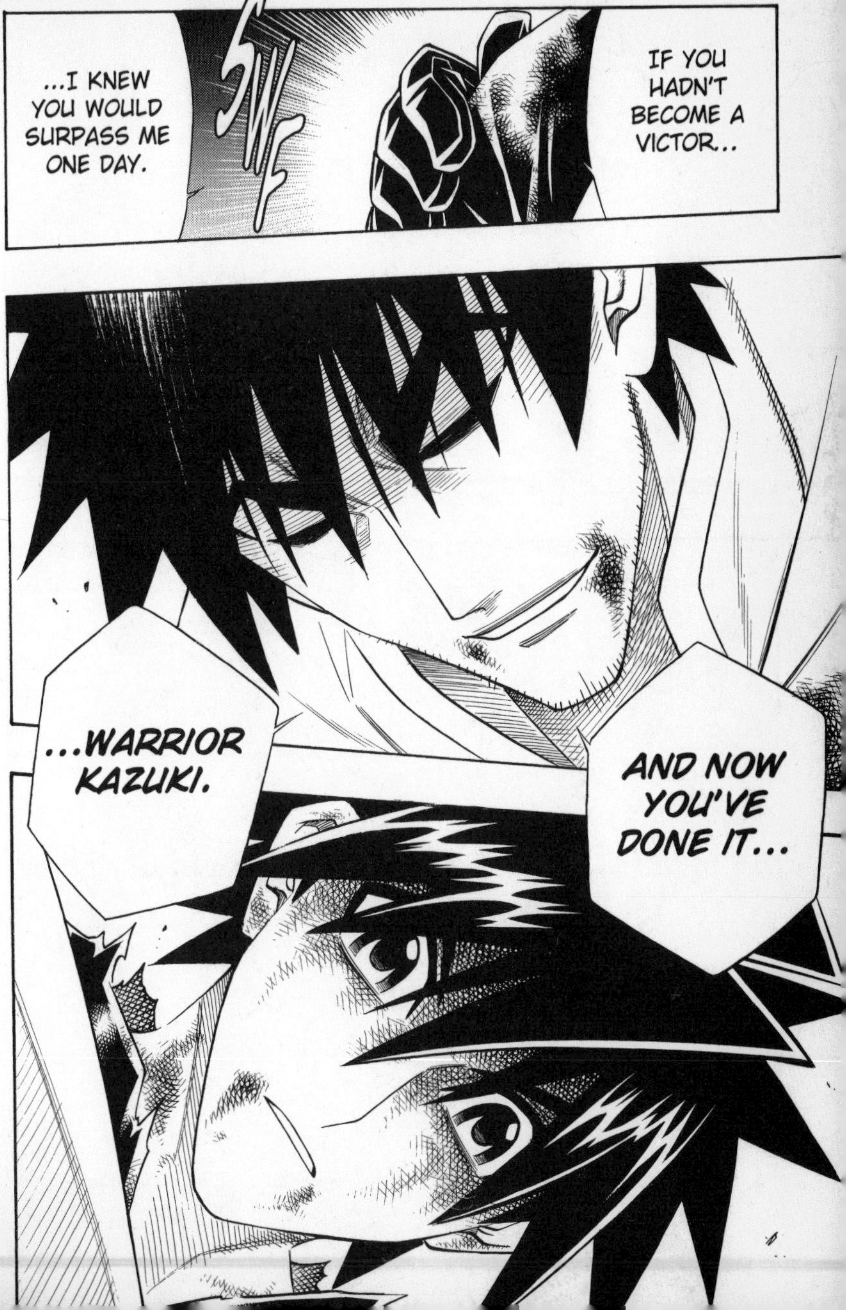
IF YOU HADN'T BECOME A VICTOR...
...I KNEW YOU WOULD SURPASS ME ONE DAY.
AND NOW YOU'VE DONE IT...
...WARRIOR KAZUKI.

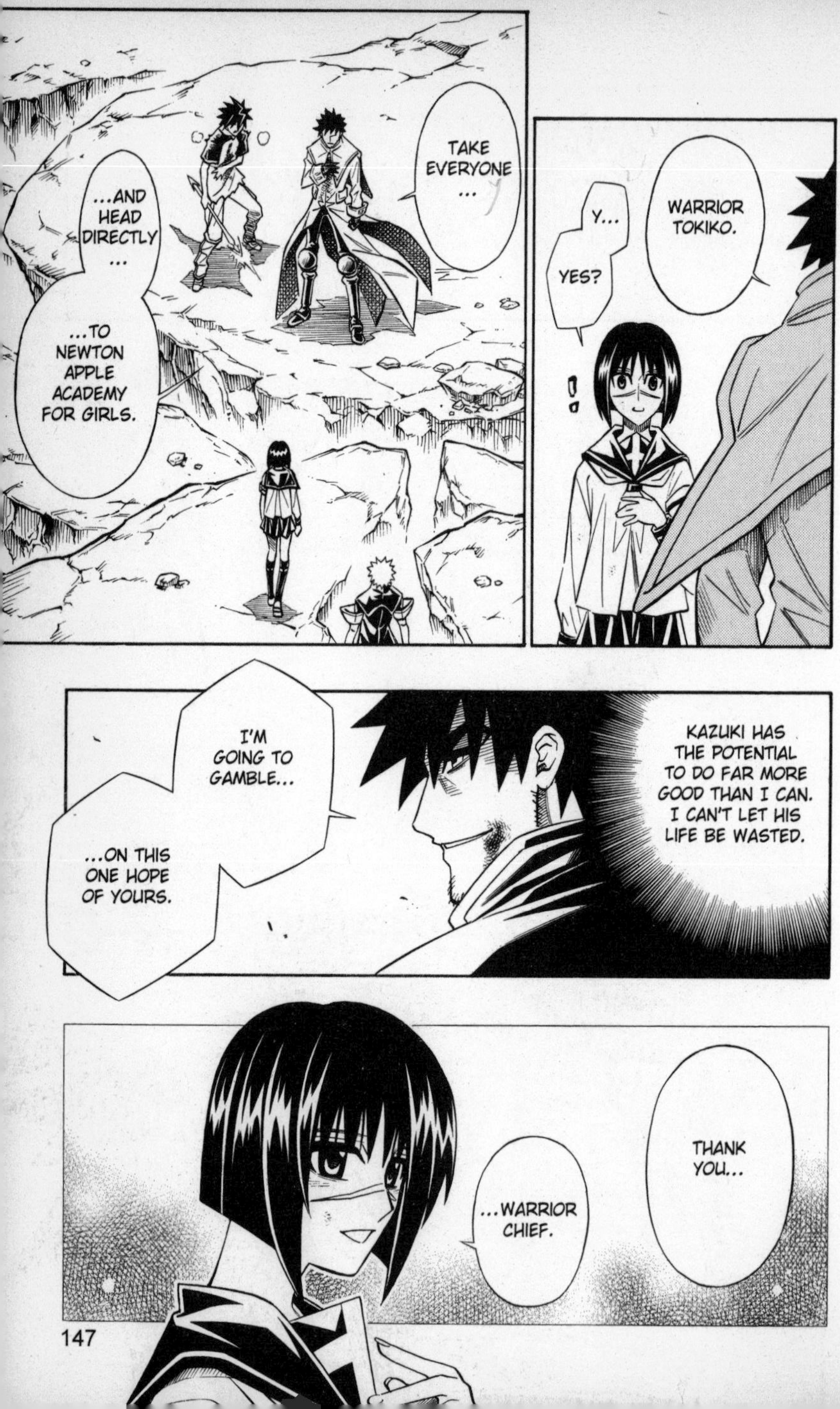
WARRIOR TOKIKO.
Y... YES?
TAKE EVERYONE ...
...AND HEAD DIRECTLY ...
...TO NEWTON APPLE ACADEMY FOR GIRLS.
KAZUKI HAS THE POTENTIAL TO DO FAR MORE GOOD THAN I CAN. I CAN'T LET HIS LIFE BE WASTED.
I'M GOING TO GAMBLE...
...ON THIS ONE HOPE OF YOURS.
THANK YOU...
...WARRIOR CHIEF.

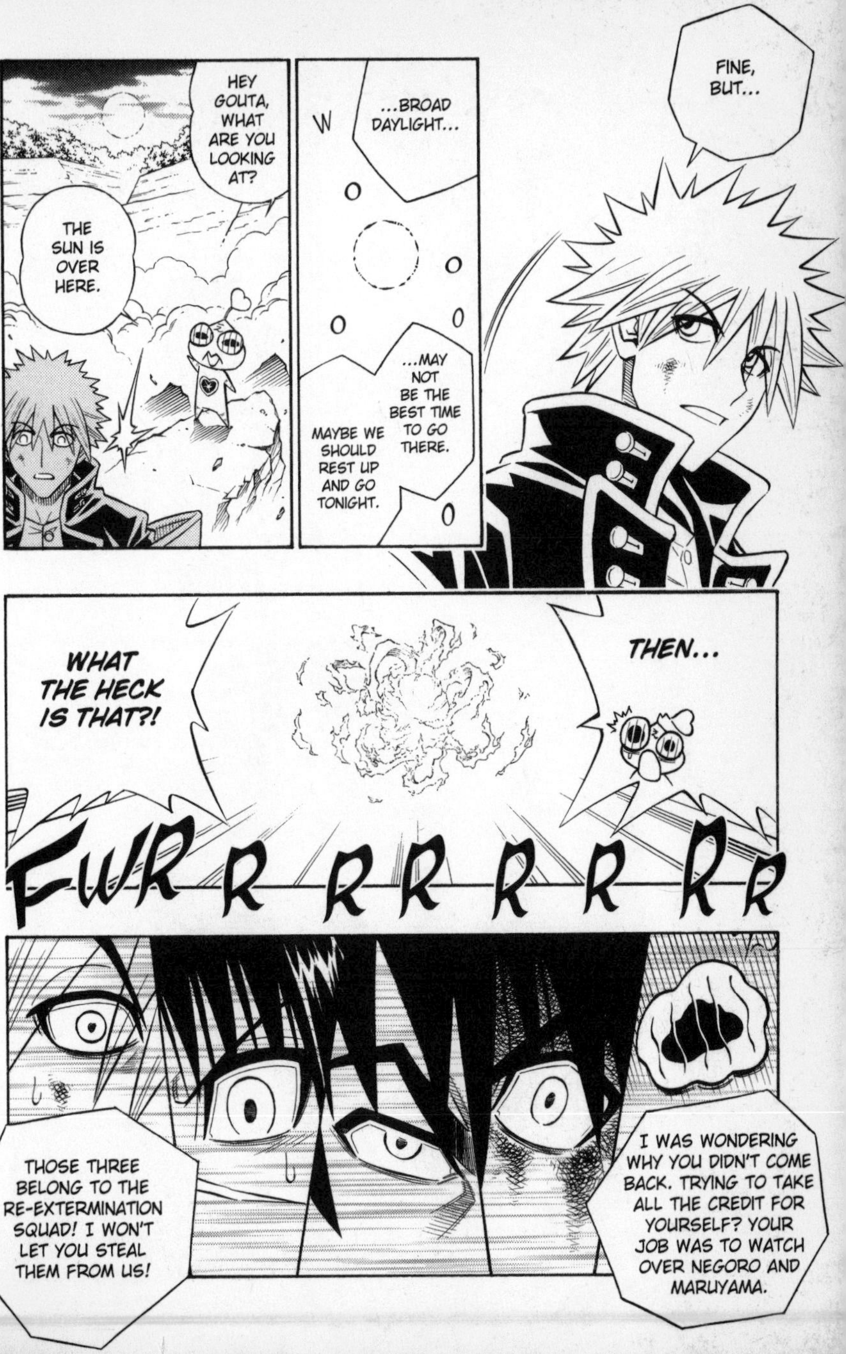
FINE, BUT...
...BROAD DAYLIGHT...
...MAY NOT BE THE BEST TIME TO GO THERE.
MAYBE WE SHOULD REST UP AND GO TONIGHT.
HEY GOUTA, WHAT ARE YOU LOOKING AT?
THE SUN IS OVER HERE.
THEN...
WHAT THE HECK IS THAT?!
FWRRRRRRRR
I WAS WONDERING WHY YOU DIDN'T COME BACK. TRYING TO TAKE ALL THE CREDIT FOR YOURSELF? YOUR JOB WAS TO WATCH OVER NEGORO AND MARUYAMA.
THOSE THREE BELONG TO THE RE-EXTERMINATION SQUAD! I WON'T LET YOU STEAL THEM FROM US!

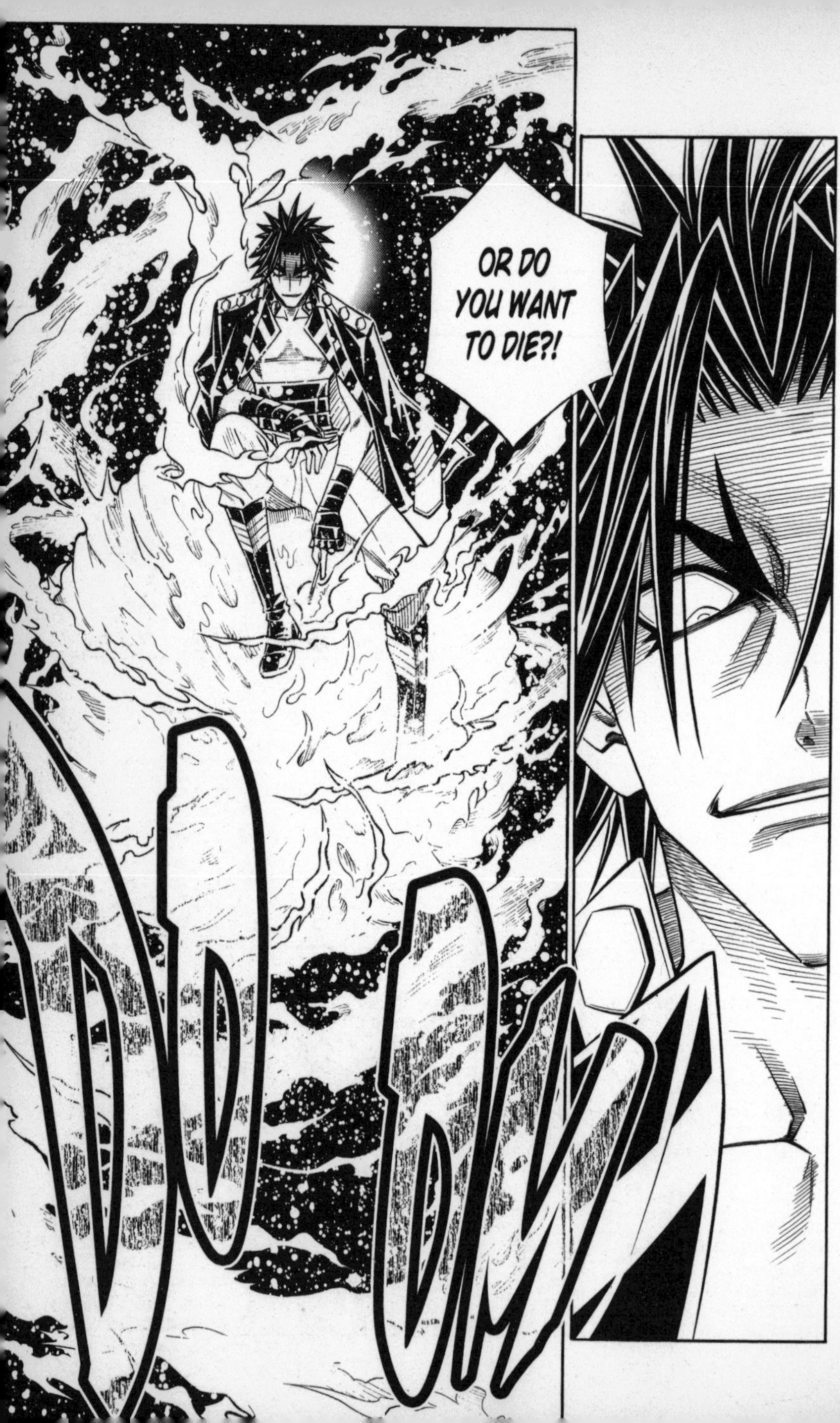
OR DO YOU WANT TO DIE?!

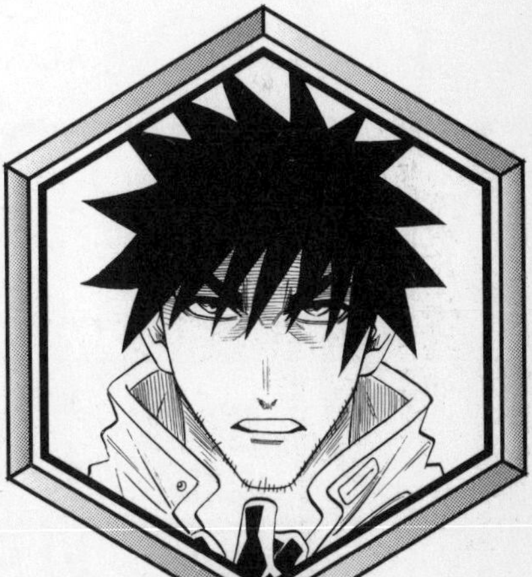

Buso Renkin
ブソウレンキン

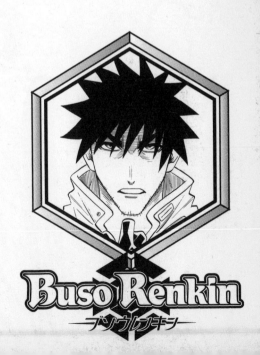

CHAPTER 72: GONE INTO FLAMES

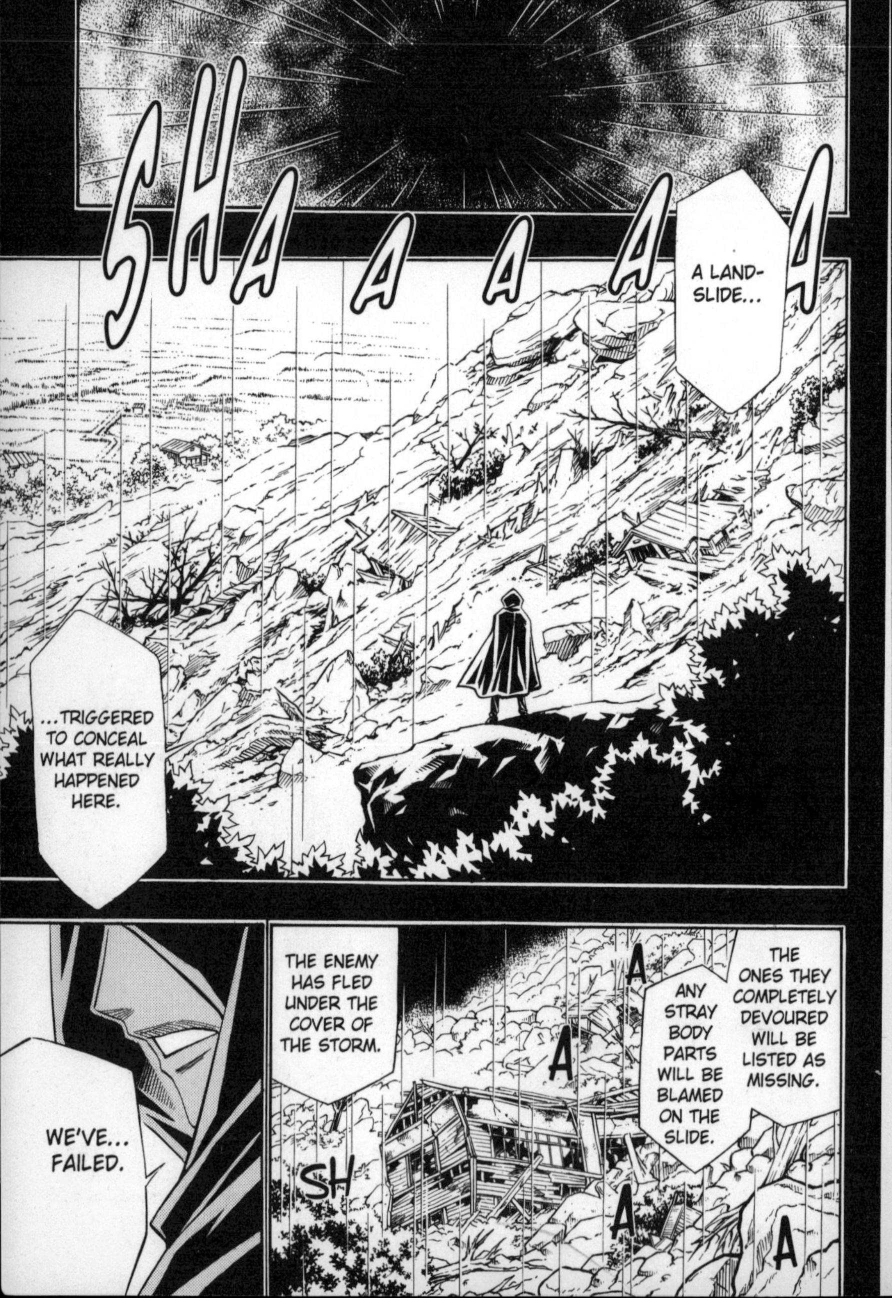
SHAAAAA
A LAND-SLIDE...
...TRIGGERED TO CONCEAL WHAT REALLY HAPPENED HERE.
THE ONES THEY COMPLETELY DEVOURED WILL BE LISTED AS MISSING.
ANY STRAY BODY PARTS WILL BE BLAMED ON THE SLIDE.
THE ENEMY HAS FLED UNDER THE COVER OF THE STORM.
SHAAAA
WE'VE... FAILED.

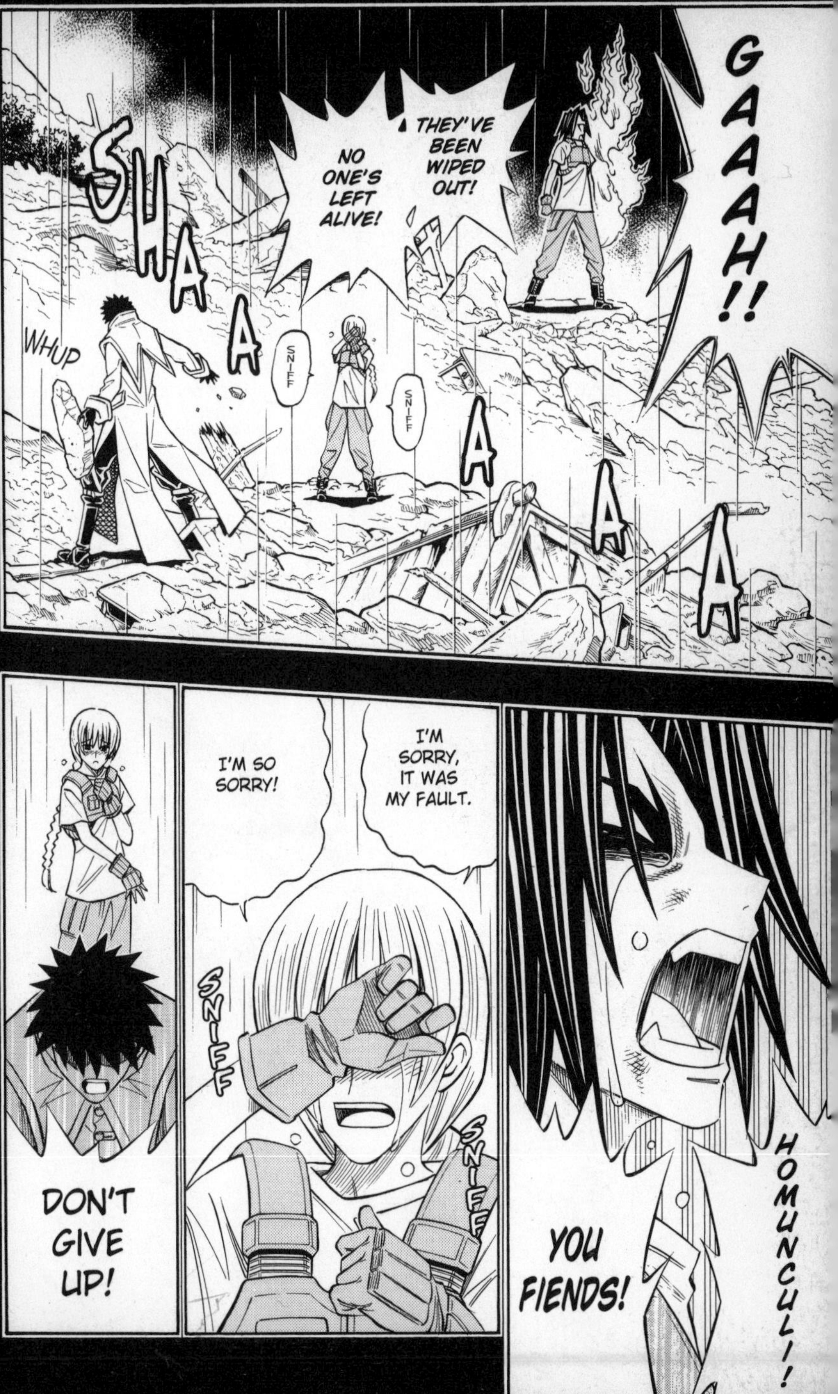
GAAAAH!!
THEY'VE BEEN WIPED OUT! NO ONE'S LEFT ALIVE!
SHAAAAAA
SNIFF
SNIFF
WHUP
HOMUNCULI!!
YOU FIENDS!
I'M SORRY, IT WAS MY FAULT.
I'M SO SORRY!
SNIFF
SNIFF
DON'T GIVE UP!

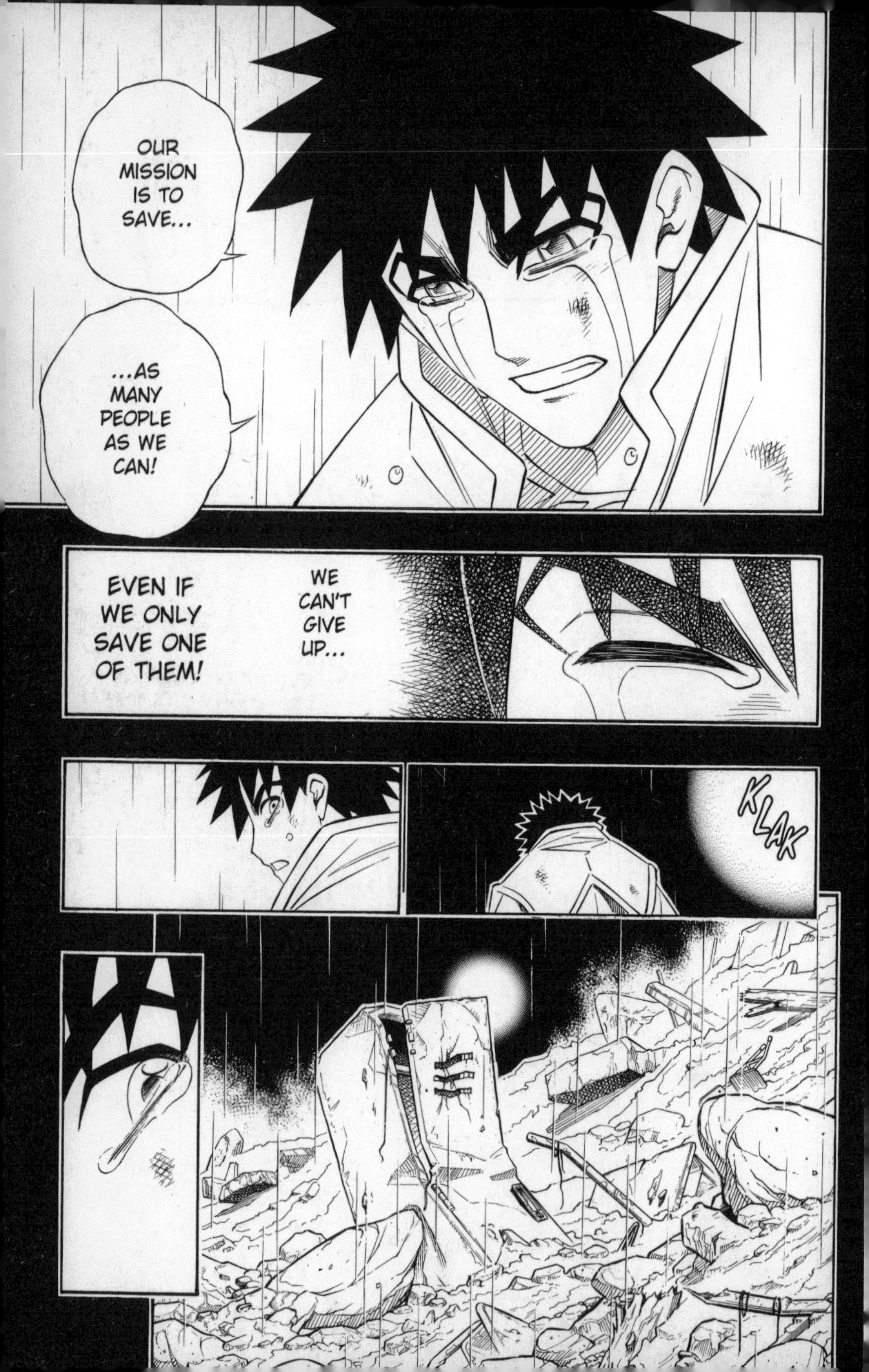
OUR MISSION IS TO SAVE...
...AS MANY PEOPLE AS WE CAN!
WE CAN'T GIVE UP...
EVEN IF WE ONLY SAVE ONE OF THEM!
KLAK

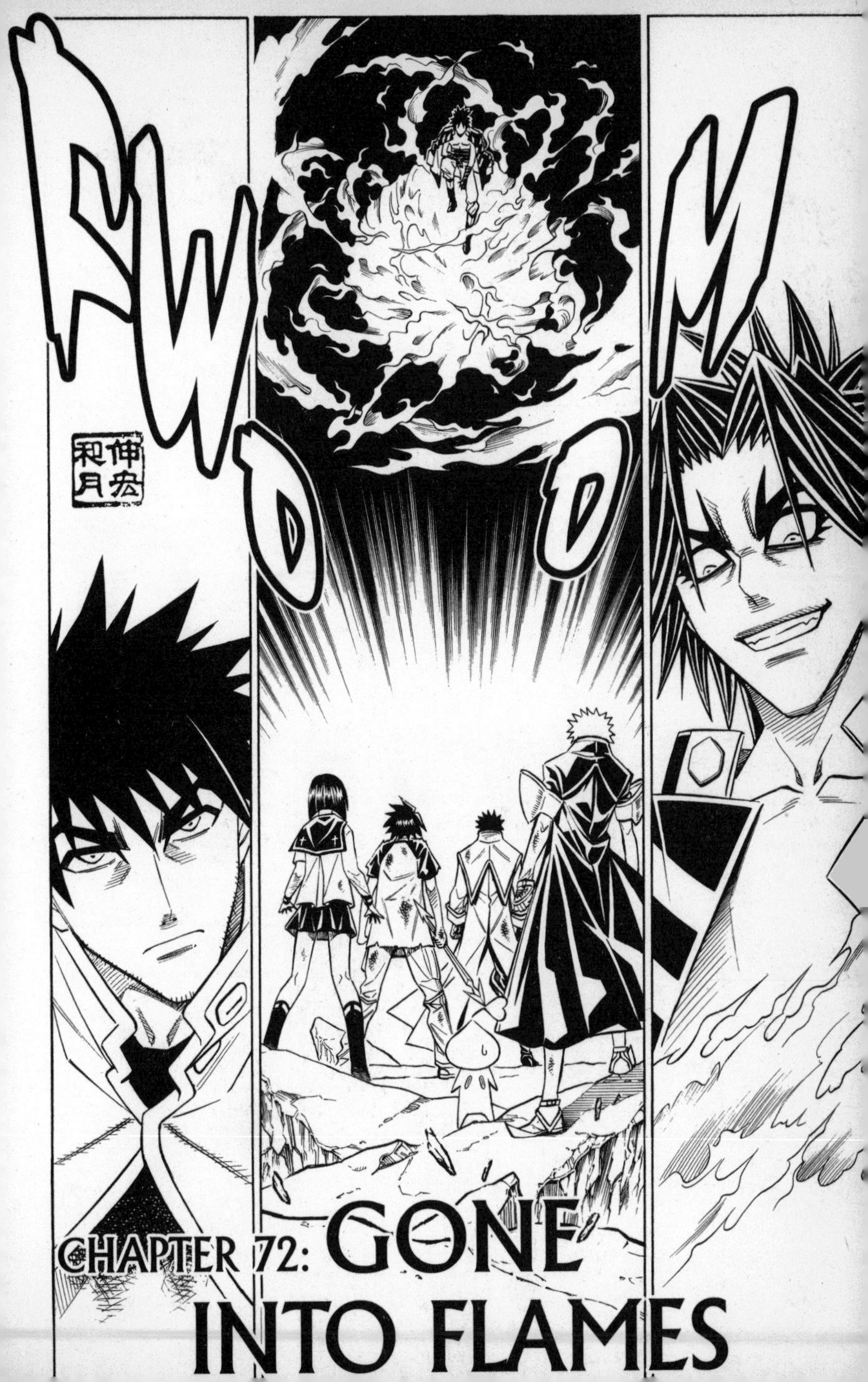
FWOOM
伸宏
和月
CHAPTER 72: GONE INTO FLAMES

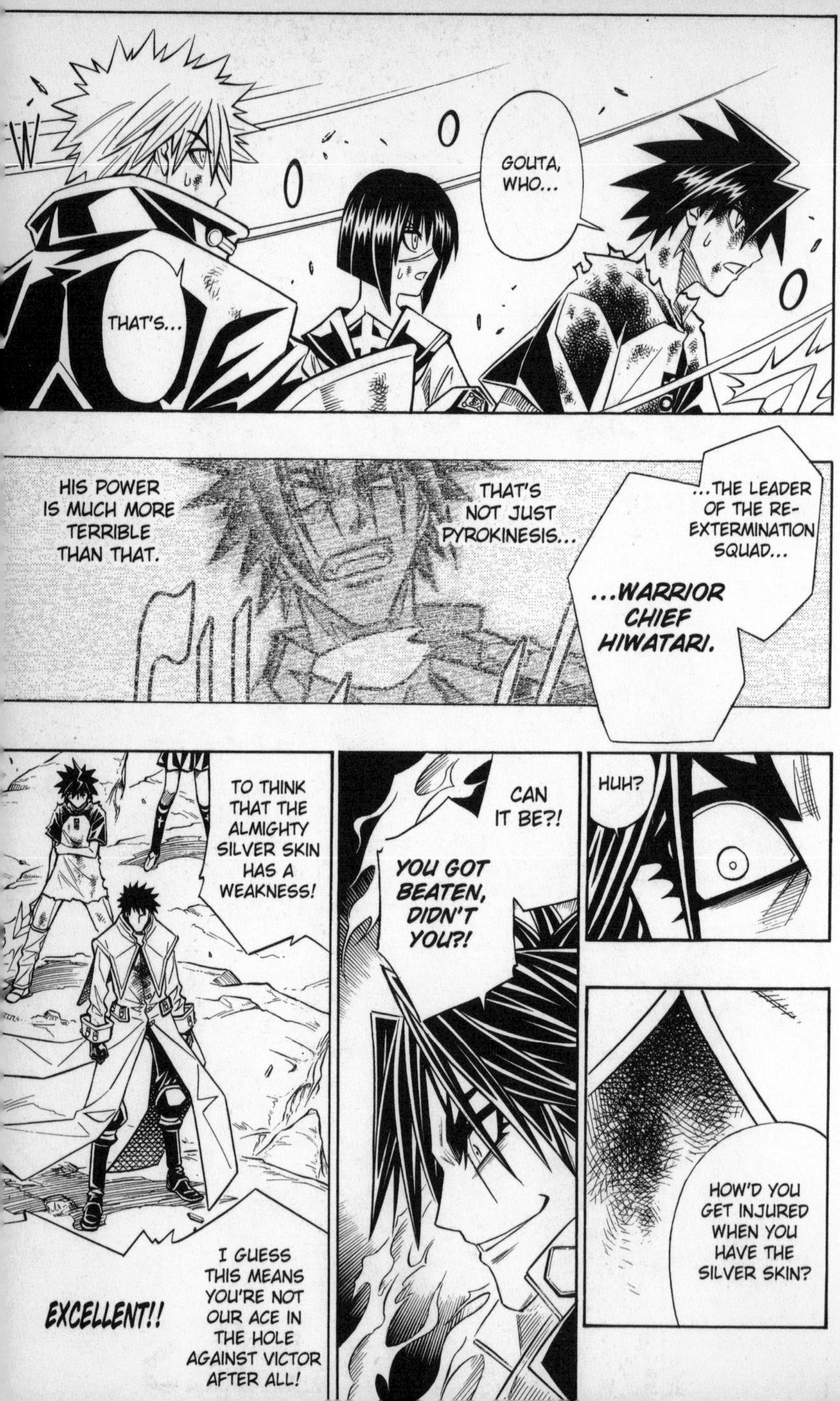
GOUTA, WHO...
THAT'S...
...THE LEADER OF THE RE-EXTERMINATION SQUAD...
...WARRIOR CHIEF HIWATARI.
THAT'S NOT JUST PYROKINESIS...
HIS POWER IS MUCH MORE TERRIBLE THAN THAT.
HUH?
HOW'D YOU GET INJURED WHEN YOU HAVE THE SILVER SKIN?
CAN IT BE?!
YOU GOT BEATEN, DIDN'T YOU?!
TO THINK THAT THE ALMIGHTY SILVER SKIN HAS A WEAKNESS!
I GUESS THIS MEANS YOU'RE NOT OUR ACE IN THE HOLE AGAINST VICTOR AFTER ALL!
EXCELLENT!!

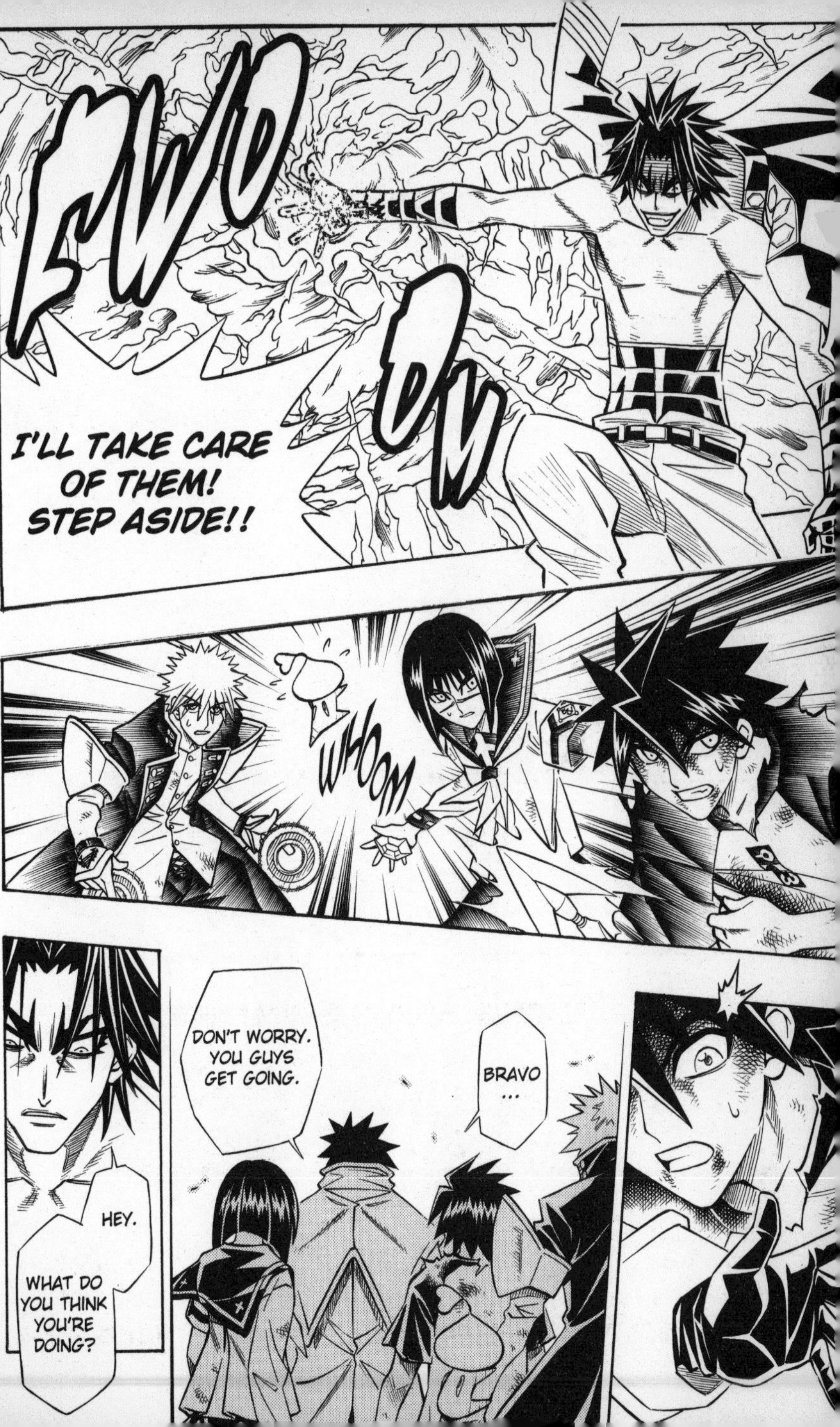
I'LL TAKE CARE OF THEM! STEP ASIDE!!
WHOOM
BRAVO ...
DON'T WORRY. YOU GUYS GET GOING.
HEY.
WHAT DO YOU THINK YOU'RE DOING?

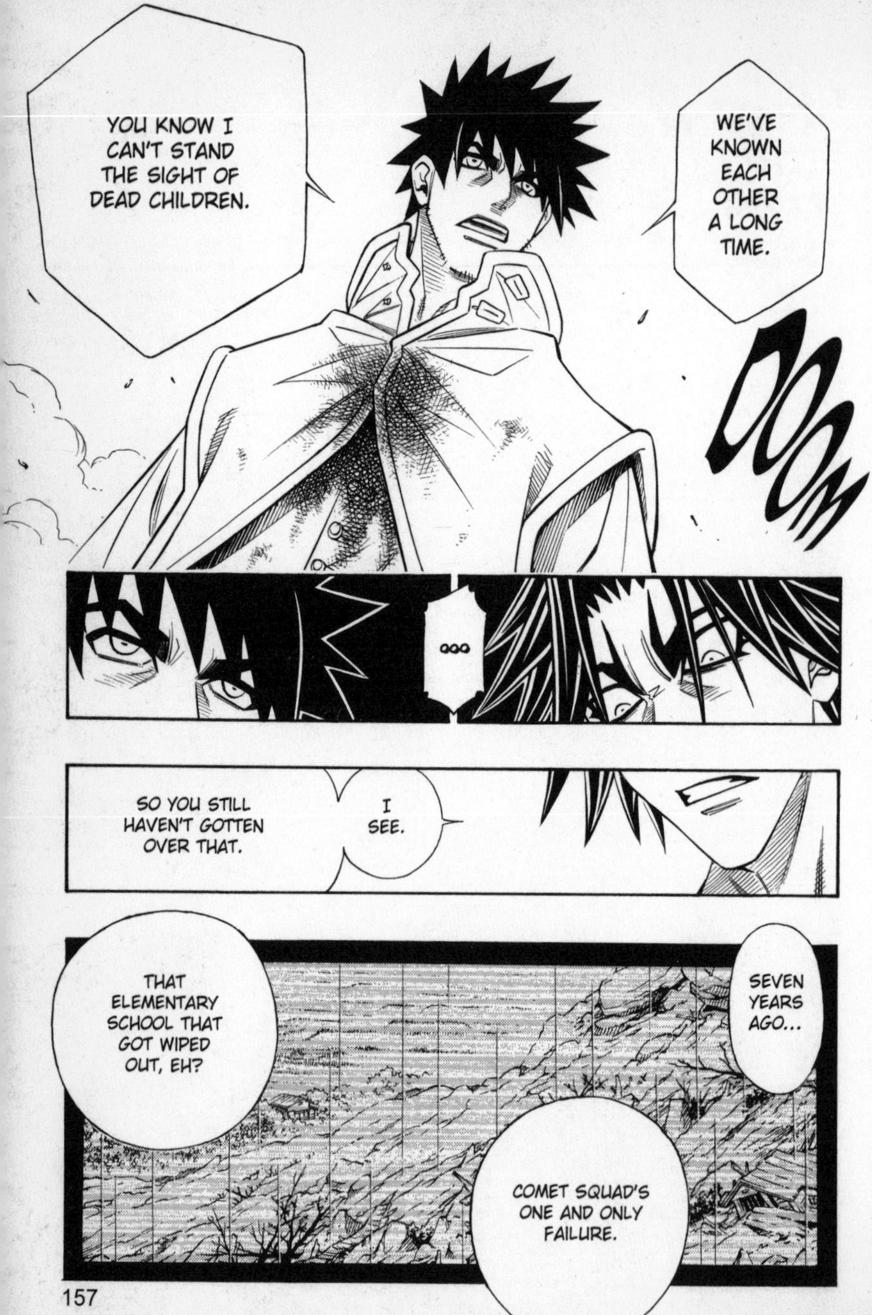
WE'VE KNOWN EACH OTHER A LONG TIME.
YOU KNOW I CAN'T STAND THE SIGHT OF DEAD CHILDREN.
DOOM
...
I SEE.
SO YOU STILL HAVEN'T GOTTEN OVER THAT.
SEVEN YEARS AGO...
THAT ELEMENTARY SCHOOL THAT GOT WIPED OUT, EH?
COMET SQUAD'S ONE AND ONLY FAILURE.

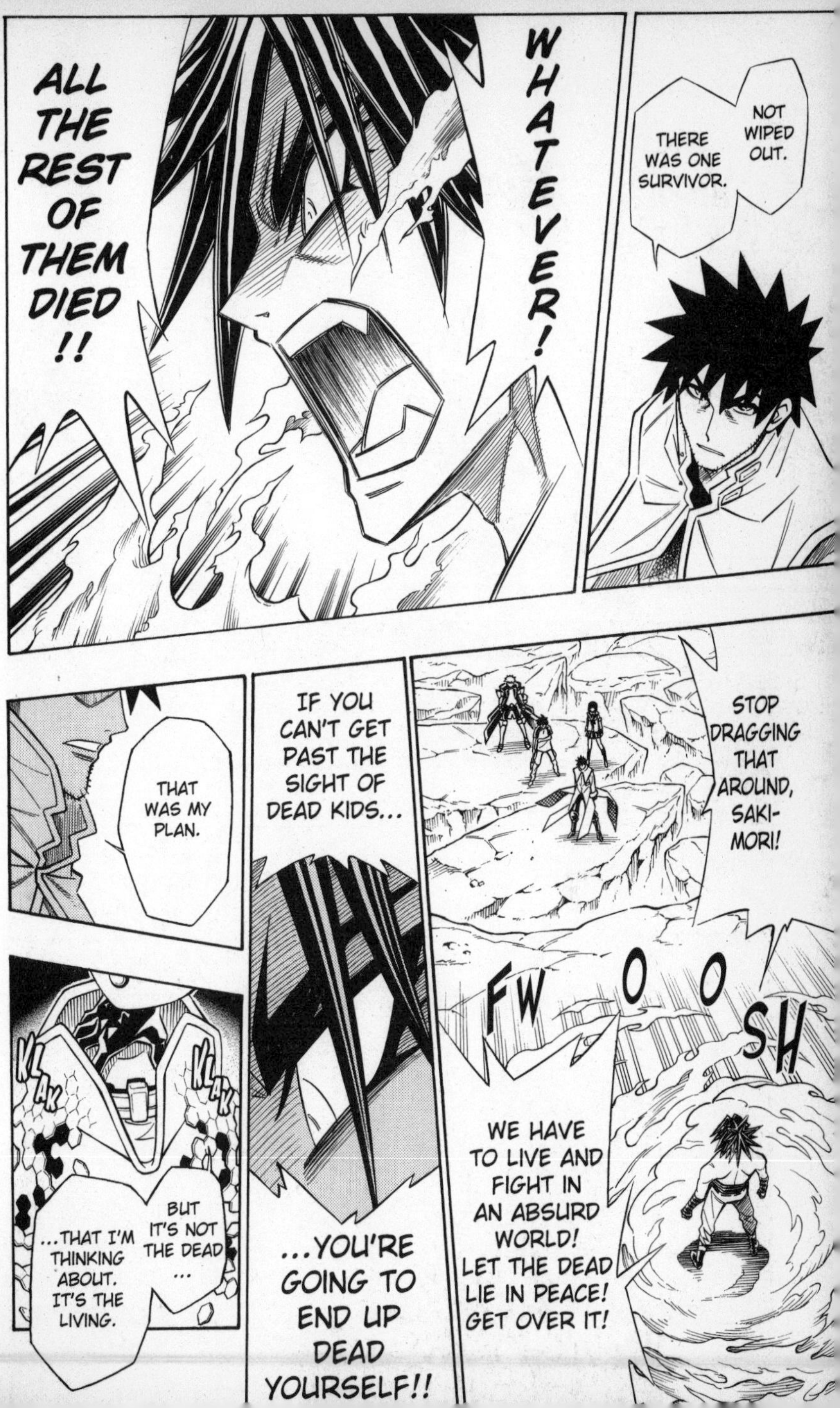
NOT WIPED OUT.
THERE WAS ONE SURVIVOR.
WHATEVER!
ALL THE REST OF THEM DIED!!
STOP DRAGGING THAT AROUND, SAKI-MORI!
FWOOOSH
WE HAVE TO LIVE AND FIGHT IN AN ABSURD WORLD! LET THE DEAD LIE IN PEACE! GET OVER IT!
IF YOU CAN'T GET PAST THE SIGHT OF DEAD KIDS...
...YOU'RE GOING TO END UP DEAD YOURSELF!!
THAT WAS MY PLAN.
KLAK
KLAK
BUT IT'S NOT THE DEAD...
...THAT I'M THINKING ABOUT. IT'S THE LIVING.

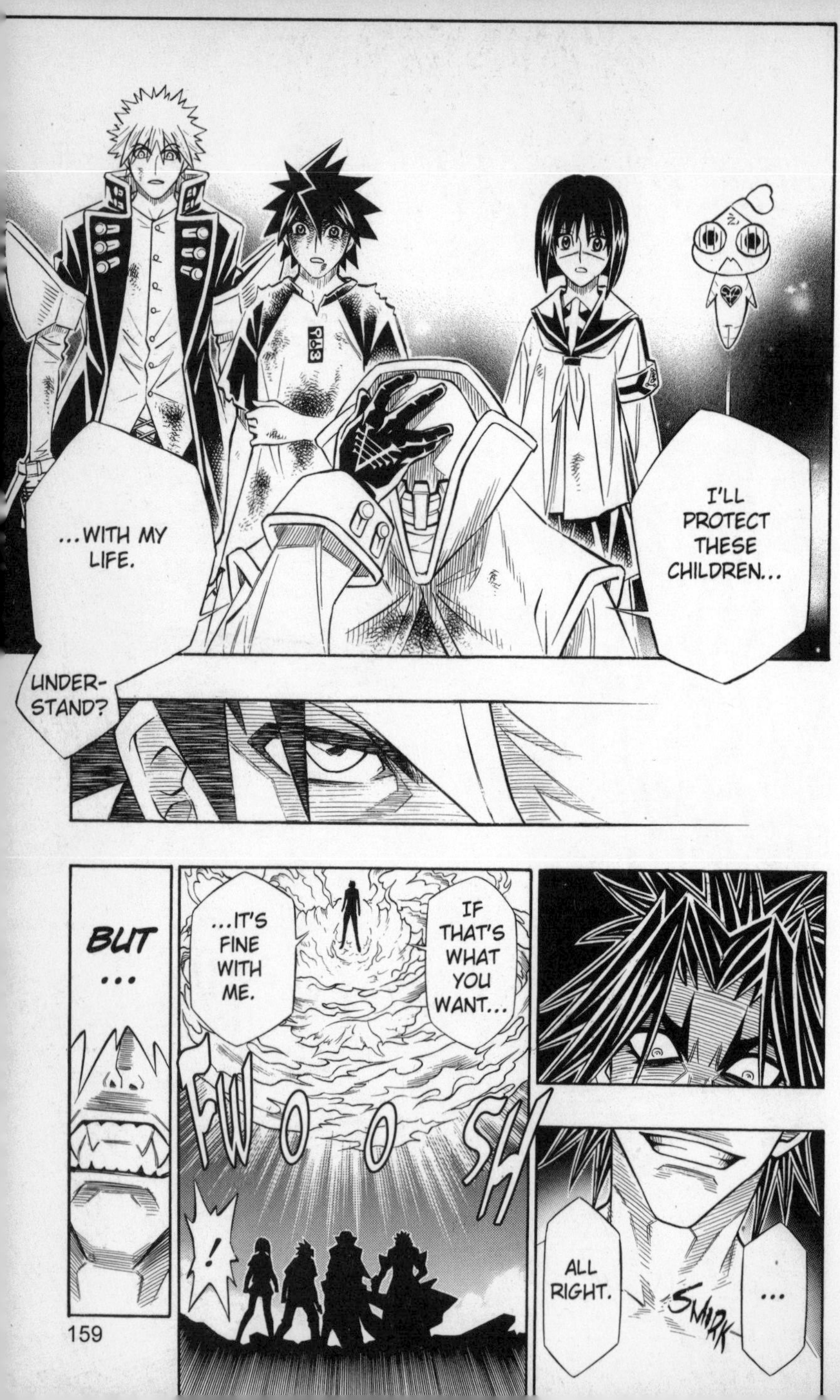
I'LL PROTECT THESE CHILDREN...
...WITH MY LIFE.
UNDER-STAND?
...
SMIRK
ALL RIGHT.
IF THAT'S WHAT YOU WANT...
...IT'S FINE WITH ME.
FWOOSH
!
BUT ...

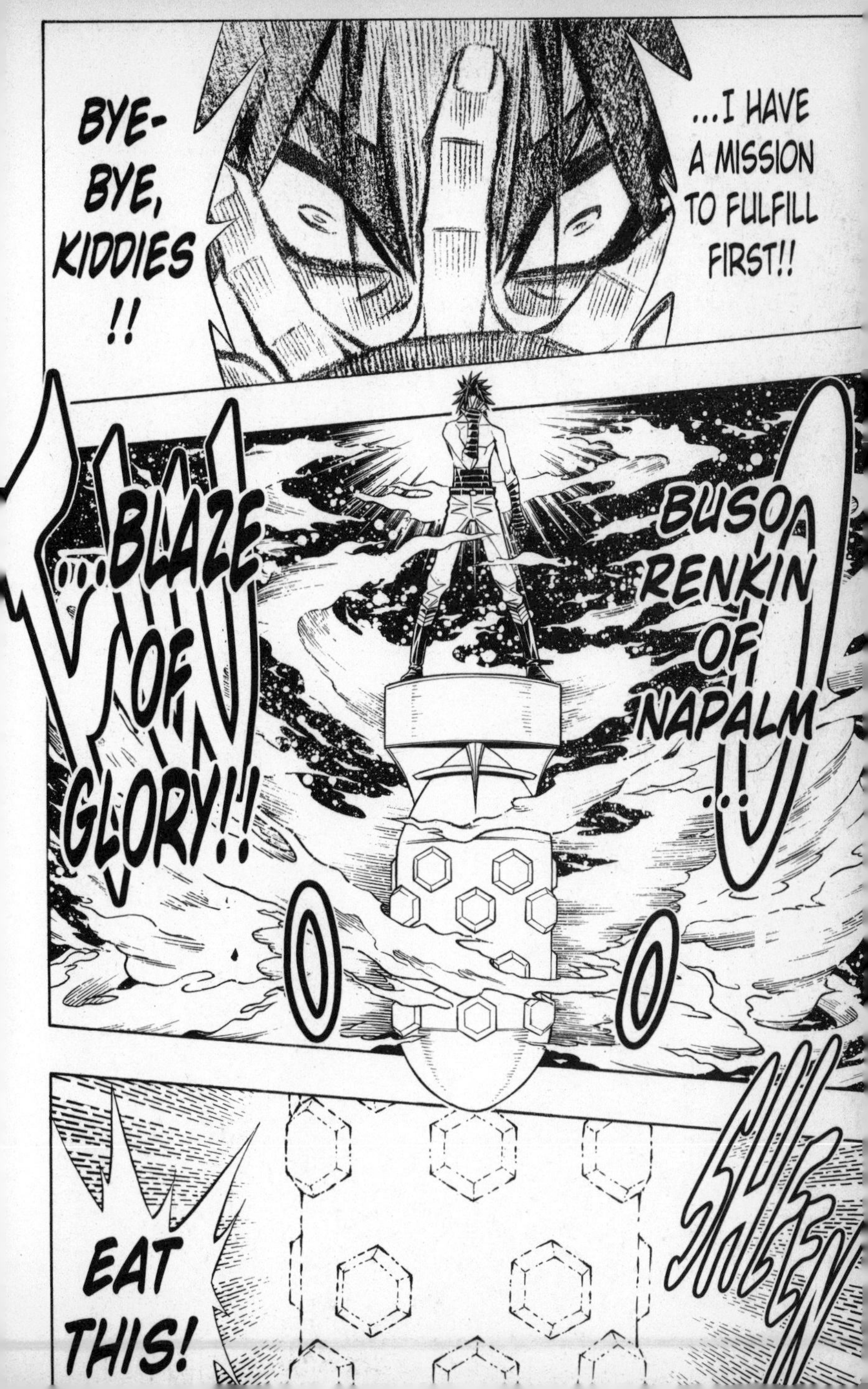
...I HAVE A MISSION TO FULFILL FIRST!!
BYE-BYE, KIDDIES!!
BUSO RENKIN OF NAPALM...
...BLAZE OF GLORY!!
EAT THIS!

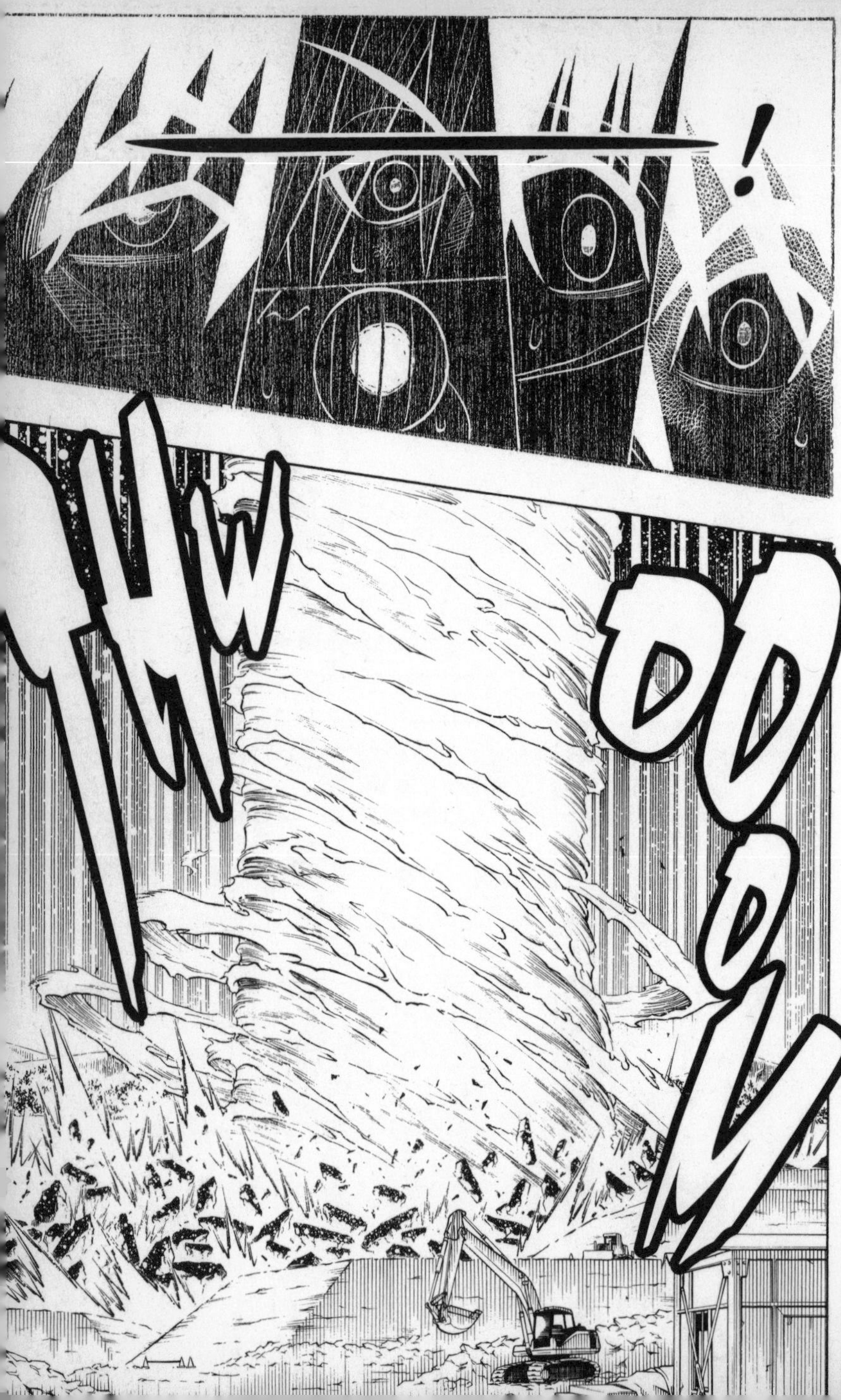
!
THWOOOM

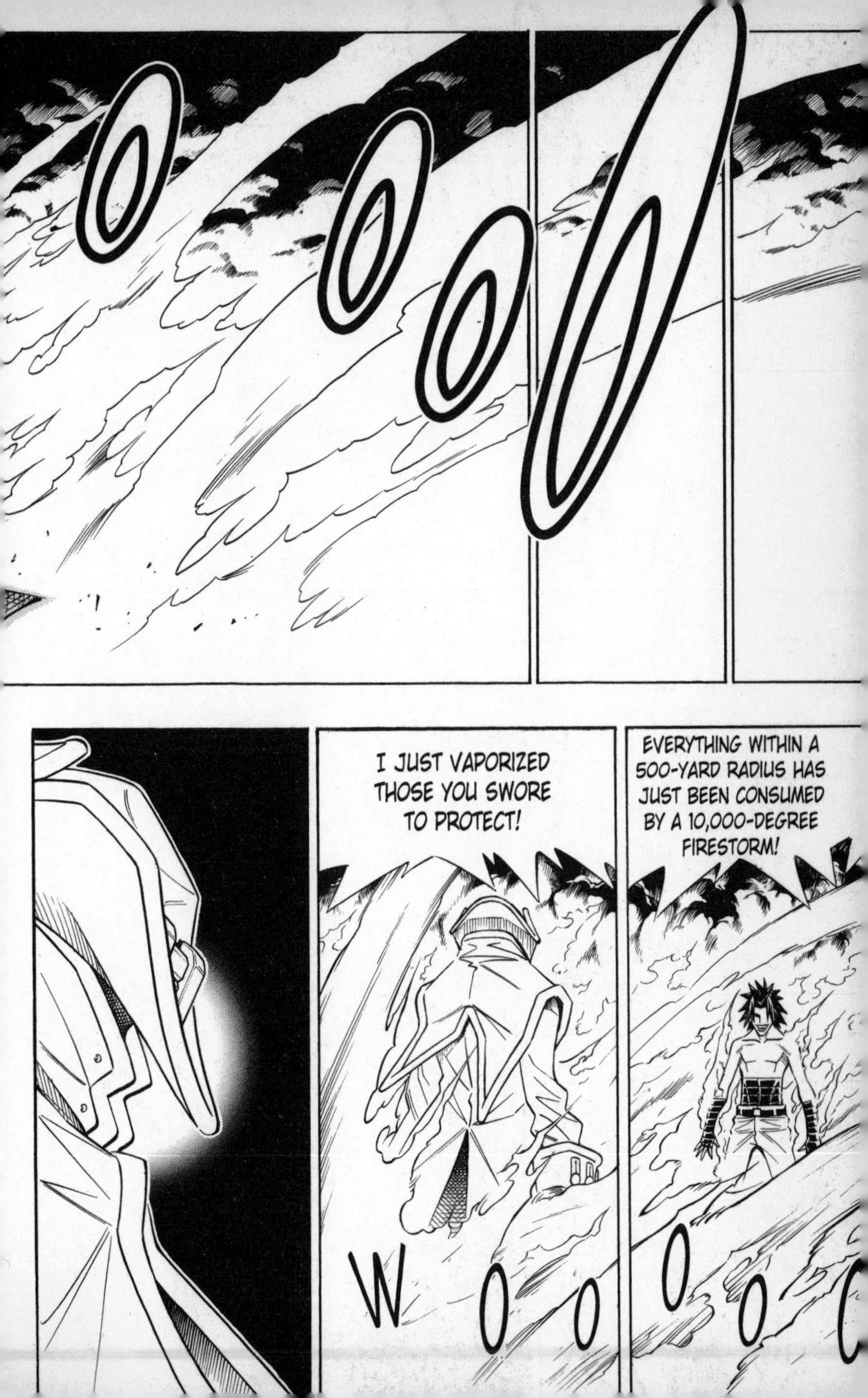
EVERYTHING WITHIN A 500-YARD RADIUS HAS JUST BEEN CONSUMED BY A 10,000-DEGREE FIRESTORM!
I JUST VAPORIZED THOSE YOU SWORE TO PROTECT!
WOOOO

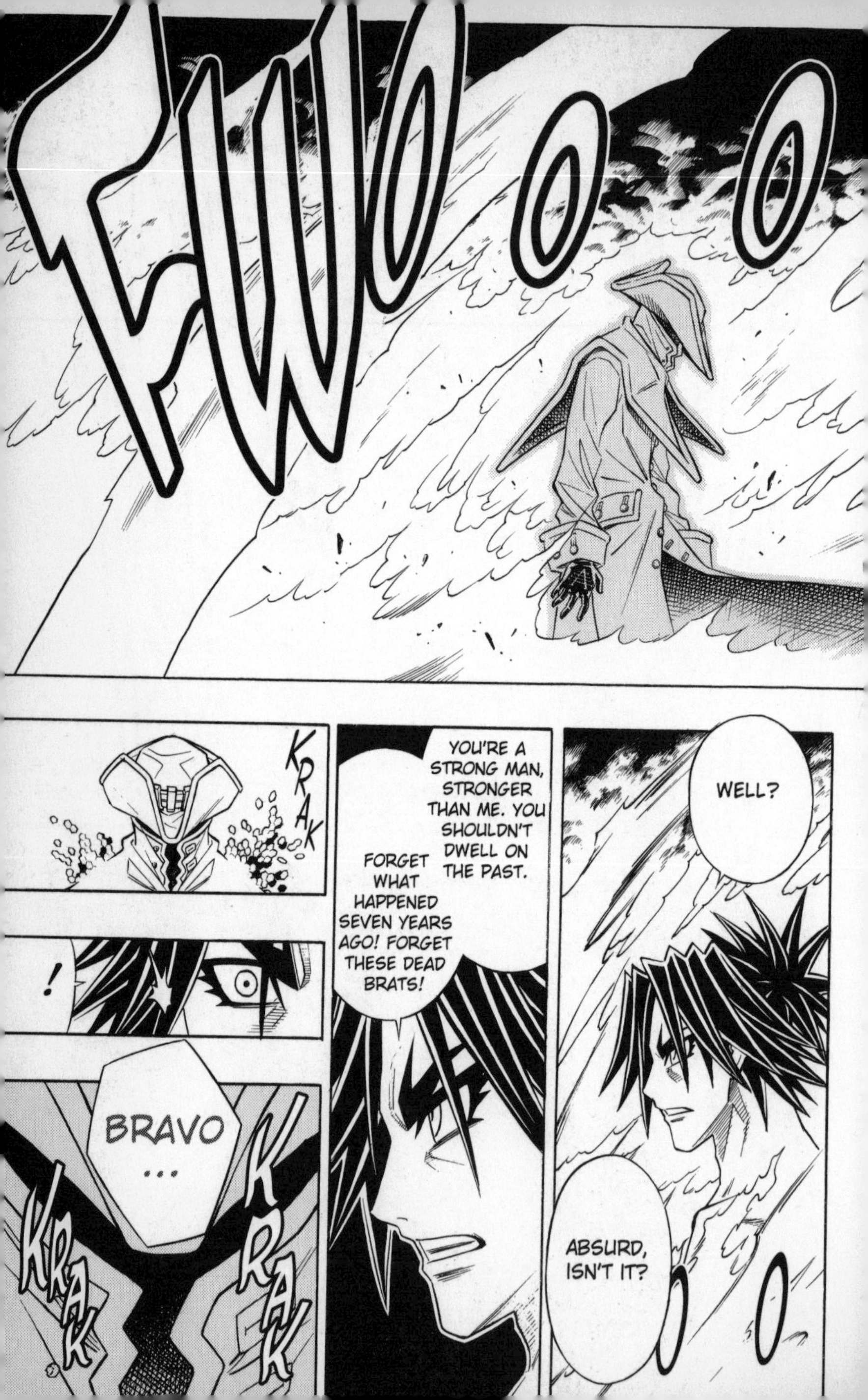
FWOOOO
WELL?
ABSURD, ISN'T IT?
YOU'RE A STRONG MAN, STRONGER THAN ME. YOU SHOULDN'T DWELL ON THE PAST.
FORGET WHAT HAPPENED SEVEN YEARS AGO! FORGET THESE DEAD BRATS!
KRAK
!
BRAVO ...
KRAK
KRAK

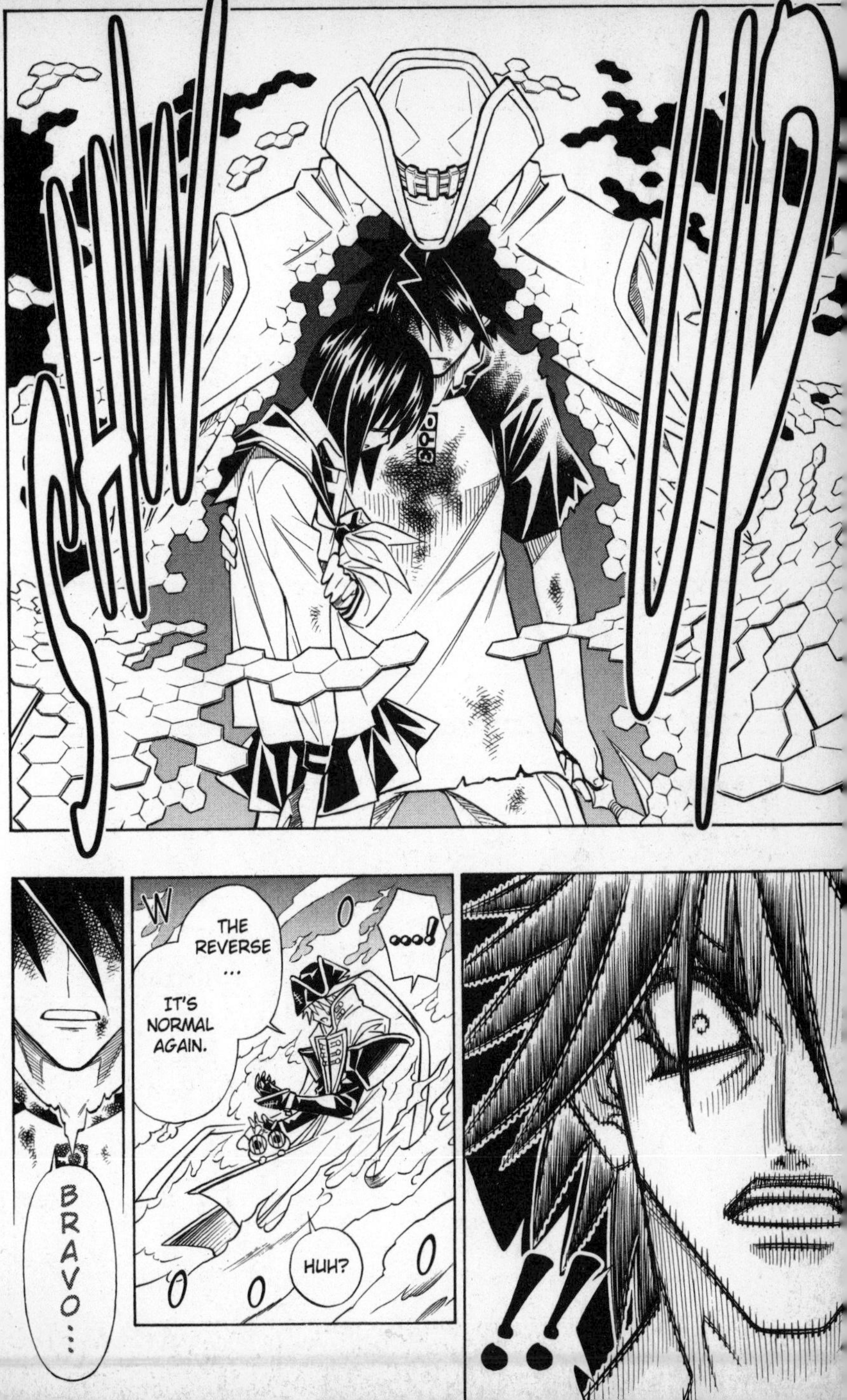
!!
...!
THE REVERSE ... IT'S NORMAL AGAIN.
HUH?
BRAVO...

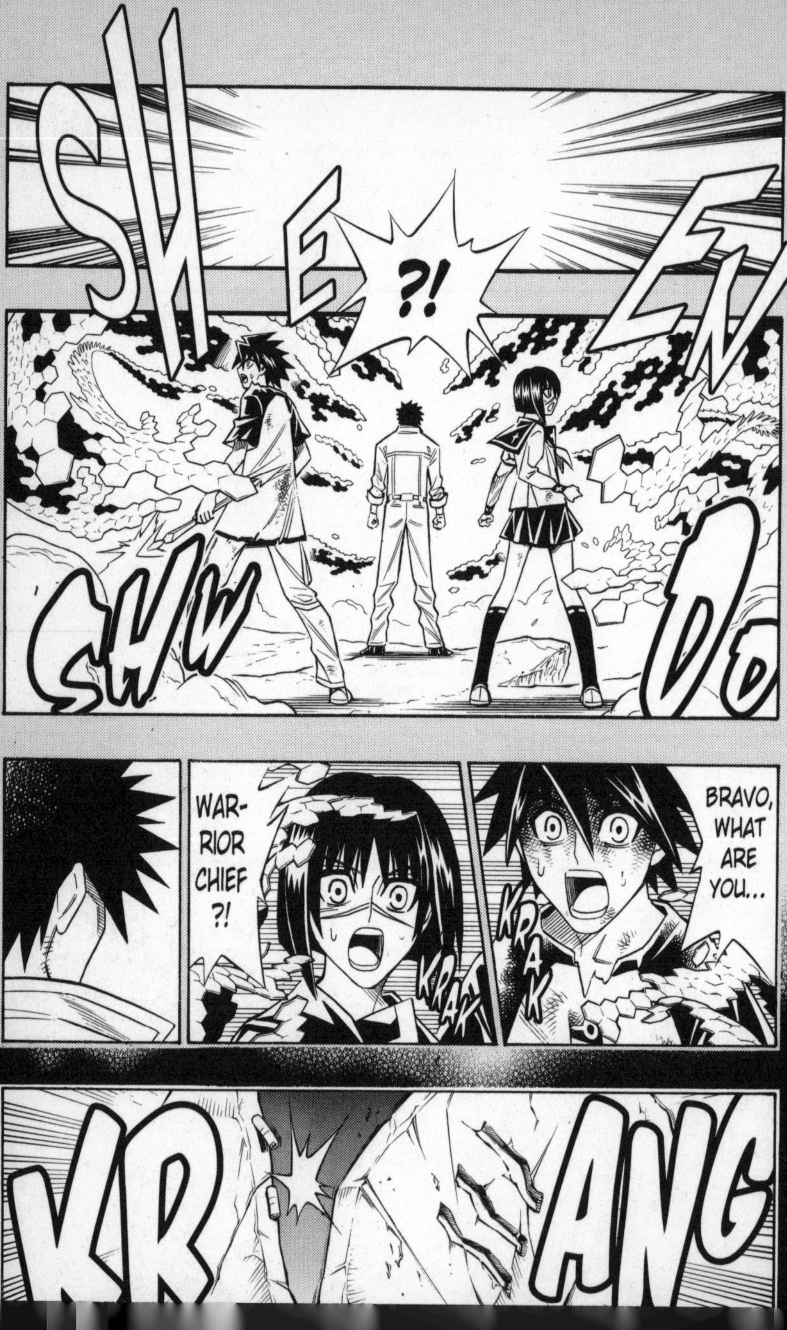
SHEEN
?!
SHWDO
BRAVO, WHAT ARE YOU...
KRAK
WAR-RIOR CHIEF ?!
KRAK
KRANG

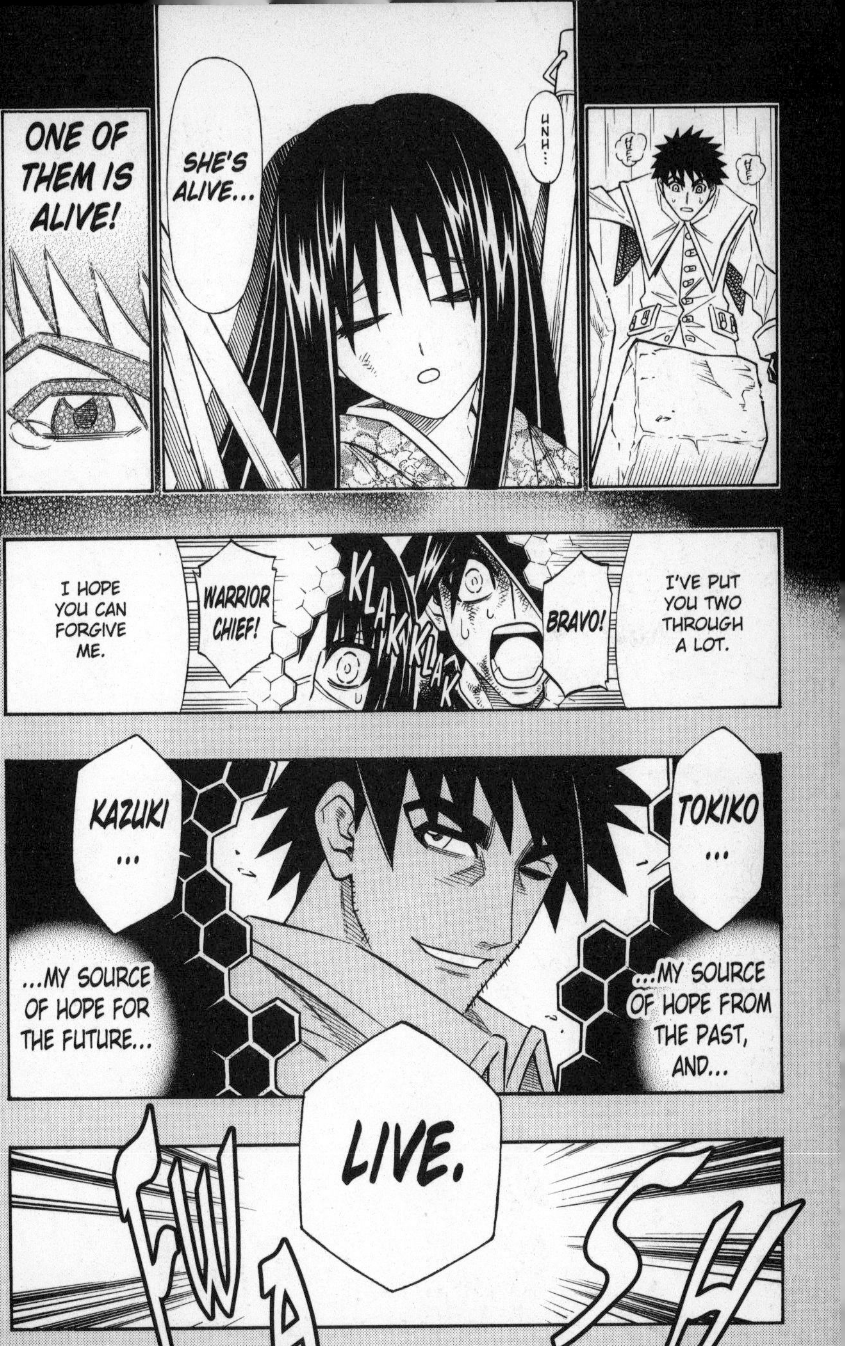
UNH...
SHE'S ALIVE...
ONE OF THEM IS ALIVE!
I'VE PUT YOU TWO THROUGH A LOT.
BRAVO!
KLAKKLAKKLAK
WARRIOR CHIEF!
I HOPE YOU CAN FORGIVE ME.
TOKIKO ...
KAZUKI ...
...MY SOURCE OF HOPE FROM THE PAST, AND...
...MY SOURCE OF HOPE FOR THE FUTURE...
LIVE.
FWASH

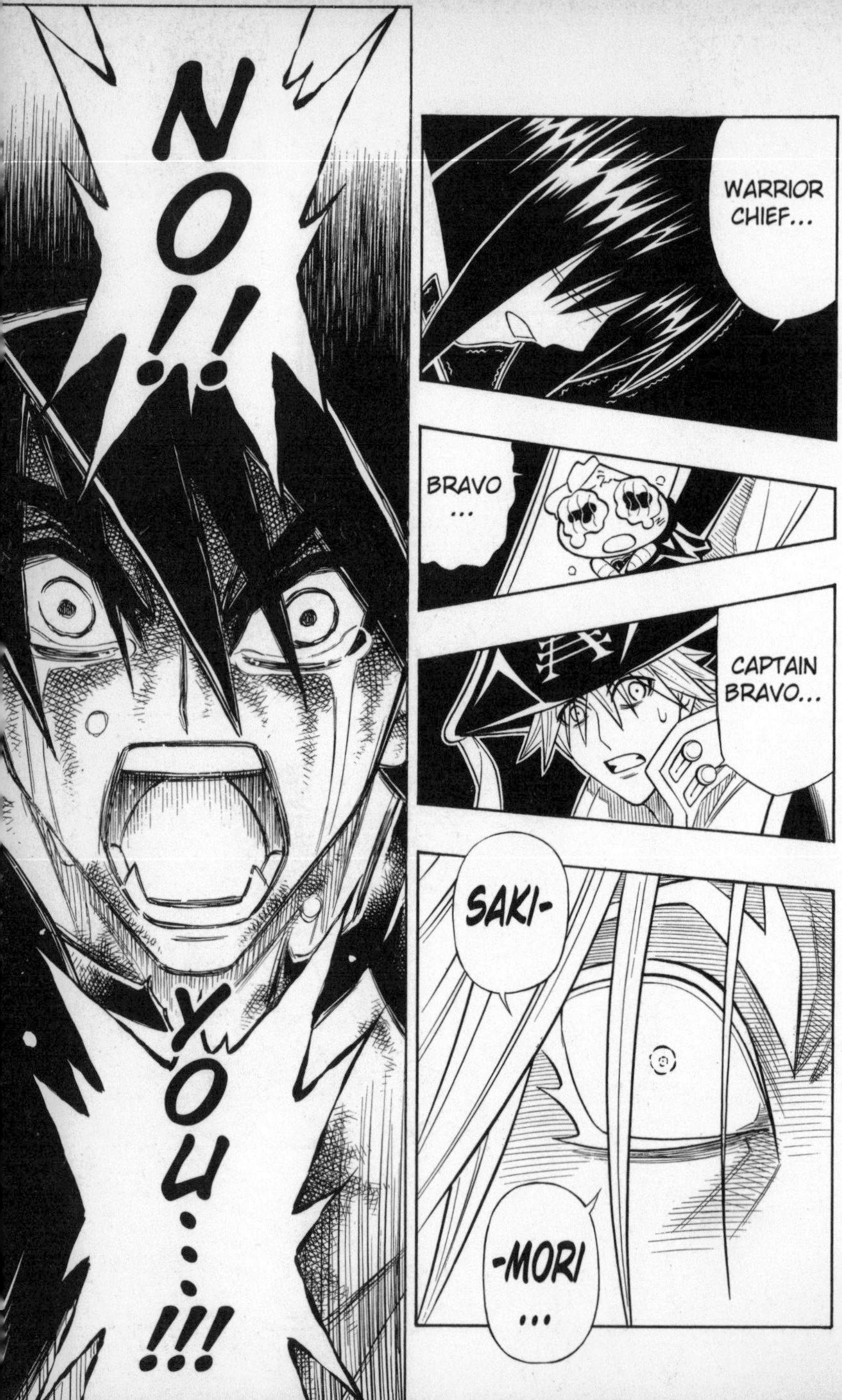
WARRIOR CHIEF...
BRAVO ...
CAPTAIN BRAVO...
SAKI-
-MORI ...
NO!!
YOU...!!!

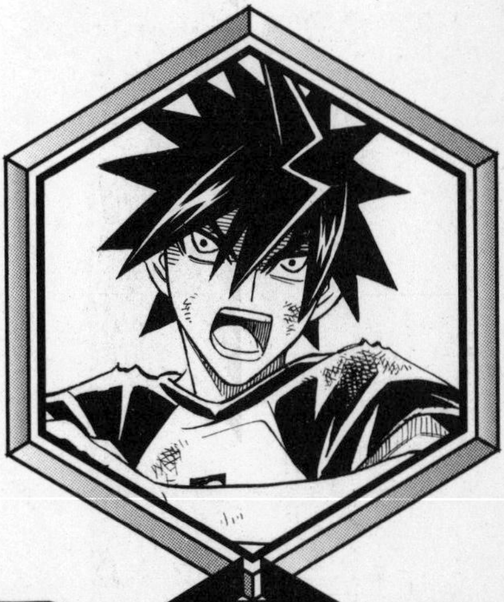

Buso Renkin
ブソウレンキン

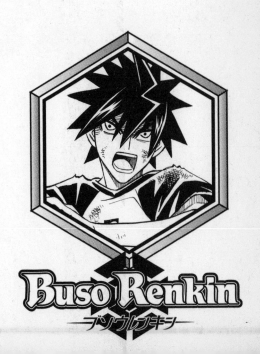

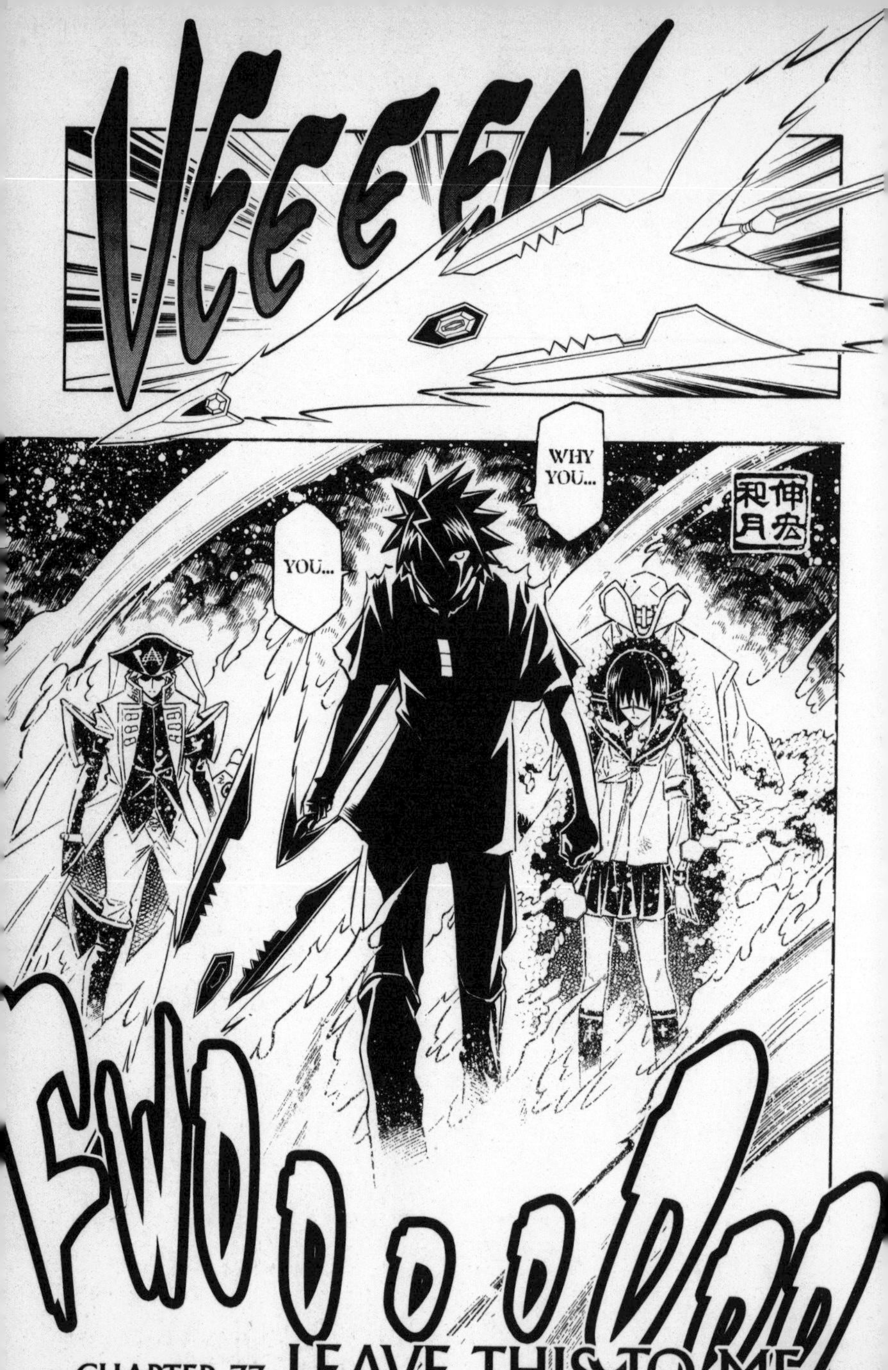
VEEEEN
WHY YOU...
YOU...

CHAPTER 73: LEAVE THIS TO ME

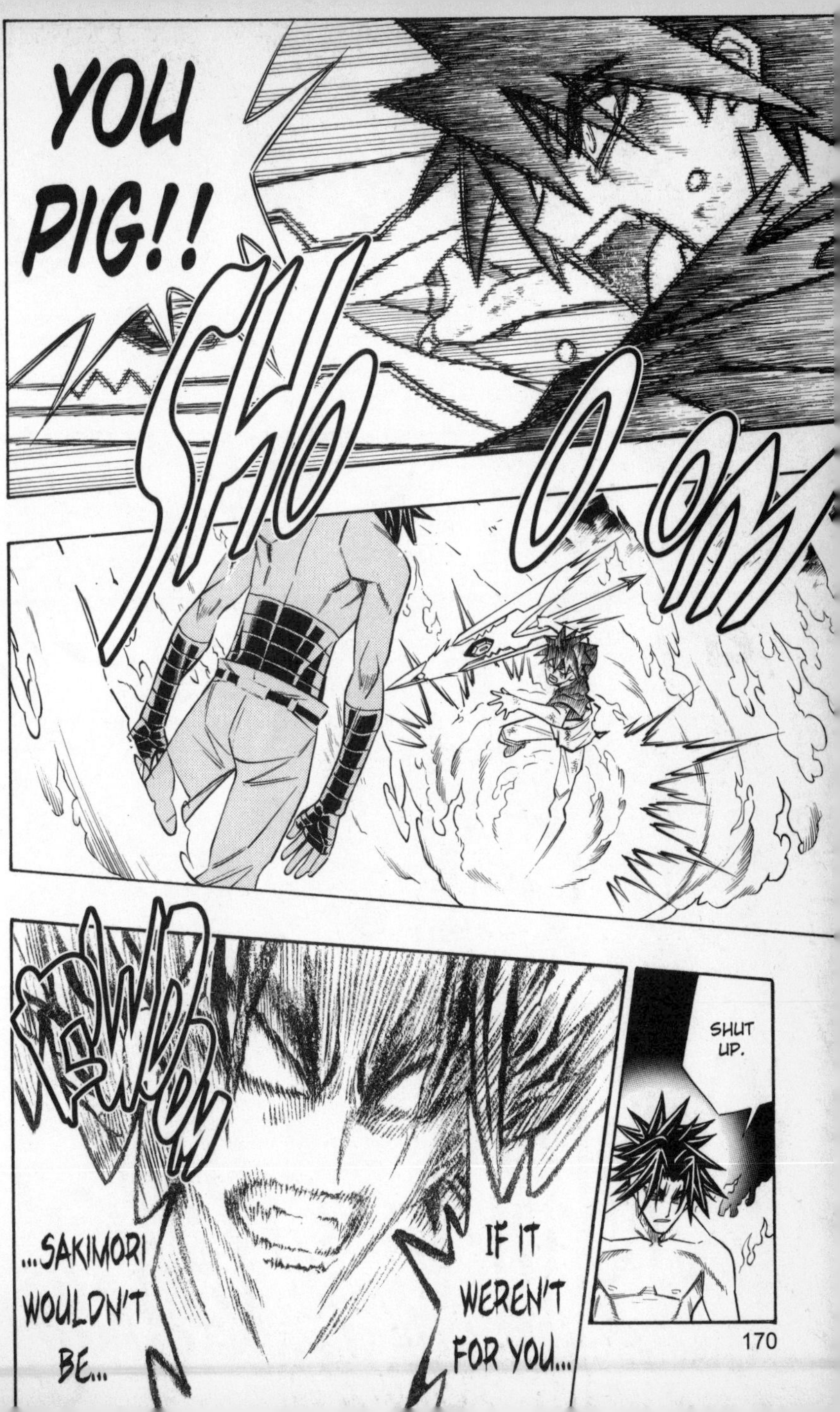
YOU PIG!!
SHOOOM
SHUT UP.
IF IT WEREN'T FOR YOU...
...SAKIMORI WOULDN'T BE...

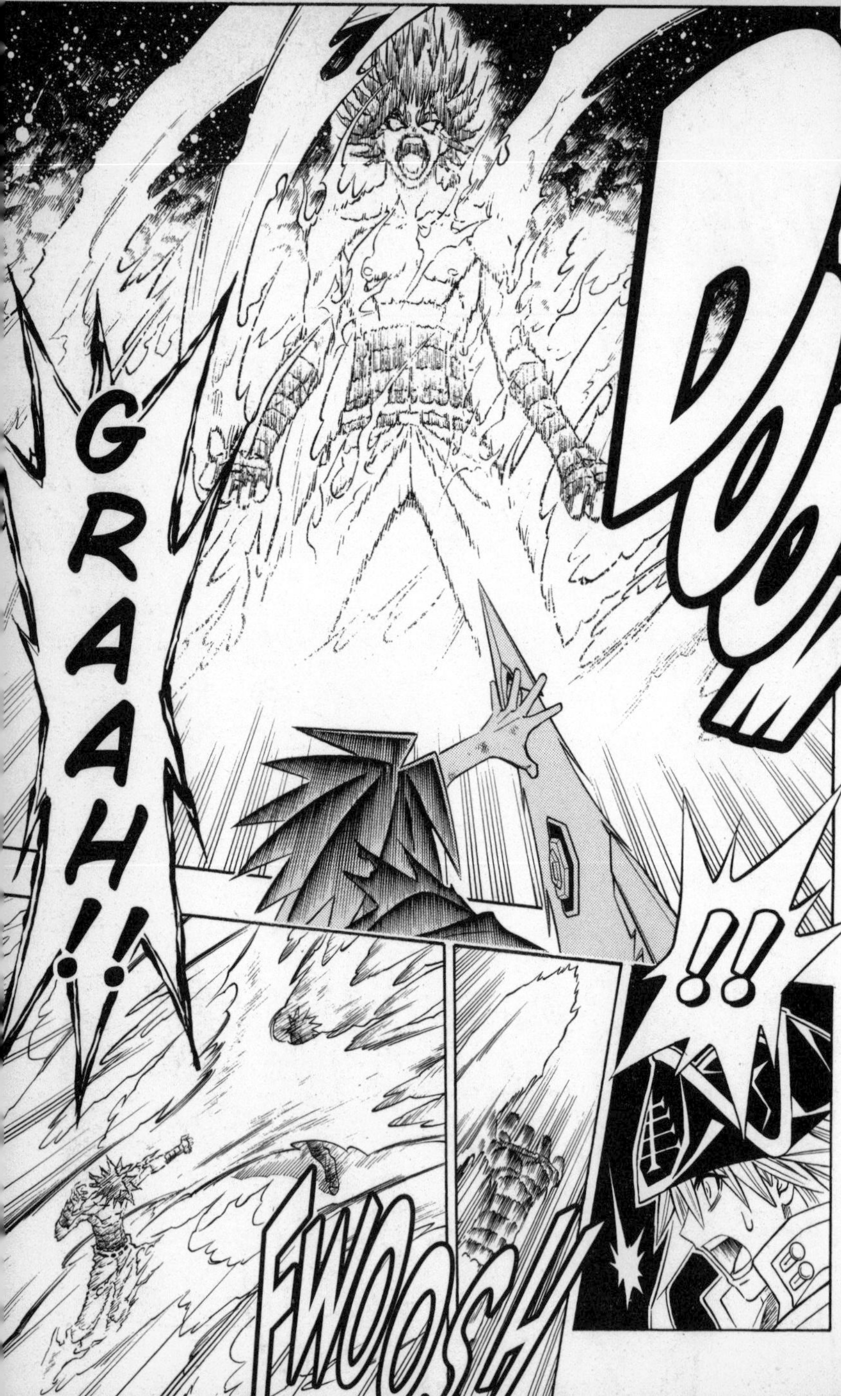
DOOM
GRAAH!!
!!
FWOOSH

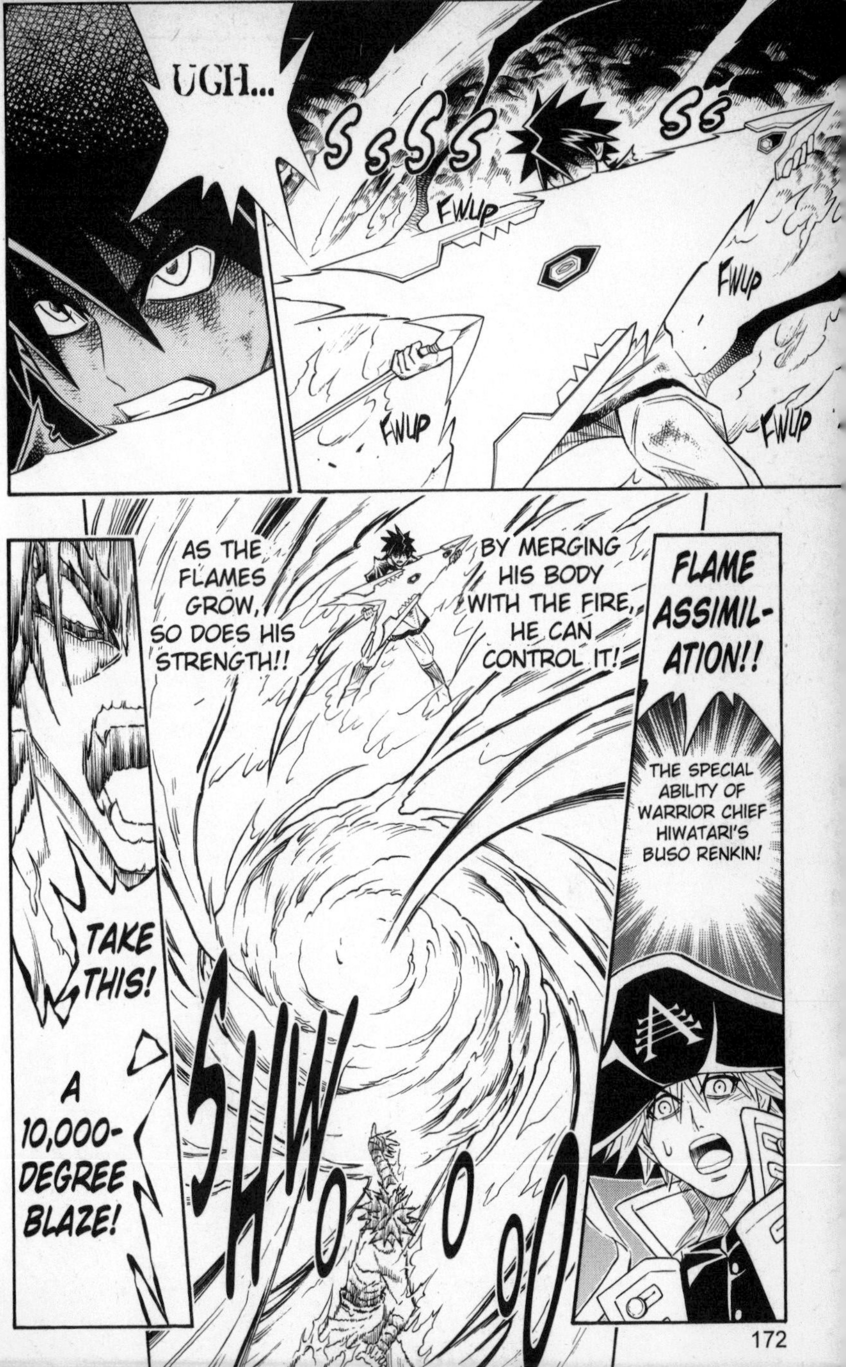
SSSS
SS
FWUP
FWUP
FWUP
FWUP
UGH...
FLAME ASSIMIL-ATION!!
THE SPECIAL ABILITY OF WARRIOR CHIEF HIWATARI'S BUSO RENKIN!
BY MERGING HIS BODY WITH THE FIRE, HE CAN CONTROL IT!
AS THE FLAMES GROW, SO DOES HIS STRENGTH!!
SHWOOOOO
TAKE THIS!
A 10,000-DEGREE BLAZE!

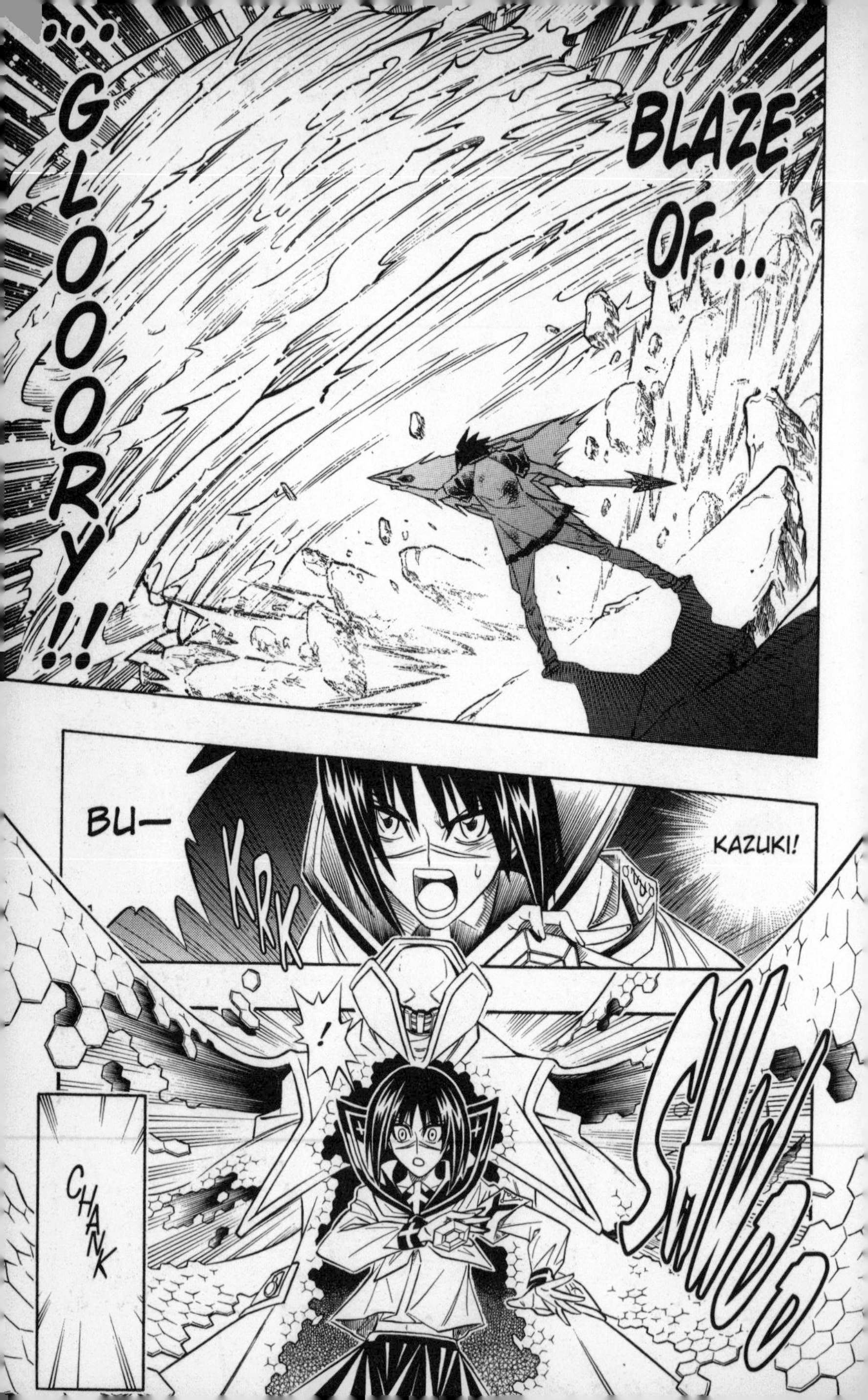
BLAZE OF...
...GLOOOORY!!
KAZUKI!
BU—
KRK
!
SHWOO
CHANK

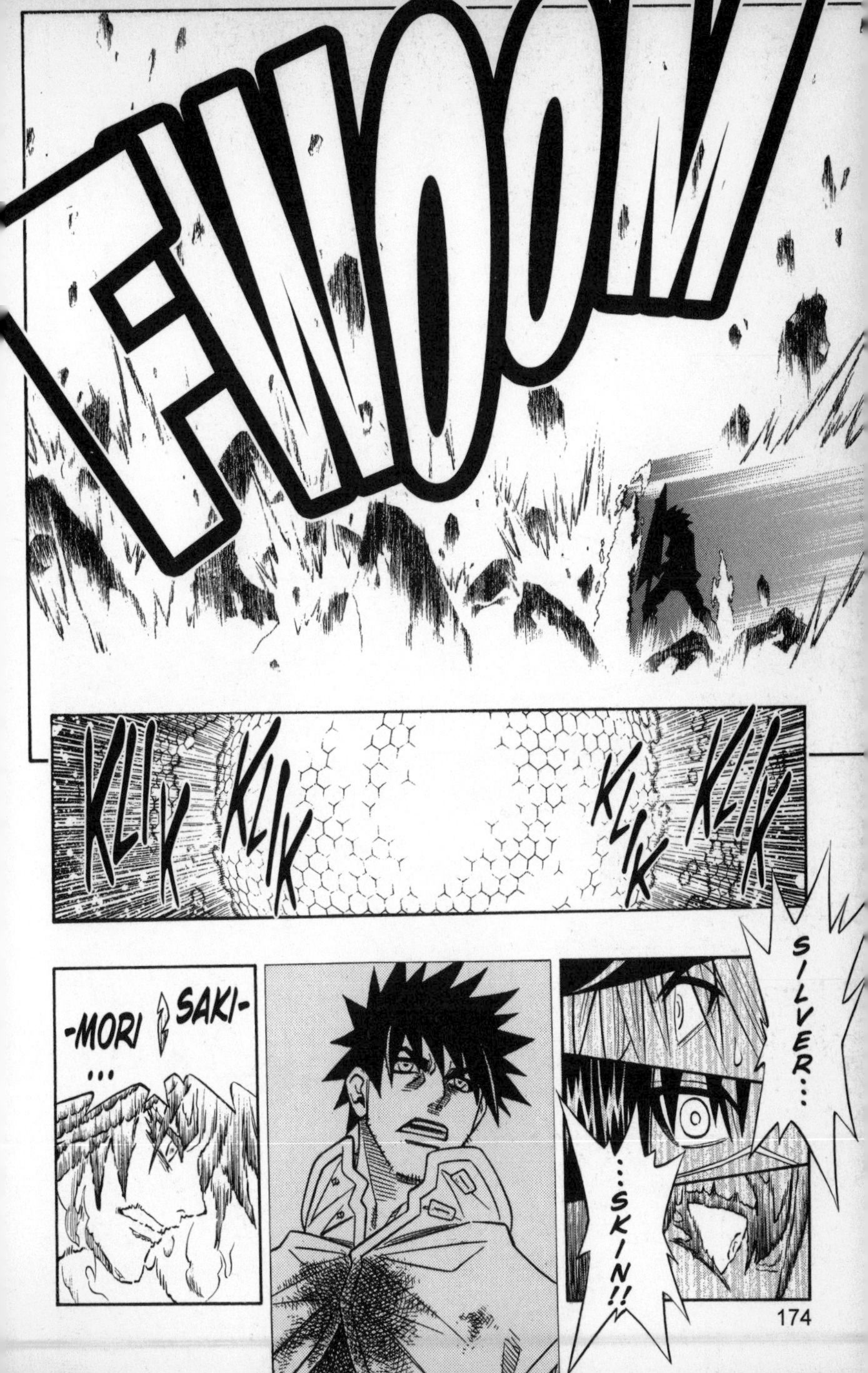
THOOM!
KLIK
KLIK
KLIK
KLIK
SILVER...
...SKIN!!
SAKI-
-MORI
...

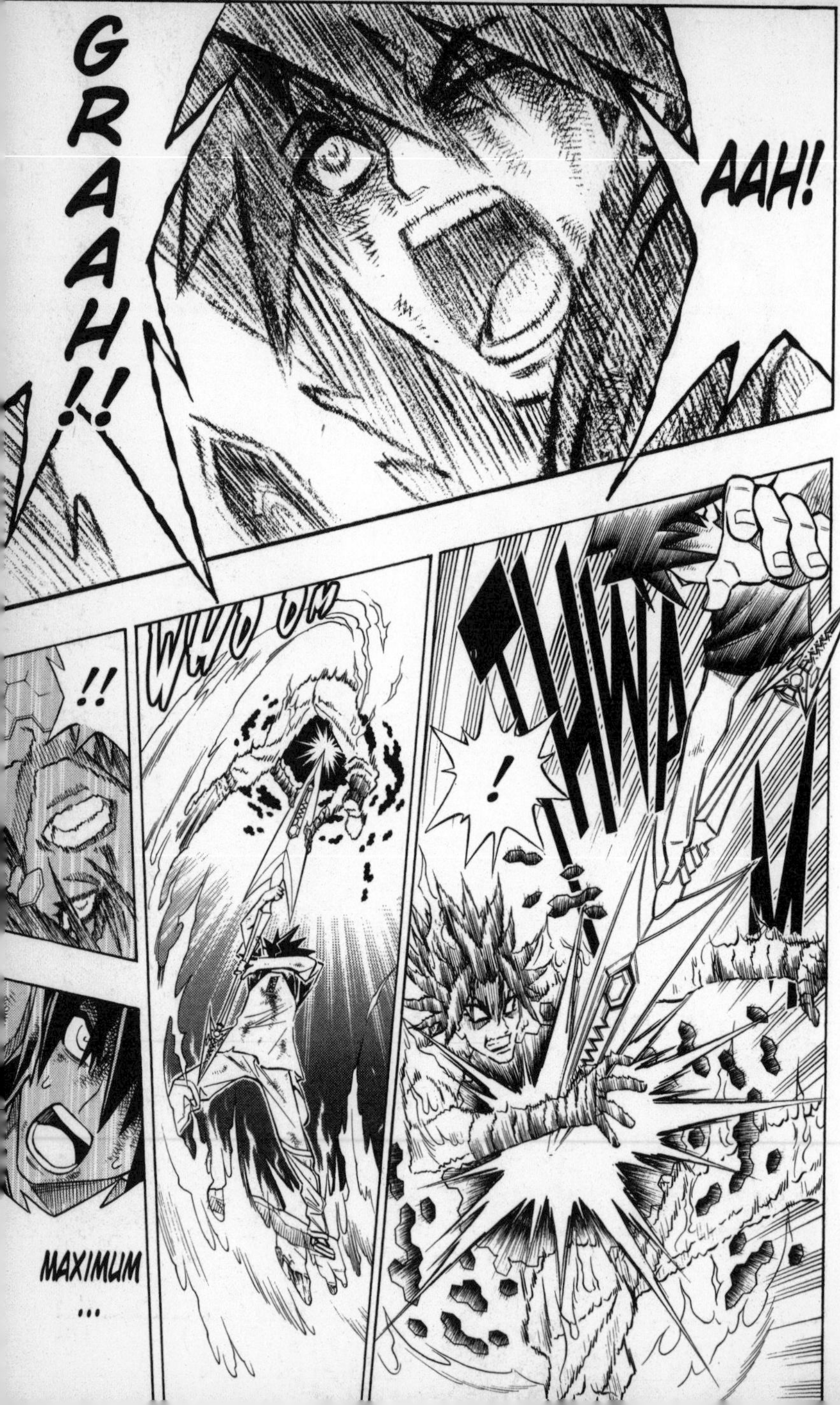
AAH!
GRAAAH!!
THWAM
!
WHOOM
!!
MAXIMUM
...

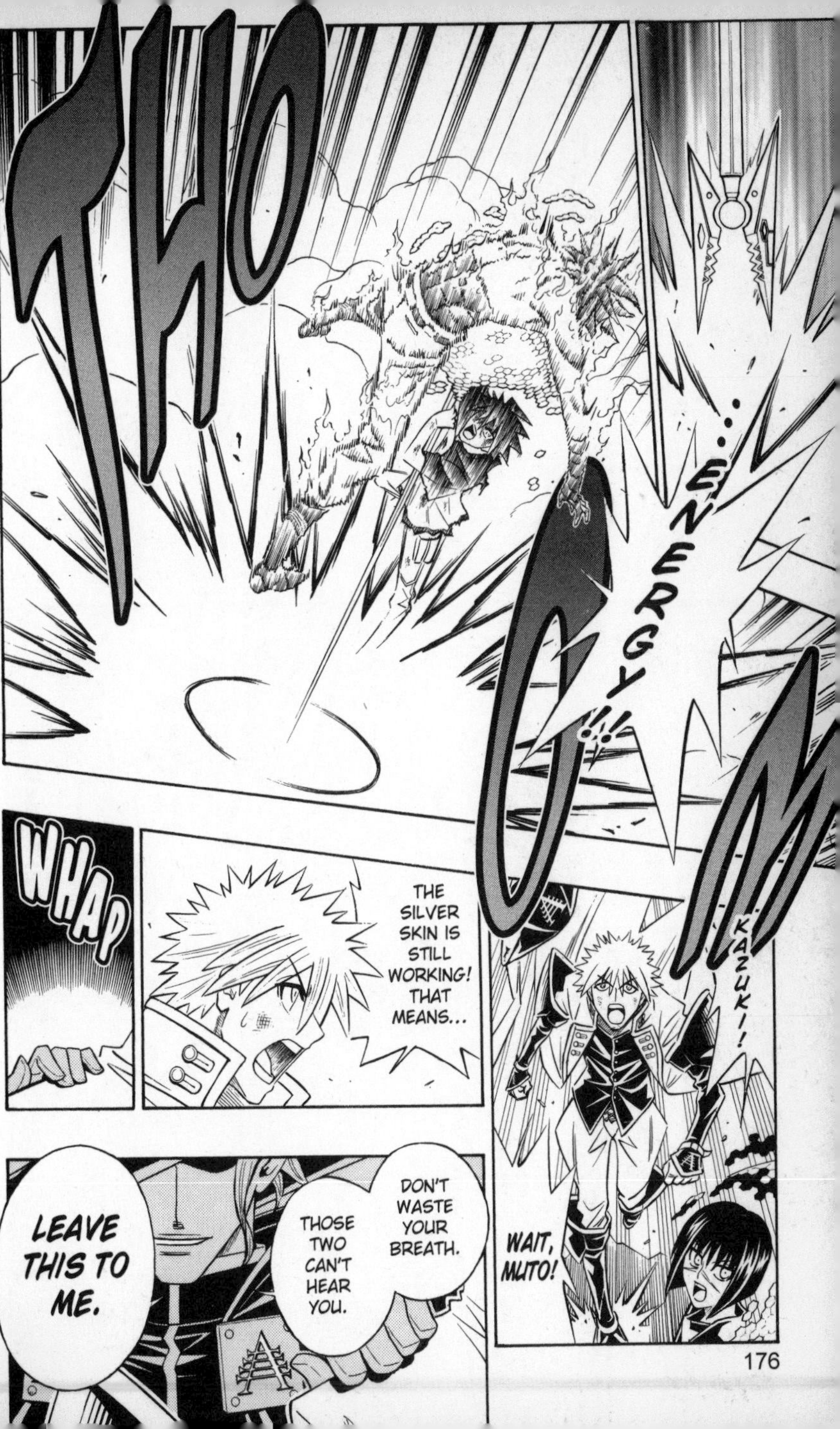
THOOM
...ENERGY!!!
KAZUKI!
THE SILVER SKIN IS STILL WORKING! THAT MEANS...
WHAP
WAIT, MUTO!
DON'T WASTE YOUR BREATH.
THOSE TWO CAN'T HEAR YOU.
LEAVE THIS TO ME.

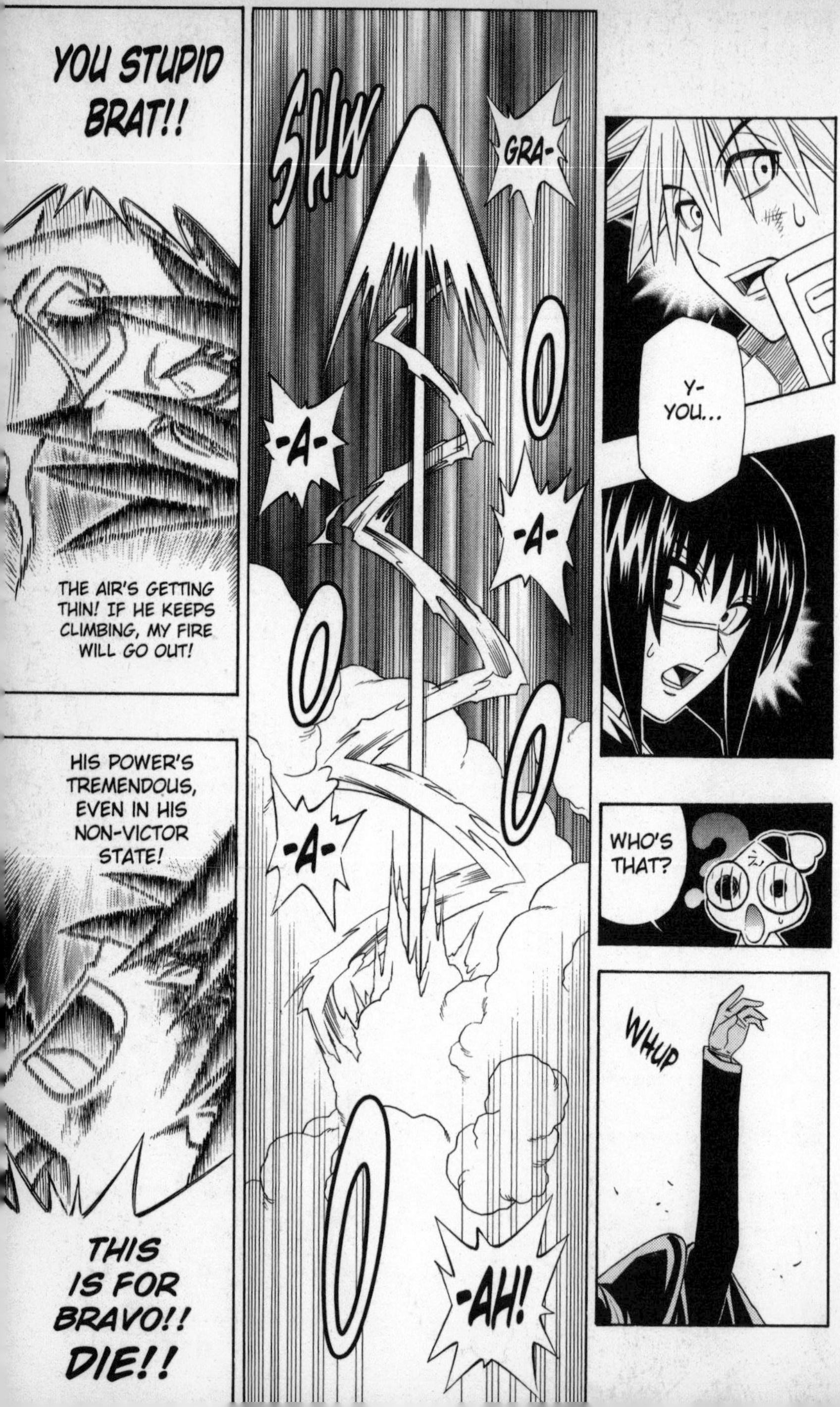
Y-YOU...
WHO'S THAT?
WHUP
SHW
GRA-
-A-
-A-
-A-
-AH!
YOU STUPID BRAT!!
THE AIR'S GETTING THIN! IF HE KEEPS CLIMBING, MY FIRE WILL GO OUT!
HIS POWER'S TREMENDOUS, EVEN IN HIS NON-VICTOR STATE!
THIS IS FOR BRAVO!! DIE!!

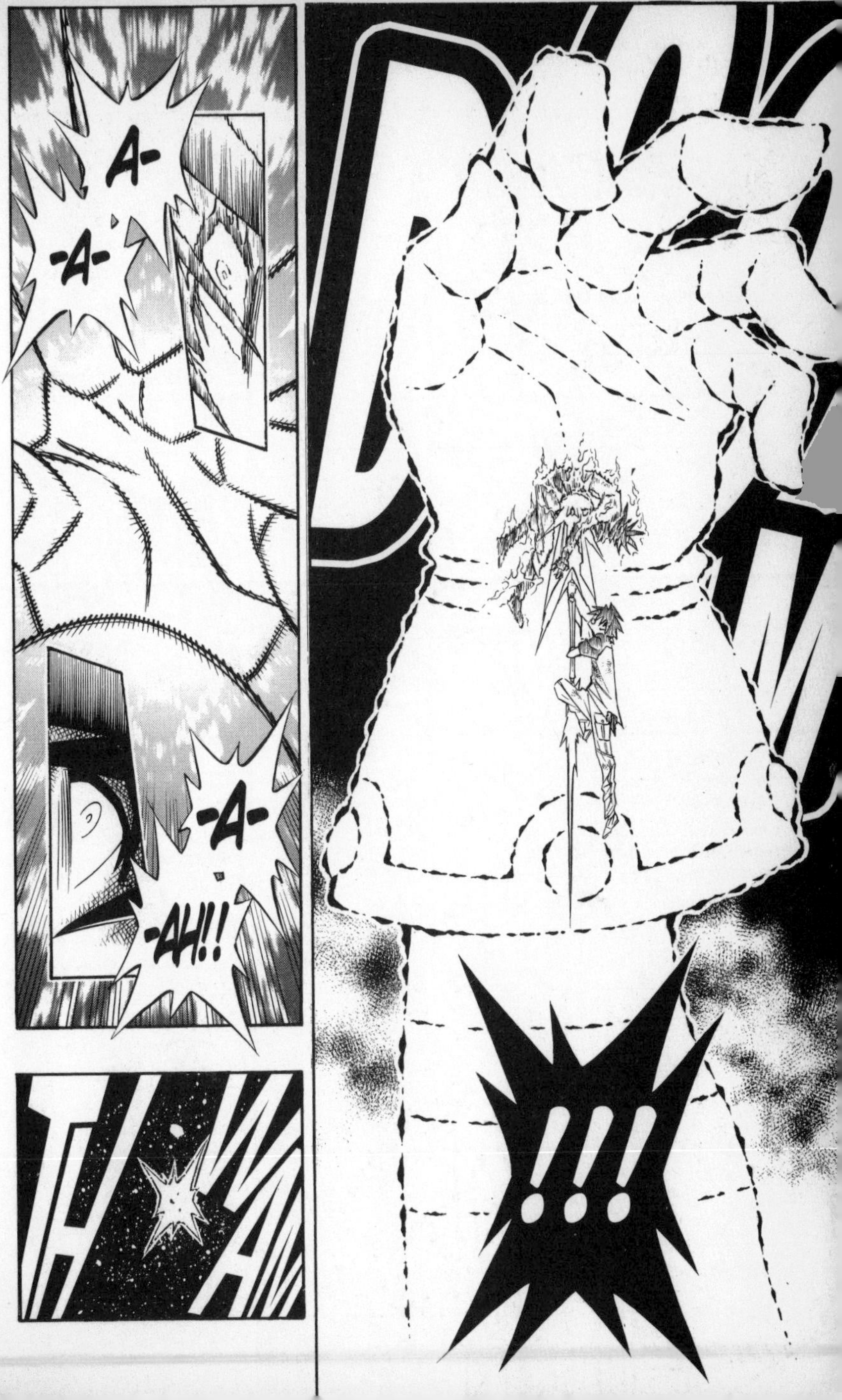
!!!
A-
-A-
-A-
-AH!!
THWAM

READ THIS WAY

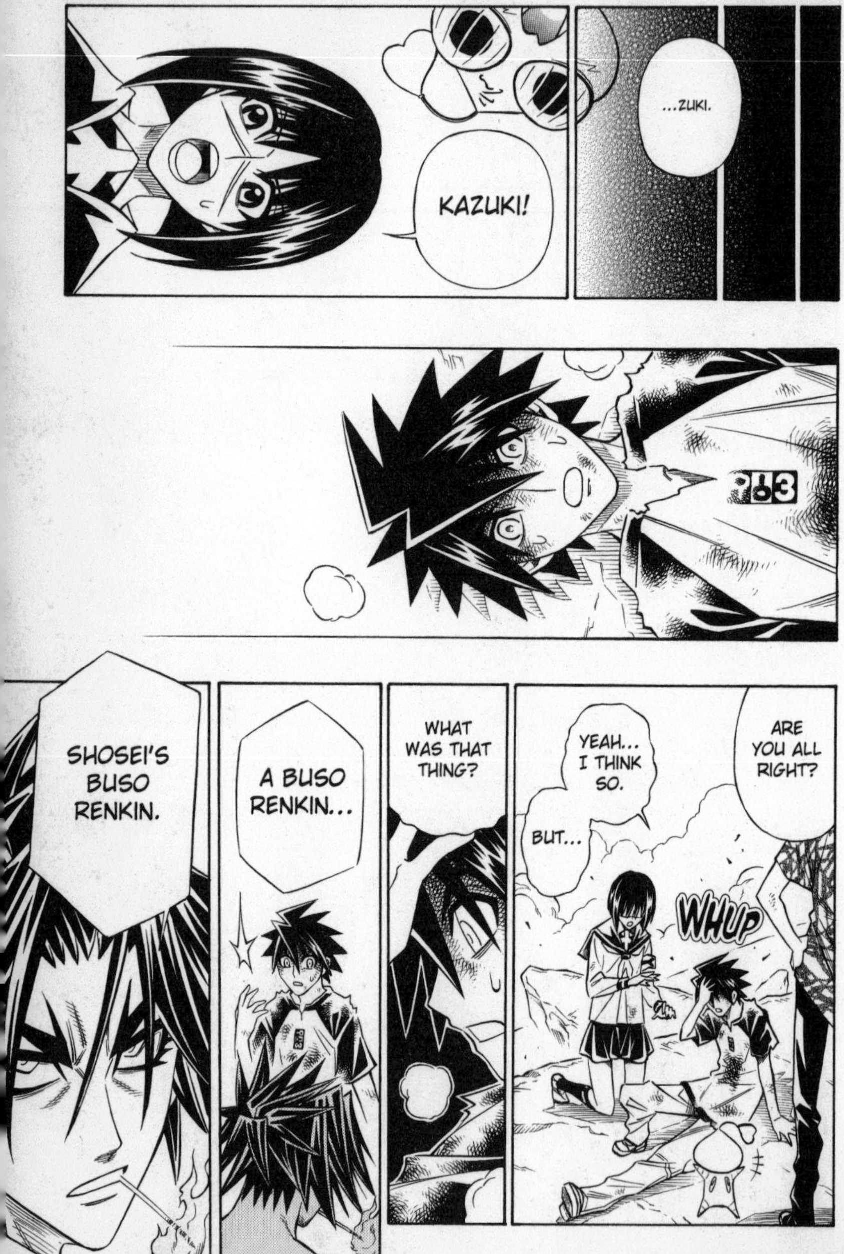
...ZUKI.
KAZUKI!
ARE YOU ALL RIGHT?
YEAH... I THINK SO.
BUT...
WHUP
WHAT WAS THAT THING?
A BUSO RENKIN...
SHOSEI'S BUSO RENKIN.

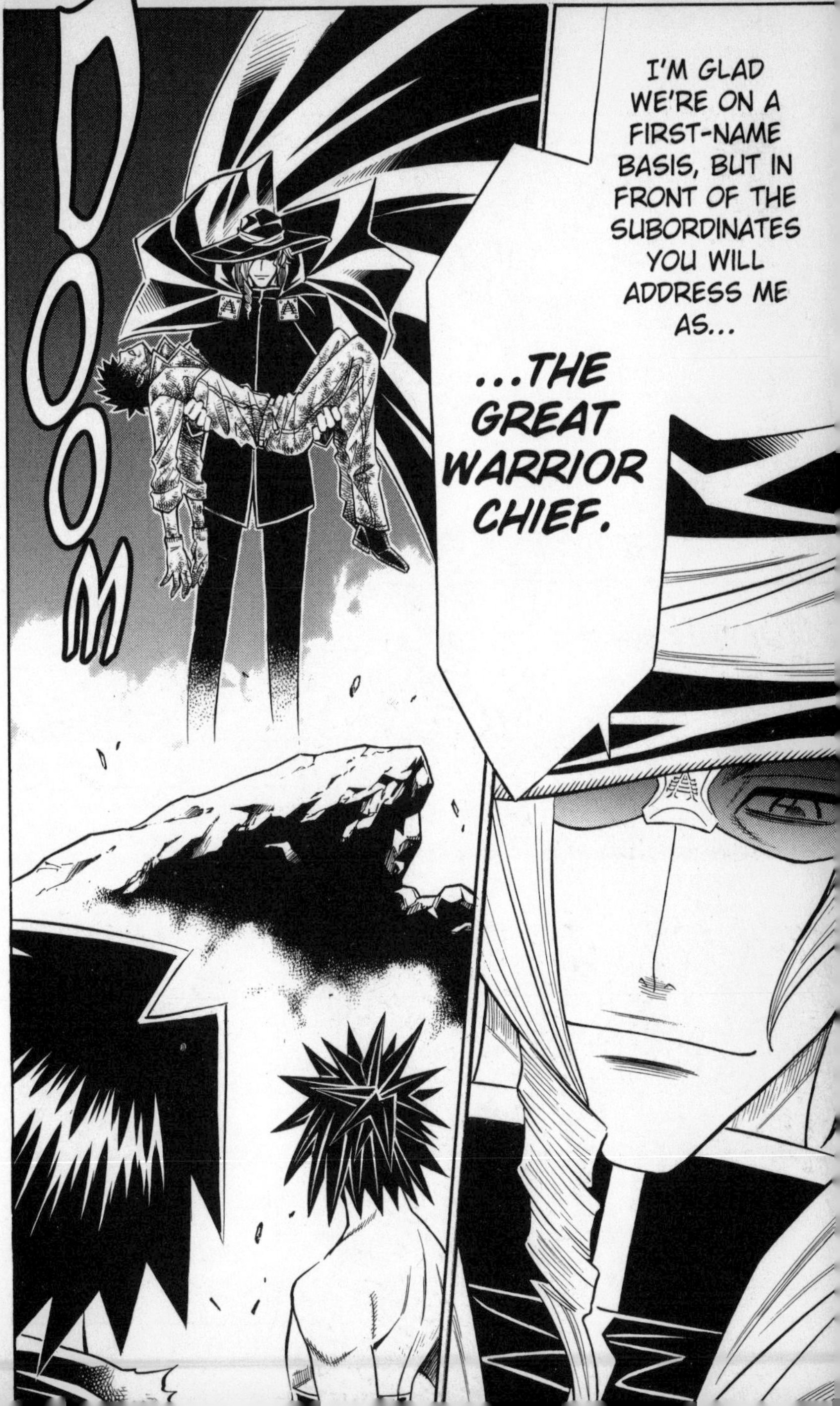
I'M GLAD WE'RE ON A FIRST-NAME BASIS, BUT IN FRONT OF THE SUBORDINATES YOU WILL ADDRESS ME AS...
...THE GREAT WARRIOR CHIEF.
DOOOM

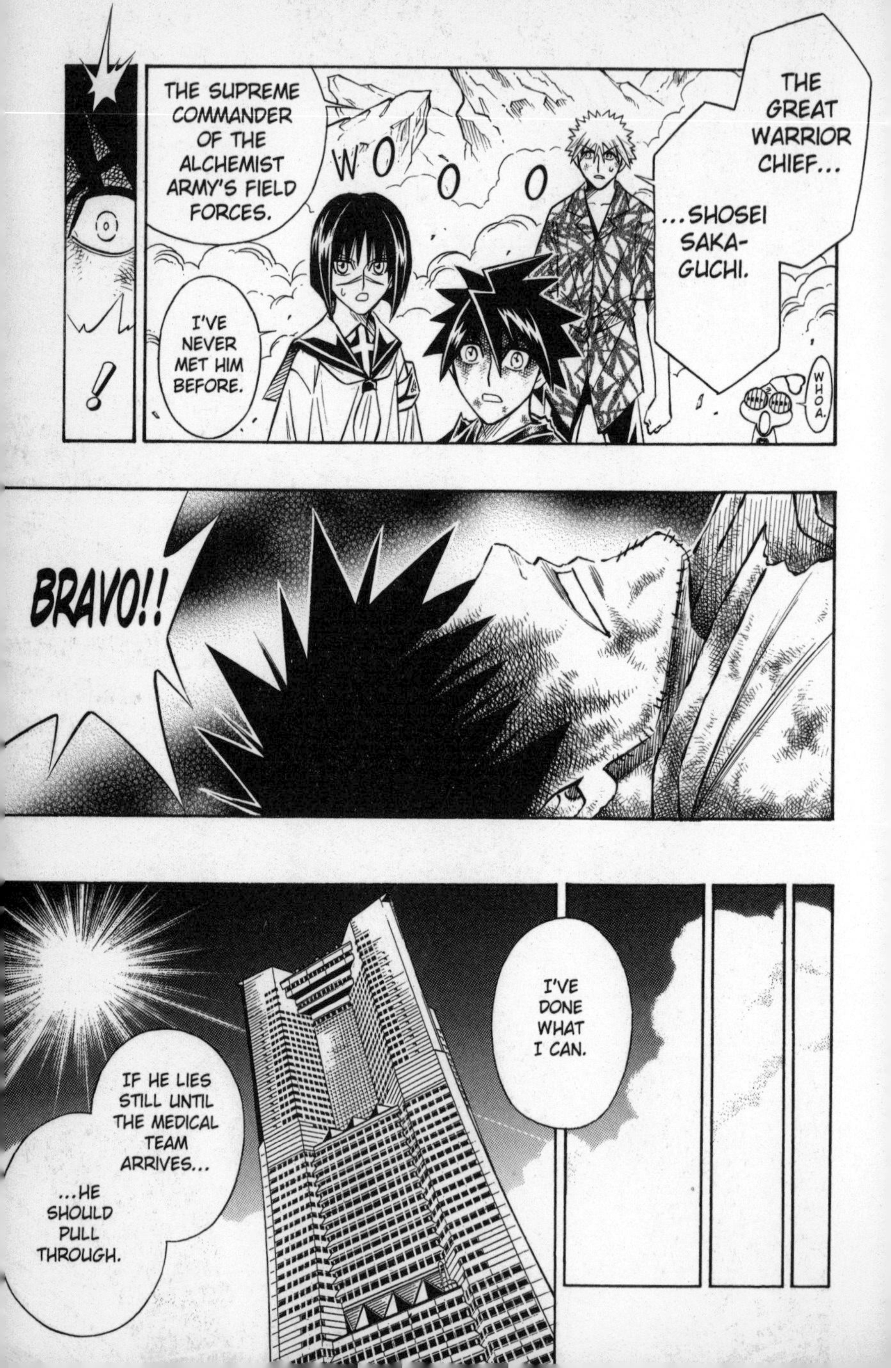
THE GREAT WARRIOR CHIEF...
...SHOSEI SAKA-GUCHI.
WHOA.
THE SUPREME COMMANDER OF THE ALCHEMIST ARMY'S FIELD FORCES.
WOOO
I'VE NEVER MET HIM BEFORE.
!
BRAVO!!
I'VE DONE WHAT I CAN.
IF HE LIES STILL UNTIL THE MEDICAL TEAM ARRIVES...
...HE SHOULD PULL THROUGH.

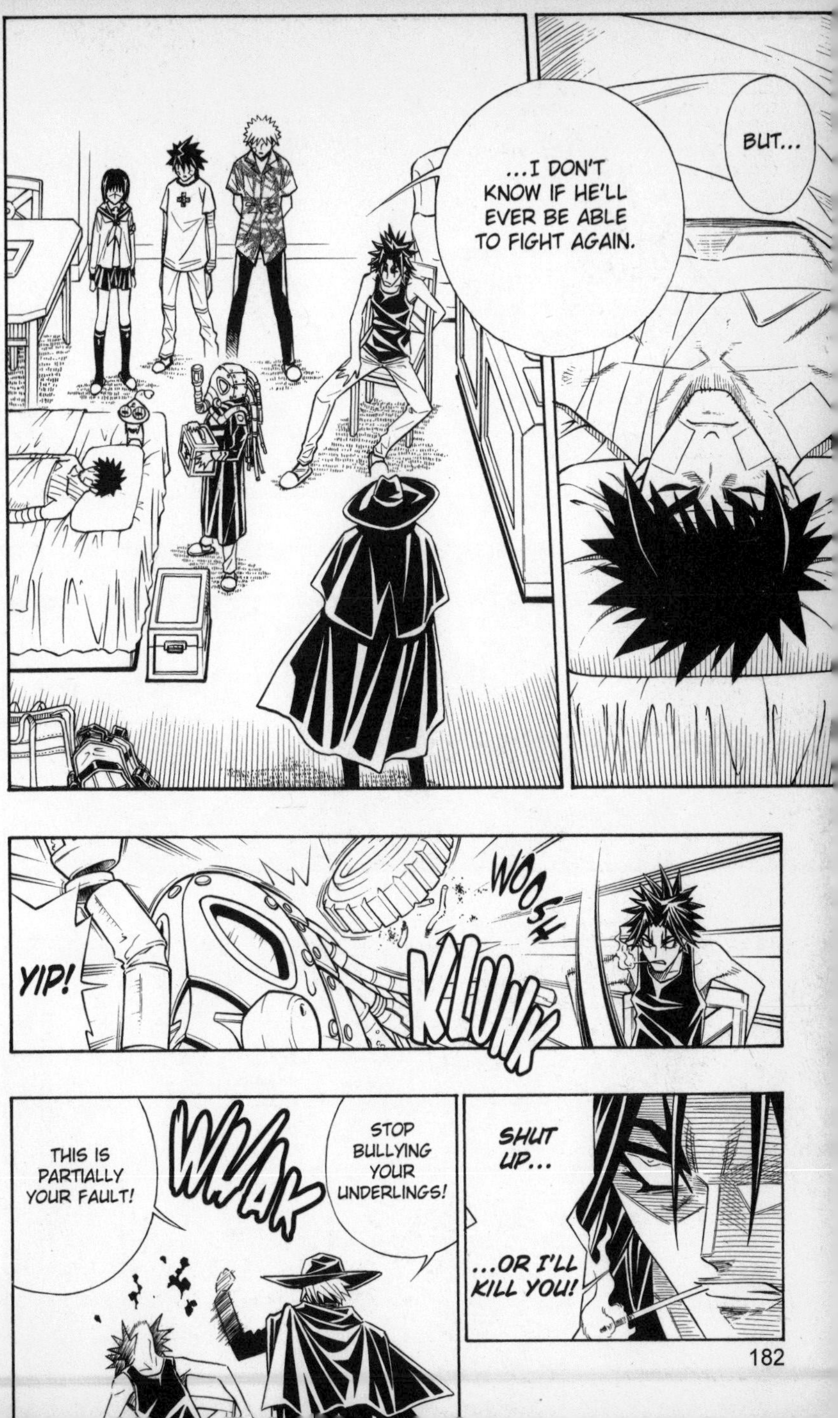
BUT...
...I DON'T KNOW IF HE'LL EVER BE ABLE TO FIGHT AGAIN.
WOOSH
KLUNK
YIP!
SHUT UP...
...OR I'LL KILL YOU!
STOP BULLYING YOUR UNDERLINGS!
WHAK
THIS IS PARTIALLY YOUR FAULT!

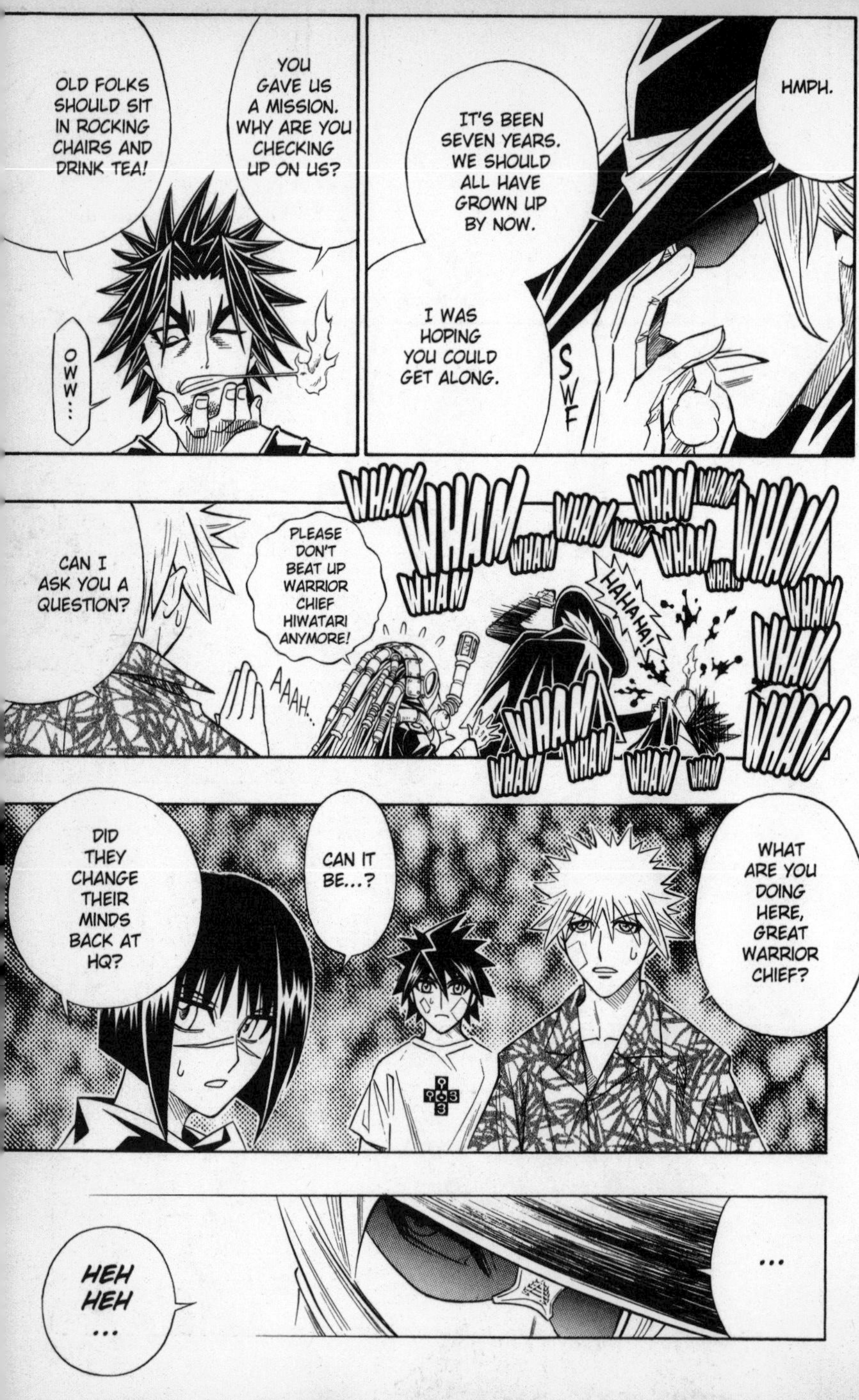
HMPH.
IT'S BEEN SEVEN YEARS. WE SHOULD ALL HAVE GROWN UP BY NOW.
I WAS HOPING YOU COULD GET ALONG.
SWF
YOU GAVE US A MISSION. WHY ARE YOU CHECKING UP ON US?
OLD FOLKS SHOULD SIT IN ROCKING CHAIRS AND DRINK TEA!
OWW...
WHAM WHAM WHAM WHAM WHAM WHAM WHAM WHAM
HAHAHA!
PLEASE DON'T BEAT UP WARRIOR CHIEF HIWATARI ANYMORE!
AAAH...
CAN I ASK YOU A QUESTION?
WHAT ARE YOU DOING HERE, GREAT WARRIOR CHIEF?
CAN IT BE...?
DID THEY CHANGE THEIR MINDS BACK AT HQ?
...
HEH HEH ...

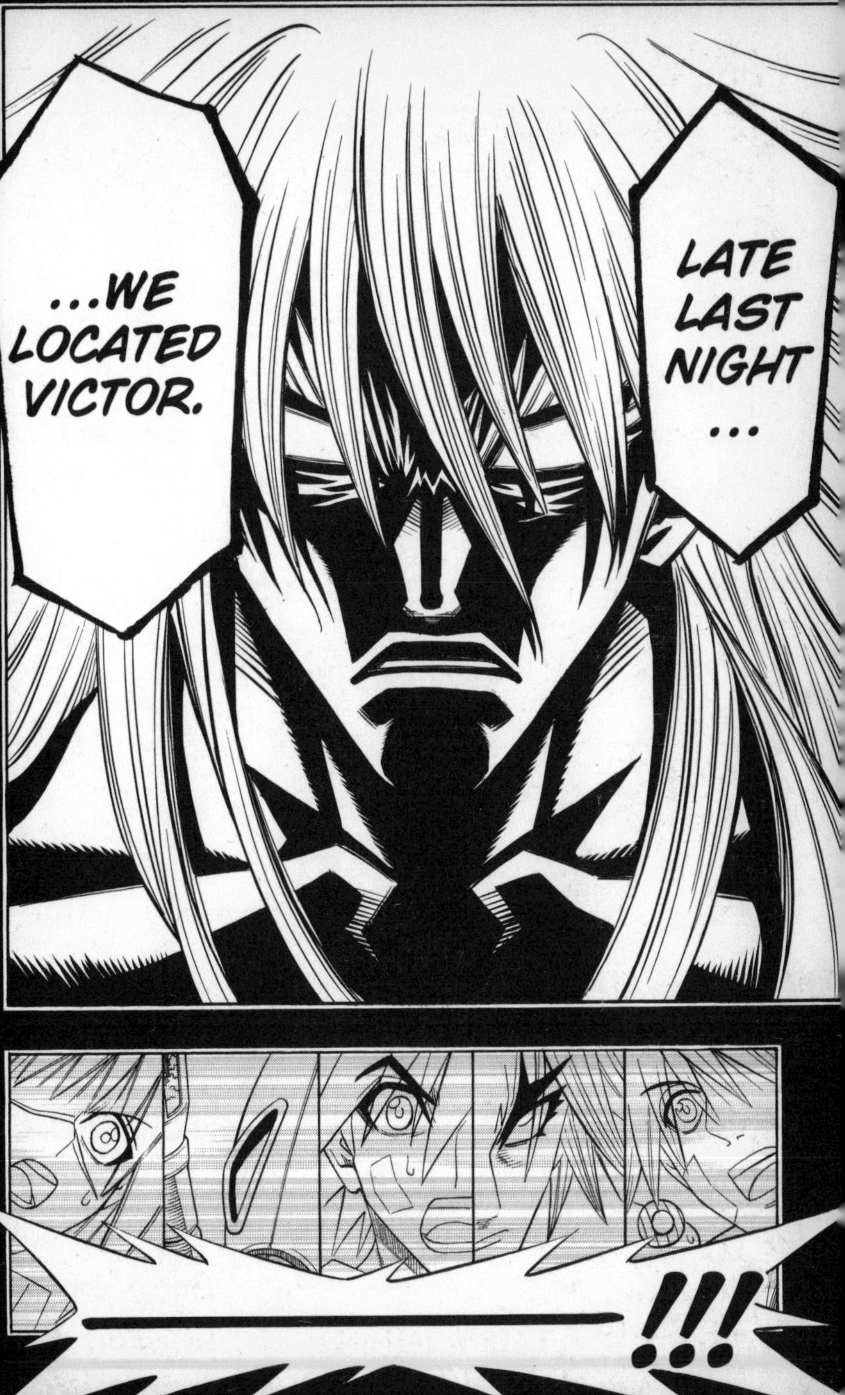
LATE LAST NIGHT ...
...WE LOCATED VICTOR.
——!!!

READ THIS WAY

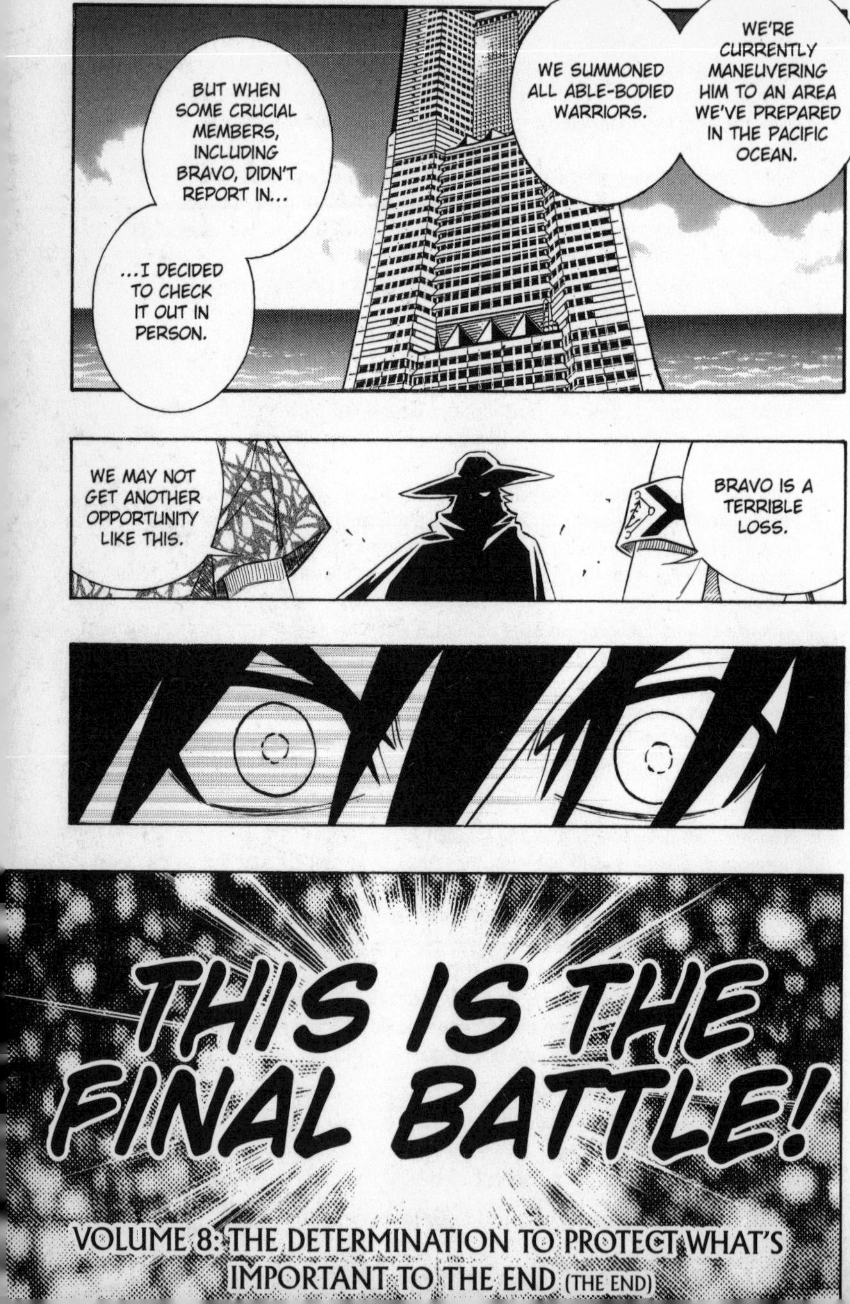
WE'RE CURRENTLY MANEUVERING HIM TO AN AREA WE'VE PREPARED IN THE PACIFIC OCEAN.
WE SUMMONED ALL ABLE-BODIED WARRIORS.
BUT WHEN SOME CRUCIAL MEMBERS, INCLUDING BRAVO, DIDN'T REPORT IN...
...I DECIDED TO CHECK IT OUT IN PERSON.
BRAVO IS A TERRIBLE LOSS.
WE MAY NOT GET ANOTHER OPPORTUNITY LIKE THIS.
THIS IS THE FINAL BATTLE!
VOLUME 8: THE DETERMINATION TO PROTECT WHAT'S IMPORTANT TO THE END (THE END)

Chapter 64: Eater

· The "Ikusabe = homunculus eater" concept seemed more like horror than action, so I tried to give the chapter a horror-like feel. But in the end, I didn't know how to make it work so I dropped the idea. The feeling you get from a horror movie is something I've been enjoying a lot lately. There's nothing like that creepy feeling…

· We haven't had any animal-based homunculi for a while. At the beginning of this series, I had a temporary assistant who did most of them for me, so having to do one myself was harder than I expected. I apologize to my assistants who had to try to mimic that style.

· Papillon's happy sigh. Nice! When I was drawing that panel, I found myself trying to do that same expression. And I have to give a happy sigh for the way it turned out.

Chapter 65: Dawn at the Graveyard

· I like the exchange between Ikusabe and Negoro when Negoro first emerges from Ikusabe's stump. The lines themselves are fairly ordinary, but I like how it turned out.

· The line where Ikusabe asks Kazuki to make a deal with him is another one I really liked in this chapter. And there was the line in which Ikusabe complimented Papillon at the end of the last volume, too. Ikusabe just seems to get the best lines. I think the right side of my brain really works overtime in some situations.

· Gouta's expression while looking at mini-Tokiko was surprisingly popular with the fans.

· Captain Bravo returns. I wanted it to be a surprise, but now that I look at it, it seems kind of predictable.

· I confess that I don't really like working on double page spreads. I don't like my working area to be bigger than a regular sheet of paper.

Chapter 66: No Regrets

· The rematch between Kazuki and Captain Bravo begins. This was another attempt at a super-battle between these two, and I took it into the air this time. It's so hard to do well…

· The line about Maruyama wanting to keep Tokiko in a cage came from the original idea that Maruyama was a psycho, but that was deemed inappropriate for a boy's manga. So I made him just a little twisted and a bit gay-seeming.

· The inside-out guts splattering scene was decided on when the decision was made to shrink Tokiko. Even though she's mellowed a lot lately, it's good to see that Tokiko's mean streak is still operational.

Chapter 67: Secret Passage of Shadows

· Though its readers are a little older than those of my other manga, *Buso Renkin* is still a Watsuki title so I couldn't show Tokiko naked. Consequently, I had to figure out a way to avoid it. I thought I should show her entire body at least once in the chapter so my first idea was to use blood to cover things up, but that was a bit much. Finally it occurred to me, "It's a graveyard. There must be some water around."

- Gouta gets an eyeful in this chapter. He's sort of an underdog so I like to throw him a bone once in a while.
- Gozen has his big moment. This is one character that I never want to make too serious. But I'm not sure it worked.

Chapter 68: Meanwhile

- This chapter begins with a status report on the characters. I used a copy machine to create this page and it was a bit more time-consuming than I expected. (We had to locate suitable shots for 13 characters, resize them, and then come up with captions.) But I recalled really liking comics that gave you these updates and reminders when I was a kid, so I thought it was worth it.
- Motor Gears vs. Secret Trail. These weapons are so different but I had to come up with some way for them to fight. The solution was to make this a battle of wits. I thought the mystery of the Secret Trail might have been a bit too hard to grasp, but it turned out to be popular with the fans.
- It isn't easy to balance Gouta's devotion to Tokiko and his growing respect for Kazuki. I want it to be a gradual change.

Chapter 69: Round Two

- Once again it's Kazuki vs. Captain Bravo. I decided to make it a double-page spread! But in the weekly serialization, there was a problem with the printing and the edges got cut off. That, along with several other problems, made it a rough time for me.
- I couldn't have Kazuki destroying a lot of graves. I didn't want a repeat of vol. 5 where Kazuki caused most of the damage to Ginsei Academy. So I moved the action to a remote location like any normal Sentai show hero would do.
- Having Kazuki propel himself with his lance was something I'd been saving for this battle. After all he'd been through, I didn't want Kazuki winning by luck. I wanted them to push each other to the limit—that was the important thing.

Chapter 70: The Determination to Protect What's Important to the End

- The Silver Skin–Alternate Type returns. All those little hexagonal plates made this an ordeal for my assistants.
- I think the explanation of how the Silver Skin could be defeated came across very well. It wasn't too long or too complicated. I was pleased that I didn't have to resort to a lot of diagrams and pages.
- After Kazuki declares that he will not use the energy-drain but that he will continue to fight for his beliefs, Bravo reveals that he intends to kill himself when this mission is over. I think that sticking to your beliefs is a good thing and I try to do it myself. The problem is that it requires a lot of tenacity, and it can make life hard for the people around you.
- "The determination to protect what's important to the end." Kazuki says this line, but it reflects how Bravo feels as well. Bravo's drive to do what he believes is right only feeds Kazuki's strength. It's a real clash of hearts and souls between these two.

Chapter 71: Excel

· Bravo's special attack, the Bravo Punch. Right after I finished drawing it, I realized that I'd depicted a Kasane Ate! I thought, "Have I used this before?" and I had to rethink things. I wish I had the strength and the will power to have gone back and fixed it.

· There's a scene where the ground splits open during the battle. I love cataclysmic scenes like this. I wanted to stretch it across two pages, but I had to do it all in one page. Someday I'd really like to do a scene of total devastation.

· Kazuki finally manages to "reach" Bravo—in every sense of the word. I liked finishing the battle this way rather than with just a tactical victory.

· Hiwatari shows up and becomes the biggest problem in this volume.

Chapter 72: Gone Into Flames

· I took the title from *Gone with the Wind*.

· One thing I realized about myself while drawing Bravo is that I see things a bit differently than I used to. Bravo says he doesn't like to see children get killed and that's how I feel too. I get really depressed when I see kids get killed in movies or in comics. (But I've killed kids in my own stories in the past.) Sometimes it's necessary in order to move the story along, but I'd rather not.

· This doesn't mean that I like to kill off adults. This episode begs the questions, "Is Bravo dead?" In the end, he survives, but readers were split about this. I got some letters that said, "It would've been better if he'd died" and others that said, "I'm glad to see he's still alive. This story isn't about death." The truth is, when I originally planned the series out, Bravo was slated to die. The scene where he sacrifices himself by putting the Silver Skin on his comrades was something I planned a long time ago. But I felt that this just wasn't the right moment and that killing him here felt almost like I was trying to glorify death or something. So I'll save the idea of the good guy dying for his friends for another time.

· Putting Bravo's flashback inside Kazuki's flashback was a bit confusing. When I talked about it with Kurosaki, she wondered if I couldn't have done it differently. All I could do was nod and ponder.

Chapter 73: Leave This to Me

· Kazuki loses it. Normally he's the type who could never truly hate anyone, but he loses it here big time.

· The Great Warrior Chief appears, and the story makes a sudden change of direction. Kazuki's battle with Bravo finishes the Re-Extermination Squad storyline, so it was time to move forward. But I guess the readers weren't ready for it because I got a lot of angry letters. I'm sorry. All I can say is that I'll try to do better next time.

· With the closing line, "This is the final battle!" I found myself wondering, "Who said that?" I'm not quite sure whether it was Kazuki or the Great Warrior Chief. In this case, even the writer doesn't know the answer.

· And so →   To be continued.

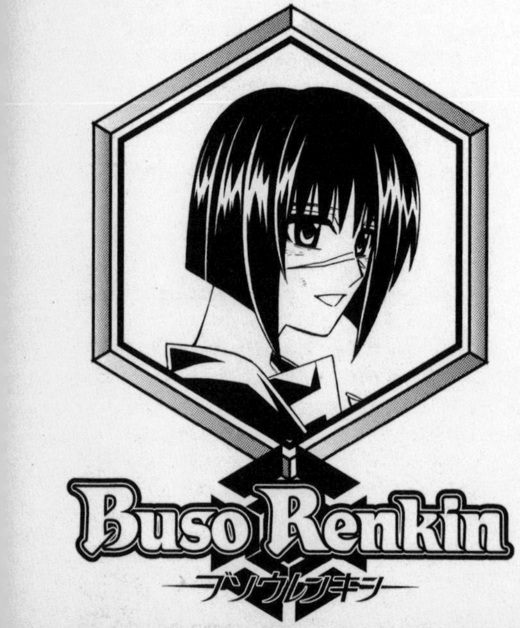

Buso Renkin

ブソウレンキン

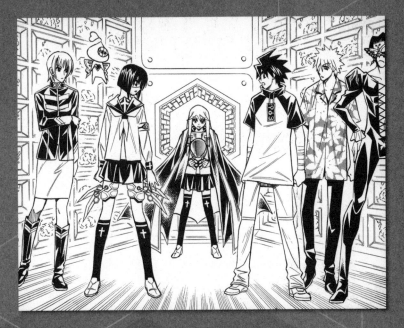

Coming Next Volume

Now that the Alchemist Army have finally tracked down Victor, they advance full force with the intent to destroy him. Meanwhile, Kazuki, Tokiko and Gouta unexpectedly meet Alexandria and Victoria, Victor's wife and daughter!

Available in December 2007!

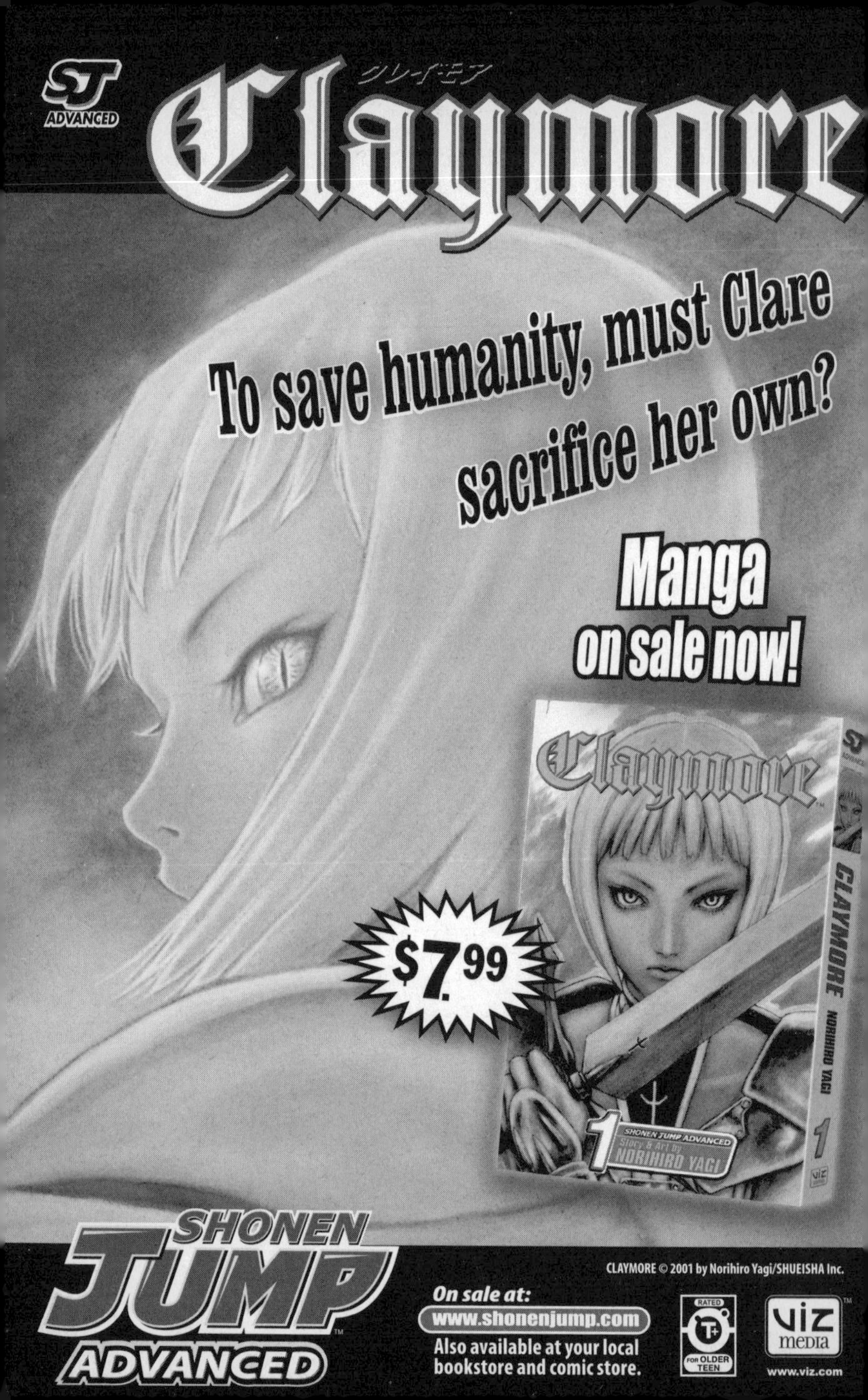
SJ ADVANCED
Claymore
クレイモア
To save humanity, must Clare sacrifice her own?
Manga on sale now!
$7.99
Claymore
CLAYMORE
NORIHIRO YAGI
1
SHONEN JUMP ADVANCED
Story & Art by NORIHIRO YAGI
SHONEN JUMP ADVANCED
CLAYMORE © 2001 by Norihiro Yagi/SHUEISHA Inc.
On sale at:
www.shonenjump.com
Also available at your local bookstore and comic store.
RATED T+ FOR OLDER TEEN
VIZ media
www.viz.com

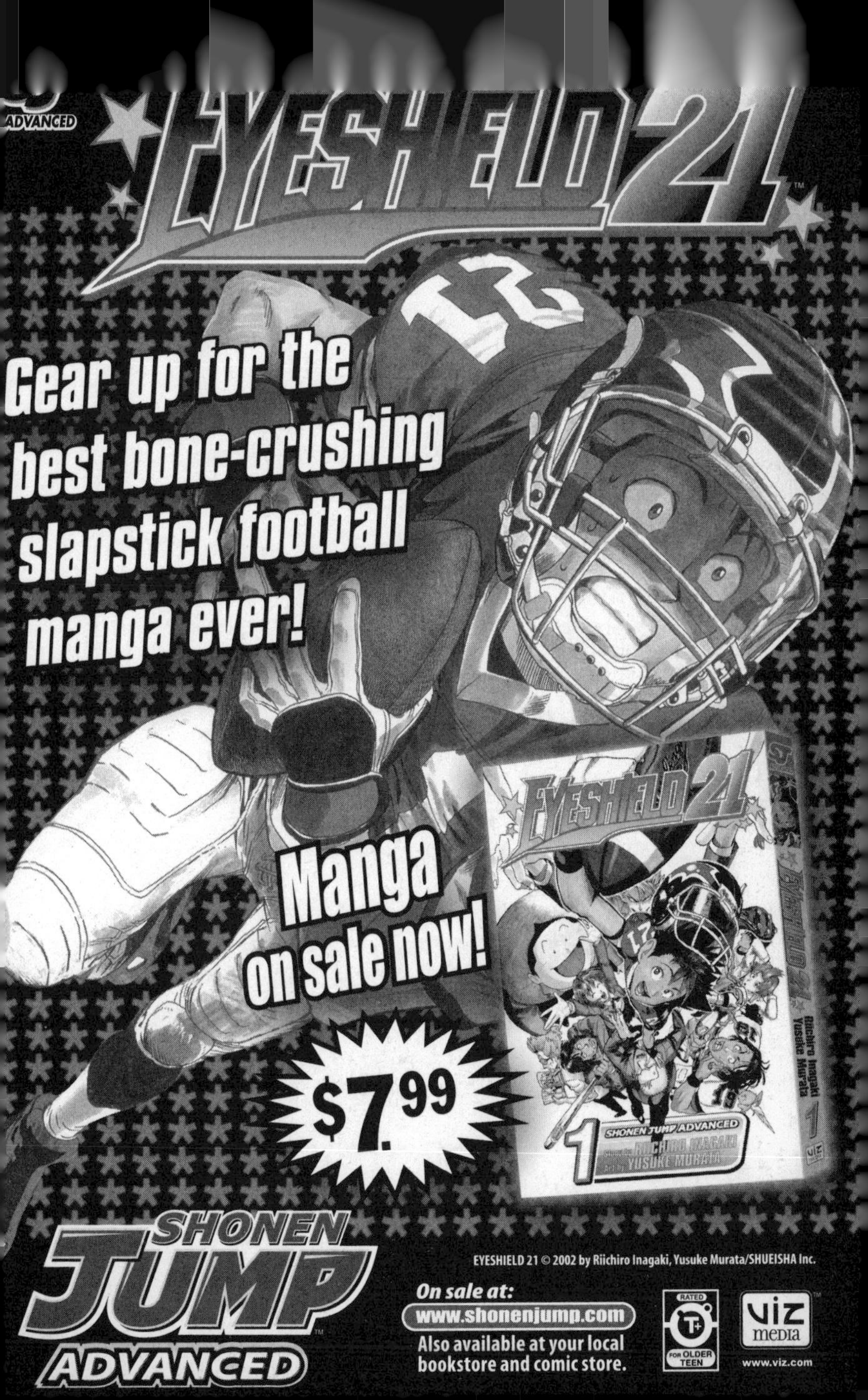
ADVANCED
EYESHIELD 21
Gear up for the best bone-crushing slapstick football manga ever!
Manga on sale now!
$7.99
SHONEN JUMP ADVANCED
EYESHIELD 21 © 2002 by Riichiro Inagaki, Yusuke Murata/SHUEISHA Inc.
On sale at:
www.shonenjump.com
Also available at your local bookstore and comic store.
RATED T+ FOR OLDER TEEN
viz media
www.viz.com

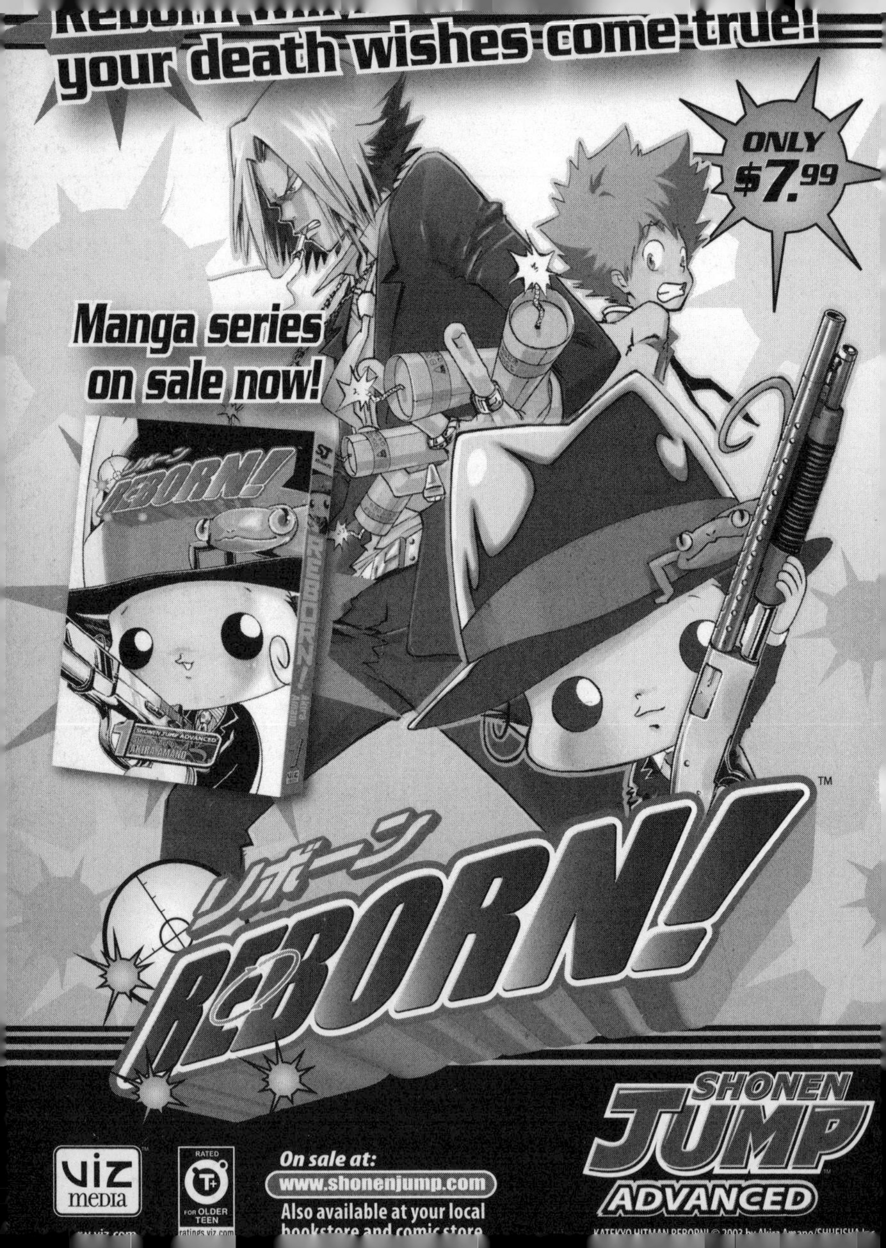
your death wishes come true!
ONLY $7.99
Manga series on sale now!
REBORN!
SHONEN JUMP ADVANCED
AKIRA AMANO
REBORN!
SHONEN JUMP ADVANCED
VIZ media
RATED T+ FOR OLDER TEEN
On sale at:
www.shonenjump.com
Also available at your local
bookstore and comic store

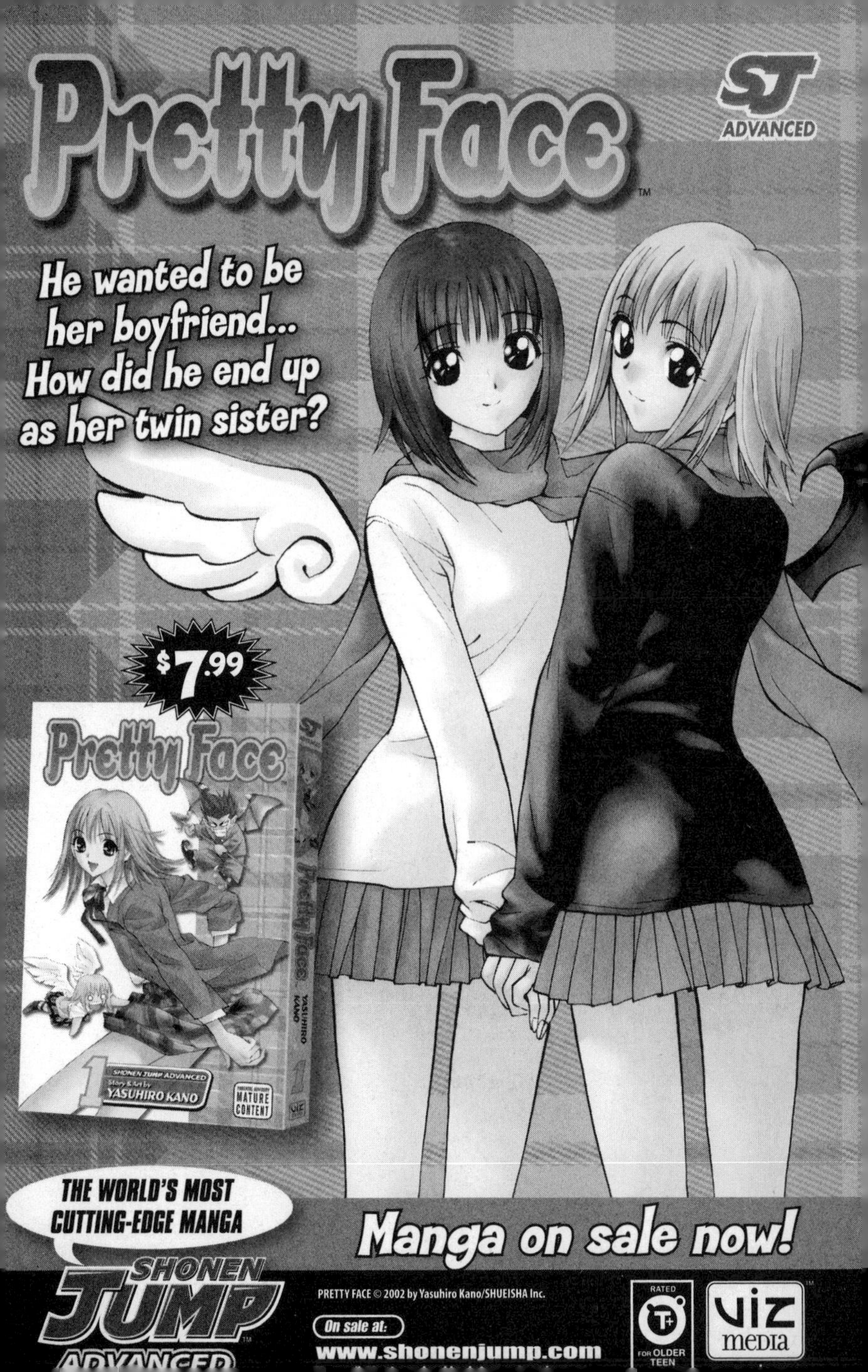
Pretty Face™
SJ ADVANCED
He wanted to be her boyfriend... How did he end up as her twin sister?
$7.99
Pretty Face
1 SHONEN JUMP ADVANCED
YASUHIRO KANO
MATURE CONTENT
THE WORLD'S MOST CUTTING-EDGE MANGA
SHONEN JUMP ADVANCED
Manga on sale now!
PRETTY FACE © 2002 by Yasuhiro Kano/SHUEISHA Inc.
On sale at:
www.shonenjump.com
RATED T+ FOR OLDER TEEN
VIZ media

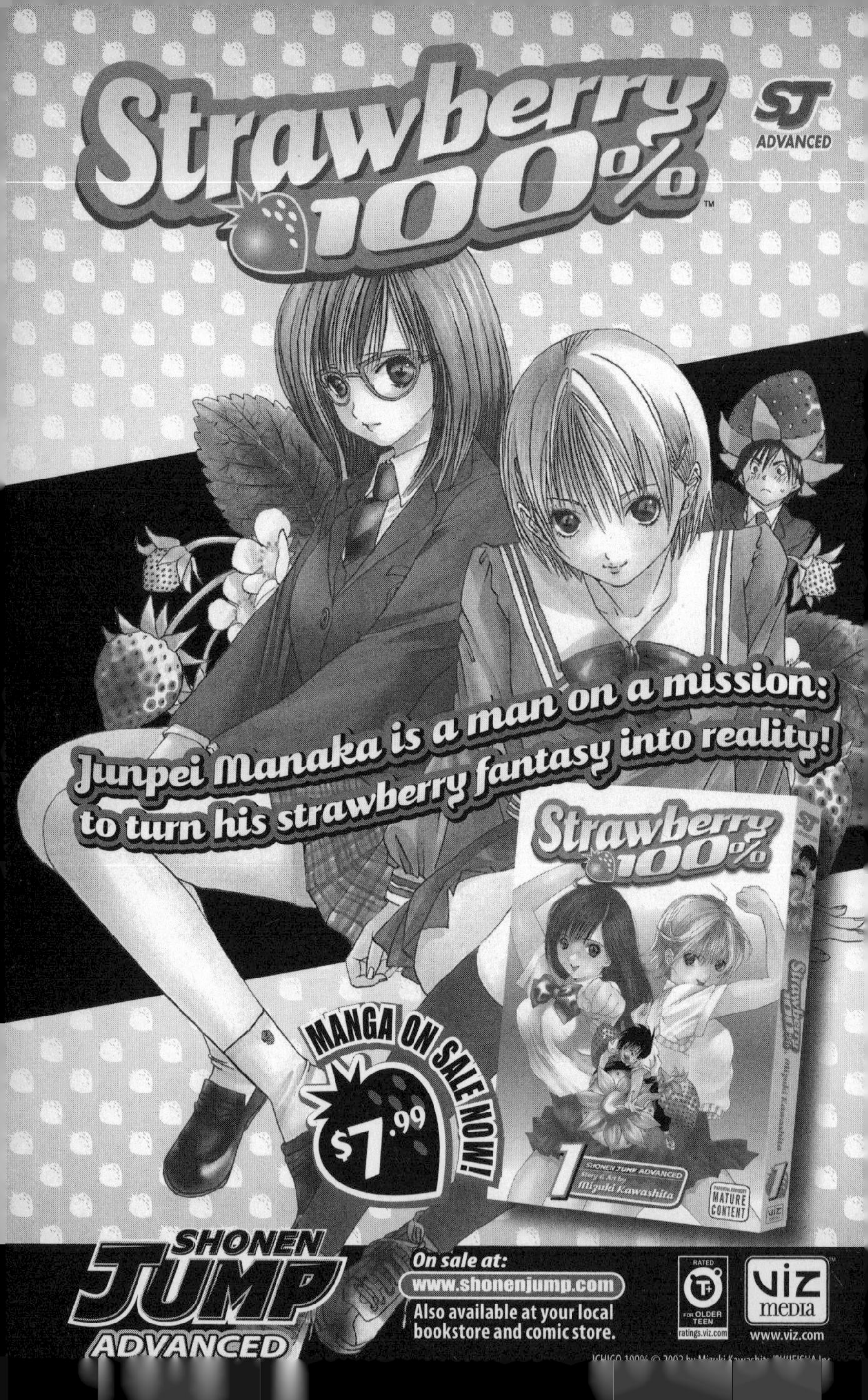
Strawberry 100%™
SJ ADVANCED
Junpei Manaka is a man on a mission: to turn his strawberry fantasy into reality!
MANGA ON SALE NOW!
$7.99
Strawberry 100%
SJ
1
SHONEN JUMP ADVANCED
Story & Art by Mizuki Kawashita
MATURE CONTENT
SHONEN JUMP ADVANCED
On sale at:
www.shonenjump.com
Also available at your local bookstore and comic store.
RATED T+ FOR OLDER TEEN
ratings.viz.com
viz media
www.viz.com
ICHIGO 100% © 2002 by Mizuki Kawashita/SHUEISHA Inc.

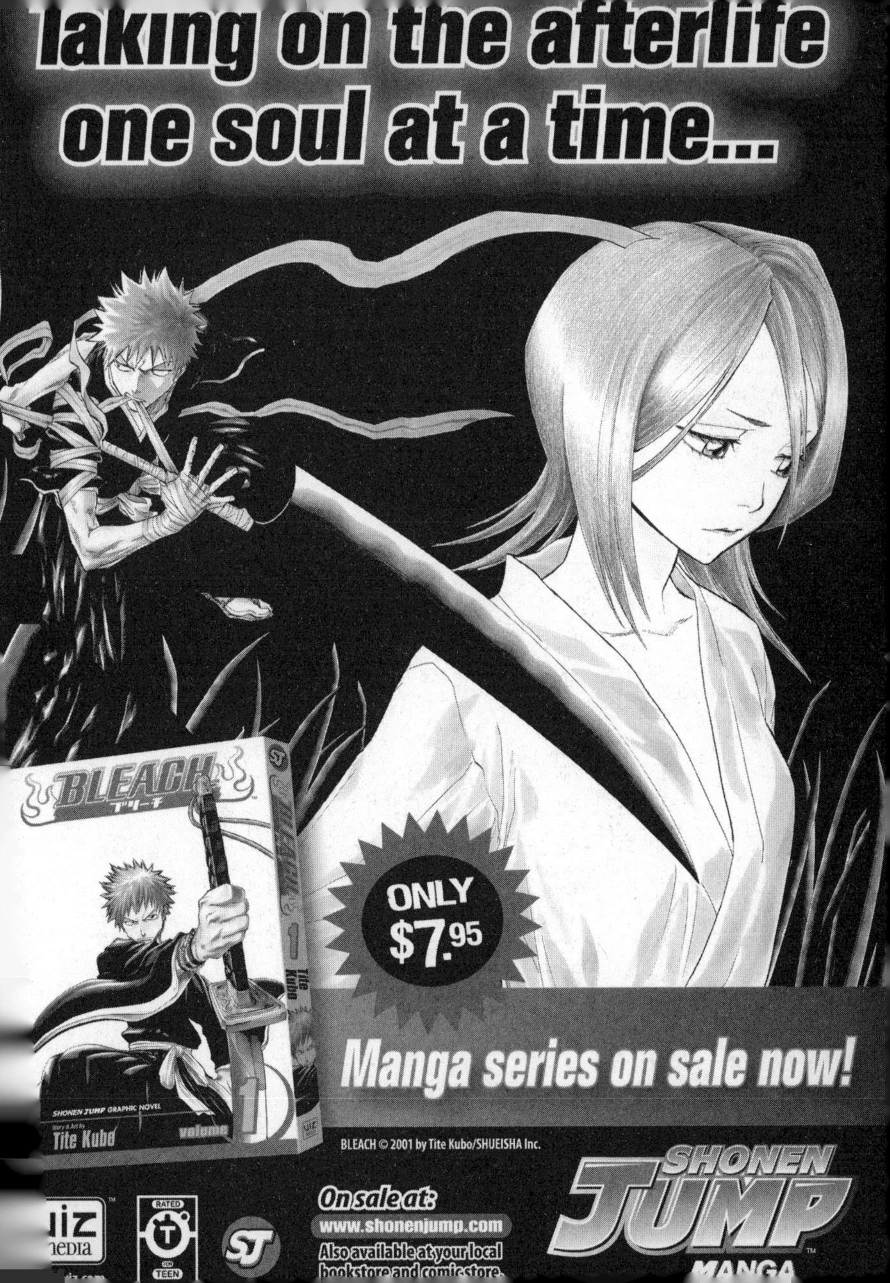

laking on the afterlife
one soul at a time...
BLEACH
ブリーチ
SHONEN JUMP GRAPHIC NOVEL
Story & Art by
Tite Kubo
volume 1
ONLY
$7.95
Manga series on sale now!
BLEACH © 2001 by Tite Kubo/SHUEISHA Inc.
On sale at:
www.shonenjump.com
Also available at your local bookstore and comic store.
RATED T FOR TEEN
SHONEN JUMP MANGA

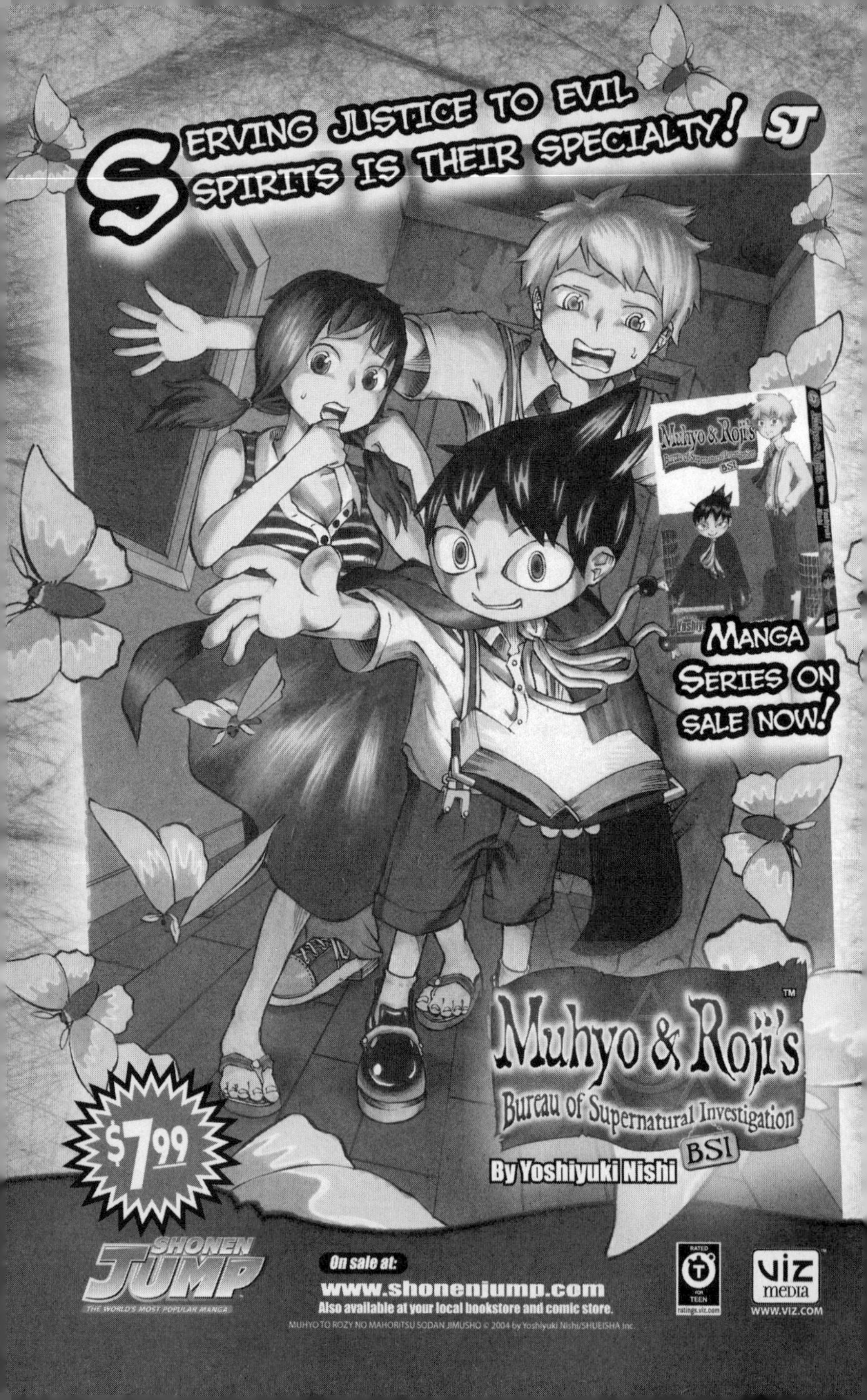

SERVING JUSTICE TO EVIL SPIRITS IS THEIR SPECIALTY!
SJ
Muhyo & Roji's Bureau of Supernatural Investigation BSI
MANGA SERIES ON SALE NOW!
Muhyo & Roji's
Bureau of Supernatural Investigation
BSI
By Yoshiyuki Nishi
$7.99
SHONEN JUMP
THE WORLD'S MOST POPULAR MANGA
On sale at:
www.shonenjump.com
Also available at your local bookstore and comic store.
RATED T FOR TEEN
ratings.viz.com
VIZ media
WWW.VIZ.COM
MUHYO TO ROZY NO MAHORITSU SODAN JIMUSHO © 2004 by Yoshiyuki Nishi/SHUEISHA Inc.

Tell us what you think about SHONEN JUMP manga!

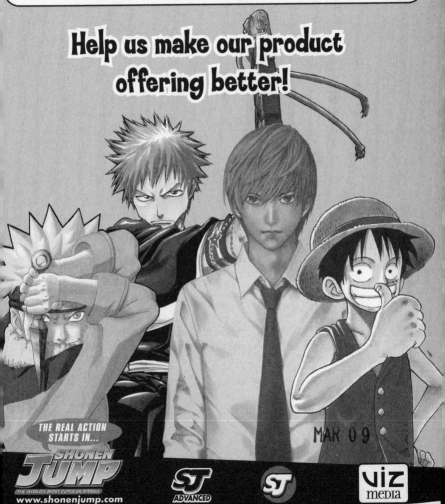

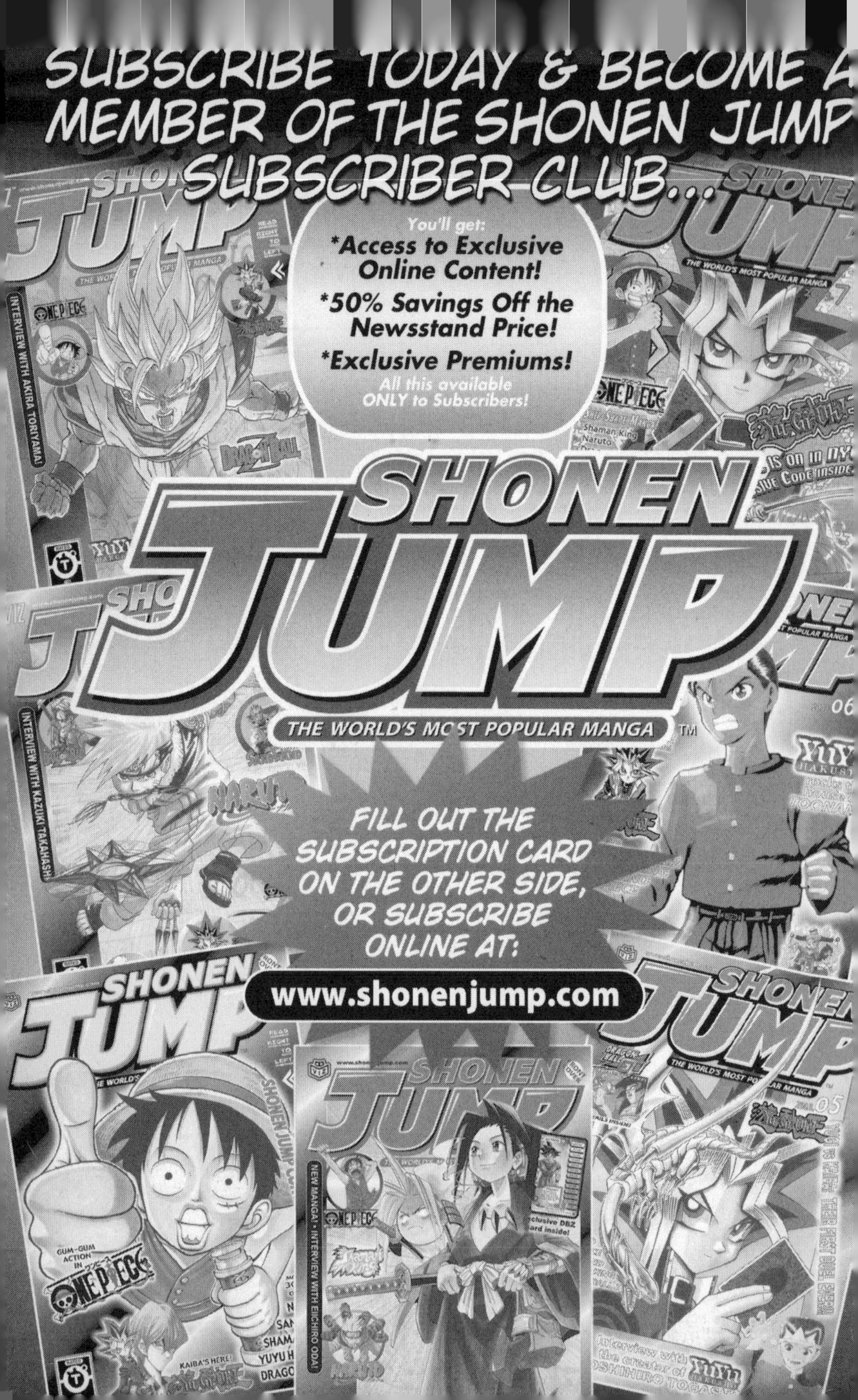
SUBSCRIBE TODAY & BECOME A MEMBER OF THE SHONEN JUMP SUBSCRIBER CLUB...
You'll get:
*Access to Exclusive Online Content!
*50% Savings Off the Newsstand Price!
*Exclusive Premiums!
All this available ONLY to Subscribers!
SHONEN JUMP
THE WORLD'S MOST POPULAR MANGA ™
FILL OUT THE SUBSCRIPTION CARD ON THE OTHER SIDE, OR SUBSCRIBE ONLINE AT:
www.shonenjump.com

SHONEN JUMP

THE WORLD'S MOST POPULAR MANGA

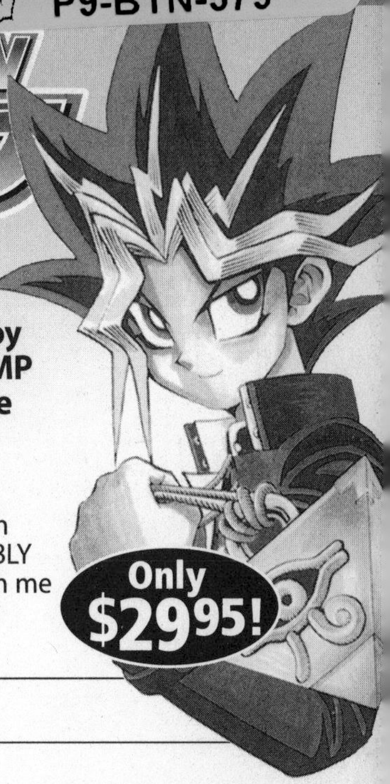

SUBSCRIBE TODAY and SAVE 50% OFF the cover price PLUS enjoy all the benefits of the SHONEN JUMP SUBSCRIBER CLUB, exclusive online content & special gifts ONLY AVAILABLE to SUBSCRIBERS!

☑**YES!** Please enter my 1 year subscription (12 issues) to *SHONEN JUMP* at the INCREDIBLY LOW SUBSCRIPTION RATE of $29.95 and sign me up for the SHONEN JUMP Subscriber Club!

Only **$29⁹⁵!**

NAME

ADDRESS

CITY   STATE   ZIP

E-MAIL ADDRESS

☐ **MY CHECK IS ENCLOSED**   ☐ **BILL ME LATER**

CREDIT CARD: ☐ **VISA**   ☐ **MASTERCARD**

ACCOUNT #   EXP. DATE

SIGNATURE

CLIP AND MAIL TO ➤   SHONEN JUMP
Subscriptions Service Dept.
P.O. Box 515
Mount Morris, IL 61054-0515

Make checks payable to: **SHONEN JUMP.**
Canada add US $12. No foreign orders. Allow 6-8 weeks for delivery.

P6SJGN   YU-GI-OH! © 1996 by Kazuki Takahashi / SHUEISHA Inc.